# White with the Red Hair

SORATA AKIDUKI

14

Rapunzel Version
SHFF
SHFF
Oh...
A prince?
What do you want?
Um, just passing by...
You've got real pretty hair, miss.
THE END

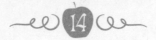

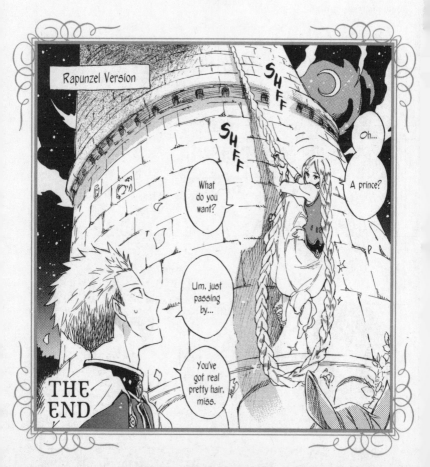

THE STORY

Shirayuki was born with beautiful hair as red as apples, but when her rare hair earns her unwanted attention from the notorious prince Raj, she's forced to flee her home. A young man named Zen helps her in the forest of the neighboring kingdom, Clarines, and it turns out he is that kingdom's second prince! Shirayuki decides to accompany Zen back to Wistal, the capital city of Clarines.

Shirayuki has met all manner of people since becoming a court herbalist, and her relationship with Zen continues to grow, as the two have finally made their feelings known to each other.

**SHIRAYUKI**

"They say that red is the color of destiny."

**PRINCE ZEN**

The second prince of the kingdom of Clarines.

Working as a court herbalist. Has feelings for Zen—feelings that he shares.

**RYU**

Shirayuki's boss. A brainy kid who became a court herbalist at a young age.

**MITSUHIDE & KIKI**

Zen's aides. They're good friends who share a strong bond.

**OBI**

Former assassin. Currently, Zen's underling. Served as Shirayuki's bodyguard for part of her stay in Lilias.

After becoming a full-fledged court herbalist, Shirayuki takes a work trip to the northern city of Lilias with her boss, Ryu. When a mysterious illness starts spreading, they investigate and figure out what's causing it. Once back in Wistal, Shirayuki and Zen go on a date, Izana gets crowned as the new king and Zen and Kiki engage in a fake courtship to satisfy Izana. With so much going on, the days fly by.

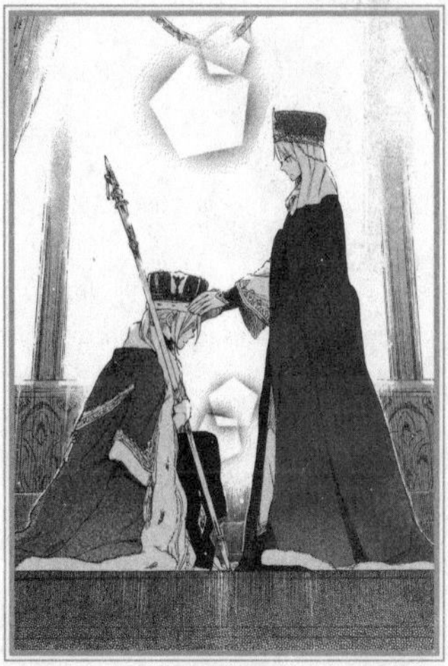

Then, Shirayuki and Ryu are ordered to relocate to Lilias for a period of two years. Shirayuki finds the resolve to make the move and do what she must, but since it will be the longest she's ever been away from Zen since coming to Clarines, she finds herself unable to hide her grief.

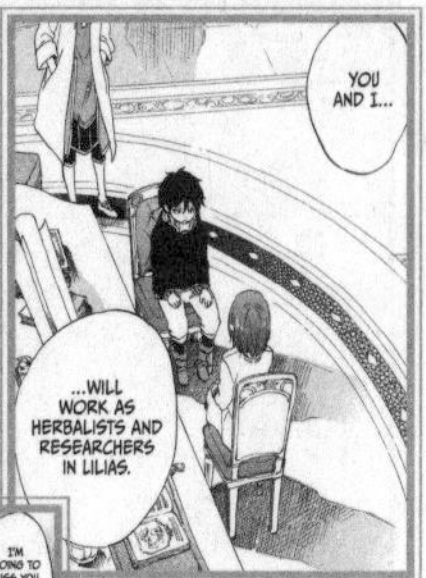
YOU AND I...
...WILL WORK AS HERBALISTS AND RESEARCHERS IN LILIAS.

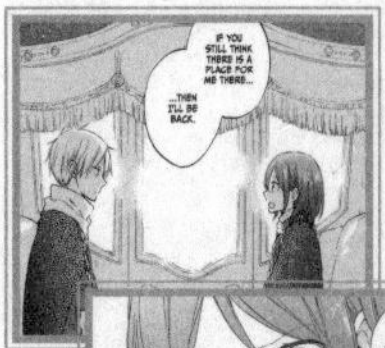
IF YOU STILL THINK THERE IS A PLACE FOR ME THERE...
...THEN I'LL BE BACK.

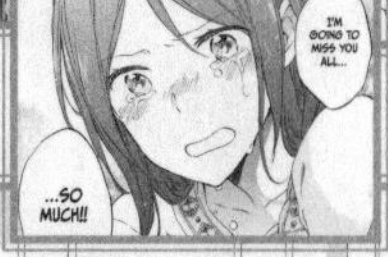
I'M GOING TO MISS YOU ALL...
...SO MUCH!!

Meanwhile, after reaffirming Obi's intentions and loyalty, Zen dispatches him to Lilias to serve at Shirayuki's side.

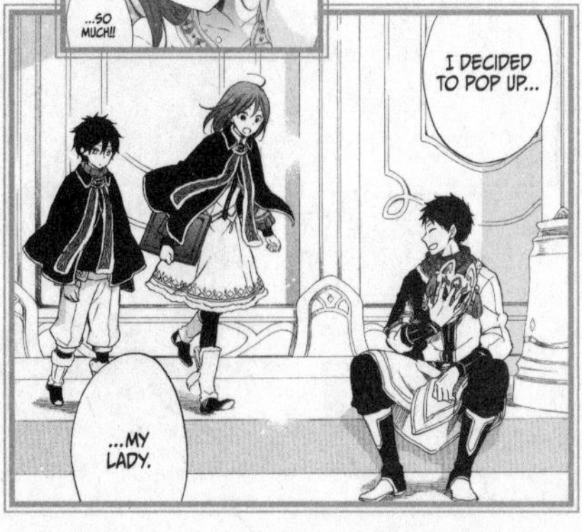
I DECIDED TO POP UP...
...MY LADY.

Snow White with the Red Hair

# VOLUME 14
## TABLE *of* CONTENTS

Chapter 61 ······························5

Chapter 62 ···························· 35

Chapter 63 ···························· 65

Chapter 64 ···························· 95

Chapter 65 ··························· 123

Bonus Chapter ······················· 141

One-Shot:
00 Days of Summer Vacation ······ 152

# Chapter 61

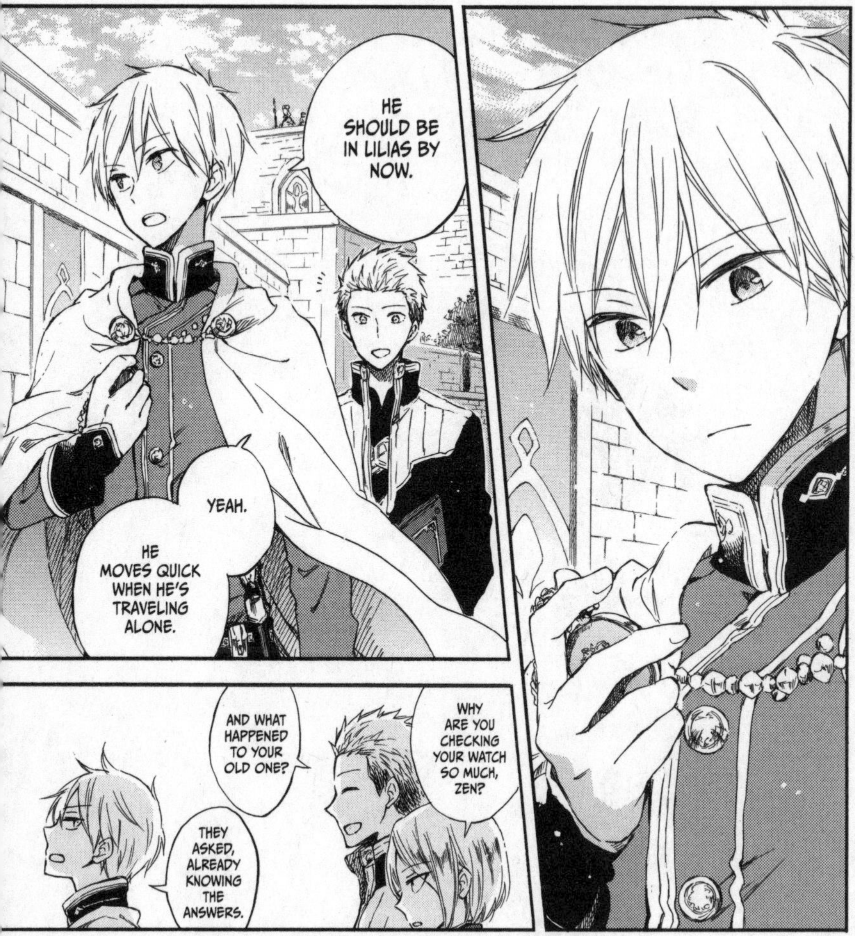
HE SHOULD BE IN LILIAS BY NOW.
YEAH.
HE MOVES QUICK WHEN HE'S TRAVELING ALONE.
WHY ARE YOU CHECKING YOUR WATCH SO MUCH, ZEN?
AND WHAT HAPPENED TO YOUR OLD ONE?
THEY ASKED, ALREADY KNOWING THE ANSWERS.

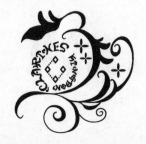

SNOW WHITE
WITH THE
RED HAIR

◇◇◇◇          RYU AND SHIRAYUKI AND ◦◦◦

Snow White
with the Red Hair LILIAS
Chapter 61

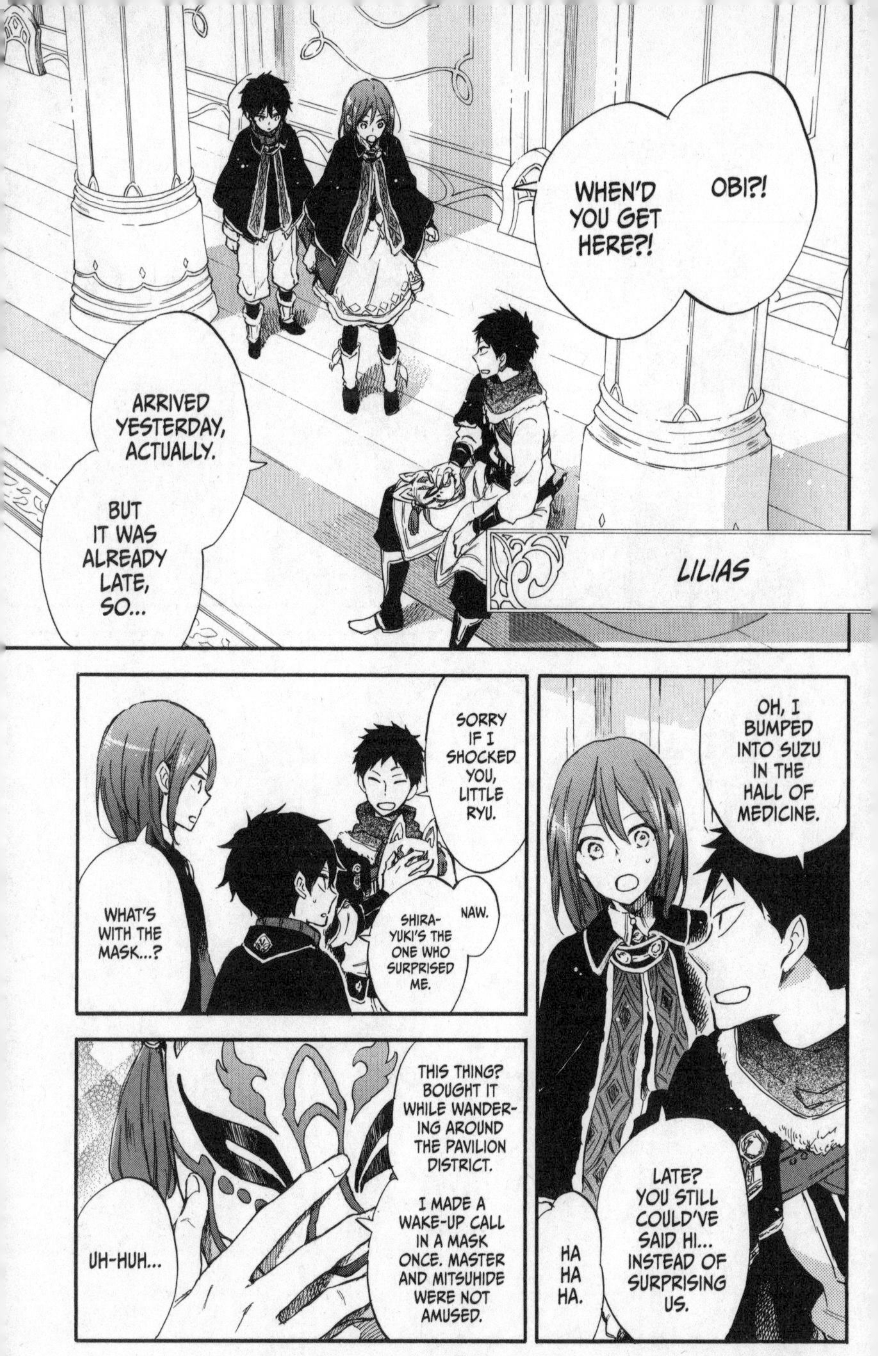
OBI?!
WHEN'D YOU GET HERE?!
LILIAS
ARRIVED YESTERDAY, ACTUALLY.
BUT IT WAS ALREADY LATE, SO...
OH, I BUMPED INTO SUZU IN THE HALL OF MEDICINE.
LATE? YOU STILL COULD'VE SAID HI... INSTEAD OF SURPRISING US.
HA HA HA.
SORRY IF I SHOCKED YOU, LITTLE RYU.
NAW.
SHIRA-YUKI'S THE ONE WHO SURPRISED ME.
WHAT'S WITH THE MASK...?
THIS THING? BOUGHT IT WHILE WANDER-ING AROUND THE PAVILION DISTRICT.
I MADE A WAKE-UP CALL IN A MASK ONCE. MASTER AND MITSUHIDE WERE NOT AMUSED.
UH-HUH...

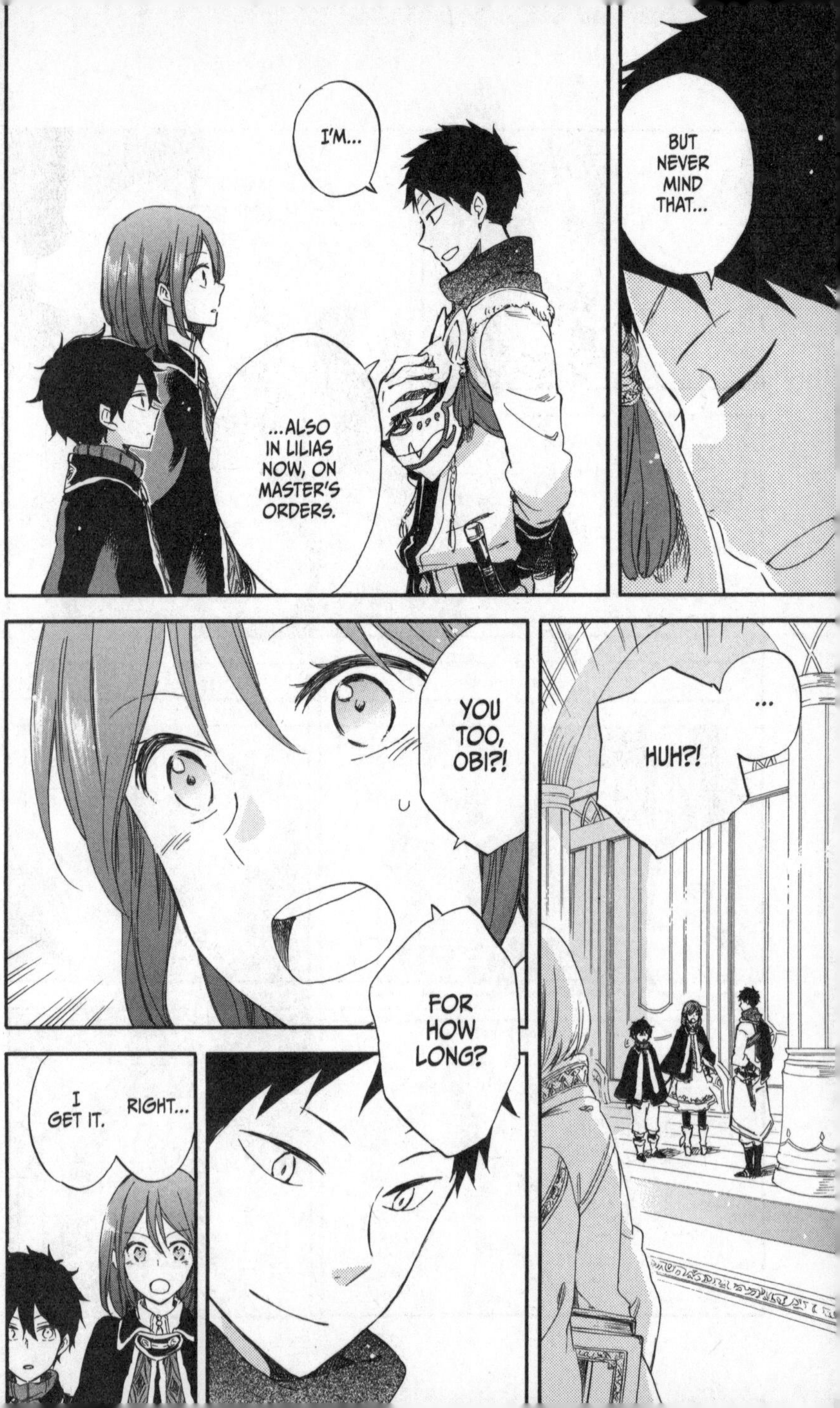
BUT NEVER MIND THAT...
I'M...
...ALSO IN LILIAS NOW, ON MASTER'S ORDERS.
...
HUH?!
YOU TOO, OBI?!
FOR HOW LONG?
RIGHT...
I GET IT.

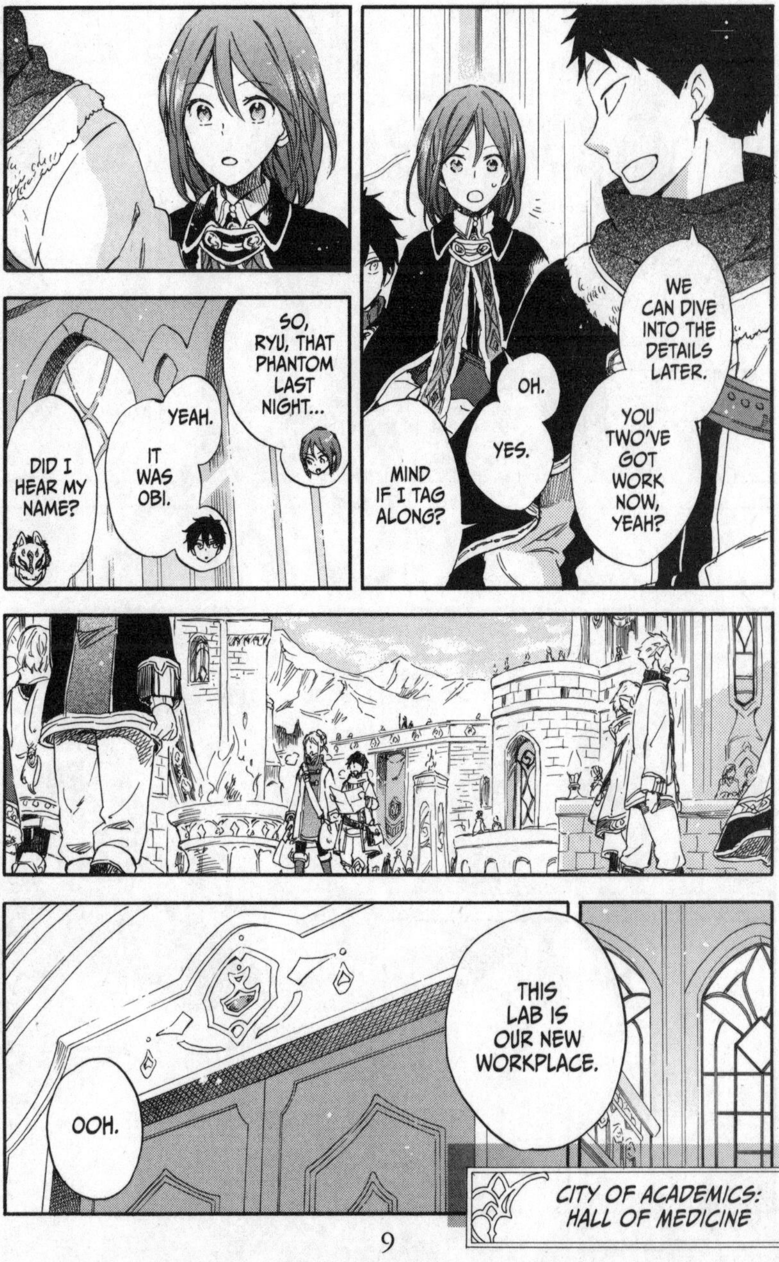
WE CAN DIVE INTO THE DETAILS LATER.
YOU TWO'VE GOT WORK NOW, YEAH?
OH.
YES.
MIND IF I TAG ALONG?
SO, RYU, THAT PHANTOM LAST NIGHT...
YEAH.
IT WAS OBI.
DID I HEAR MY NAME?
CITY OF ACADEMICS: HALL OF MEDICINE
THIS LAB IS OUR NEW WORKPLACE.
OOH.

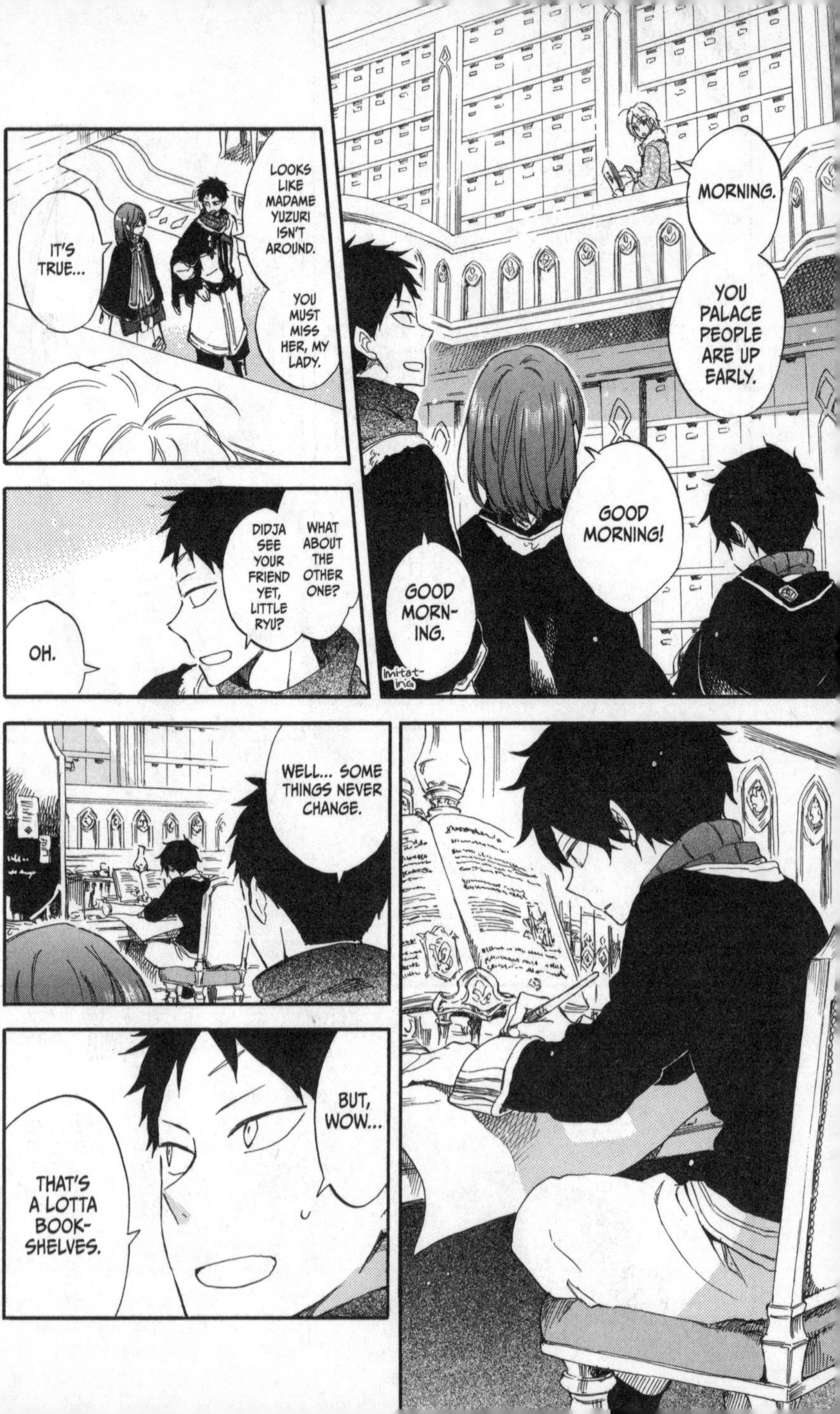
MORNING.
YOU PALACE PEOPLE ARE UP EARLY.
GOOD MORNING!
GOOD MORNING.
Imitating
LOOKS LIKE MADAME YUZURI ISN'T AROUND.
YOU MUST MISS HER, MY LADY.
IT'S TRUE...
WHAT ABOUT THE OTHER ONE?
DIDJA SEE YOUR FRIEND YET, LITTLE RYU?
OH.
WELL... SOME THINGS NEVER CHANGE.
BUT, WOW...
THAT'S A LOTTA BOOK-SHELVES.

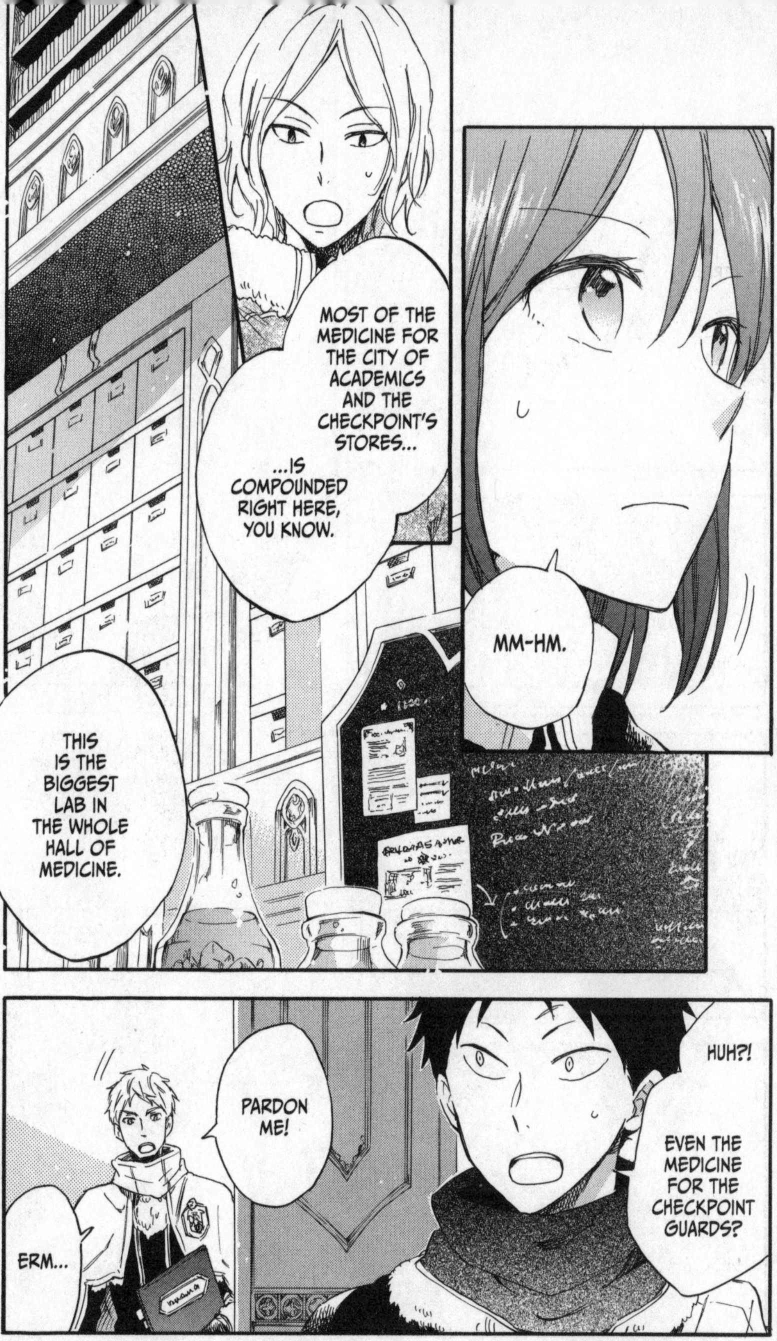
MOST OF THE MEDICINE FOR THE CITY OF ACADEMICS AND THE CHECKPOINT'S STORES...
...IS COMPOUNDED RIGHT HERE, YOU KNOW.
MM-HM.
THIS IS THE BIGGEST LAB IN THE WHOLE HALL OF MEDICINE.
HUH?!
EVEN THE MEDICINE FOR THE CHECKPOINT GUARDS?
PARDON ME!
ERM...

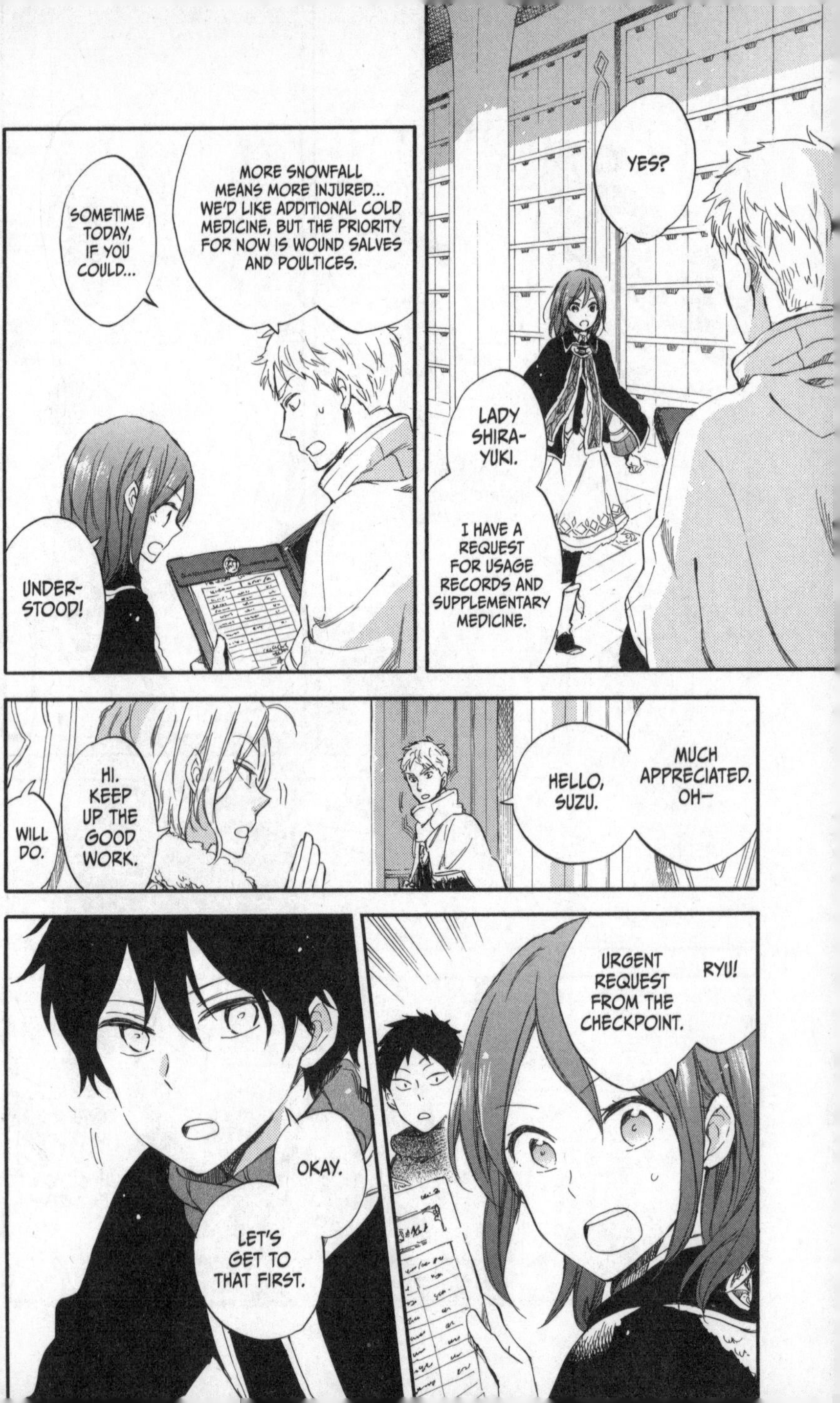
YES?
LADY SHIRA-YUKI.
I HAVE A REQUEST FOR USAGE RECORDS AND SUPPLEMENTARY MEDICINE.
MORE SNOWFALL MEANS MORE INJURED... WE'D LIKE ADDITIONAL COLD MEDICINE, BUT THE PRIORITY FOR NOW IS WOUND SALVES AND POULTICES.
SOMETIME TODAY, IF YOU COULD...
UNDER-STOOD!
MUCH APPRECIATED. OH—
HELLO, SUZU.
HI. KEEP UP THE GOOD WORK.
WILL DO.
RYU!
URGENT REQUEST FROM THE CHECKPOINT.
OKAY.
LET'S GET TO THAT FIRST.

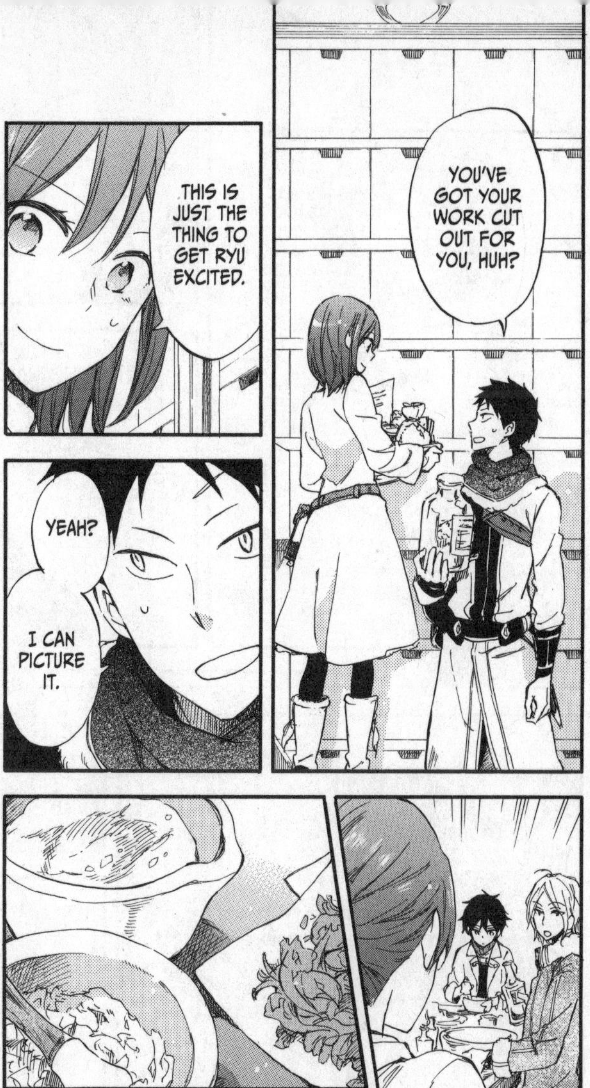
YOU'VE GOT YOUR WORK CUT OUT FOR YOU, HUH?
THIS IS JUST THE THING TO GET RYU EXCITED.
YEAH?
I CAN PICTURE IT.

## GREETINGS

Hello there! Akiduki, here. It's summer!

Thank you for picking up volume 14 of Snow White with the Red Hair!

1 4

Shirayuki and Kiki are gracing the cover with their presence. Phew.

About a month after submitting the cover, I saw a colored sample and noticed that Kiki's sword was sort of... um... Forget it... Just forget it...

This volume contains the usual chapters, plus a bonus chapter and a one-shot story. I hope you enjoy it!

Maybe the next cover will showcase the boys...

Rejected.

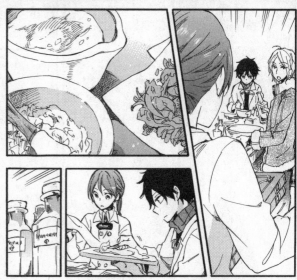

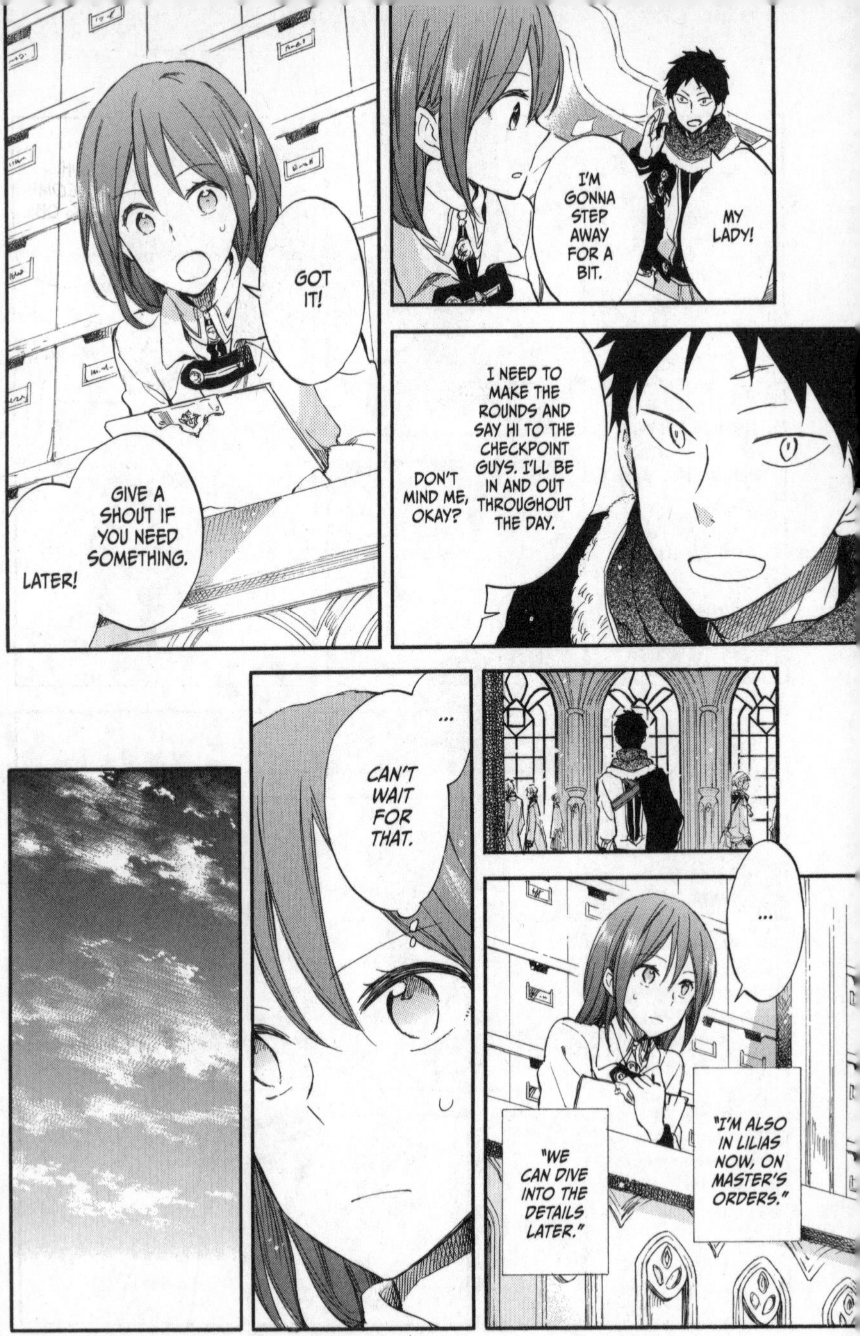
MY LADY!
I'M GONNA STEP AWAY FOR A BIT.
I NEED TO MAKE THE ROUNDS AND SAY HI TO THE CHECKPOINT GUYS. I'LL BE IN AND OUT THROUGHOUT THE DAY.
DON'T MIND ME, OKAY?
GOT IT!
GIVE A SHOUT IF YOU NEED SOMETHING.
LATER!
...
"I'M ALSO IN LILIAS NOW, ON MASTER'S ORDERS."
"WE CAN DIVE INTO THE DETAILS LATER."
...
CAN'T WAIT FOR THAT.

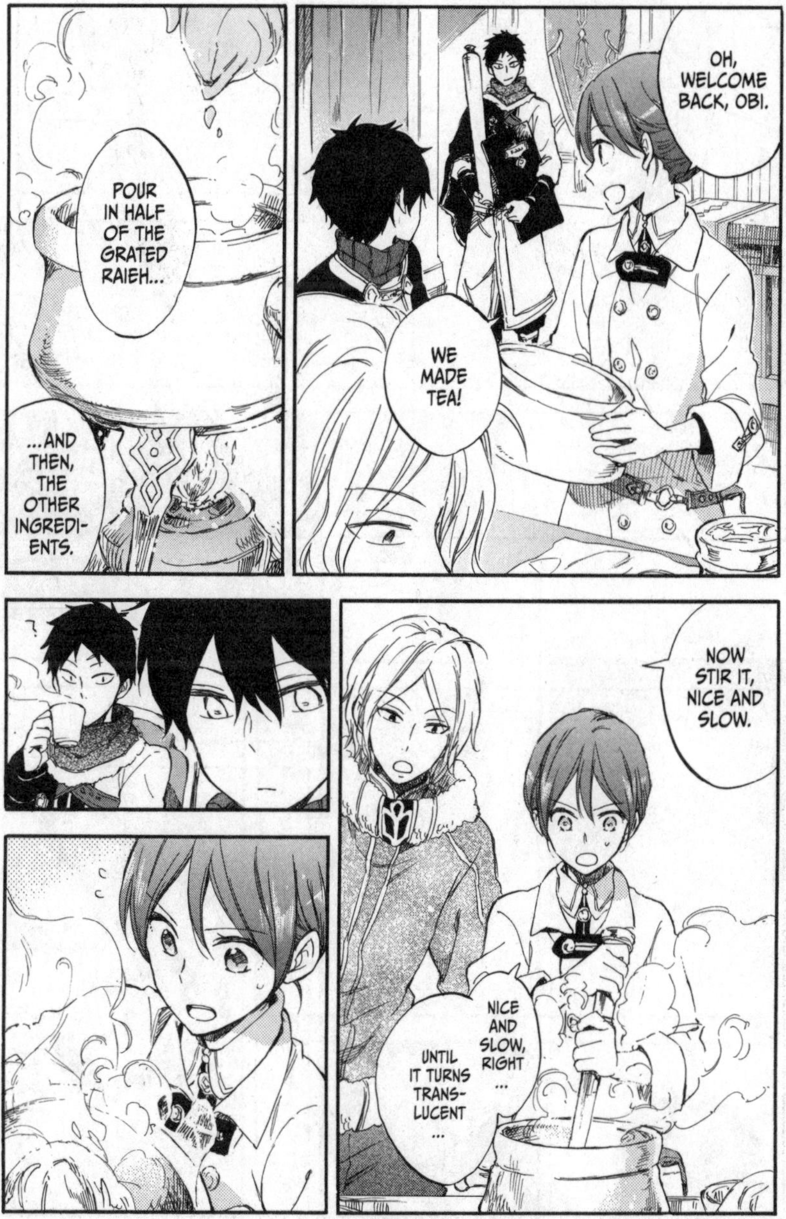
OH, WELCOME BACK, OBI.
WE MADE TEA!
POUR IN HALF OF THE GRATED RAIEH...
...AND THEN, THE OTHER INGREDIENTS.
NOW STIR IT, NICE AND SLOW.
NICE AND SLOW, RIGHT...
UNTIL IT TURNS TRANSLUCENT...
?

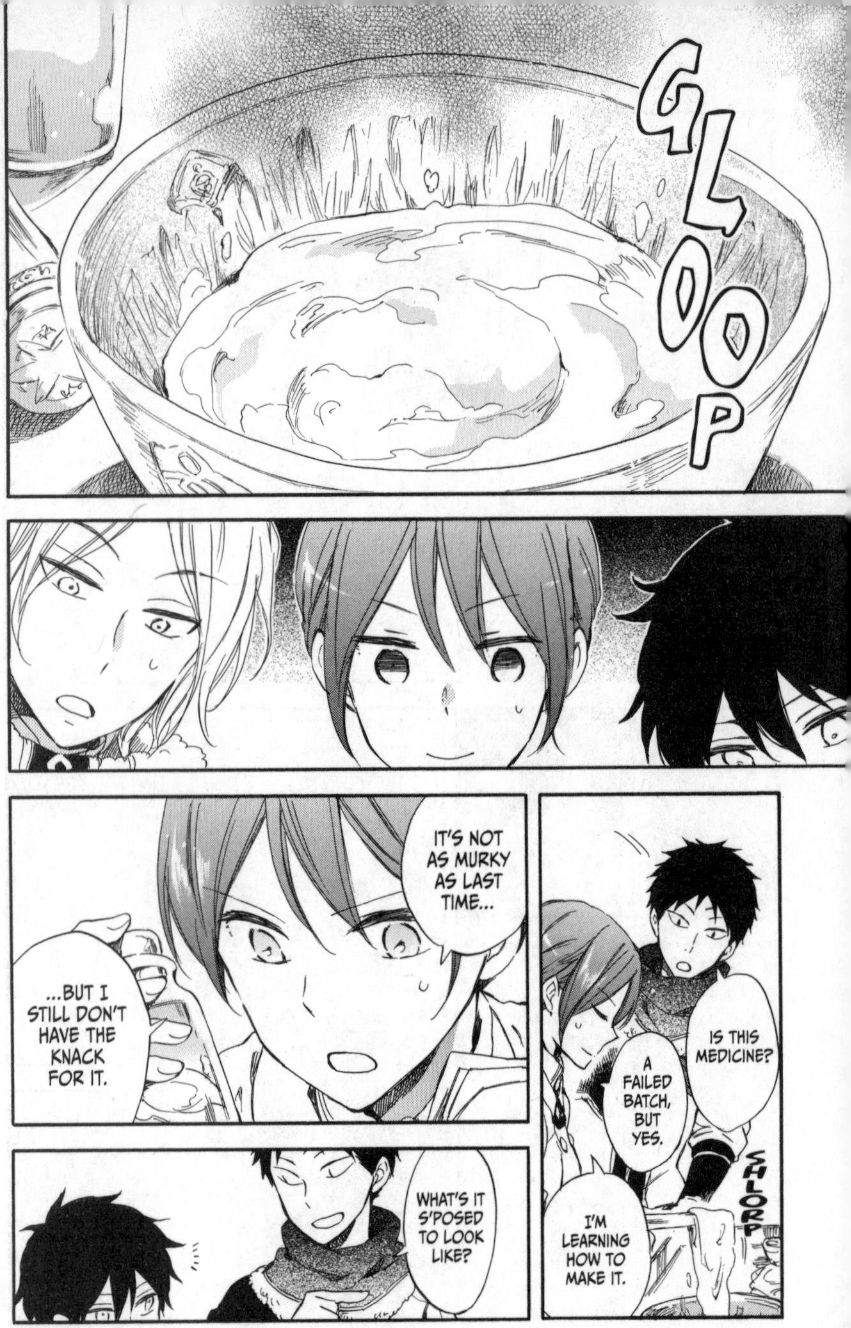
GLOOP
IS THIS MEDICINE?
A FAILED BATCH, BUT YES.
SHLORP
I'M LEARNING HOW TO MAKE IT.
IT'S NOT AS MURKY AS LAST TIME...
...BUT I STILL DON'T HAVE THE KNACK FOR IT.
WHAT'S IT S'POSED TO LOOK LIKE?

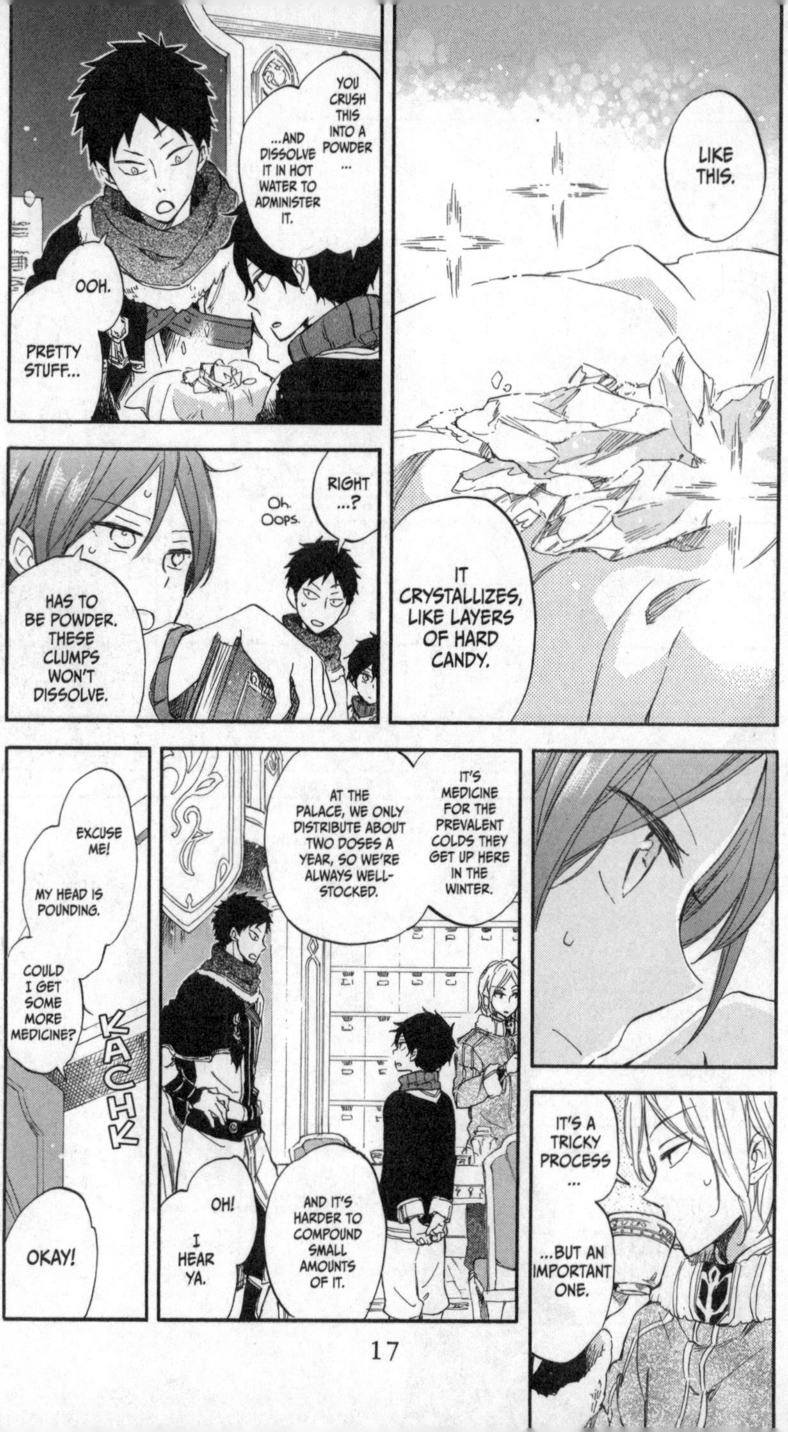
LIKE THIS.
IT CRYSTALLIZES, LIKE LAYERS OF HARD CANDY.
YOU CRUSH THIS INTO A POWDER ...
...AND DISSOLVE IT IN HOT WATER TO ADMINISTER IT.
OOH.
PRETTY STUFF...
RIGHT ...?
Oh. Oops.
HAS TO BE POWDER. THESE CLUMPS WON'T DISSOLVE.
IT'S A TRICKY PROCESS ...
...BUT AN IMPORTANT ONE.
IT'S MEDICINE FOR THE PREVALENT COLDS THEY GET UP HERE IN THE WINTER.
AT THE PALACE, WE ONLY DISTRIBUTE ABOUT TWO DOSES A YEAR, SO WE'RE ALWAYS WELL-STOCKED.
AND IT'S HARDER TO COMPOUND SMALL AMOUNTS OF IT.
OH!
I HEAR YA.
EXCUSE ME!
MY HEAD IS POUNDING.
COULD I GET SOME MORE MEDICINE?
KACHK
OKAY!

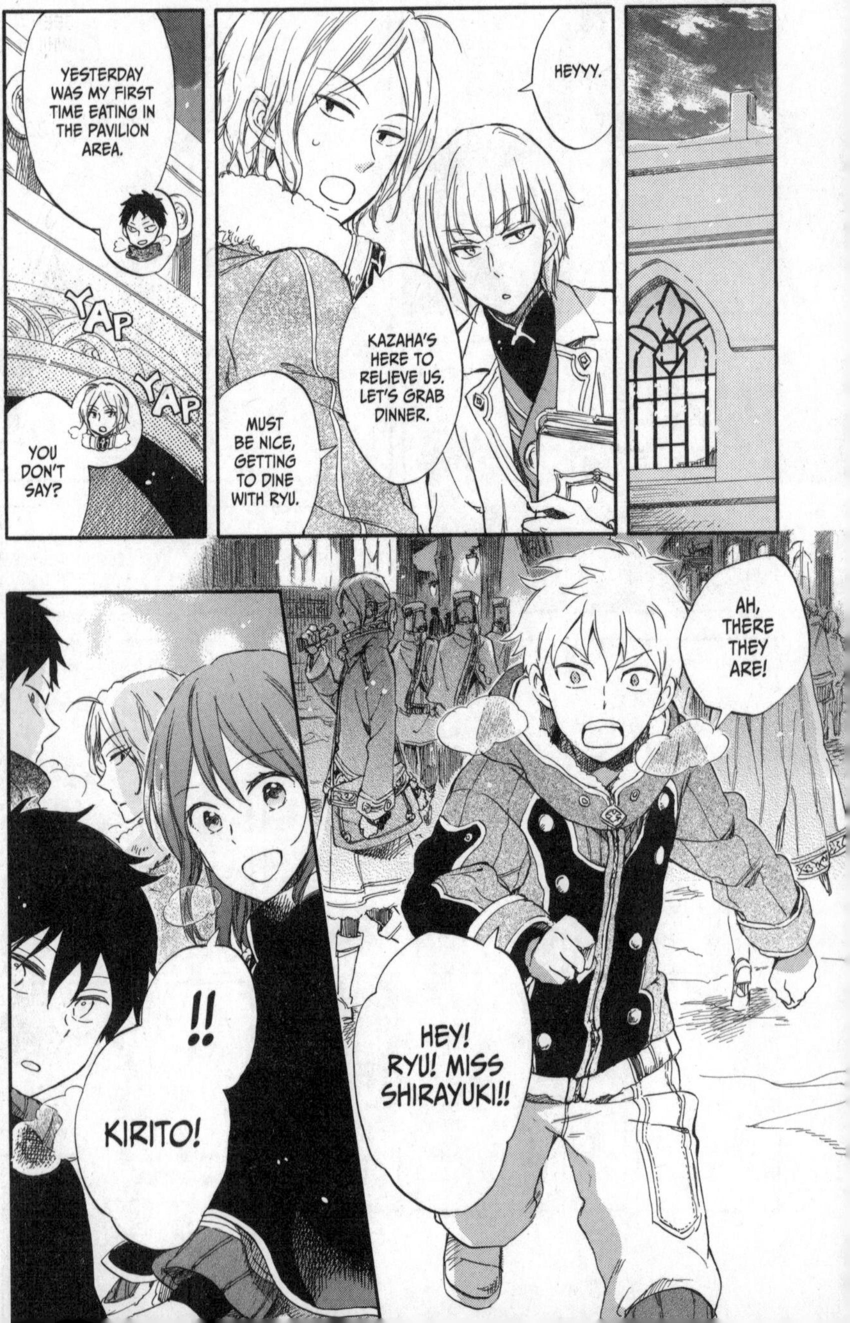
HEYYY.
KAZAHA'S HERE TO RELIEVE US. LET'S GRAB DINNER.
MUST BE NICE, GETTING TO DINE WITH RYU.
YESTERDAY WAS MY FIRST TIME EATING IN THE PAVILION AREA.
YAP
YAP
YOU DON'T SAY?
AH, THERE THEY ARE!
HEY! RYU! MISS SHIRAYUKI!!
!!
KIRITO!

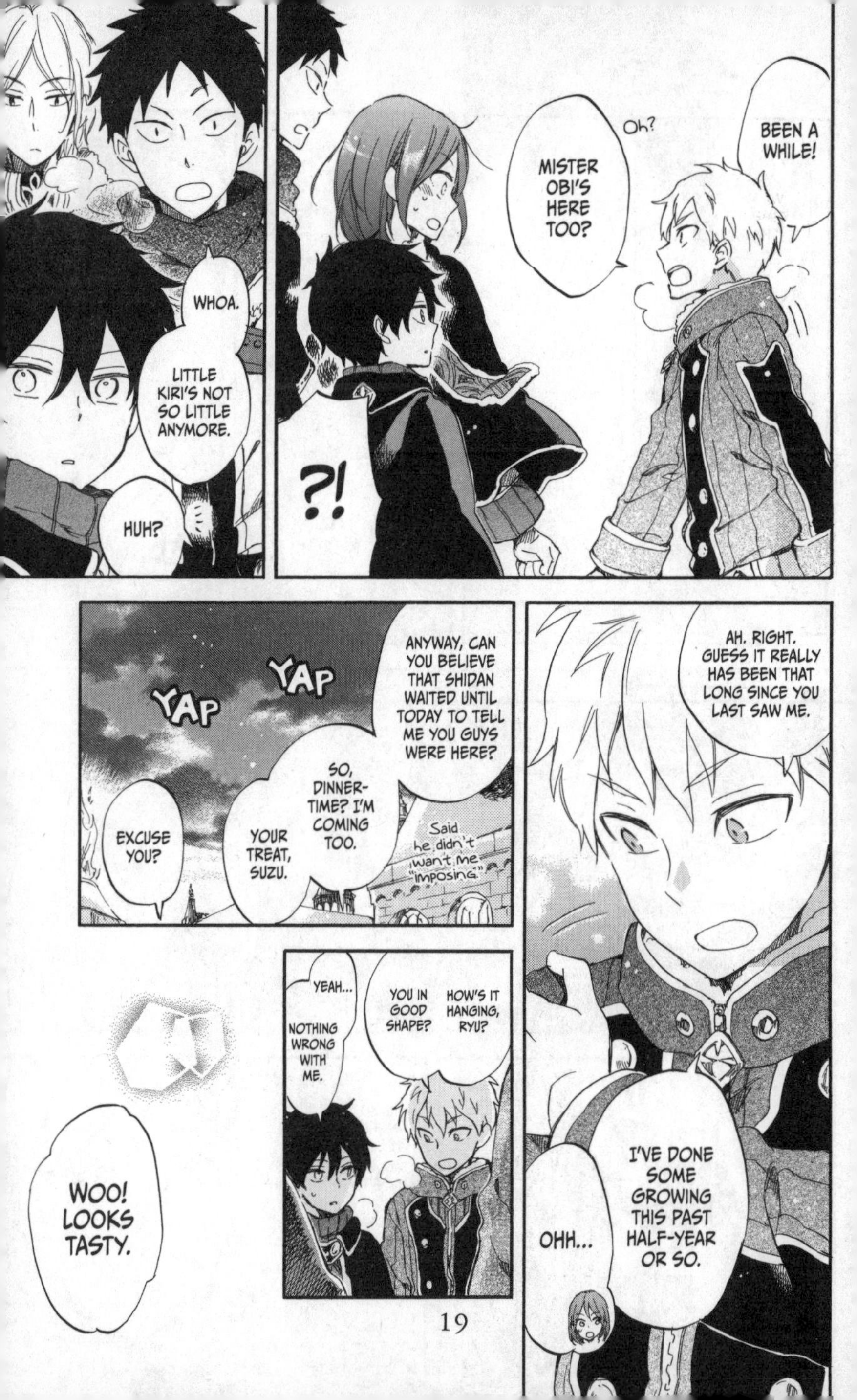
BEEN A WHILE!
Oh?
MISTER OBI'S HERE TOO?
?!
WHOA.
LITTLE KIRI'S NOT SO LITTLE ANYMORE.
HUH?
AH. RIGHT. GUESS IT REALLY HAS BEEN THAT LONG SINCE YOU LAST SAW ME.
I'VE DONE SOME GROWING THIS PAST HALF-YEAR OR SO.
OHH...
ANYWAY, CAN YOU BELIEVE THAT SHIDAN WAITED UNTIL TODAY TO TELL ME YOU GUYS WERE HERE?
YAP
YAP
SO, DINNER-TIME? I'M COMING TOO.
Said he didn't want me "imposing"
YOUR TREAT, SUZU.
EXCUSE YOU?
HOW'S IT HANGING, RYU?
YOU IN GOOD SHAPE?
YEAH...
NOTHING WRONG WITH ME.
WOO! LOOKS TASTY.

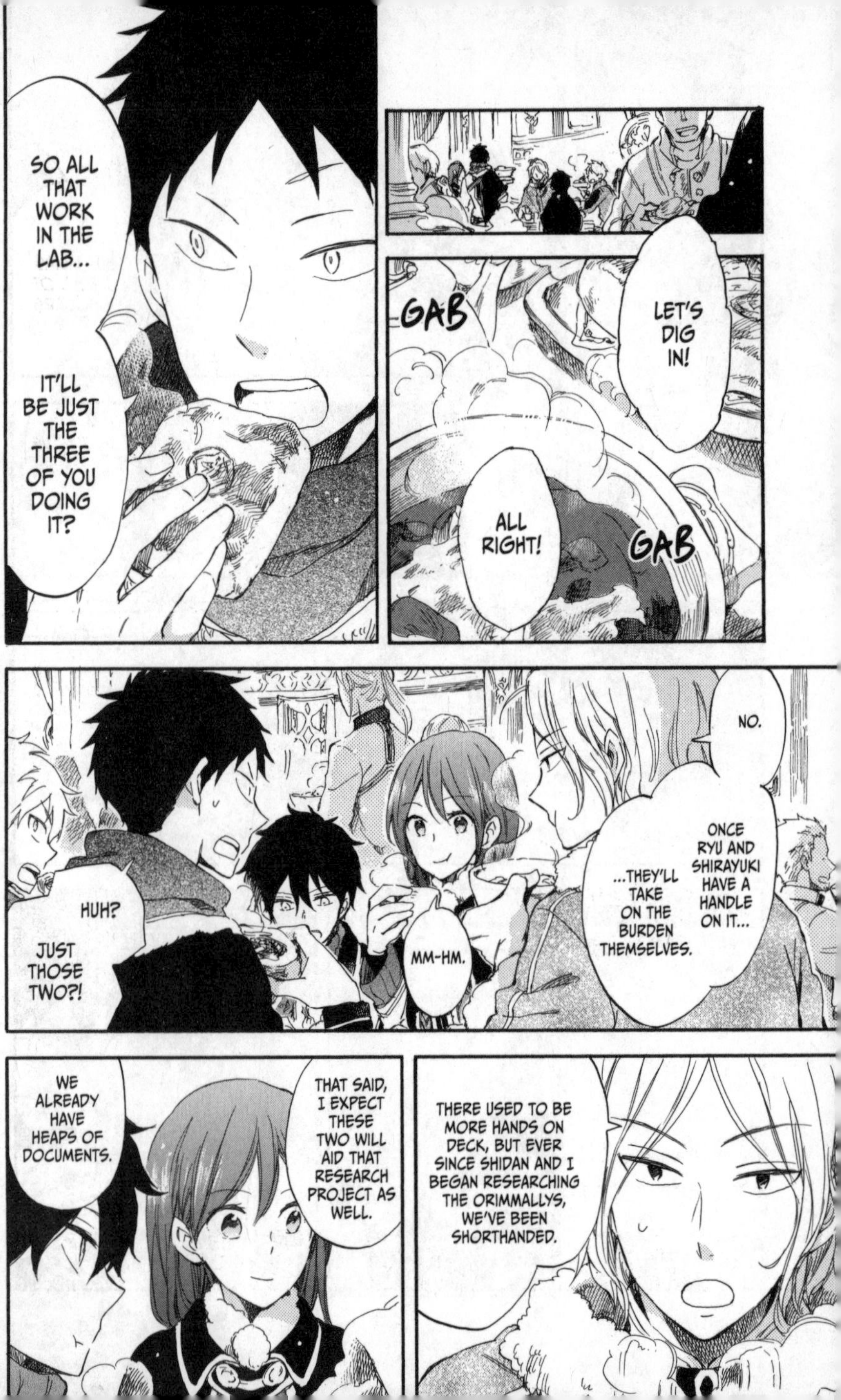
LET'S DIG IN!
GAB
GAB
ALL RIGHT!
SO ALL THAT WORK IN THE LAB...
IT'LL BE JUST THE THREE OF YOU DOING IT?
NO.
ONCE RYU AND SHIRAYUKI HAVE A HANDLE ON IT...
...THEY'LL TAKE ON THE BURDEN THEMSELVES.
MM-HM.
HUH?
JUST THOSE TWO?!
THERE USED TO BE MORE HANDS ON DECK, BUT EVER SINCE SHIDAN AND I BEGAN RESEARCHING THE ORIMMALLYS, WE'VE BEEN SHORTHANDED.
THAT SAID, I EXPECT THESE TWO WILL AID THAT RESEARCH PROJECT AS WELL.
WE ALREADY HAVE HEAPS OF DOCUMENTS.

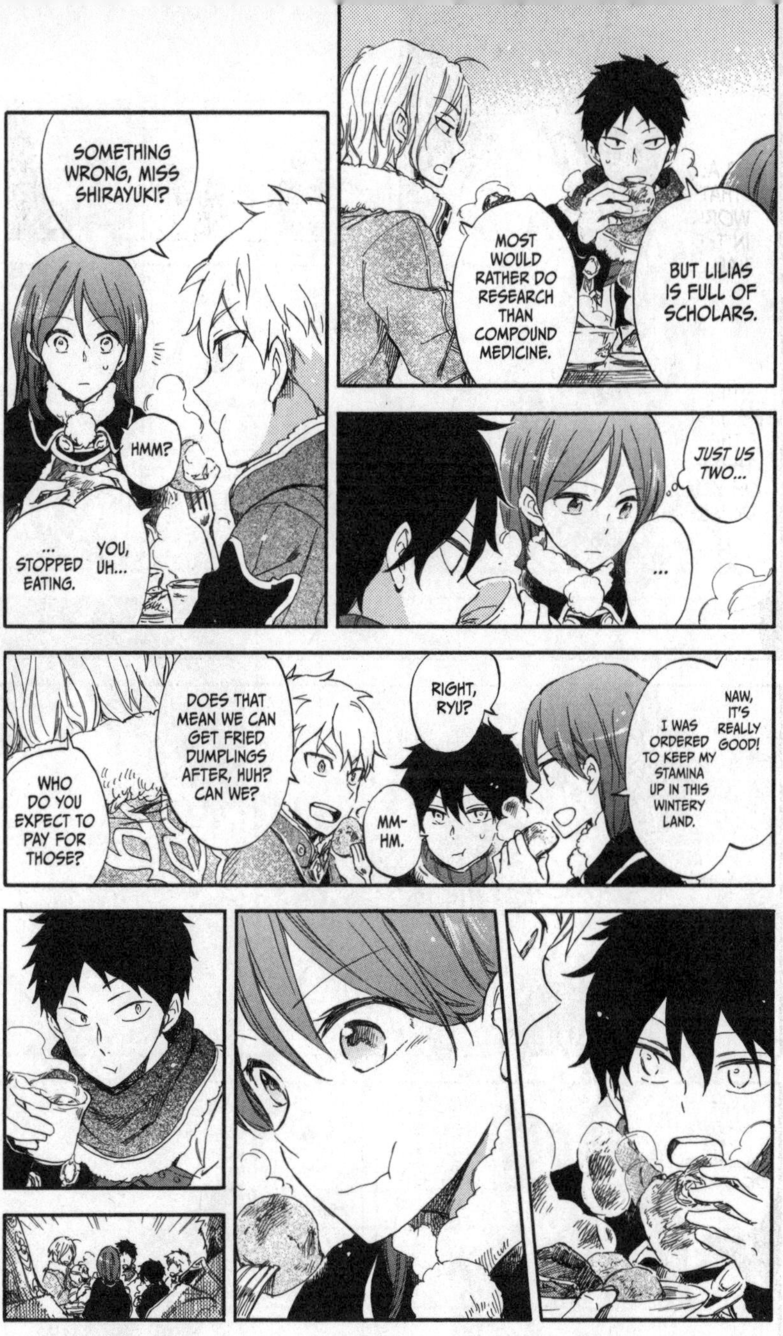

BUT LILIAS IS FULL OF SCHOLARS.
MOST WOULD RATHER DO RESEARCH THAN COMPOUND MEDICINE.
JUST US TWO...
...
SOMETHING WRONG, MISS SHIRAYUKI?
HMM?
YOU, UH...
... STOPPED EATING.
NAW, IT'S REALLY GOOD!
I WAS ORDERED TO KEEP MY STAMINA UP IN THIS WINTERY LAND.
RIGHT, RYU?
MM-HM.
DOES THAT MEAN WE CAN GET FRIED DUMPLINGS AFTER, HUH? CAN WE?
WHO DO YOU EXPECT TO PAY FOR THOSE?

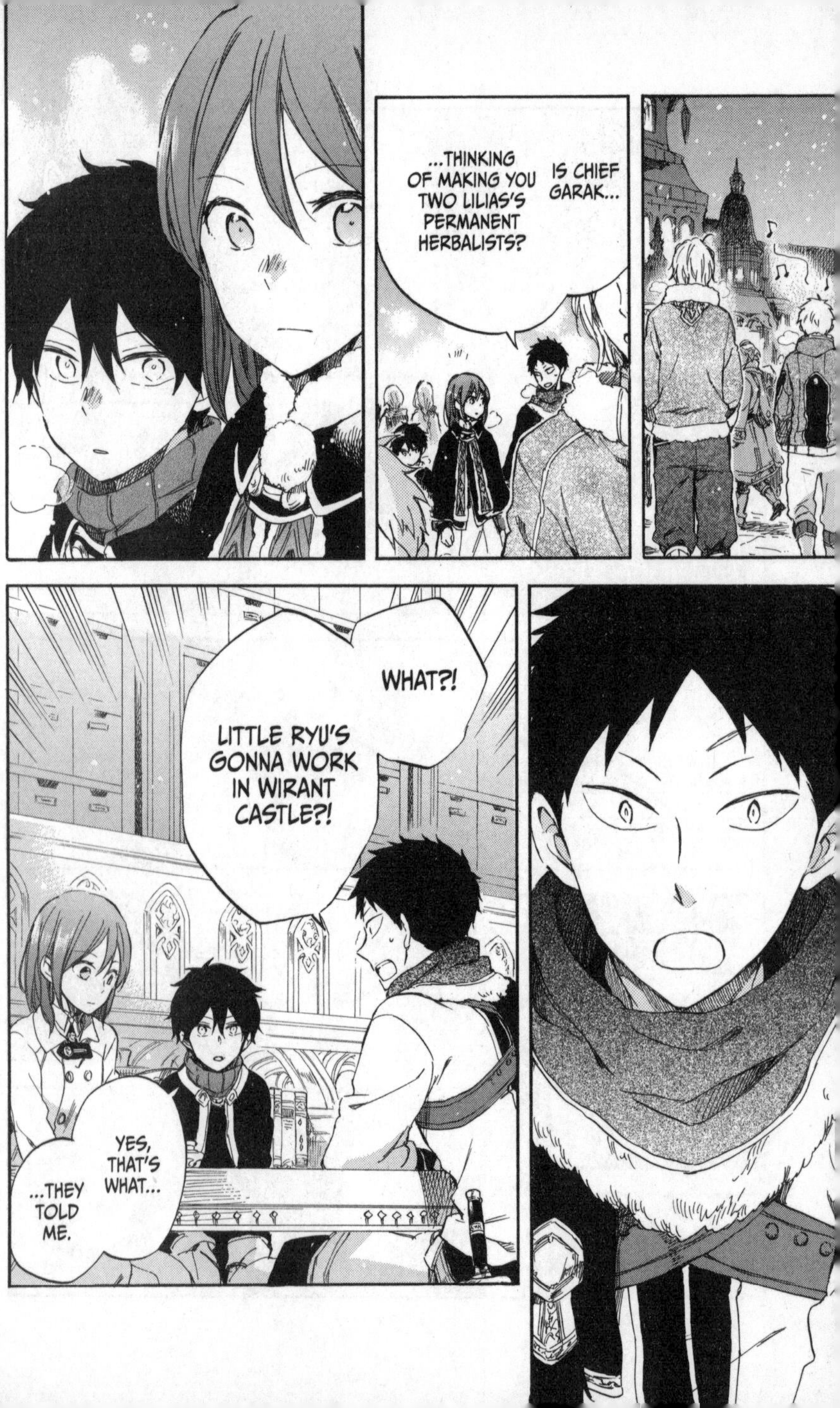
IS CHIEF GARAK...
...THINKING OF MAKING YOU TWO LILIAS'S PERMANENT HERBALISTS?
WHAT?!
LITTLE RYU'S GONNA WORK IN WIRANT CASTLE?!
YES, THAT'S WHAT...
...THEY TOLD ME.

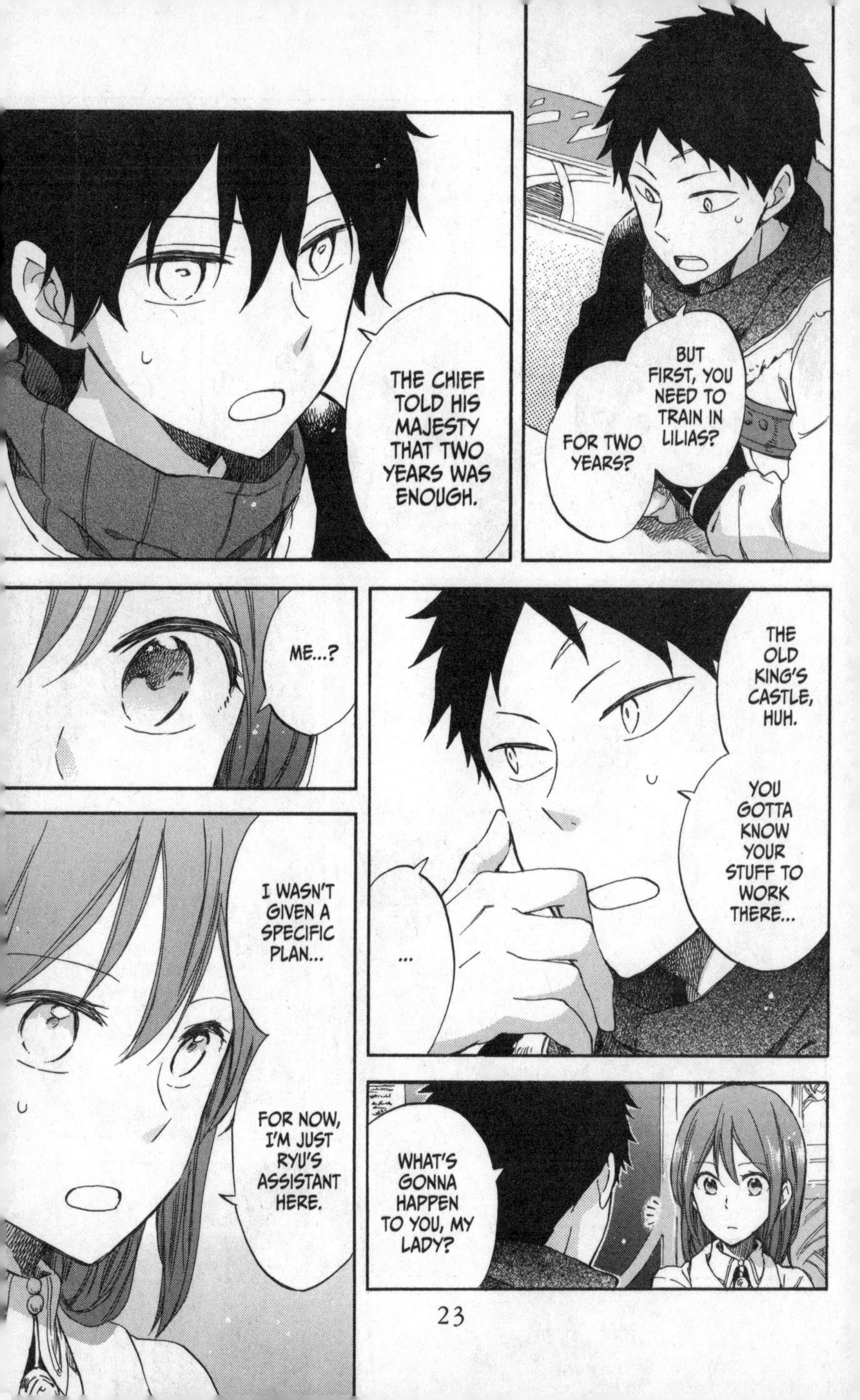
BUT FIRST, YOU NEED TO TRAIN IN LILIAS?
FOR TWO YEARS?
THE CHIEF TOLD HIS MAJESTY THAT TWO YEARS WAS ENOUGH.
THE OLD KING'S CASTLE, HUH.
YOU GOTTA KNOW YOUR STUFF TO WORK THERE...
...
WHAT'S GONNA HAPPEN TO YOU, MY LADY?
ME...?
I WASN'T GIVEN A SPECIFIC PLAN...
FOR NOW, I'M JUST RYU'S ASSISTANT HERE.

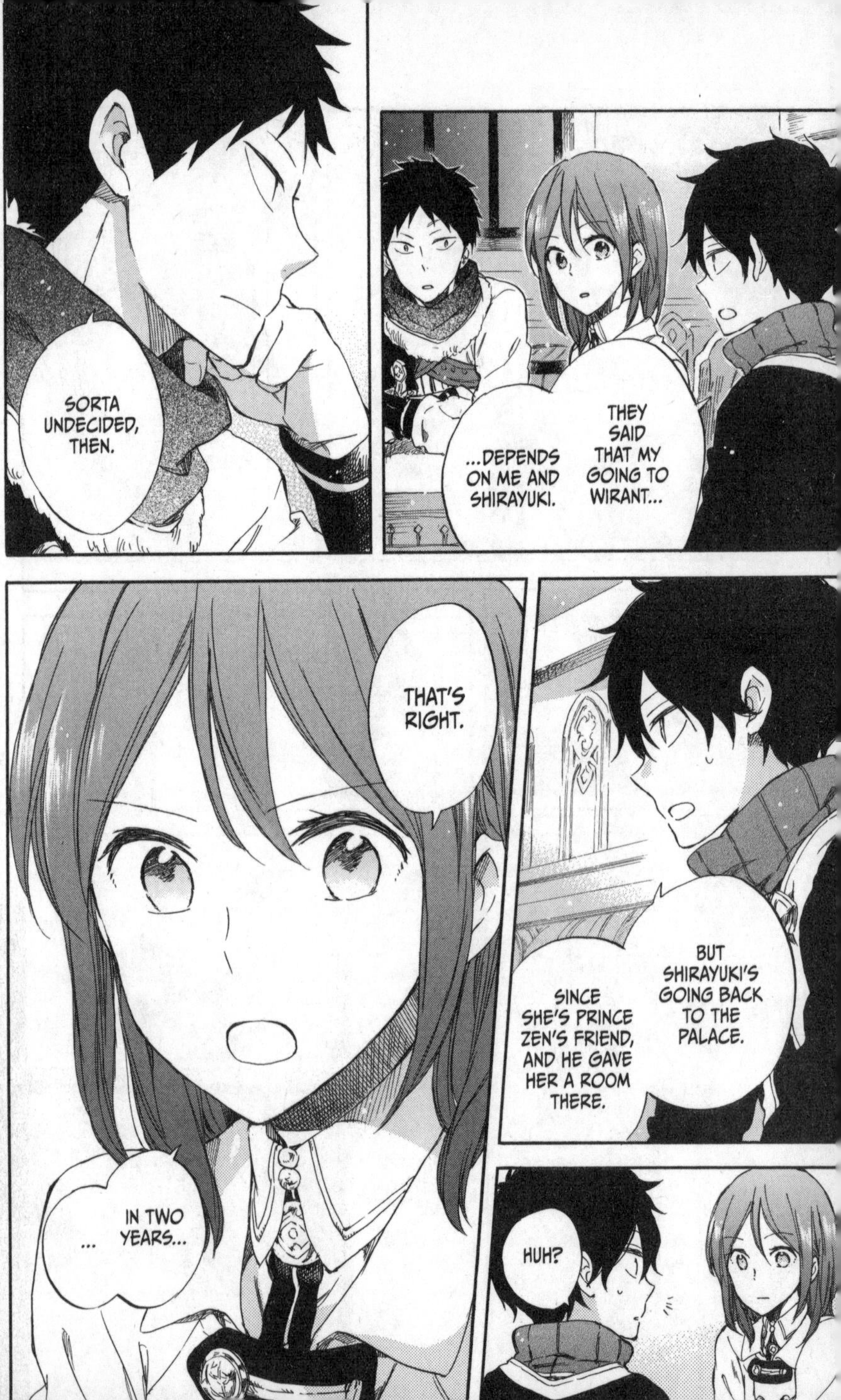
THEY SAID THAT MY GOING TO WIRANT...
...DEPENDS ON ME AND SHIRAYUKI.
SORTA UNDECIDED, THEN.
BUT SHIRAYUKI'S GOING BACK TO THE PALACE.
SINCE SHE'S PRINCE ZEN'S FRIEND, AND HE GAVE HER A ROOM THERE.
HUH?
THAT'S RIGHT.
...
IN TWO YEARS...

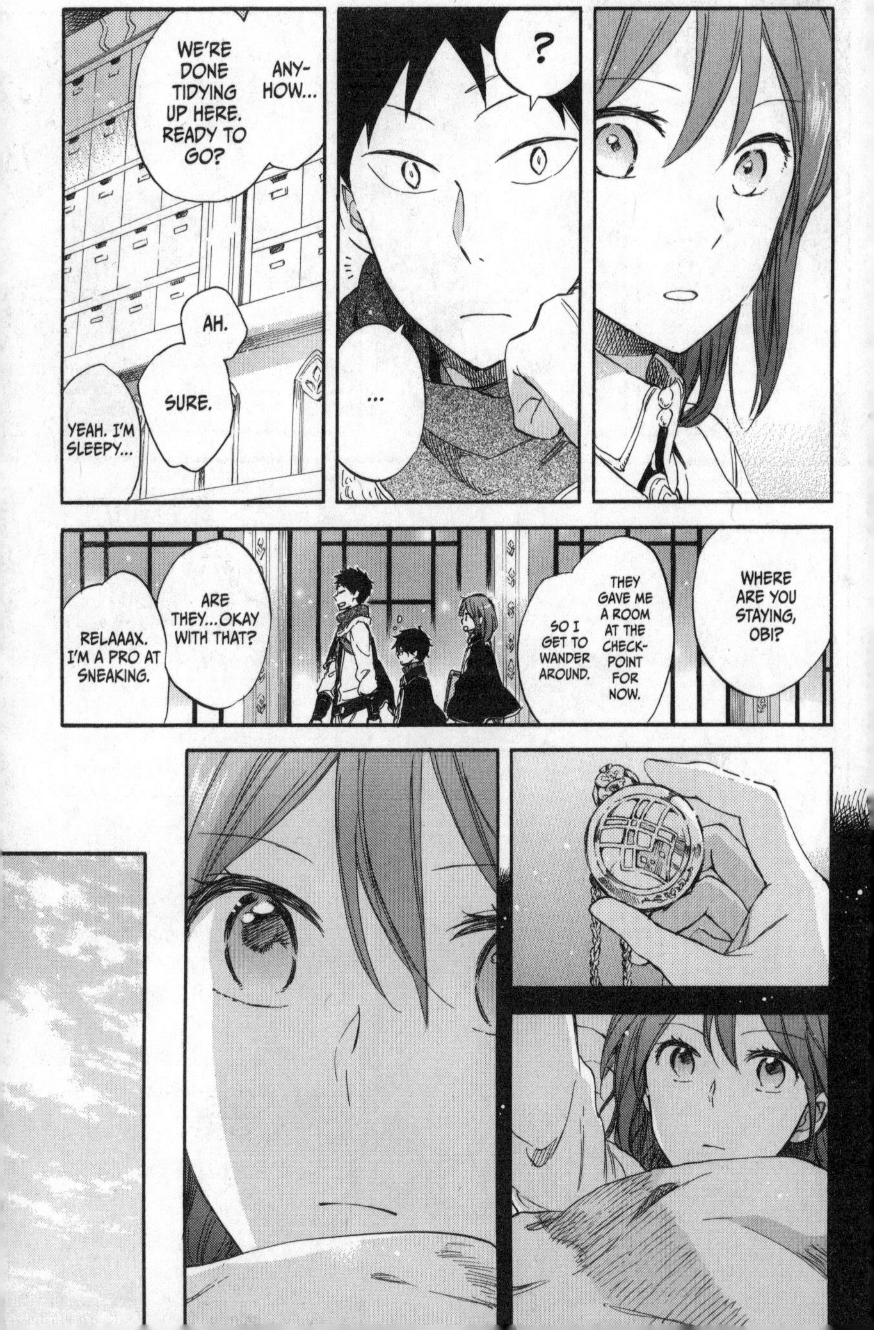
?
...
ANY-HOW...
WE'RE DONE TIDYING UP HERE. READY TO GO?
AH.
SURE.
YEAH. I'M SLEEPY...
WHERE ARE YOU STAYING, OBI?
THEY GAVE ME A ROOM AT THE CHECK-POINT FOR NOW.
SO I GET TO WANDER AROUND.
ARE THEY...OKAY WITH THAT?
RELAAAX. I'M A PRO AT SNEAKING.

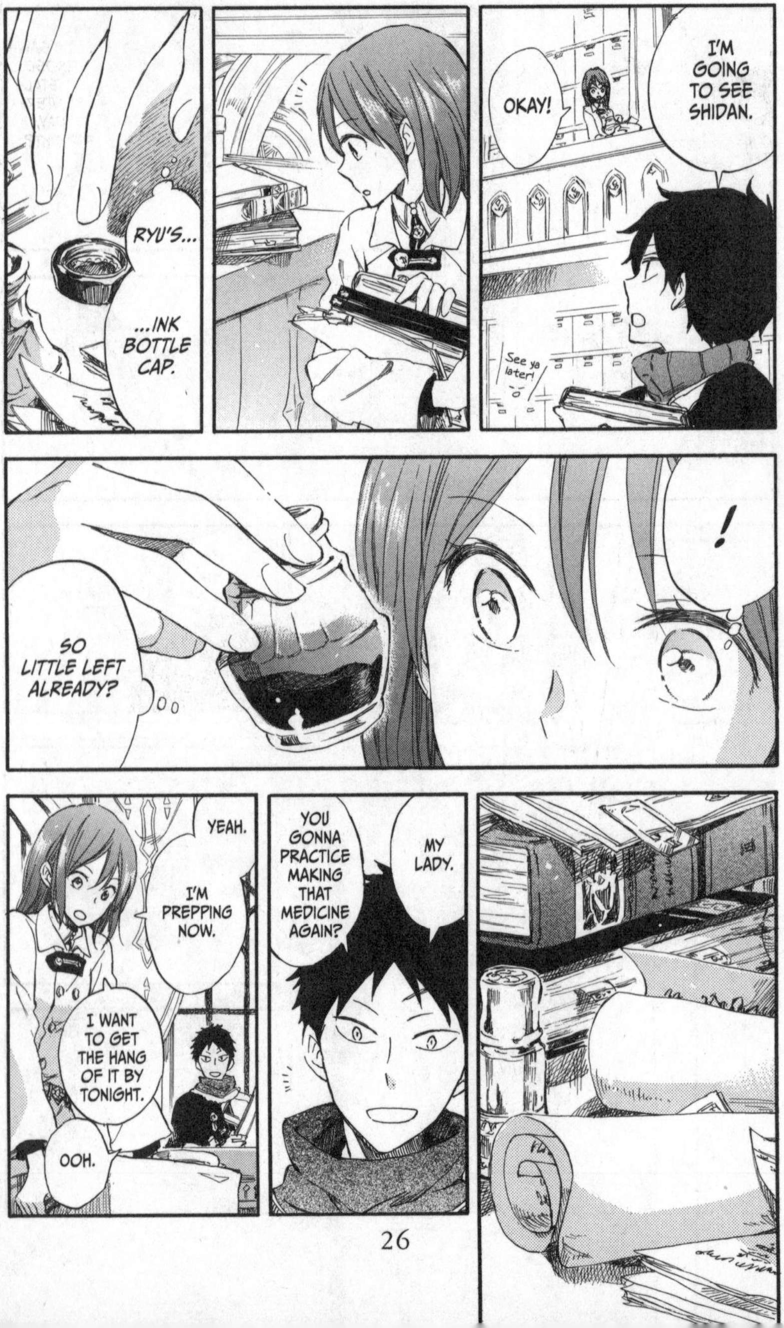
I'M GOING TO SEE SHIDAN.
OKAY!
See ya later!
RYU'S...
...INK BOTTLE CAP.
!
SO LITTLE LEFT ALREADY?
MY LADY.
YOU GONNA PRACTICE MAKING THAT MEDICINE AGAIN?
YEAH.
I'M PREPPING NOW.
I WANT TO GET THE HANG OF IT BY TONIGHT.
OOH.

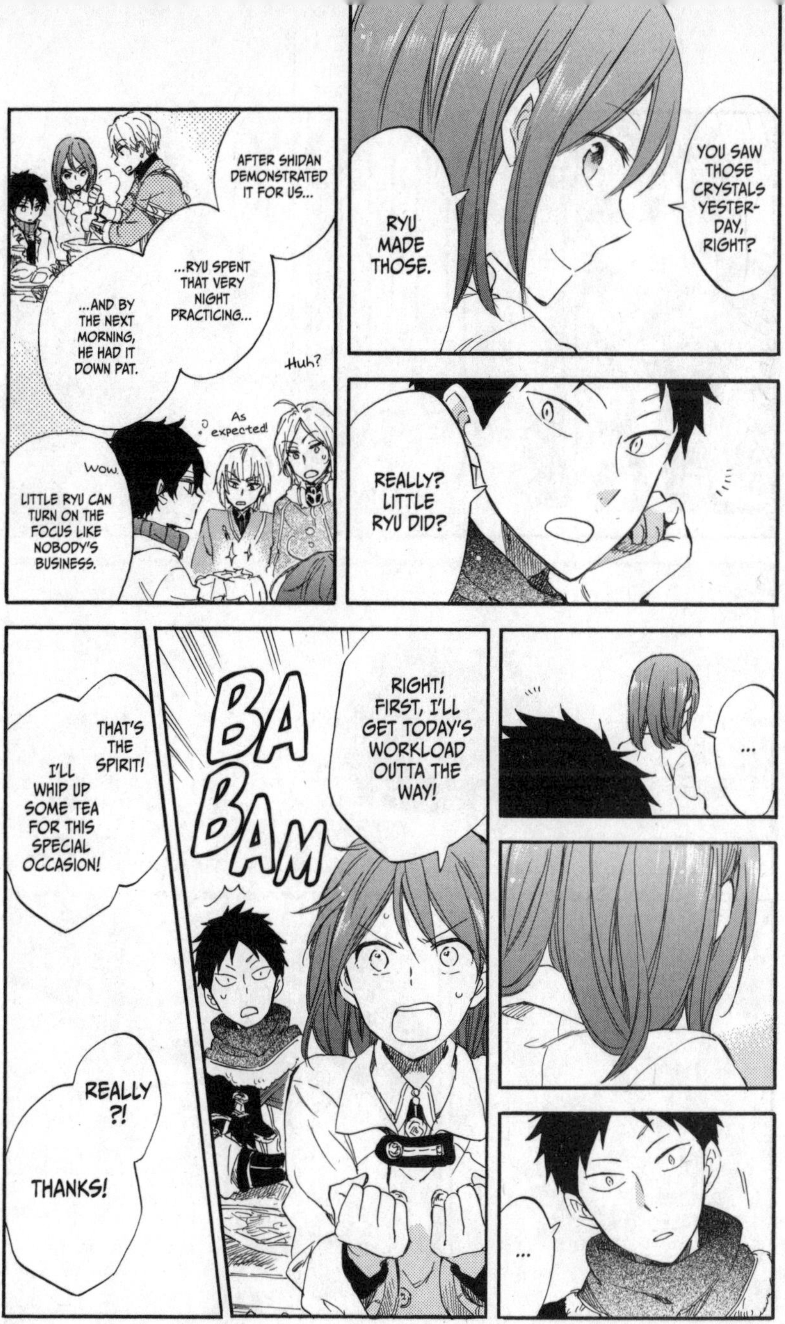
YOU SAW THOSE CRYSTALS YESTER-DAY, RIGHT?
RYU MADE THOSE.
REALLY? LITTLE RYU DID?
AFTER SHIDAN DEMONSTRATED IT FOR US...
...RYU SPENT THAT VERY NIGHT PRACTICING...
...AND BY THE NEXT MORNING, HE HAD IT DOWN PAT.
Huh?
As expected!
Wow.
LITTLE RYU CAN TURN ON THE FOCUS LIKE NOBODY'S BUSINESS.
...
...
RIGHT! FIRST, I'LL GET TODAY'S WORKLOAD OUTTA THE WAY!
BA BAM
THAT'S THE SPIRIT!
I'LL WHIP UP SOME TEA FOR THIS SPECIAL OCCASION!
REALLY?!
THANKS!

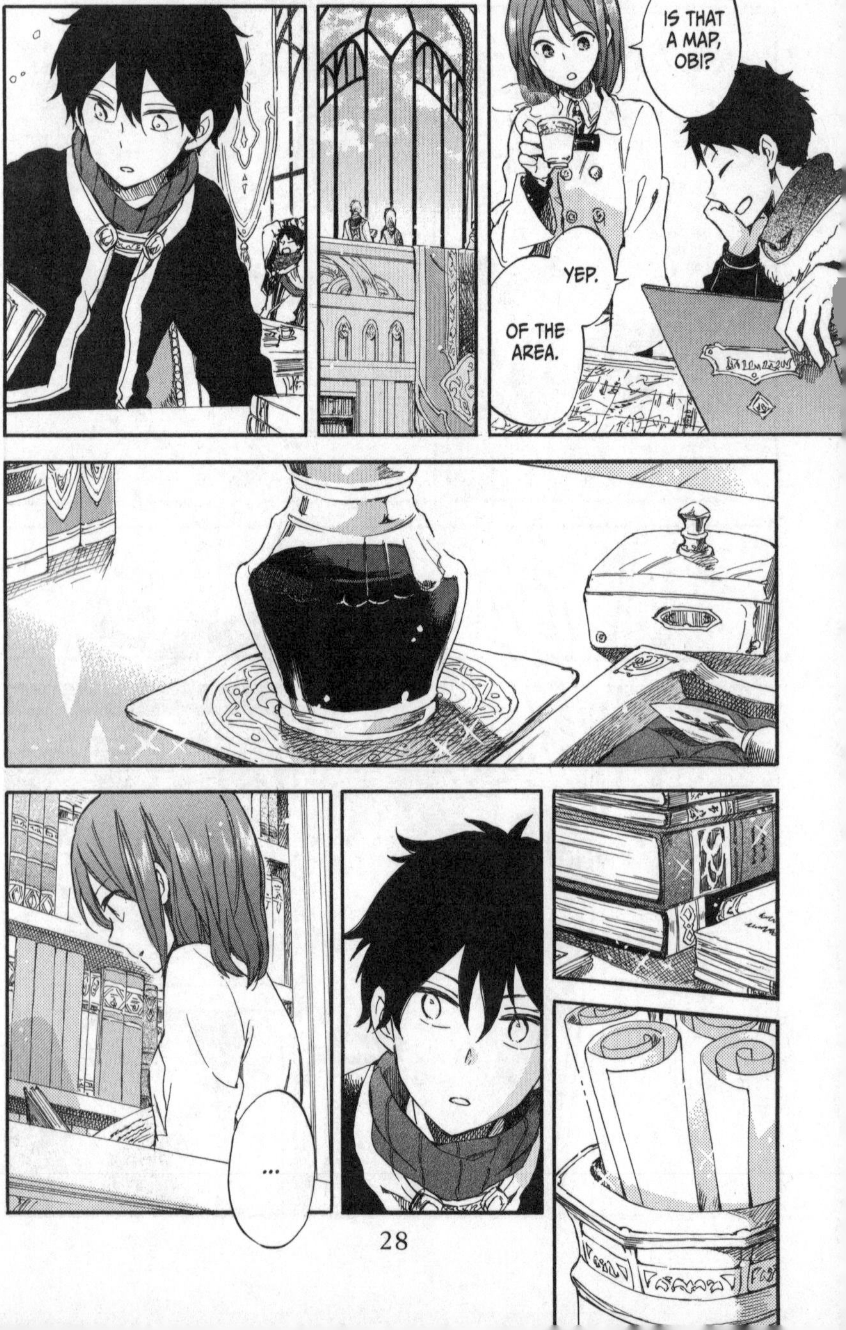
IS THAT A MAP, OBI?
YEP.
OF THE AREA.
...

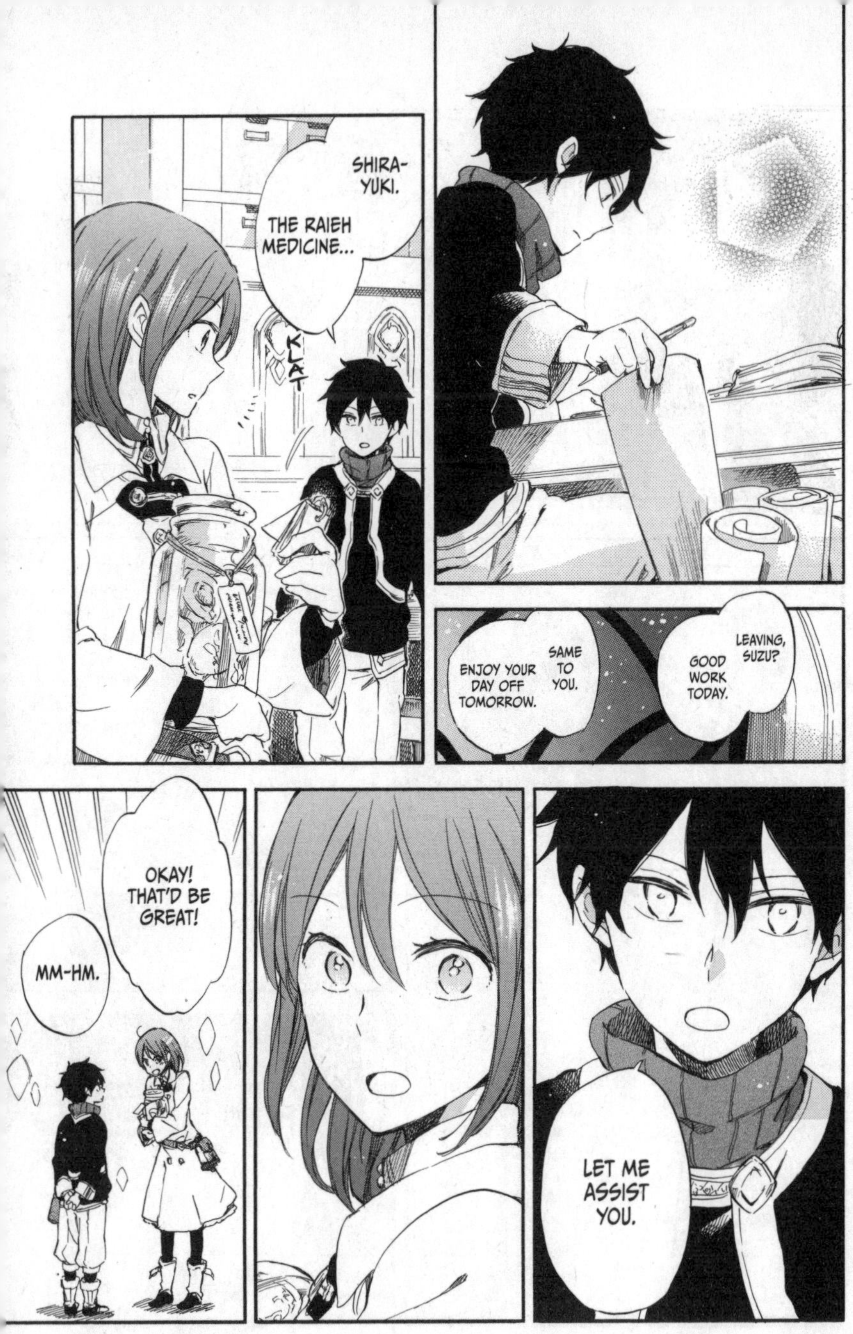
LEAVING, SUZU?
GOOD WORK TODAY.
SAME TO YOU.
ENJOY YOUR DAY OFF TOMORROW.
SHIRA-YUKI.
THE RAIEH MEDICINE...
KLAT
LET ME ASSIST YOU.
OKAY! THAT'D BE GREAT!
MM-HM.

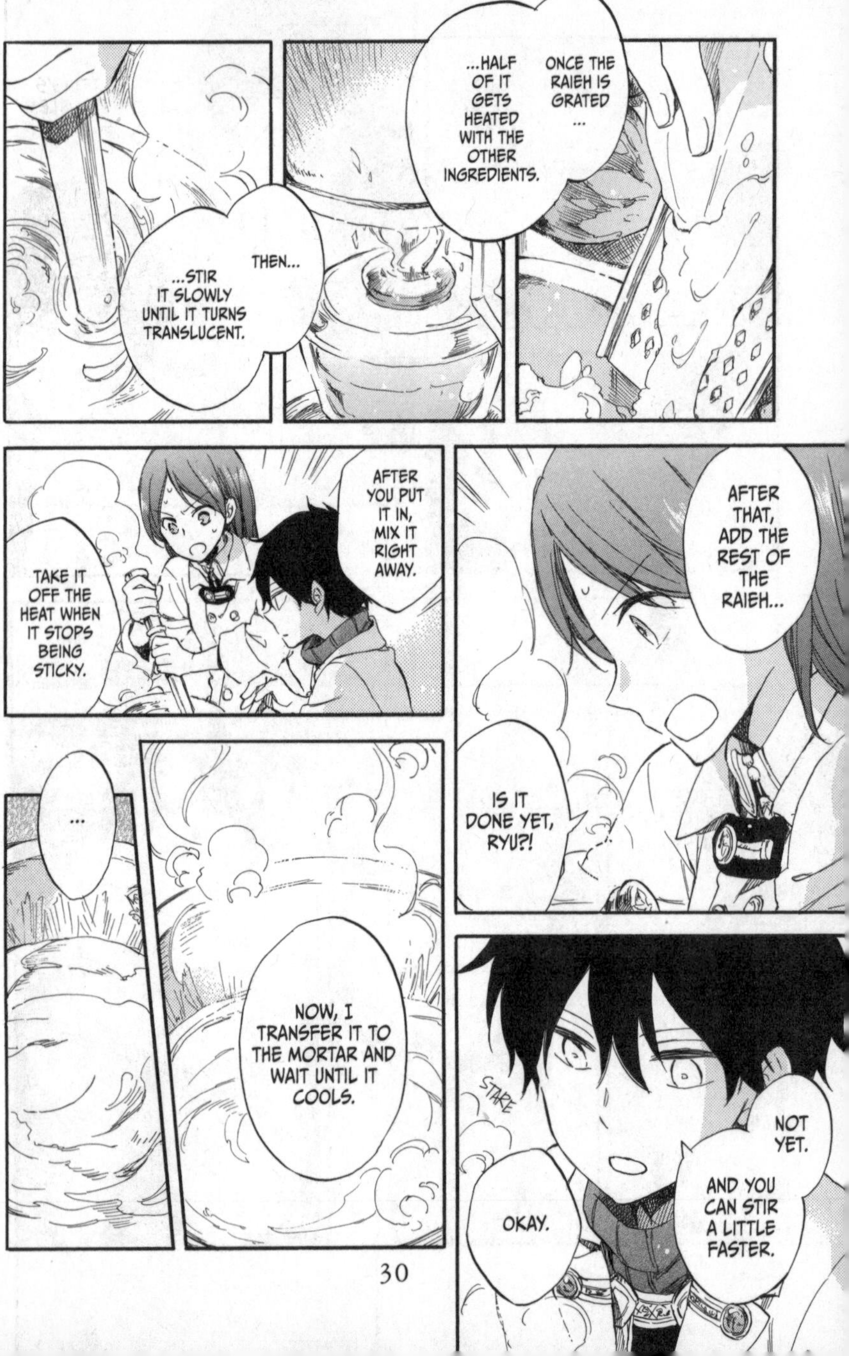
ONCE THE RAIEH IS GRATED...
...HALF OF IT GETS HEATED WITH THE OTHER INGREDIENTS.
THEN...
...STIR IT SLOWLY UNTIL IT TURNS TRANSLUCENT.
AFTER THAT, ADD THE REST OF THE RAIEH...
IS IT DONE YET, RYU?!
AFTER YOU PUT IT IN, MIX IT RIGHT AWAY.
TAKE IT OFF THE HEAT WHEN IT STOPS BEING STICKY.
STARE
NOT YET.
AND YOU CAN STIR A LITTLE FASTER.
OKAY.
NOW, I TRANSFER IT TO THE MORTAR AND WAIT UNTIL IT COOLS.
...

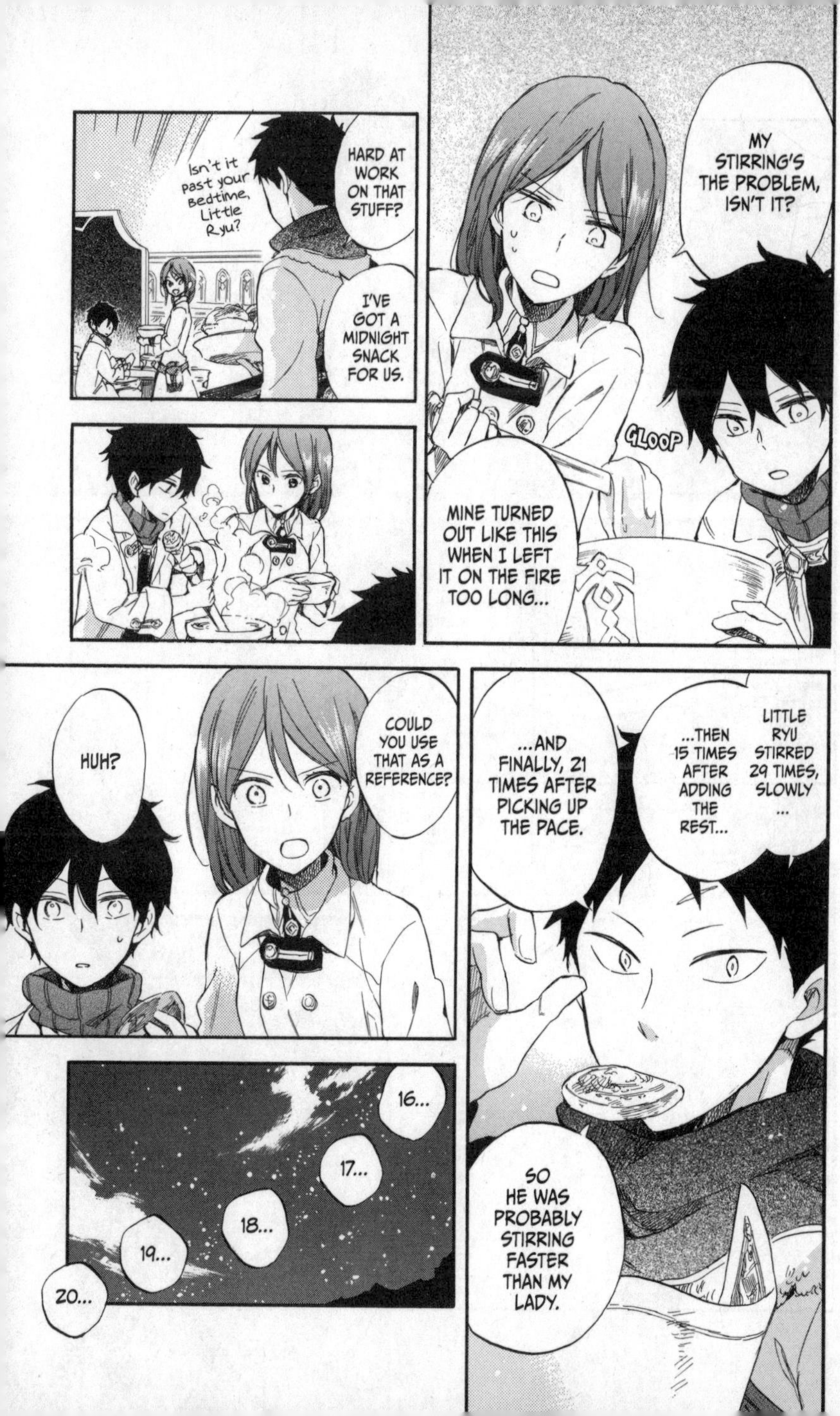
MY STIRRING'S THE PROBLEM, ISN'T IT?
GLOOP
MINE TURNED OUT LIKE THIS WHEN I LEFT IT ON THE FIRE TOO LONG...
HARD AT WORK ON THAT STUFF?
Isn't it past your bedtime, Little Ryu?
I'VE GOT A MIDNIGHT SNACK FOR US.
LITTLE RYU STIRRED 29 TIMES, SLOWLY...
...THEN 15 TIMES AFTER ADDING THE REST...
...AND FINALLY, 21 TIMES AFTER PICKING UP THE PACE.
SO HE WAS PROBABLY STIRRING FASTER THAN MY LADY.
COULD YOU USE THAT AS A REFERENCE?
HUH?
16...
17...
18...
19...
20...

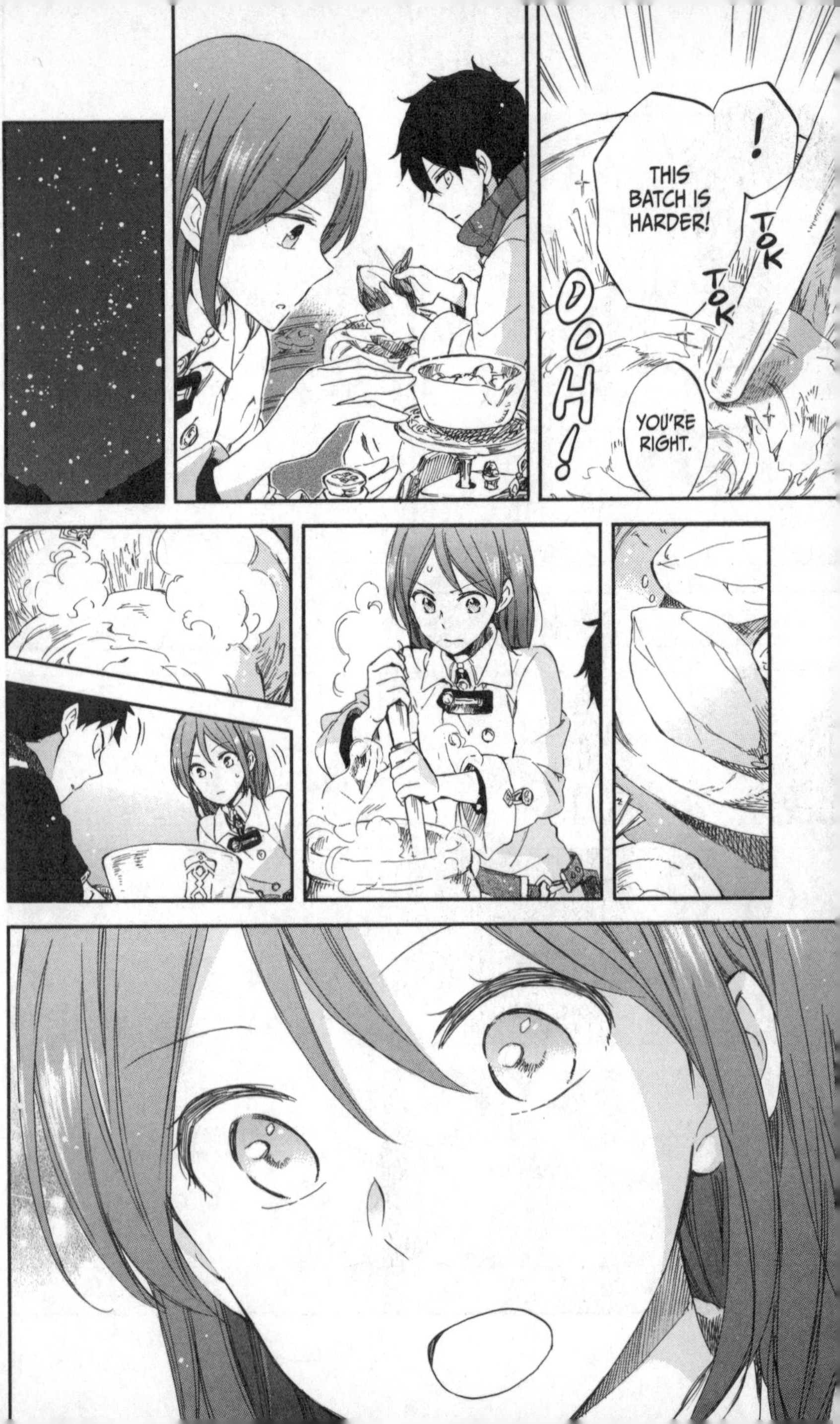
!
THIS BATCH IS HARDER!
TOK
TOK
OOOH!
YOU'RE RIGHT.

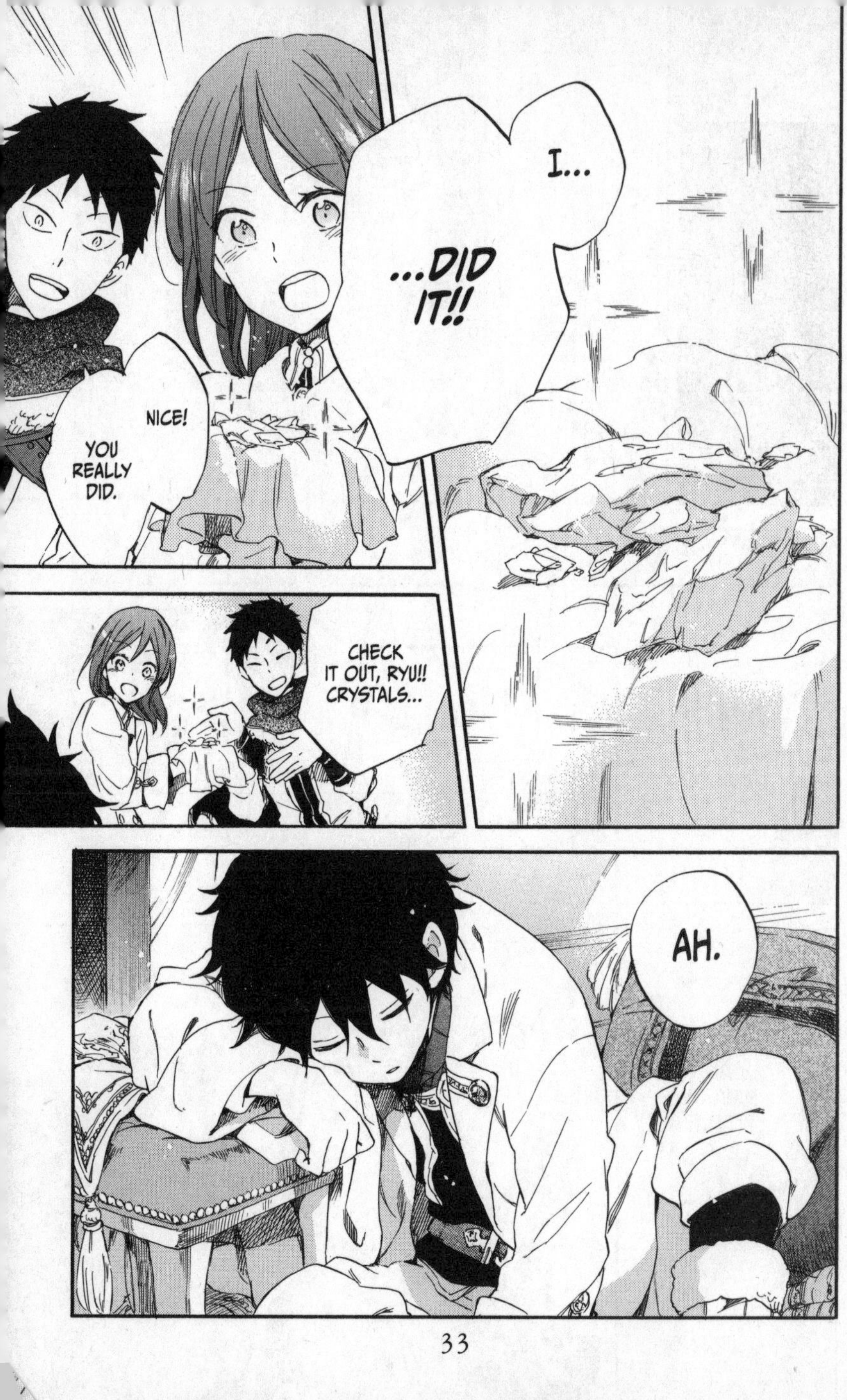
I...
...DID IT!!
NICE!
YOU REALLY DID.
CHECK IT OUT, RYU!! CRYSTALS...
AH.

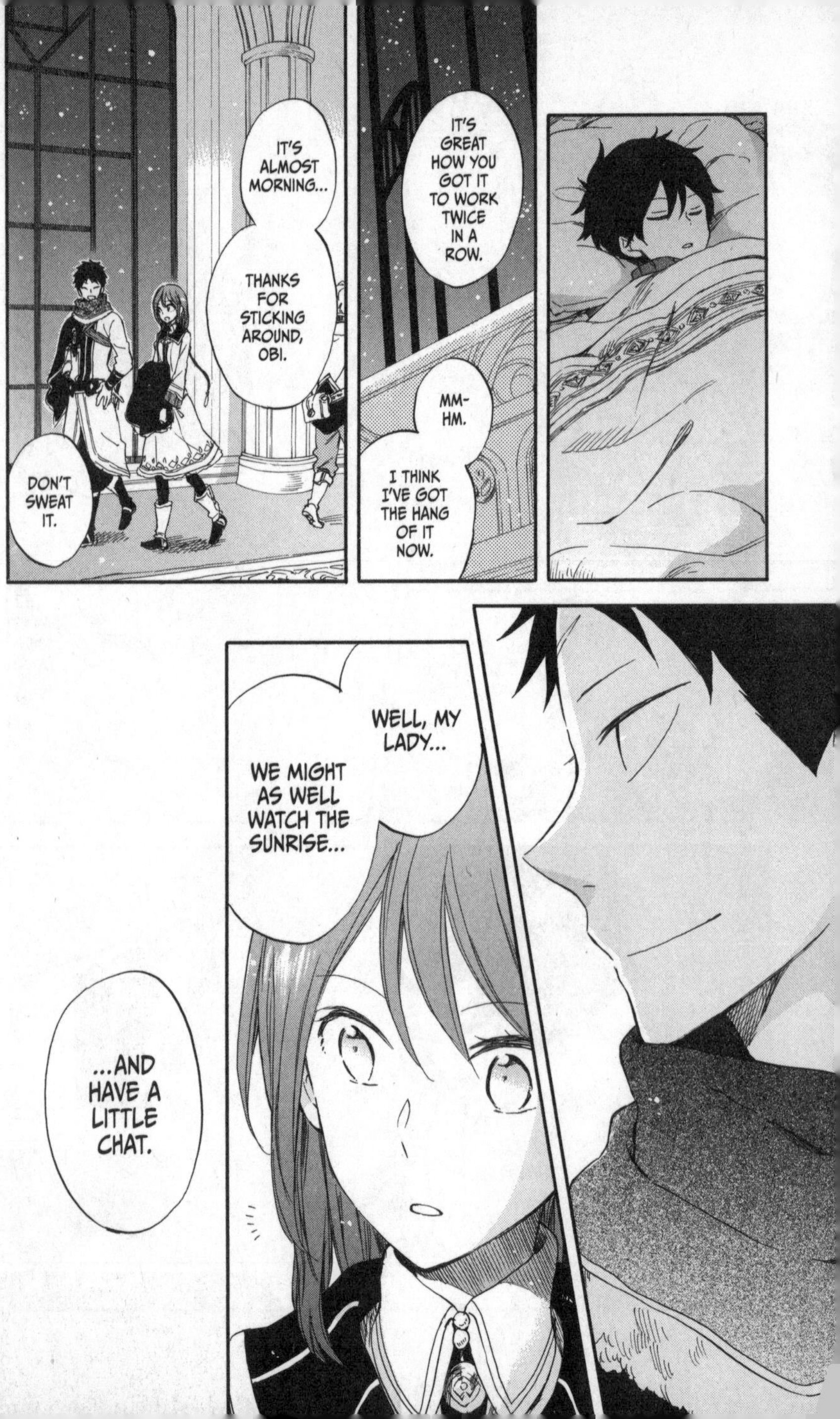
IT'S GREAT HOW YOU GOT IT TO WORK TWICE IN A ROW.
MM-HM.
I THINK I'VE GOT THE HANG OF IT NOW.
IT'S ALMOST MORNING...
THANKS FOR STICKING AROUND, OBI.
DON'T SWEAT IT.
WELL, MY LADY...
WE MIGHT AS WELL WATCH THE SUNRISE...
...AND HAVE A LITTLE CHAT.

# Chapter 62

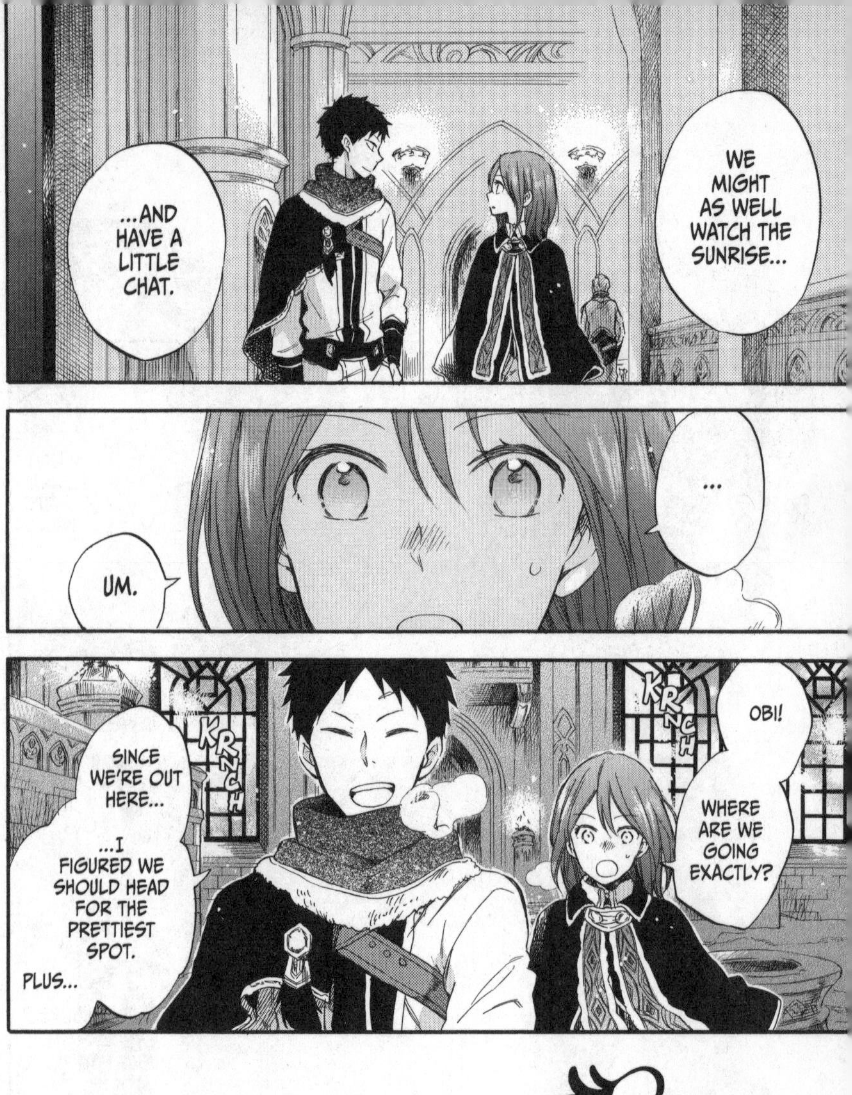
WE MIGHT AS WELL WATCH THE SUNRISE...
...AND HAVE A LITTLE CHAT.
...
UM.
OBI!
WHERE ARE WE GOING EXACTLY?
KRNCH
KRNCH
SINCE WE'RE OUT HERE...
...I FIGURED WE SHOULD HEAD FOR THE PRETTIEST SPOT.
PLUS...

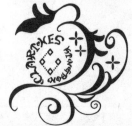

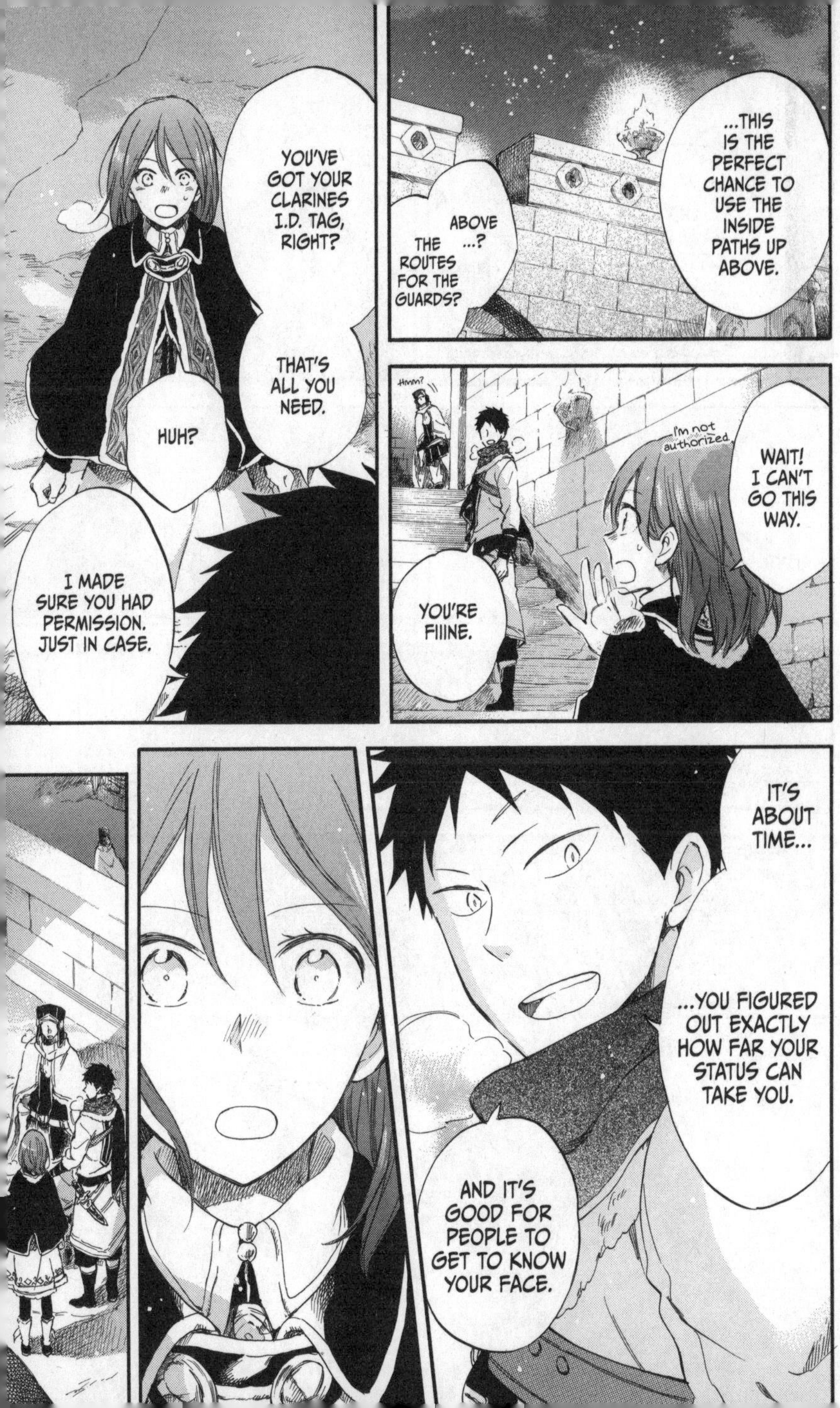
...THIS IS THE PERFECT CHANCE TO USE THE INSIDE PATHS UP ABOVE.
ABOVE ...?
THE ROUTES FOR THE GUARDS?
Hmm?
I'm not authorized
WAIT! I CAN'T GO THIS WAY.
YOU'RE FIIINE.
YOU'VE GOT YOUR CLARINES I.D. TAG, RIGHT?
THAT'S ALL YOU NEED.
HUH?
I MADE SURE YOU HAD PERMISSION. JUST IN CASE.
IT'S ABOUT TIME...
...YOU FIGURED OUT EXACTLY HOW FAR YOUR STATUS CAN TAKE YOU.
AND IT'S GOOD FOR PEOPLE TO GET TO KNOW YOUR FACE.

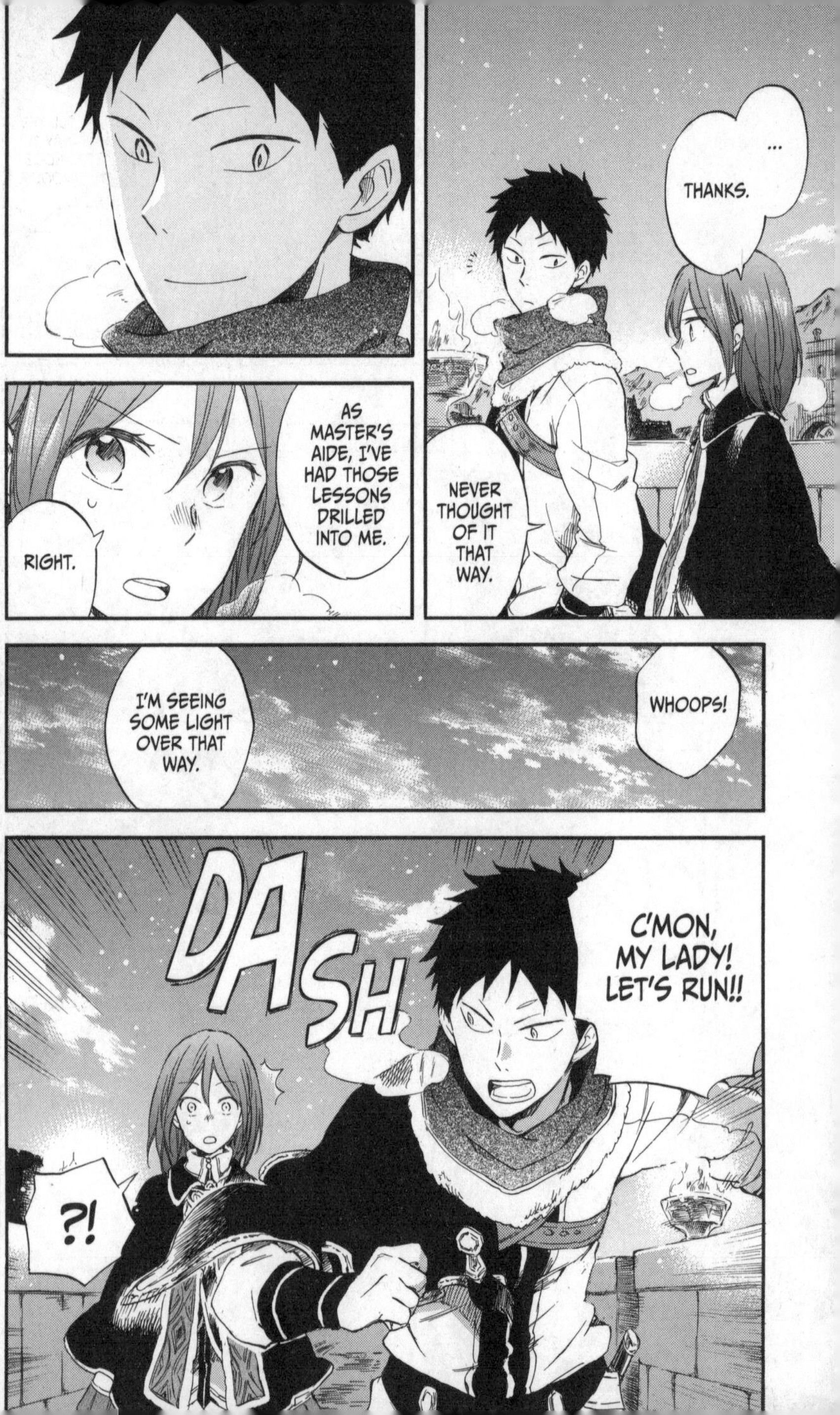
...
THANKS.
NEVER THOUGHT OF IT THAT WAY.
AS MASTER'S AIDE, I'VE HAD THOSE LESSONS DRILLED INTO ME.
RIGHT.
WHOOPS!
I'M SEEING SOME LIGHT OVER THAT WAY.
C'MON, MY LADY! LET'S RUN!!
DASH
?!

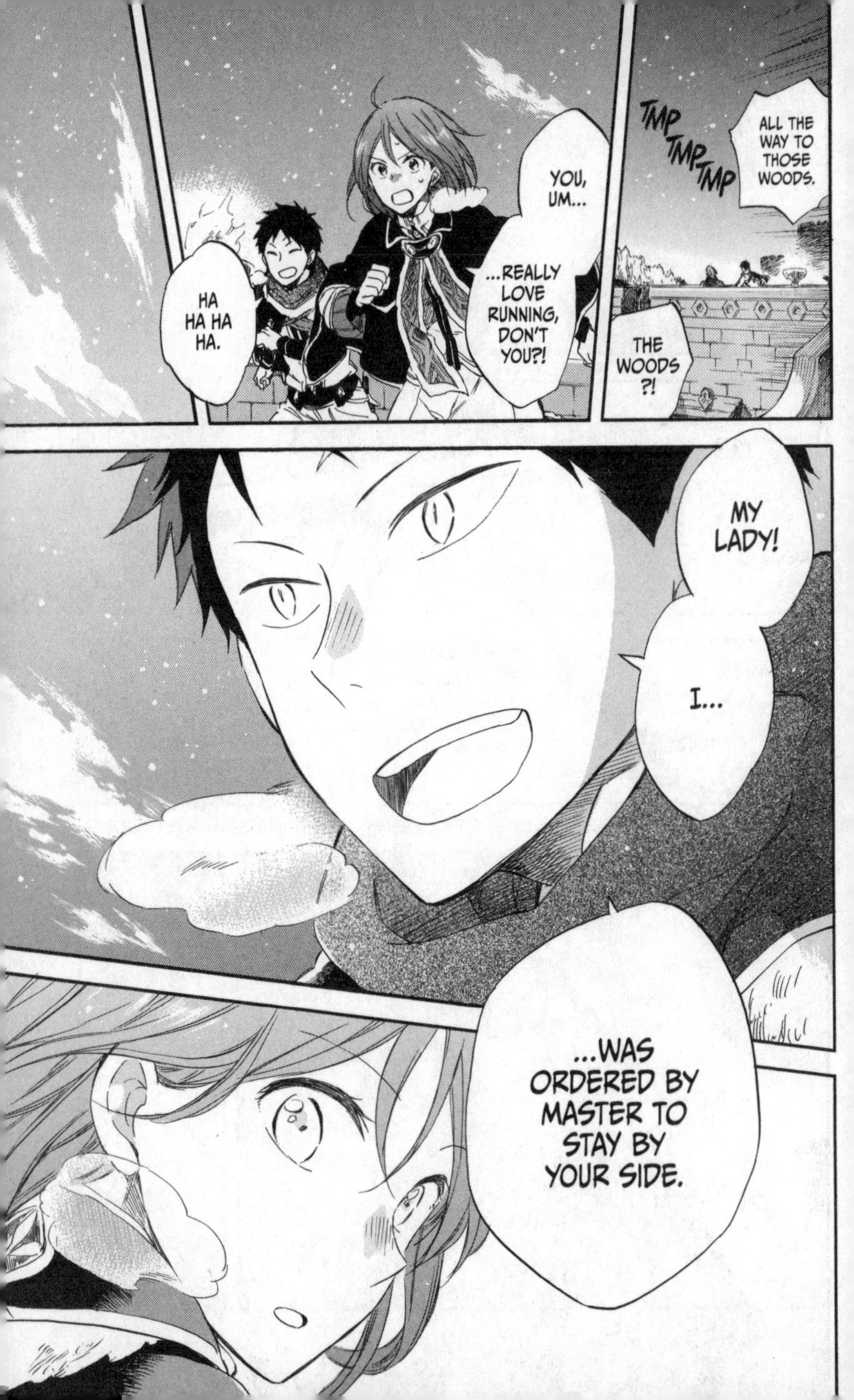
ALL THE WAY TO THOSE WOODS.
TMP TMP TMP
THE WOODS ?!
YOU, UM...
...REALLY LOVE RUNNING, DON'T YOU?!
HA HA HA HA.
MY LADY!
I...
...WAS ORDERED BY MASTER TO STAY BY YOUR SIDE.

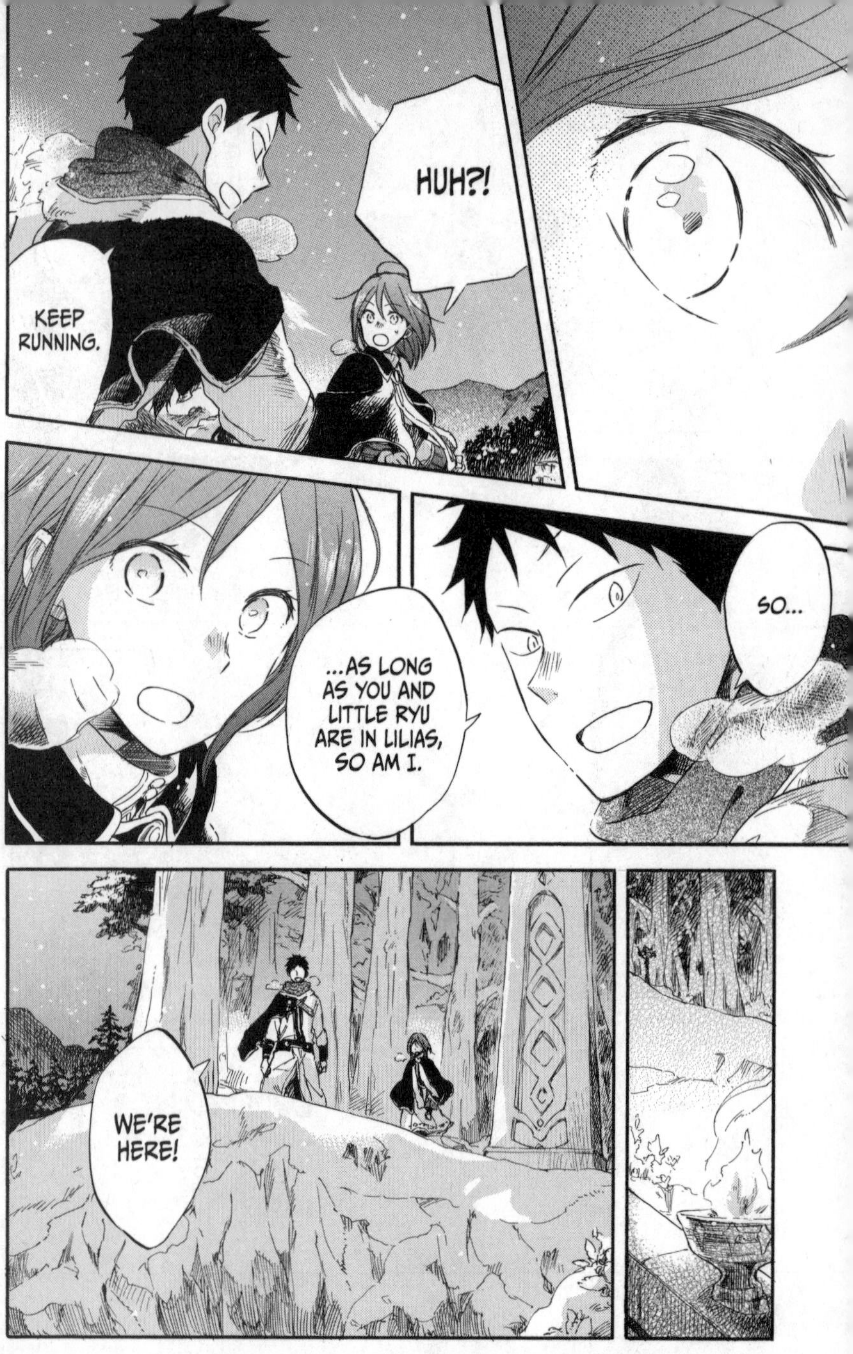
HUH?!
KEEP RUNNING.
SO...
...AS LONG AS YOU AND LITTLE RYU ARE IN LILIAS, SO AM I.
WE'RE HERE!

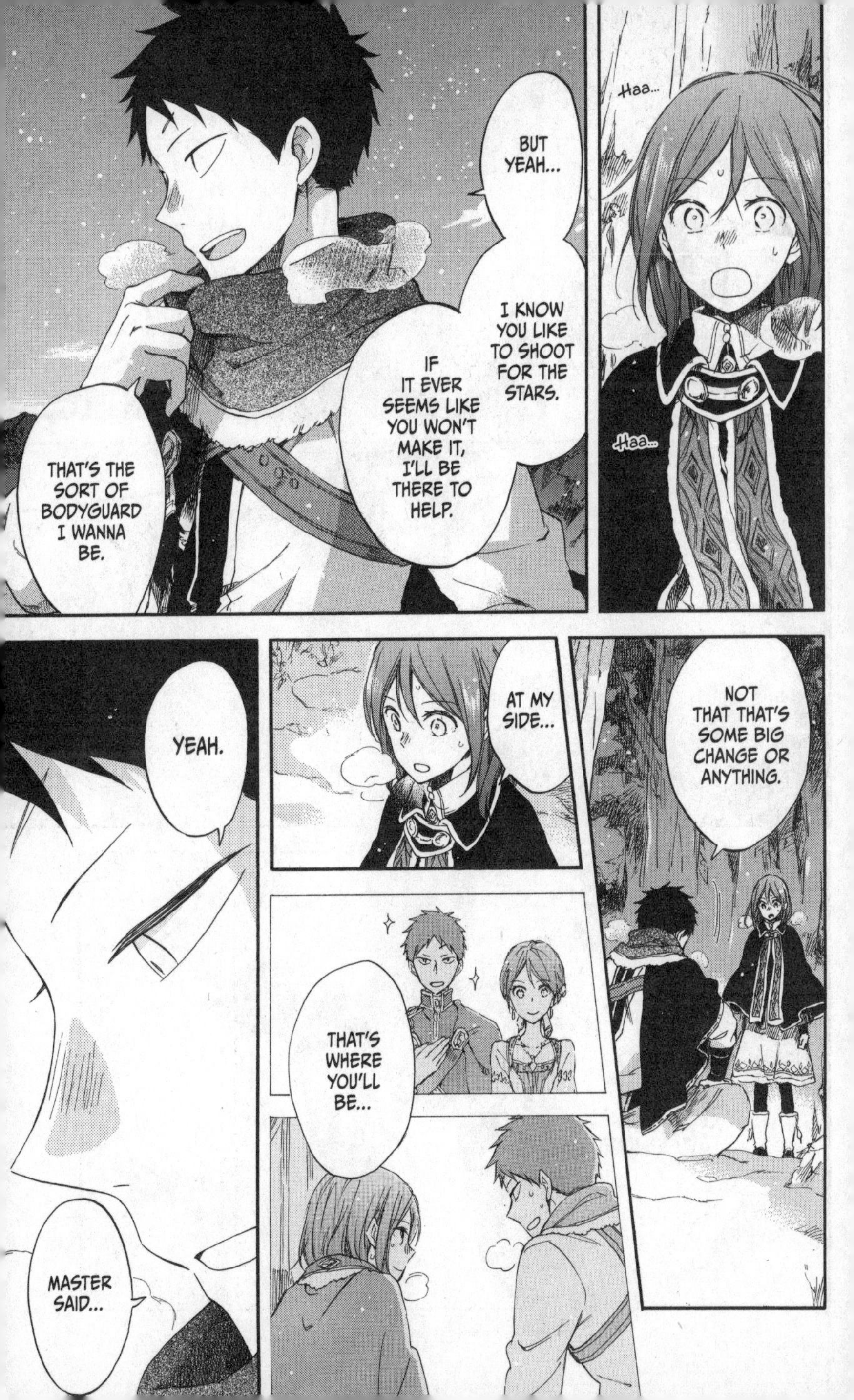
Haa...
Haa...
BUT YEAH...
I KNOW YOU LIKE TO SHOOT FOR THE STARS.
IF IT EVER SEEMS LIKE YOU WON'T MAKE IT, I'LL BE THERE TO HELP.
THAT'S THE SORT OF BODYGUARD I WANNA BE.
NOT THAT THAT'S SOME BIG CHANGE OR ANYTHING.
AT MY SIDE...
THAT'S WHERE YOU'LL BE...
YEAH.
MASTER SAID...

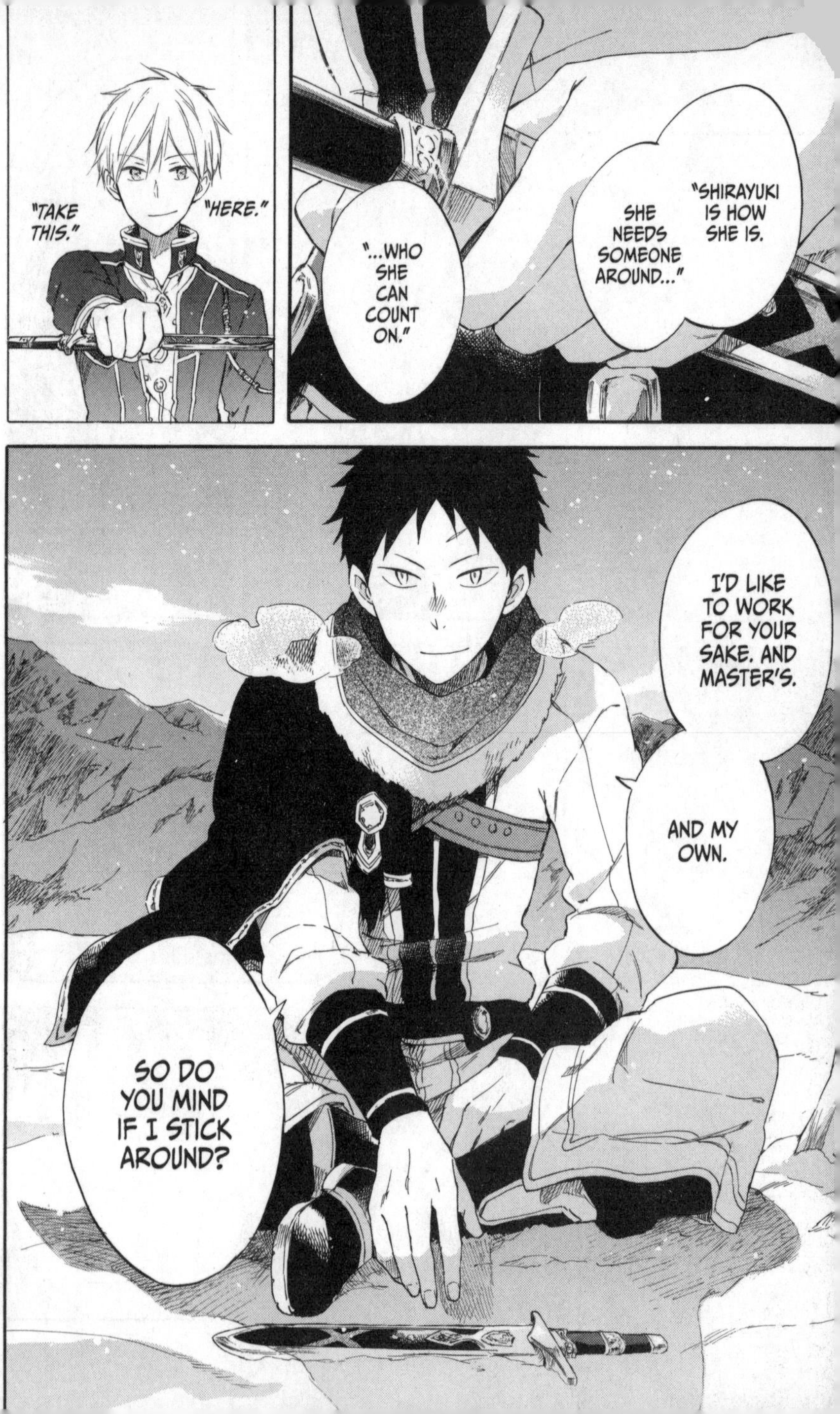
"SHIRAYUKI IS HOW SHE IS.
SHE NEEDS SOMEONE AROUND..."
"...WHO SHE CAN COUNT ON."
"HERE."
"TAKE THIS."
I'D LIKE TO WORK FOR YOUR SAKE. AND MASTER'S.
AND MY OWN.
SO DO YOU MIND IF I STICK AROUND?

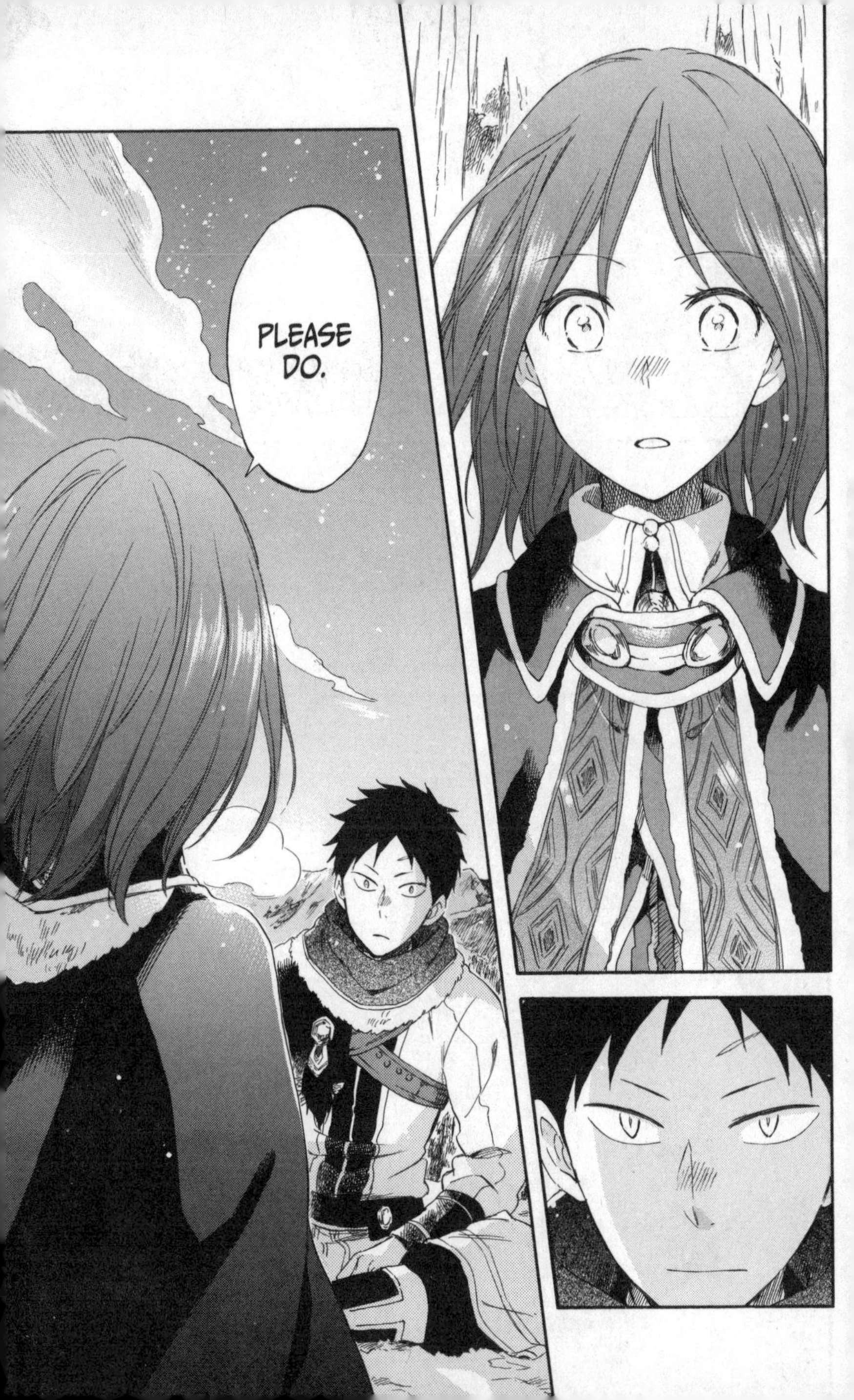
PLEASE DO.

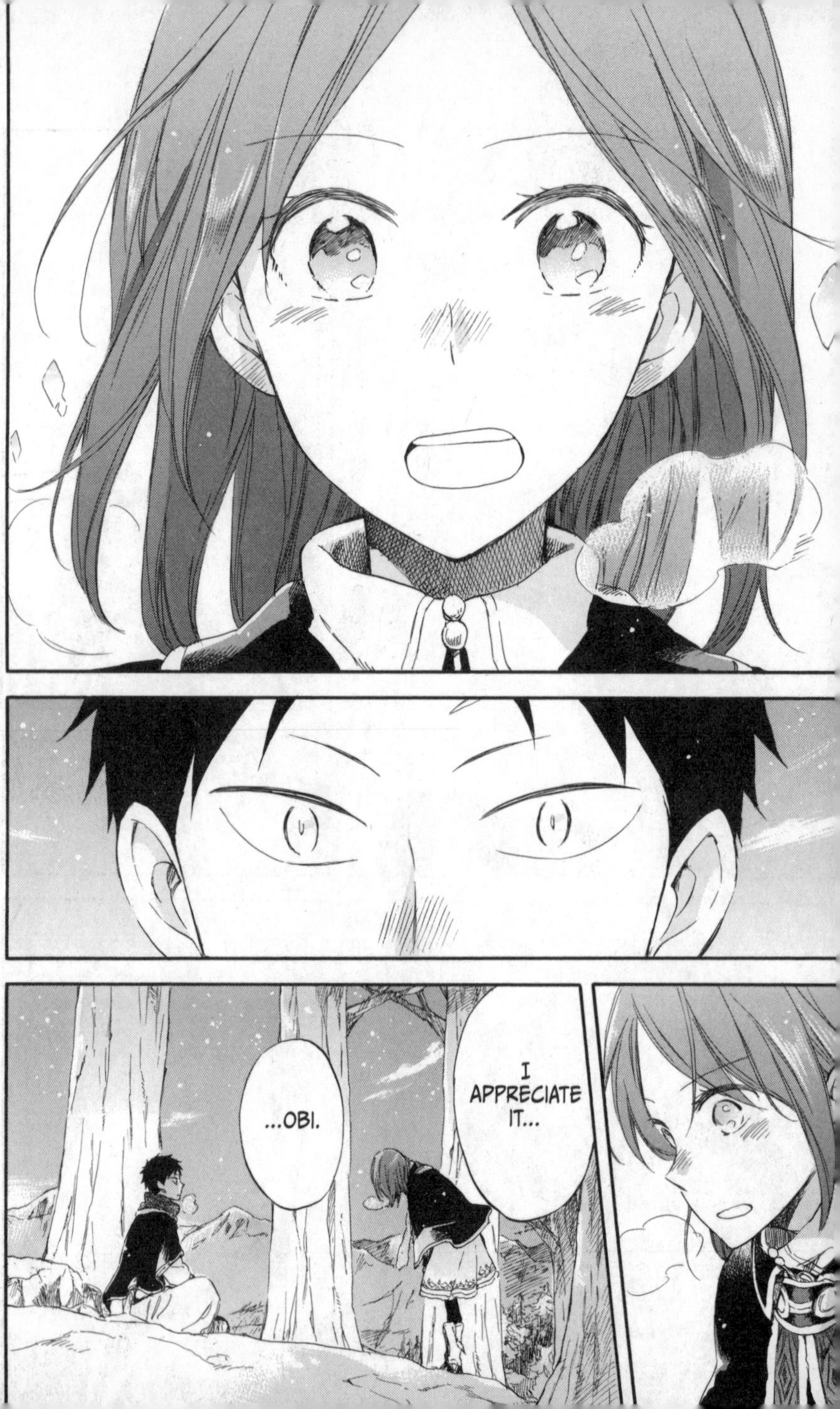
I APPRECIATE IT...
...OBI.

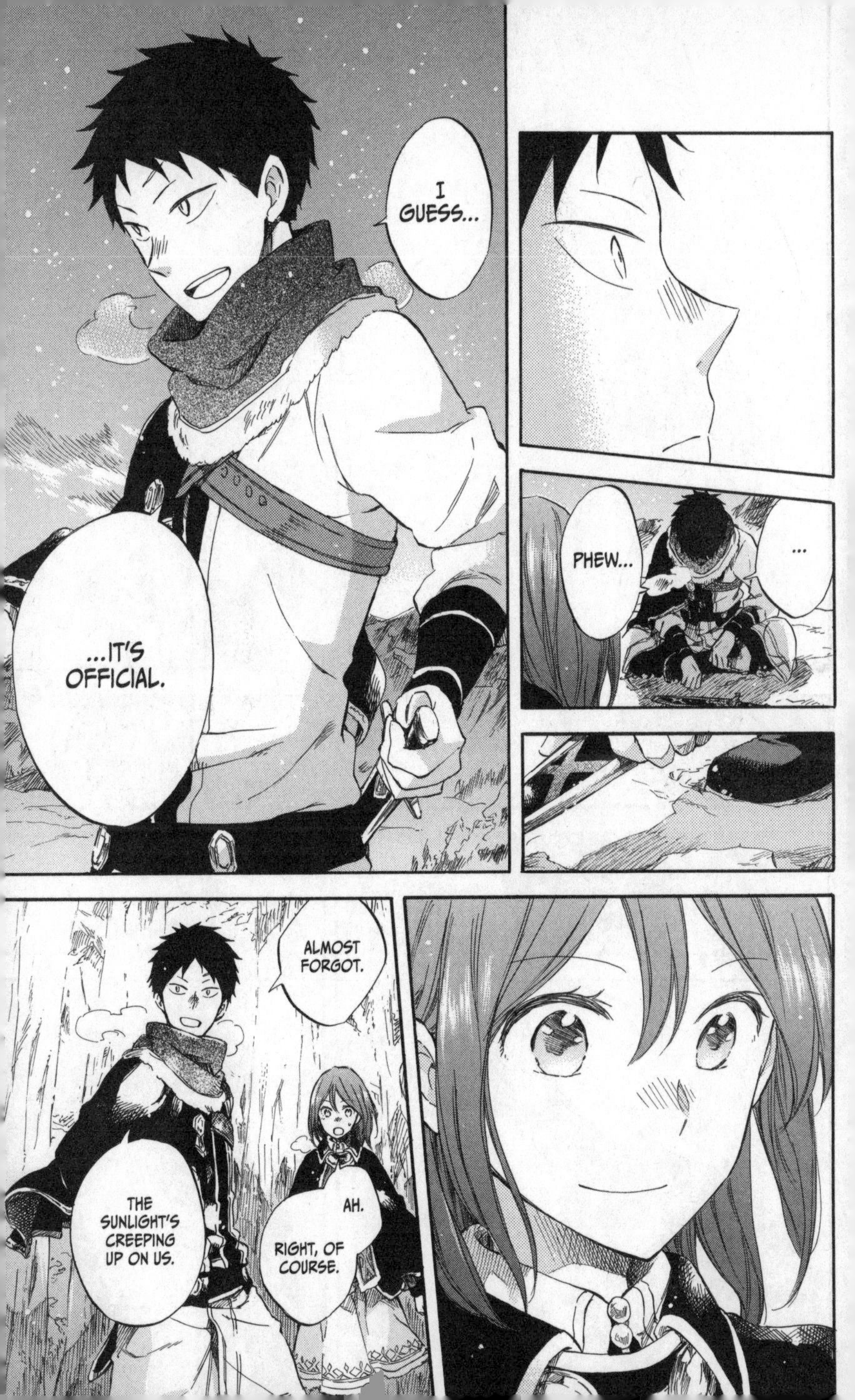
...
PHEW...
I GUESS...
...IT'S OFFICIAL.
ALMOST FORGOT.
AH.
RIGHT, OF COURSE.
THE SUNLIGHT'S CREEPING UP ON US.

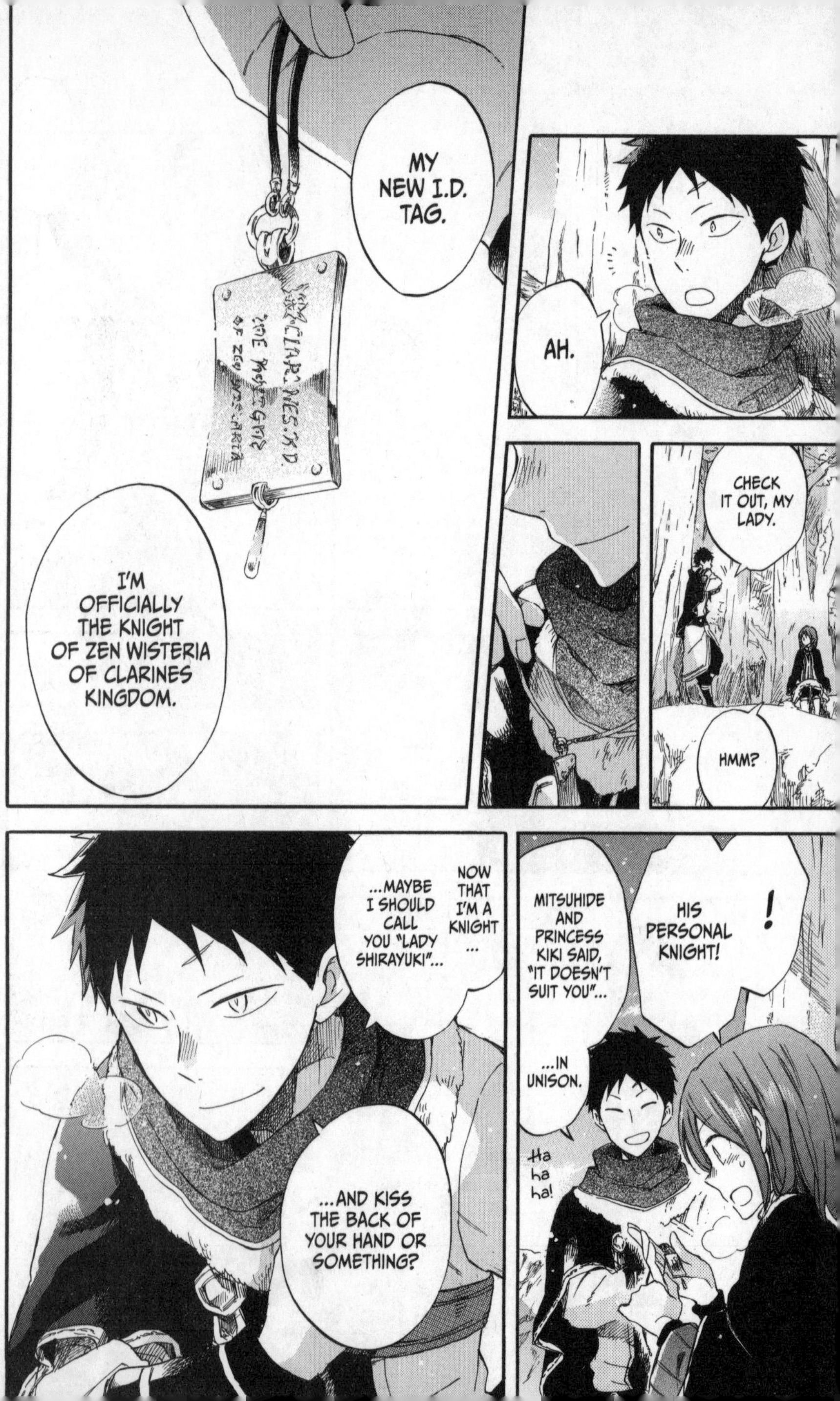
AH.
CHECK IT OUT, MY LADY.
HMM?
MY NEW I.D. TAG.
I'M OFFICIALLY THE KNIGHT OF ZEN WISTERIA OF CLARINES KINGDOM.
HIS PERSONAL KNIGHT!
!
MITSUHIDE AND PRINCESS KIKI SAID, "IT DOESN'T SUIT YOU"...
...IN UNISON.
Ha ha ha!
NOW THAT I'M A KNIGHT...
...MAYBE I SHOULD CALL YOU "LADY SHIRAYUKI"...
...AND KISS THE BACK OF YOUR HAND OR SOMETHING?

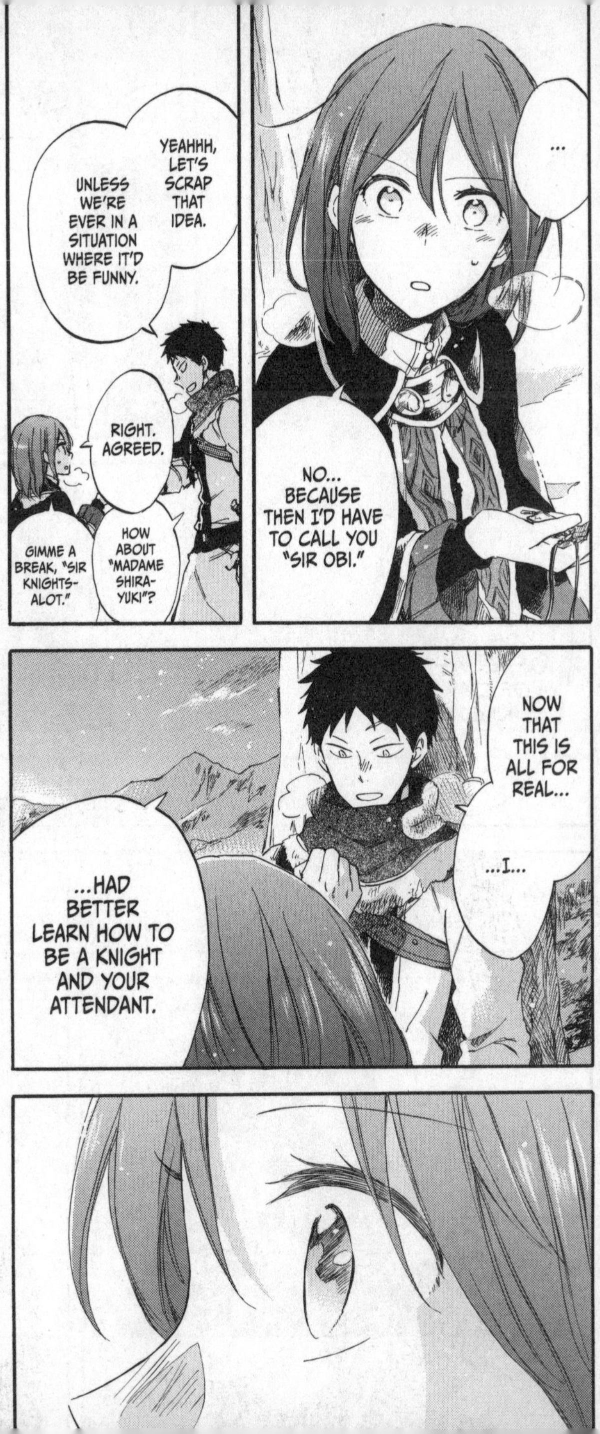
...
NO... BECAUSE THEN I'D HAVE TO CALL YOU "SIR OBI."
YEAHHH, LET'S SCRAP THAT IDEA.
UNLESS WE'RE EVER IN A SITUATION WHERE IT'D BE FUNNY.
RIGHT. AGREED.
HOW ABOUT "MADAME SHIRAYUKI"?
GIMME A BREAK, "SIR KNIGHTS-ALOT."
NOW THAT THIS IS ALL FOR REAL...
...I...
...HAD BETTER LEARN HOW TO BE A KNIGHT AND YOUR ATTENDANT.

2

*THE "WHAT IF" SERIES*

I'm talking, of course, about the first page of this volume...

I originally considered using "Beauty and the Beast" for this book, but when I thought about it, I realized I wasn't that familiar with the story. So I did some research on the original version of the tale and decided to go with "Rapunzel" instead after finding this summary...

Summary:
A castle-owning beast and a girl spend time together and fall in love. While she's away from the castle, the beast dies under a huge mountain of cabbage. What a happy ending!
~Fin~

Cabbage...? Really?

Where can I read this story in full?

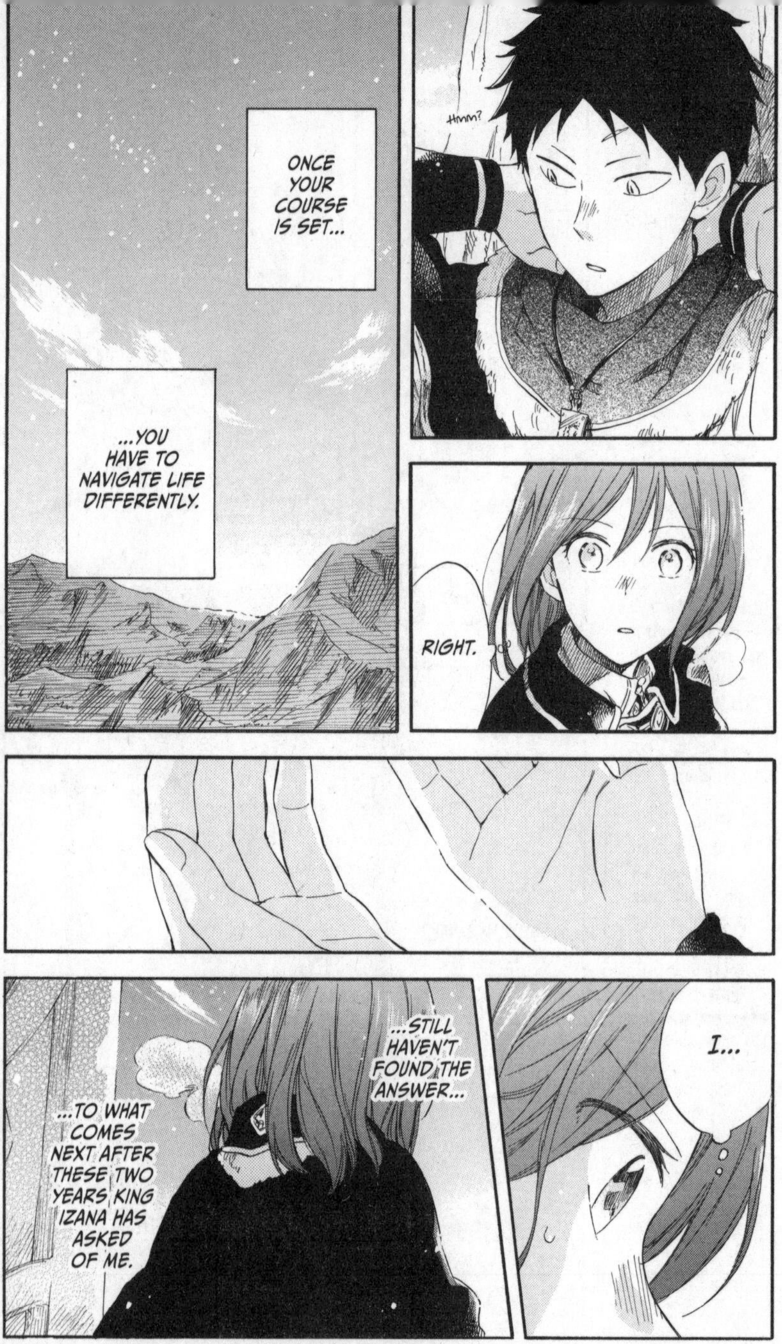
Hmm?
RIGHT.
ONCE YOUR COURSE IS SET...
...YOU HAVE TO NAVIGATE LIFE DIFFERENTLY.
I...
...STILL HAVEN'T FOUND THE ANSWER...
...TO WHAT COMES NEXT AFTER THESE TWO YEARS KING IZANA HAS ASKED OF ME.

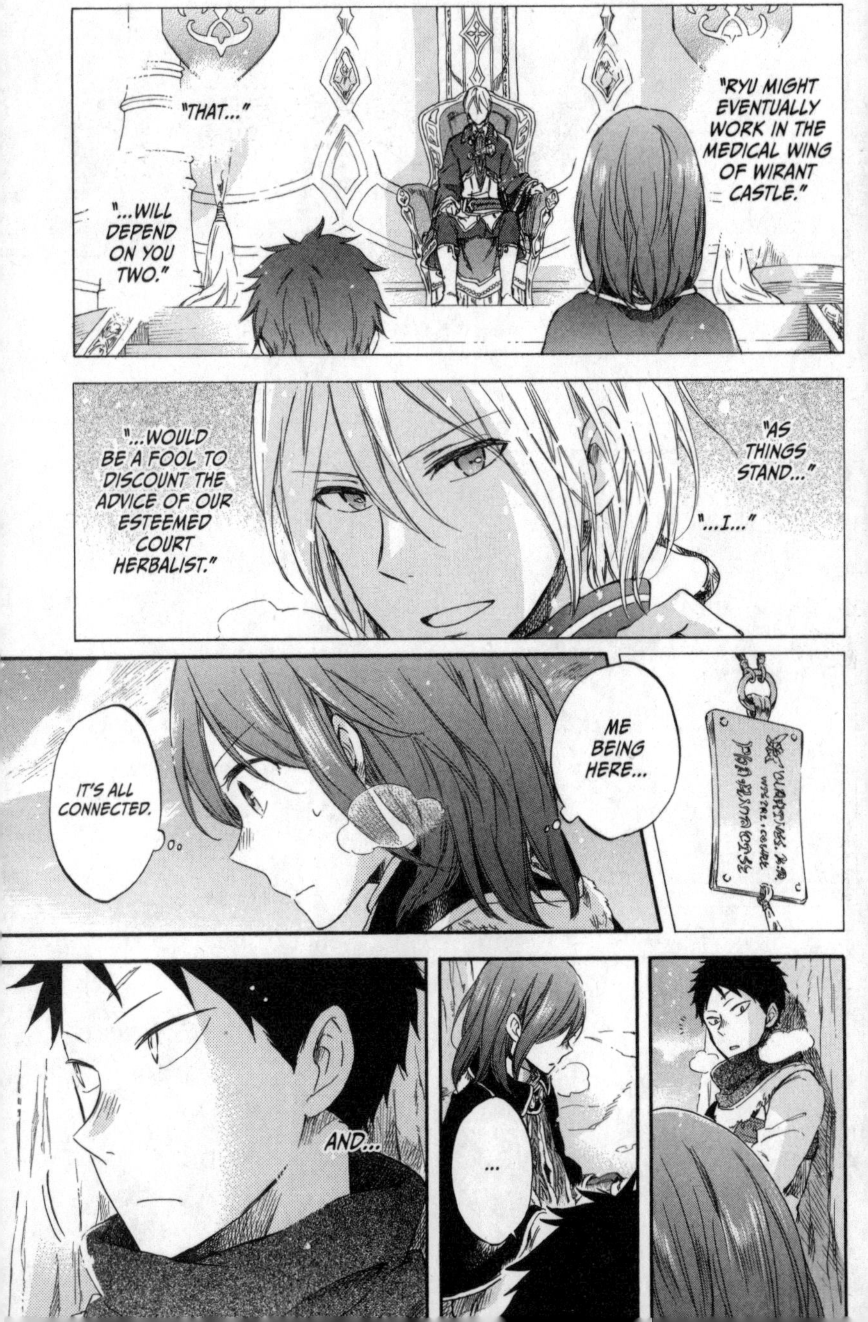
"RYU MIGHT EVENTUALLY WORK IN THE MEDICAL WING OF WIRANT CASTLE."
"THAT..."
"...WILL DEPEND ON YOU TWO."
"AS THINGS STAND..."
"...I..."
"...WOULD BE A FOOL TO DISCOUNT THE ADVICE OF OUR ESTEEMED COURT HERBALIST."
ME BEING HERE...
IT'S ALL CONNECTED.
AND...
...

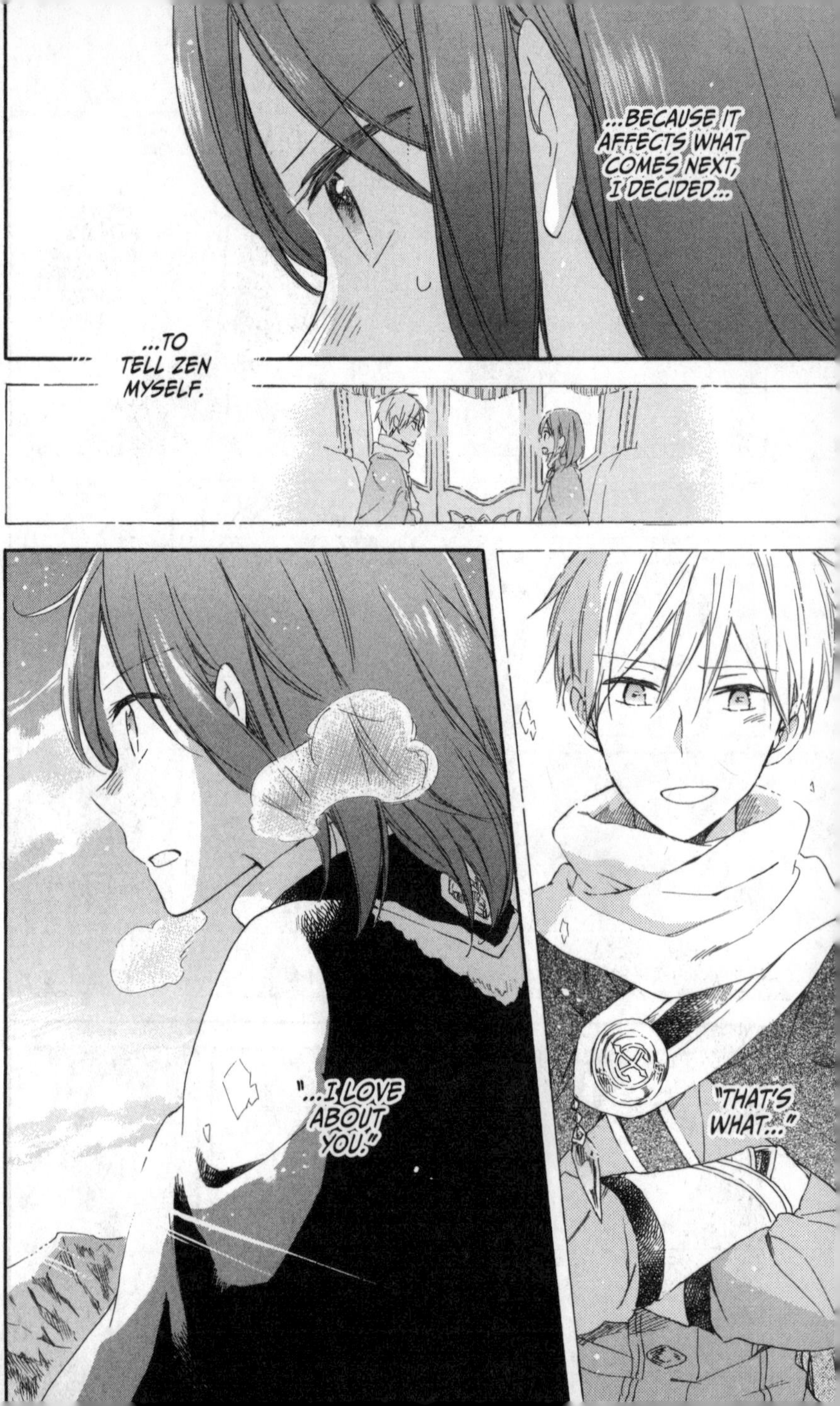
...BECAUSE IT AFFECTS WHAT COMES NEXT, I DECIDED...
...TO TELL ZEN MYSELF.
"THAT'S WHAT..."
"...I LOVE ABOUT YOU."

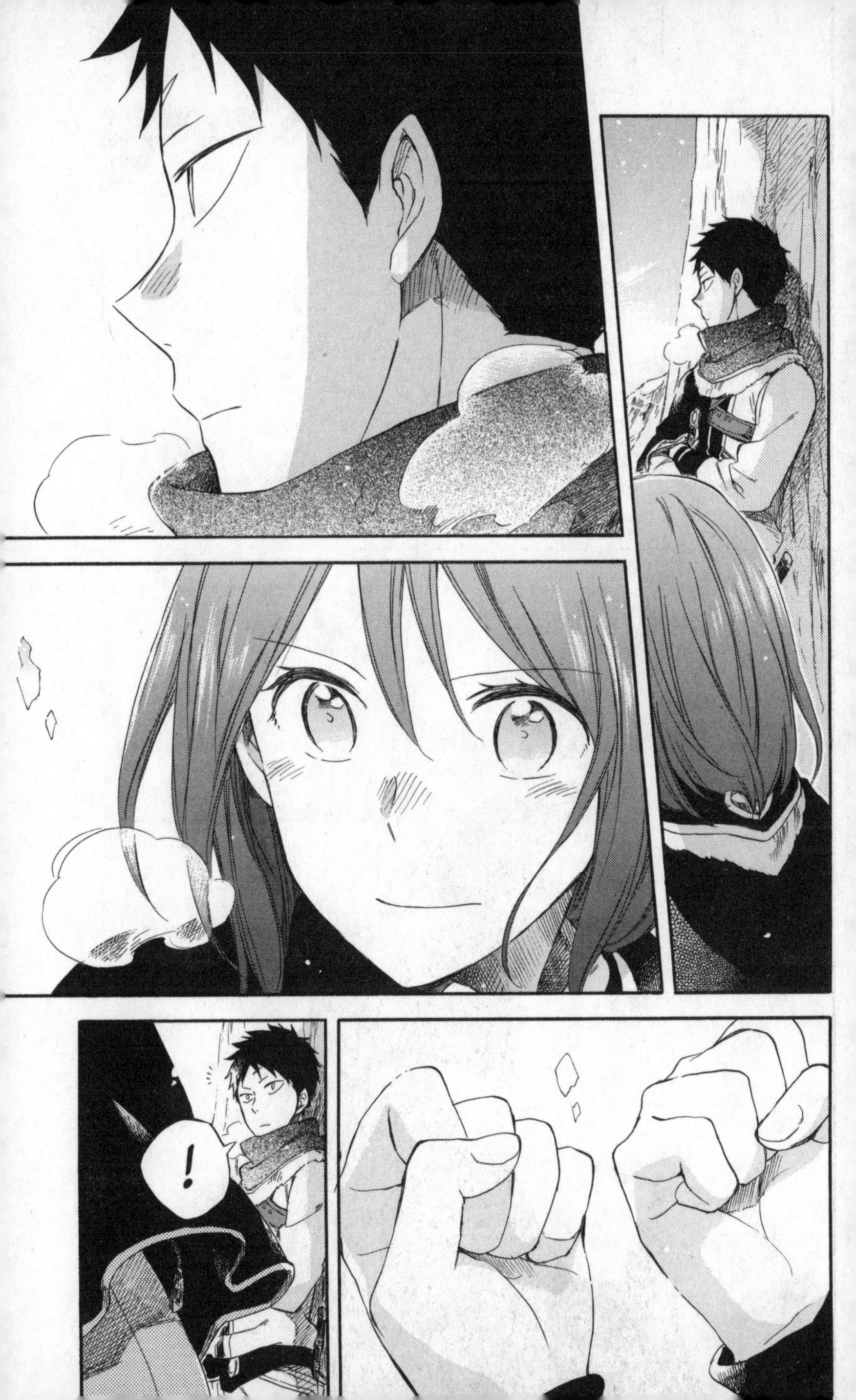
!

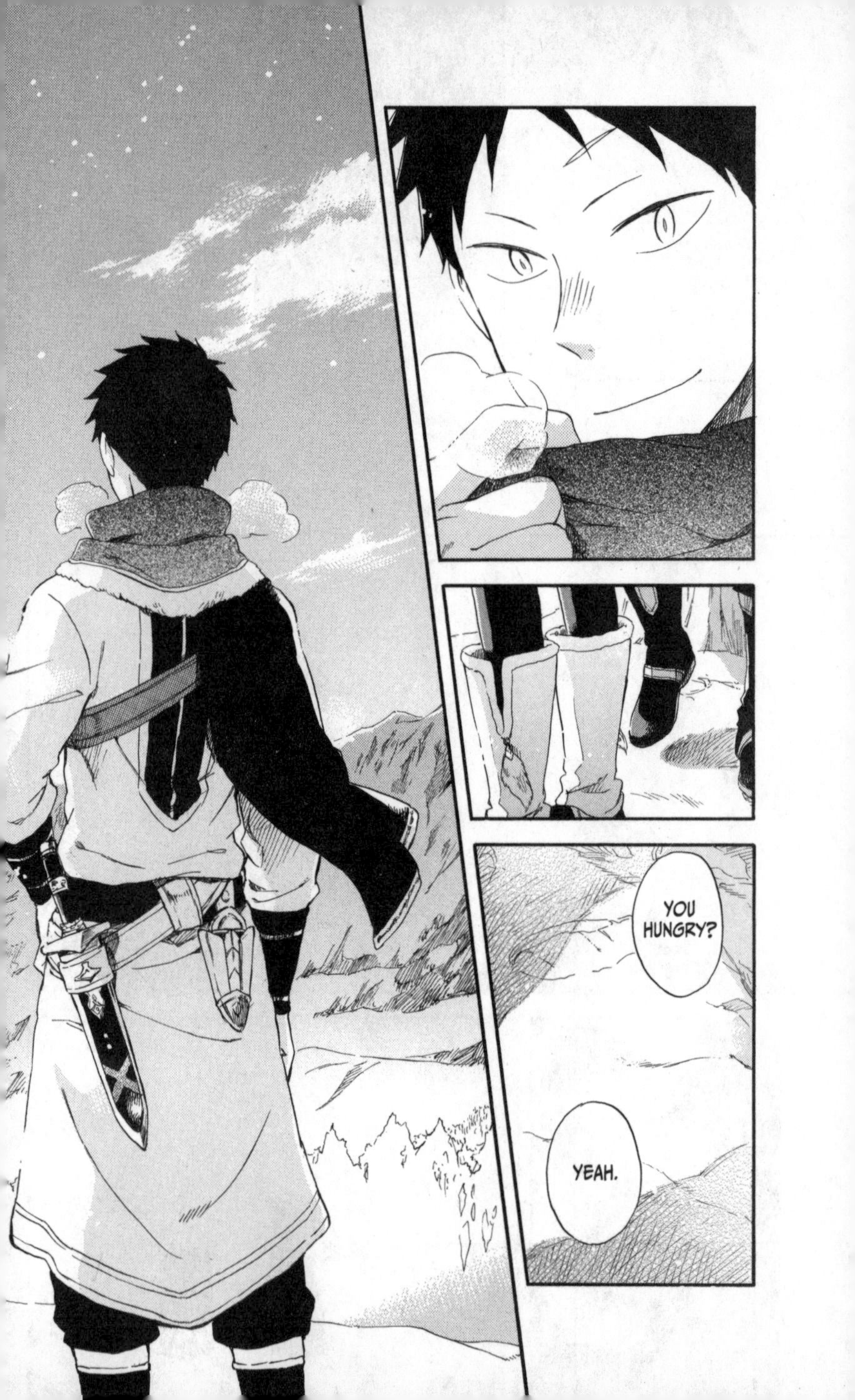
YOU HUNGRY?
YEAH.

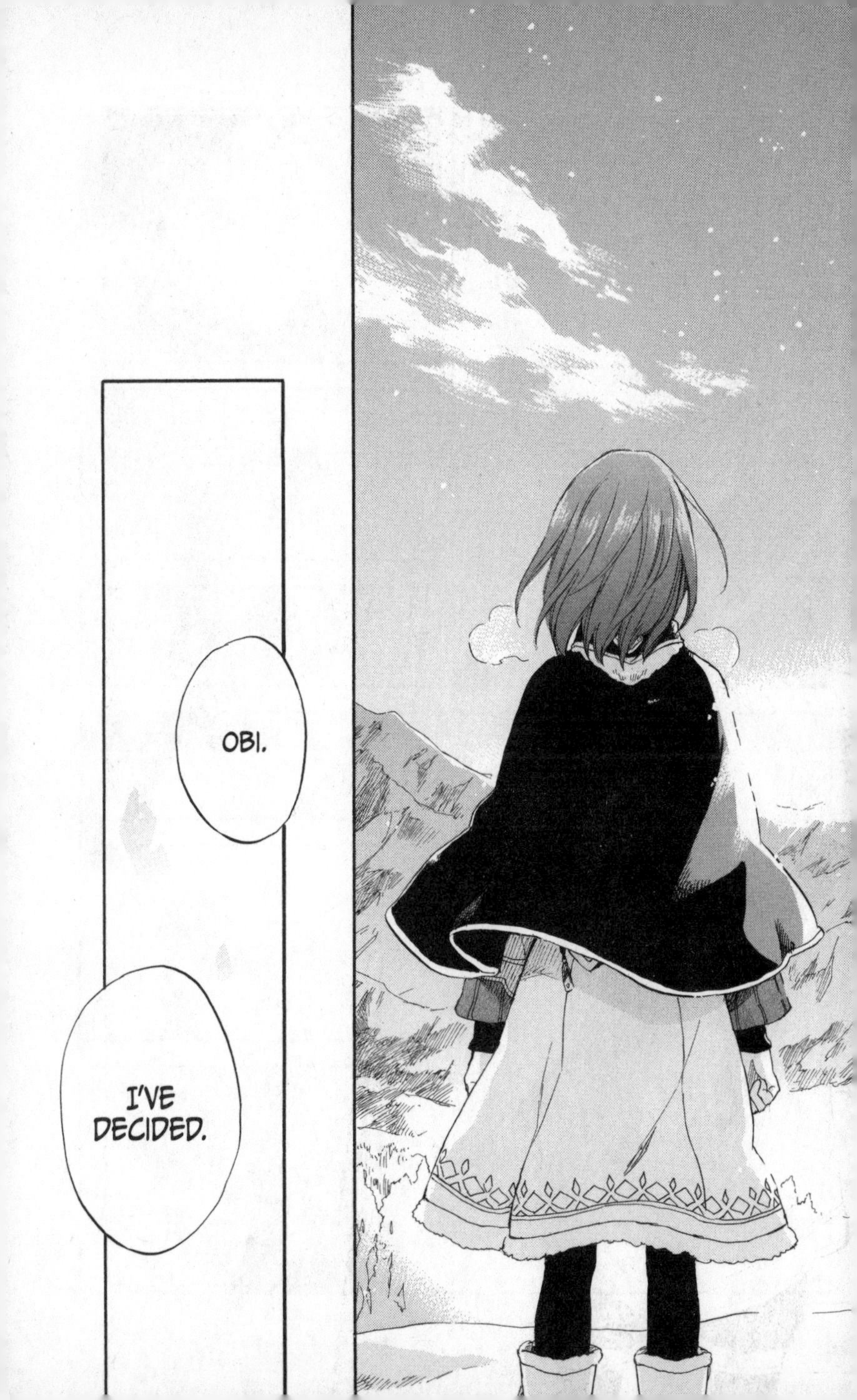
OBI.
I'VE DECIDED.

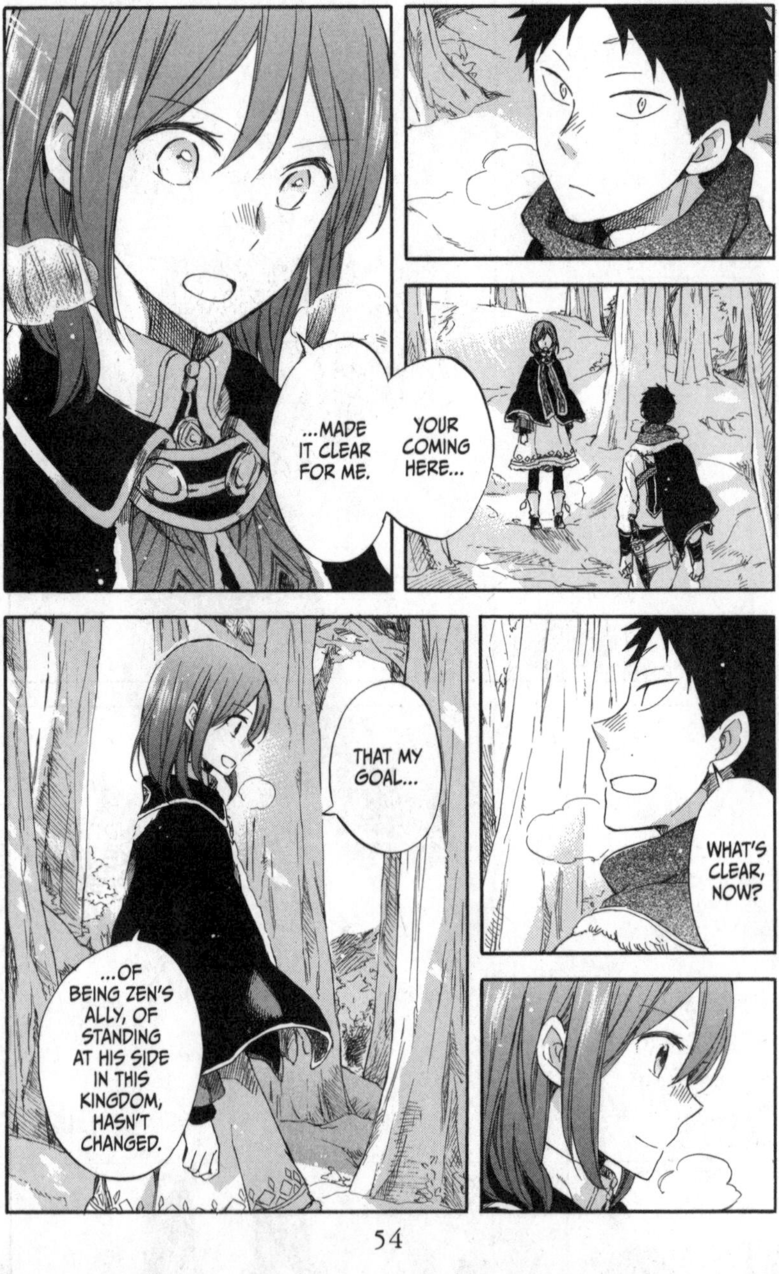
YOUR COMING HERE...
...MADE IT CLEAR FOR ME.
WHAT'S CLEAR, NOW?
THAT MY GOAL...
...OF BEING ZEN'S ALLY, OF STANDING AT HIS SIDE IN THIS KINGDOM, HASN'T CHANGED.

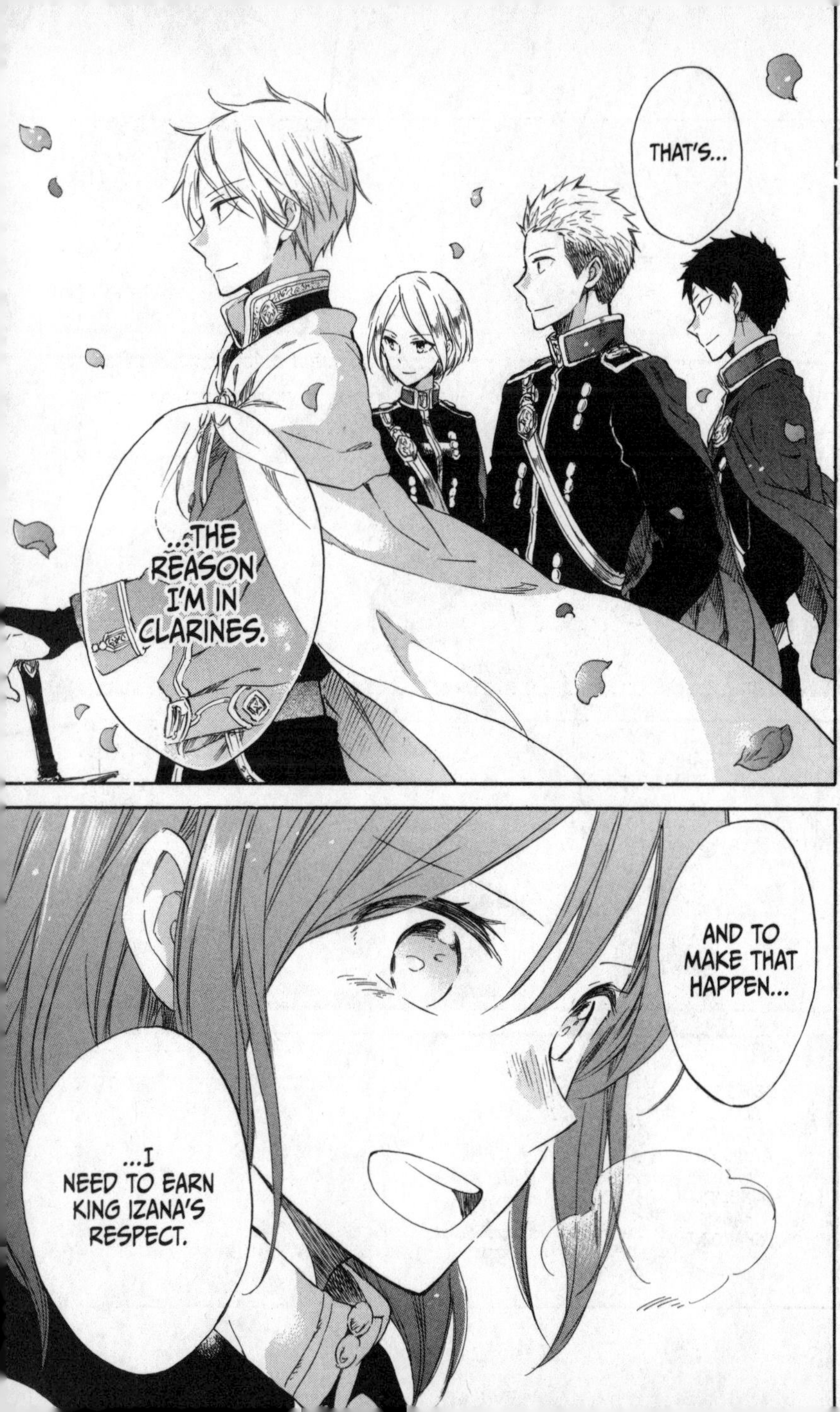
THAT'S...
...THE REASON I'M IN CLARINES.
AND TO MAKE THAT HAPPEN...
...I NEED TO EARN KING IZANA'S RESPECT.

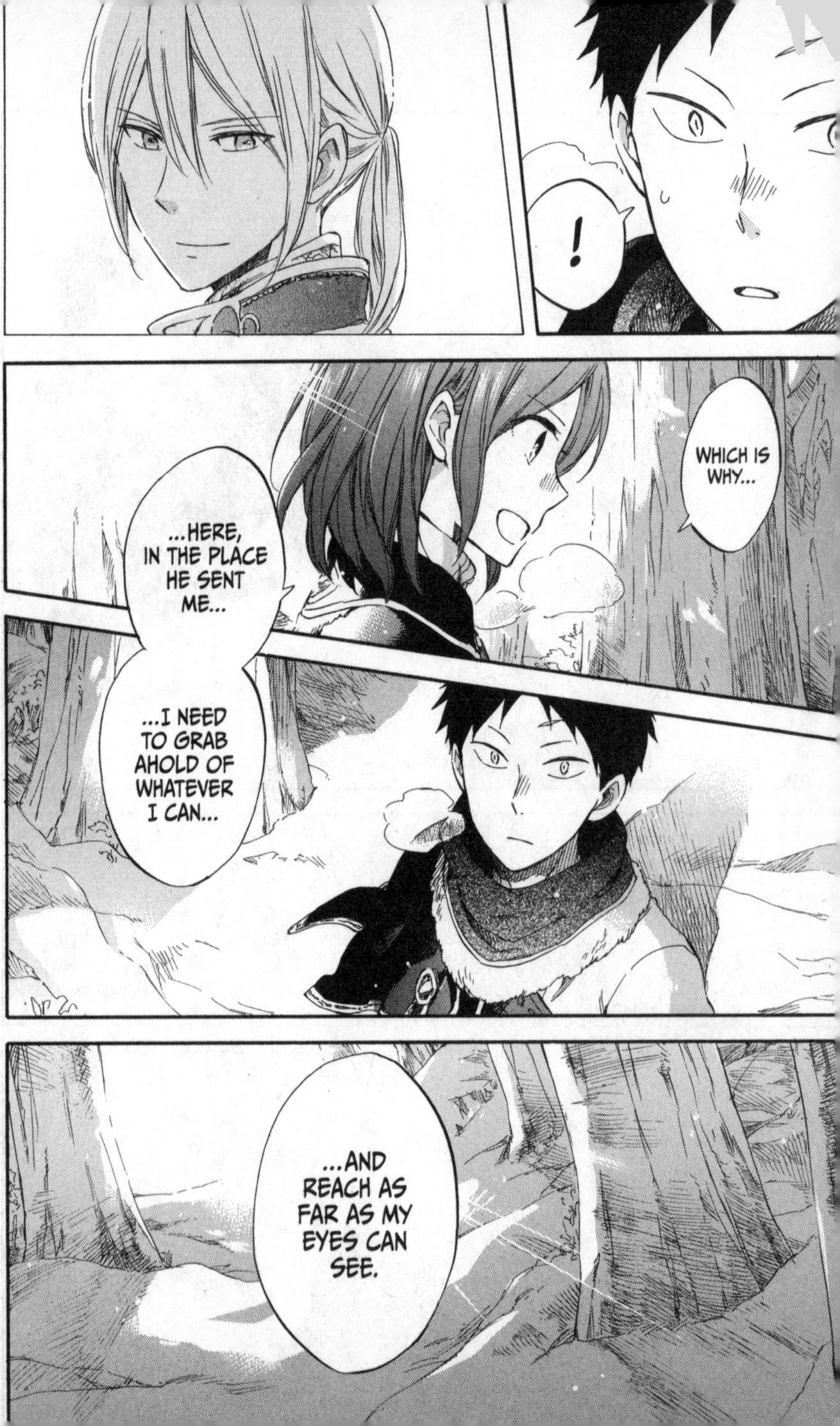
!
WHICH IS WHY...
...HERE, IN THE PLACE HE SENT ME...
...I NEED TO GRAB AHOLD OF WHATEVER I CAN...
...AND REACH AS FAR AS MY EYES CAN SEE.

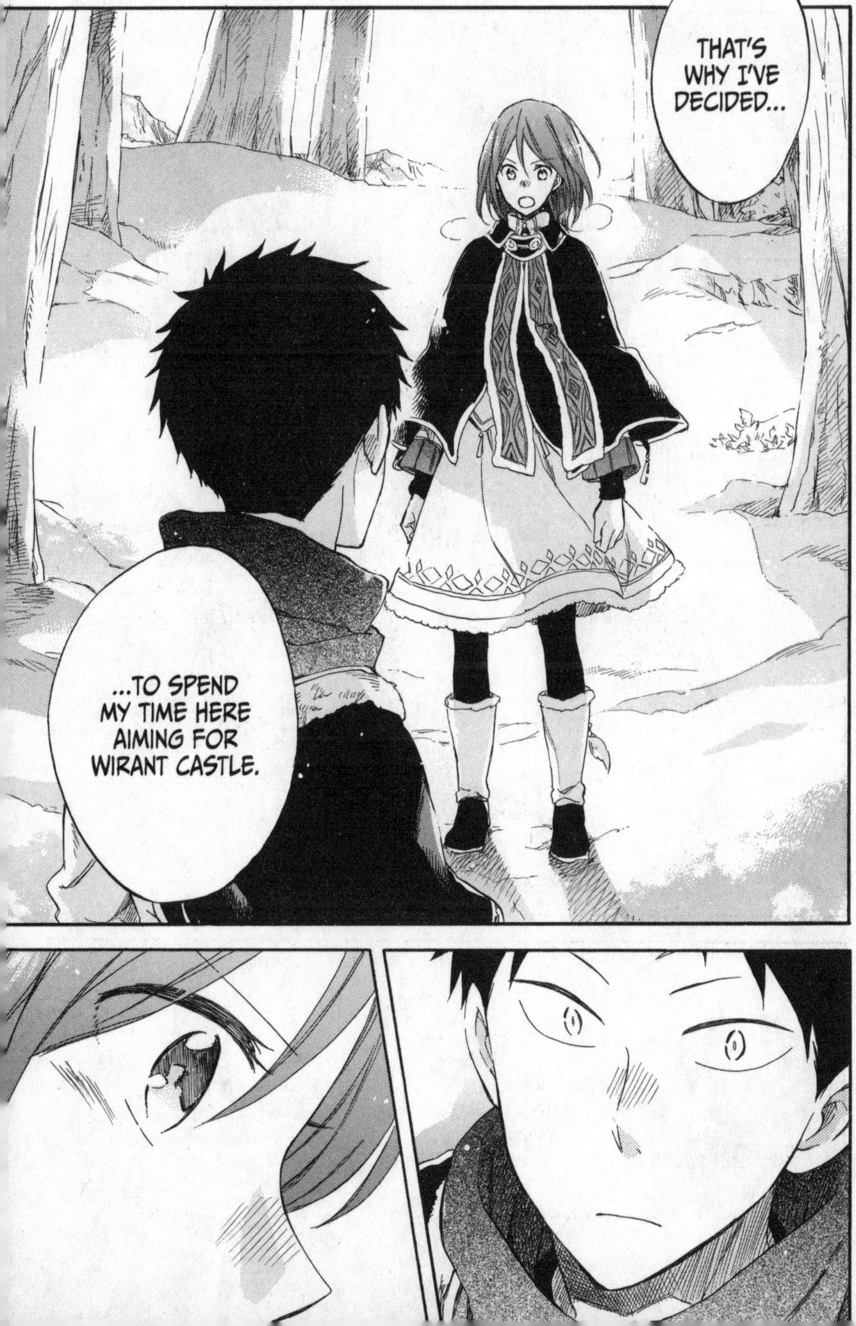
THAT'S WHY I'VE DECIDED...
...TO SPEND MY TIME HERE AIMING FOR WIRANT CASTLE.

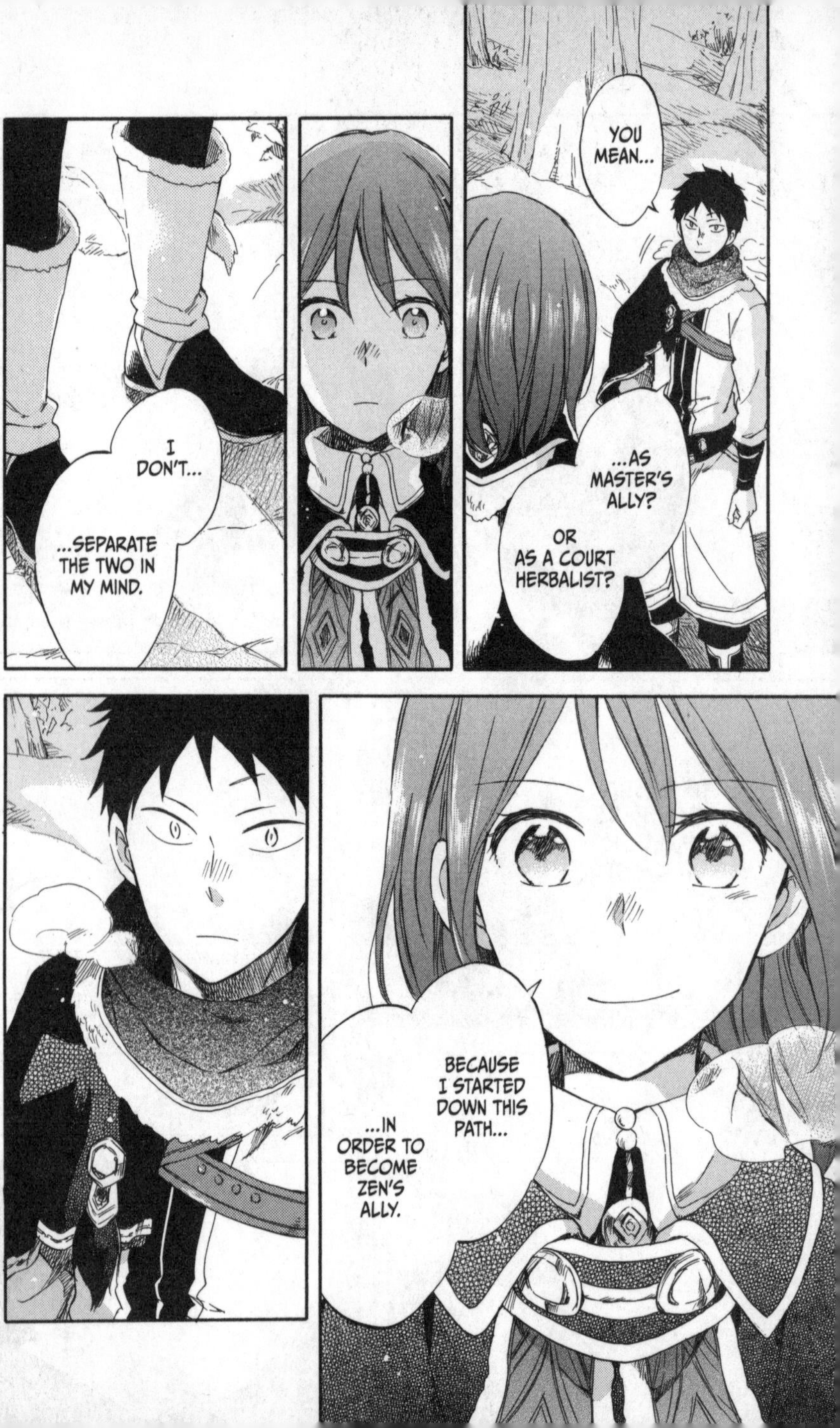
YOU MEAN...
...AS MASTER'S ALLY?
OR AS A COURT HERBALIST?
I DON'T...
...SEPARATE THE TWO IN MY MIND.
BECAUSE I STARTED DOWN THIS PATH...
...IN ORDER TO BECOME ZEN'S ALLY.

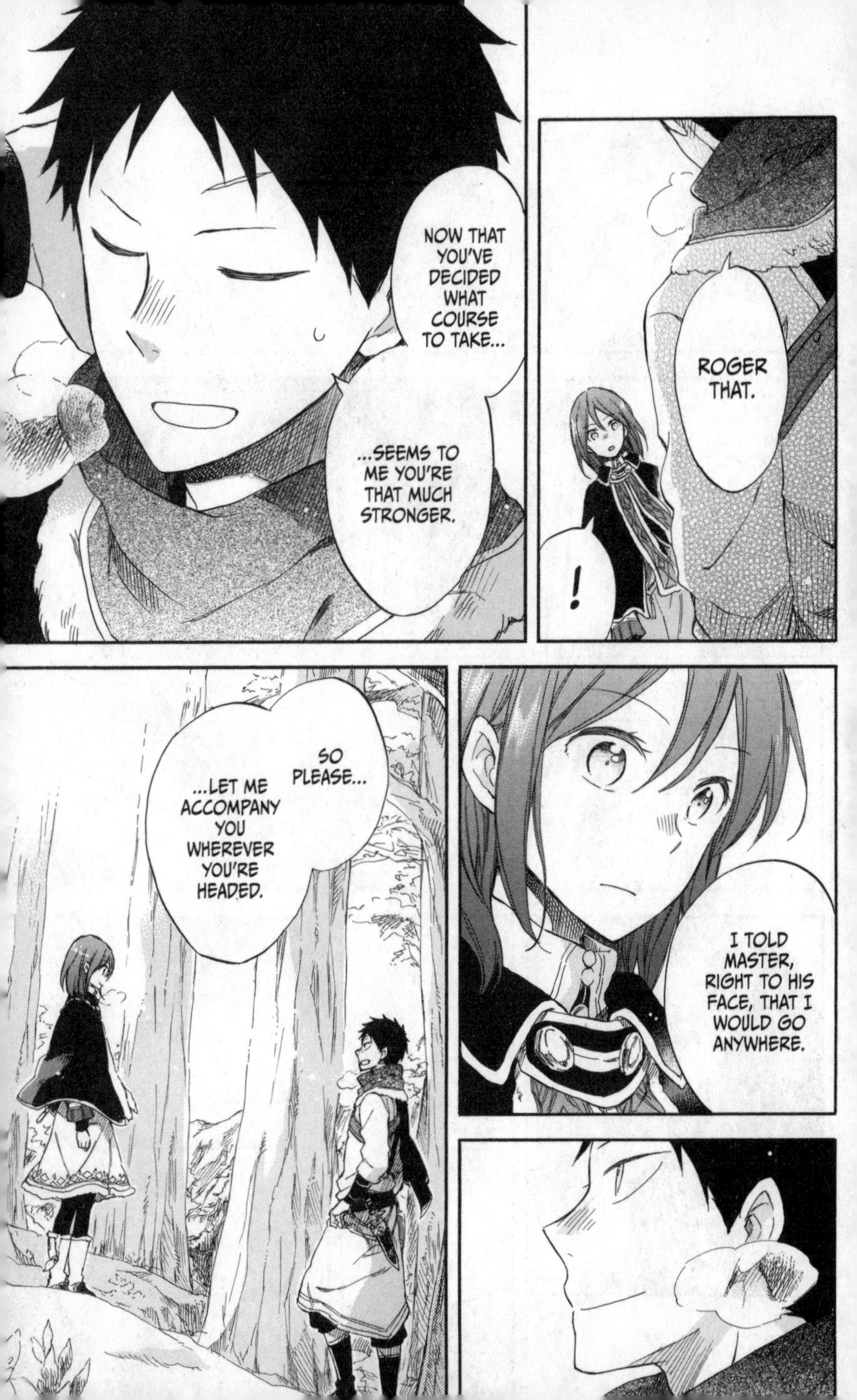
ROGER THAT.
!
NOW THAT YOU'VE DECIDED WHAT COURSE TO TAKE...
...SEEMS TO ME YOU'RE THAT MUCH STRONGER.
I TOLD MASTER, RIGHT TO HIS FACE, THAT I WOULD GO ANYWHERE.
SO PLEASE...
...LET ME ACCOMPANY YOU WHEREVER YOU'RE HEADED.

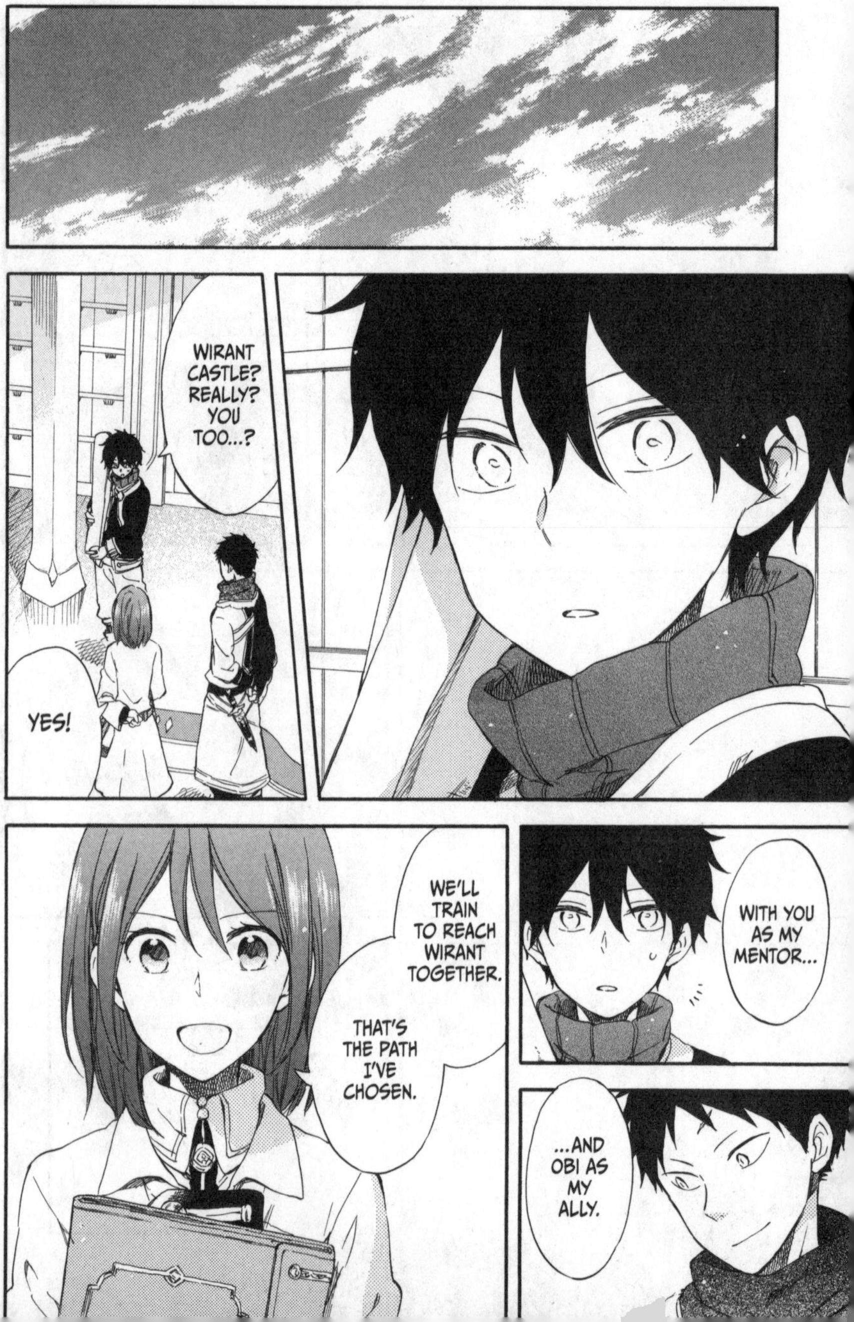
WIRANT CASTLE? REALLY? YOU TOO...?
YES!
WITH YOU AS MY MENTOR...
...AND OBI AS MY ALLY.
WE'LL TRAIN TO REACH WIRANT TOGETHER.
THAT'S THE PATH I'VE CHOSEN.

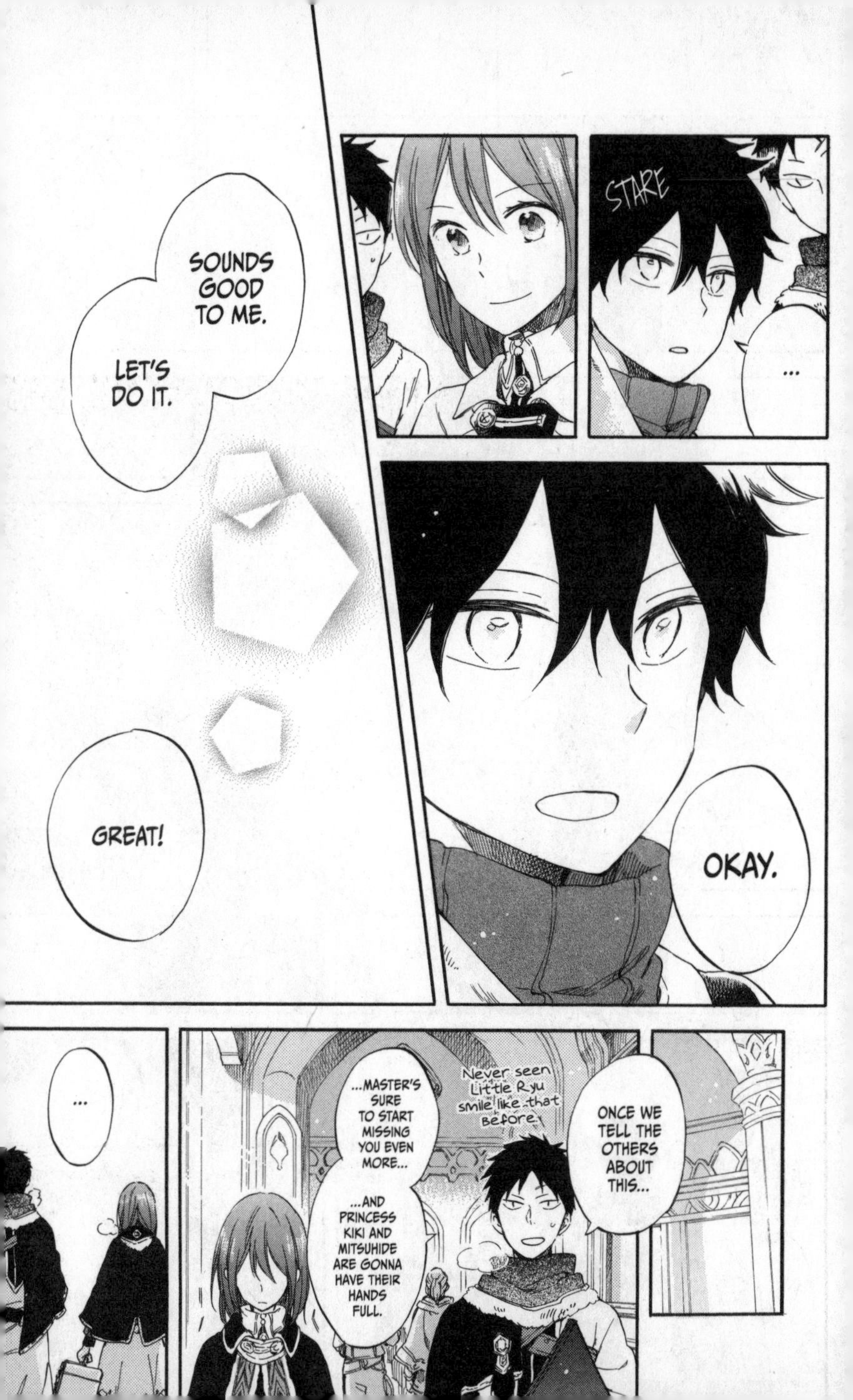
STARE
...
OKAY.
SOUNDS GOOD TO ME.
LET'S DO IT.
GREAT!
ONCE WE TELL THE OTHERS ABOUT THIS...
Never seen Little Ryu smile like that before.
...MASTER'S SURE TO START MISSING YOU EVEN MORE...
...AND PRINCESS KIKI AND MITSUHIDE ARE GONNA HAVE THEIR HANDS FULL.
...

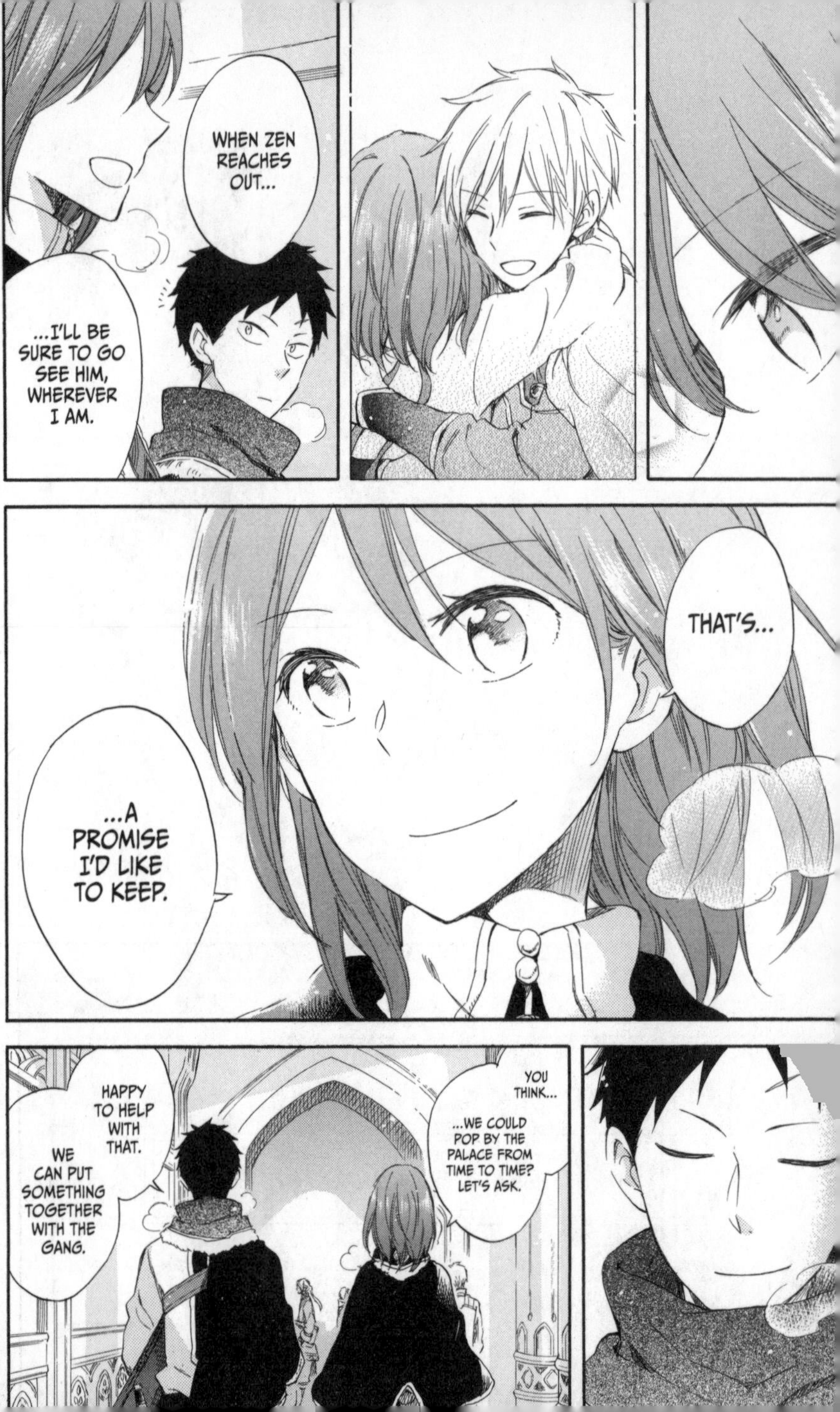
WHEN ZEN REACHES OUT...
...I'LL BE SURE TO GO SEE HIM, WHEREVER I AM.
THAT'S...
...A PROMISE I'D LIKE TO KEEP.
YOU THINK...
...WE COULD POP BY THE PALACE FROM TIME TO TIME? LET'S ASK.
HAPPY TO HELP WITH THAT.
WE CAN PUT SOMETHING TOGETHER WITH THE GANG.

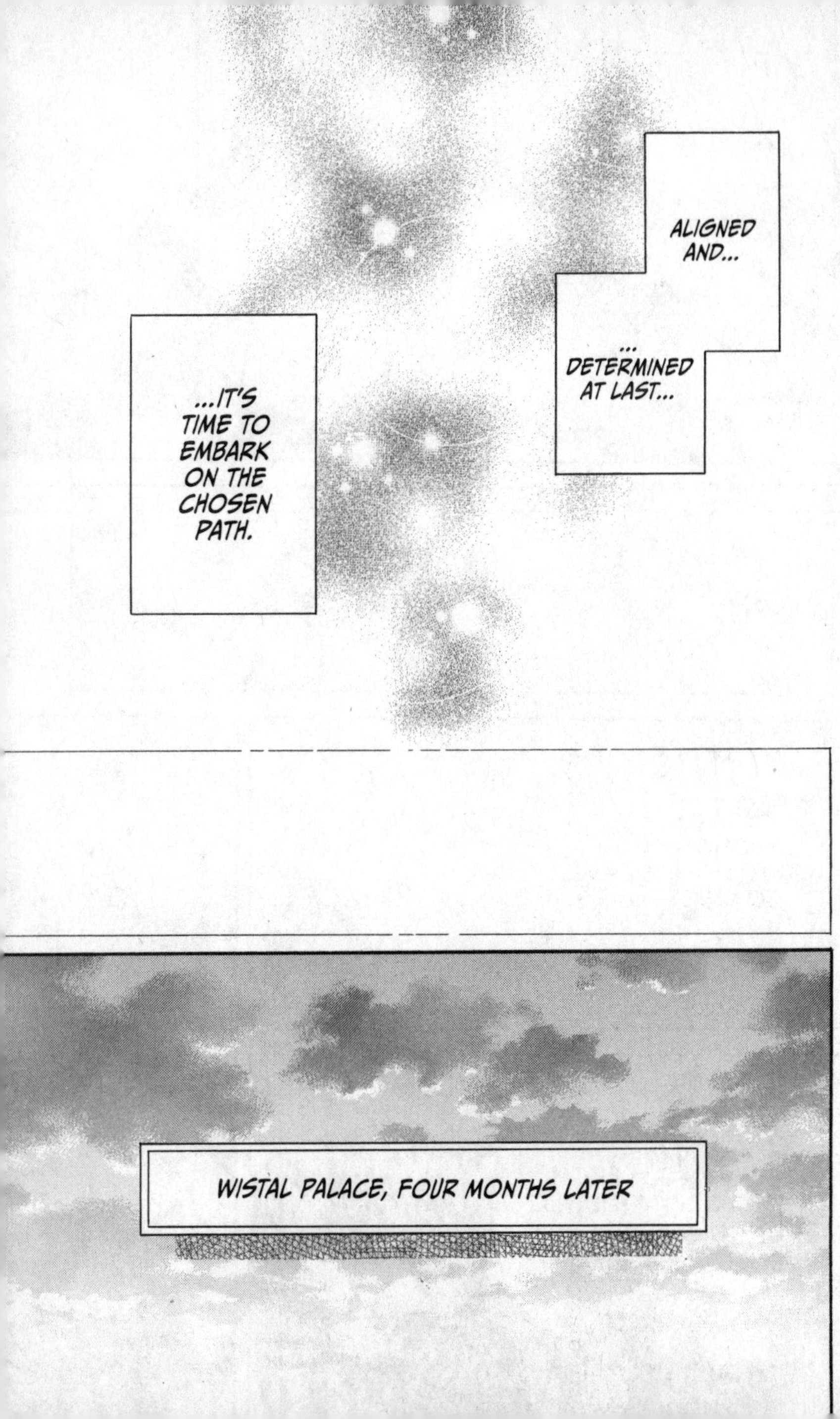
ALIGNED AND...
...DETERMINED AT LAST...
...IT'S TIME TO EMBARK ON THE CHOSEN PATH.
WISTAL PALACE, FOUR MONTHS LATER

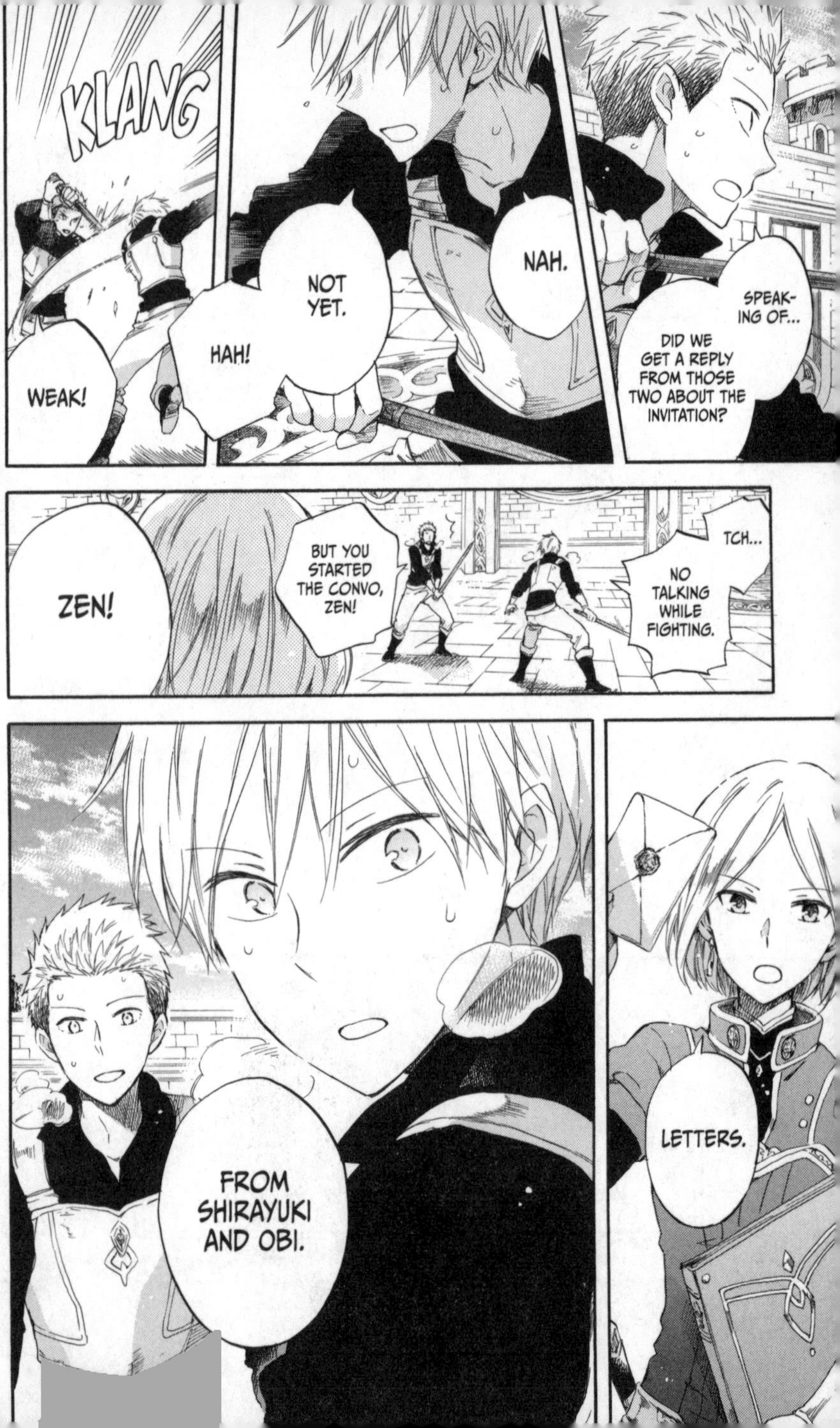
SPEAK-ING OF...
DID WE GET A REPLY FROM THOSE TWO ABOUT THE INVITATION?
NAH.
NOT YET.
HAH!
KLANG
WEAK!
TCH...
NO TALKING WHILE FIGHTING.
BUT YOU STARTED THE CONVO, ZEN!
ZEN!
LETTERS.
FROM SHIRAYUKI AND OBI.

# Chapter 63

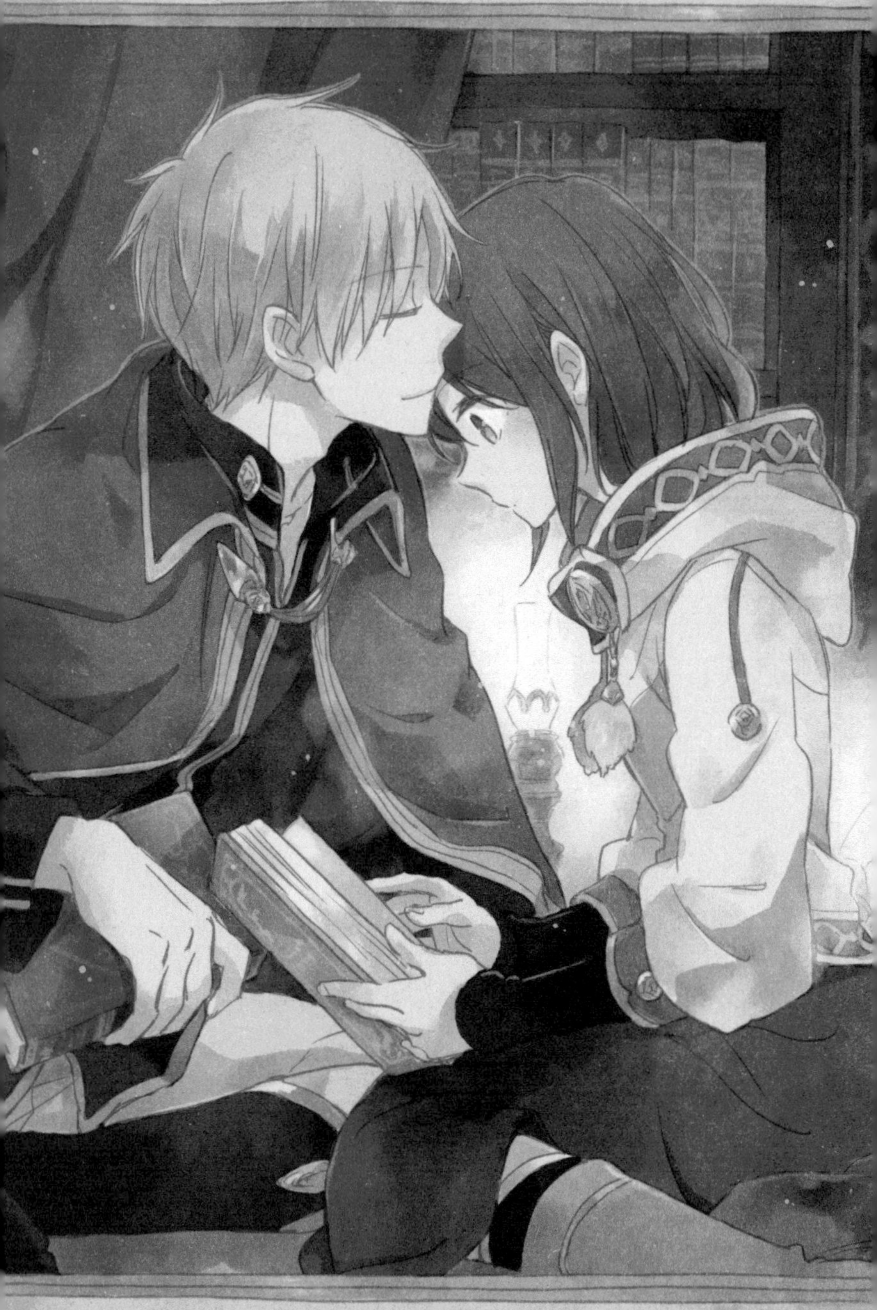

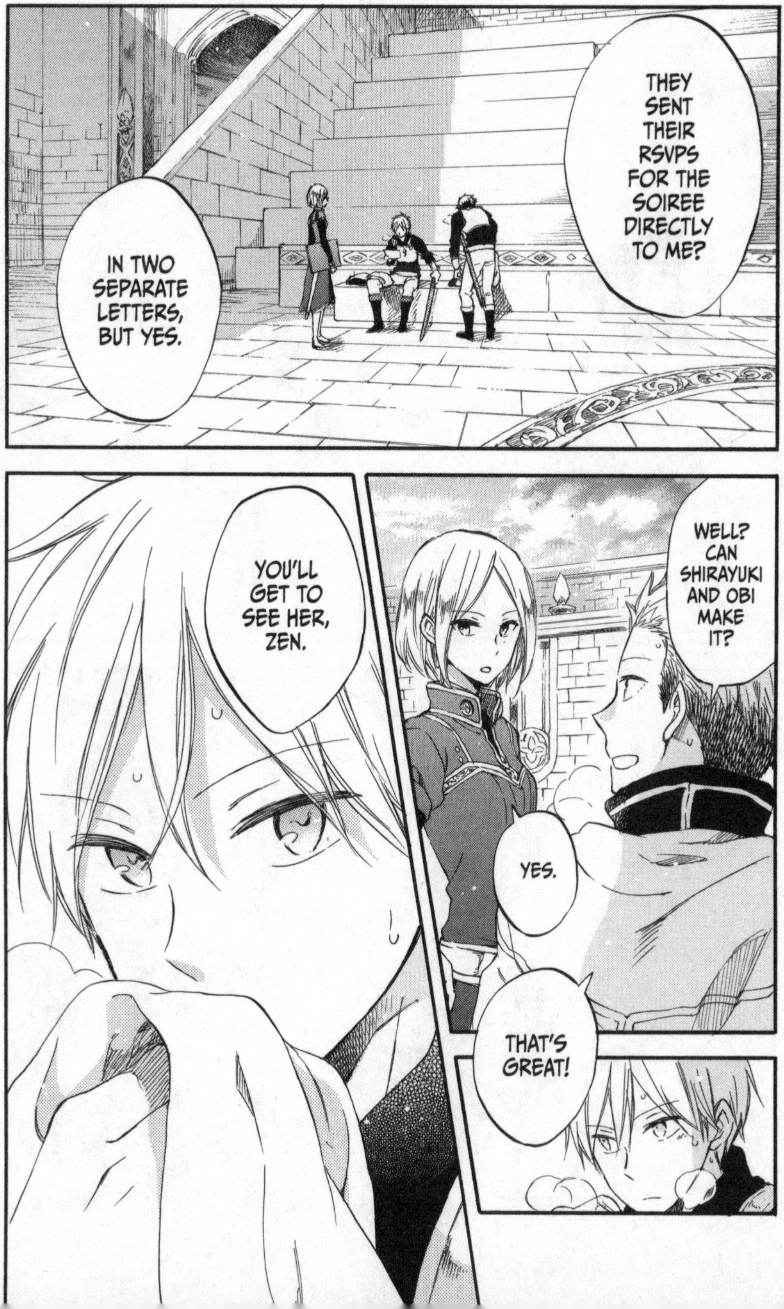
THEY SENT THEIR RSVPS FOR THE SOIREE DIRECTLY TO ME?
IN TWO SEPARATE LETTERS, BUT YES.
WELL? CAN SHIRAYUKI AND OBI MAKE IT?
YES.
THAT'S GREAT!
YOU'LL GET TO SEE HER, ZEN.

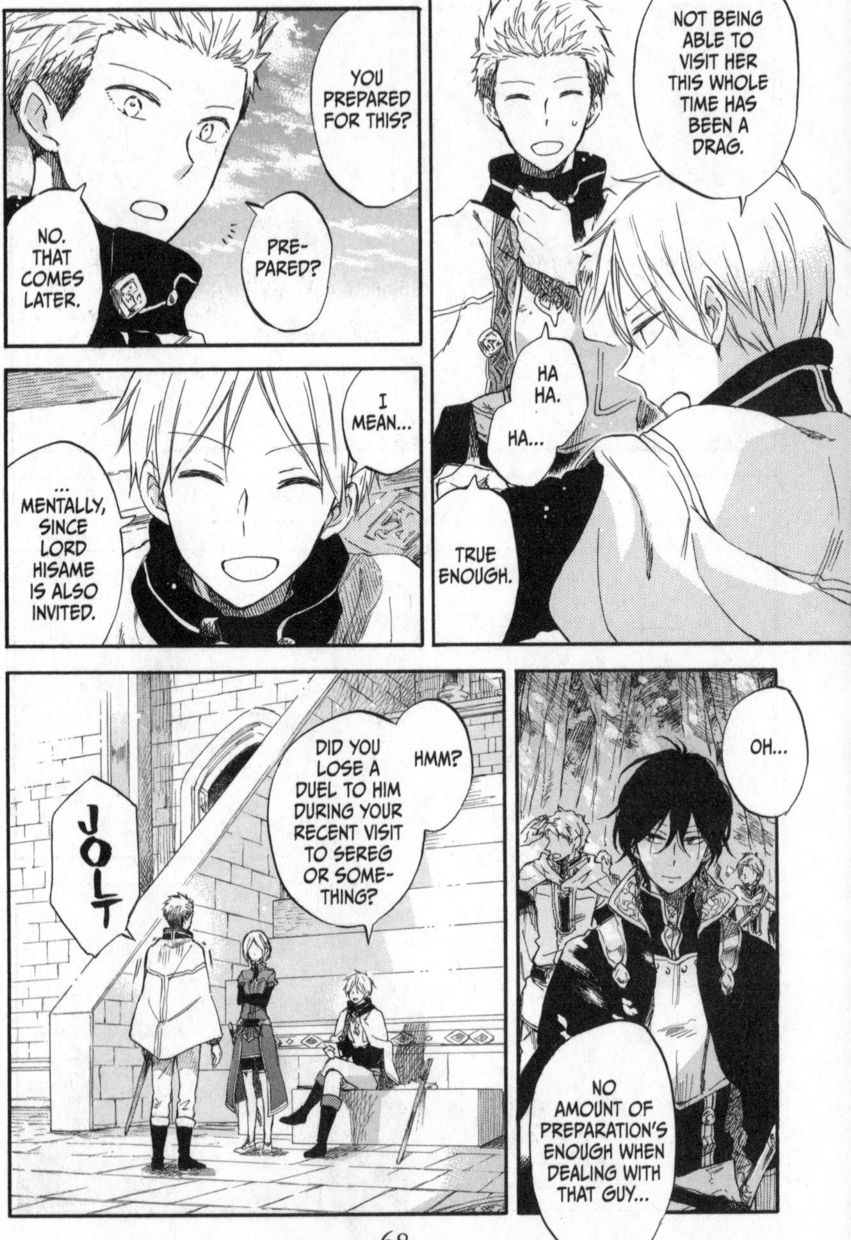
NOT BEING ABLE TO VISIT HER THIS WHOLE TIME HAS BEEN A DRAG.
HA HA.
HA...
TRUE ENOUGH.
YOU PREPARED FOR THIS?
PRE-PARED?
NO. THAT COMES LATER.
I MEAN...
...MENTALLY, SINCE LORD HISAME IS ALSO INVITED.
OH...
NO AMOUNT OF PREPARATION'S ENOUGH WHEN DEALING WITH THAT GUY...
HMM?
DID YOU LOSE A DUEL TO HIM DURING YOUR RECENT VISIT TO SEREG OR SOME-THING?
JOLT

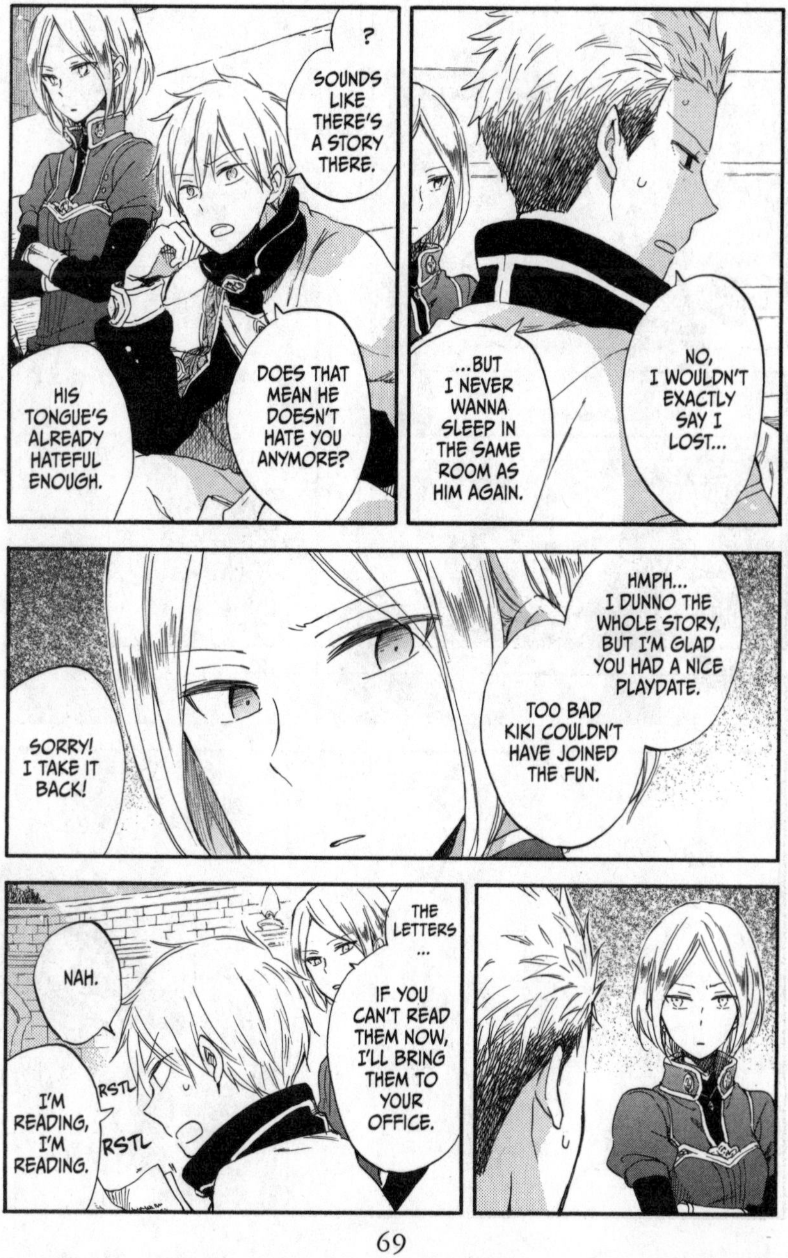
NO, I WOULDN'T EXACTLY SAY I LOST...
...BUT I NEVER WANNA SLEEP IN THE SAME ROOM AS HIM AGAIN.
?
SOUNDS LIKE THERE'S A STORY THERE.
DOES THAT MEAN HE DOESN'T HATE YOU ANYMORE?
HIS TONGUE'S ALREADY HATEFUL ENOUGH.
HMPH... I DUNNO THE WHOLE STORY, BUT I'M GLAD YOU HAD A NICE PLAYDATE.
TOO BAD KIKI COULDN'T HAVE JOINED THE FUN.
SORRY! I TAKE IT BACK!
THE LETTERS ...
IF YOU CAN'T READ THEM NOW, I'LL BRING THEM TO YOUR OFFICE.
NAH.
RSTL
RSTL
I'M READING, I'M READING.

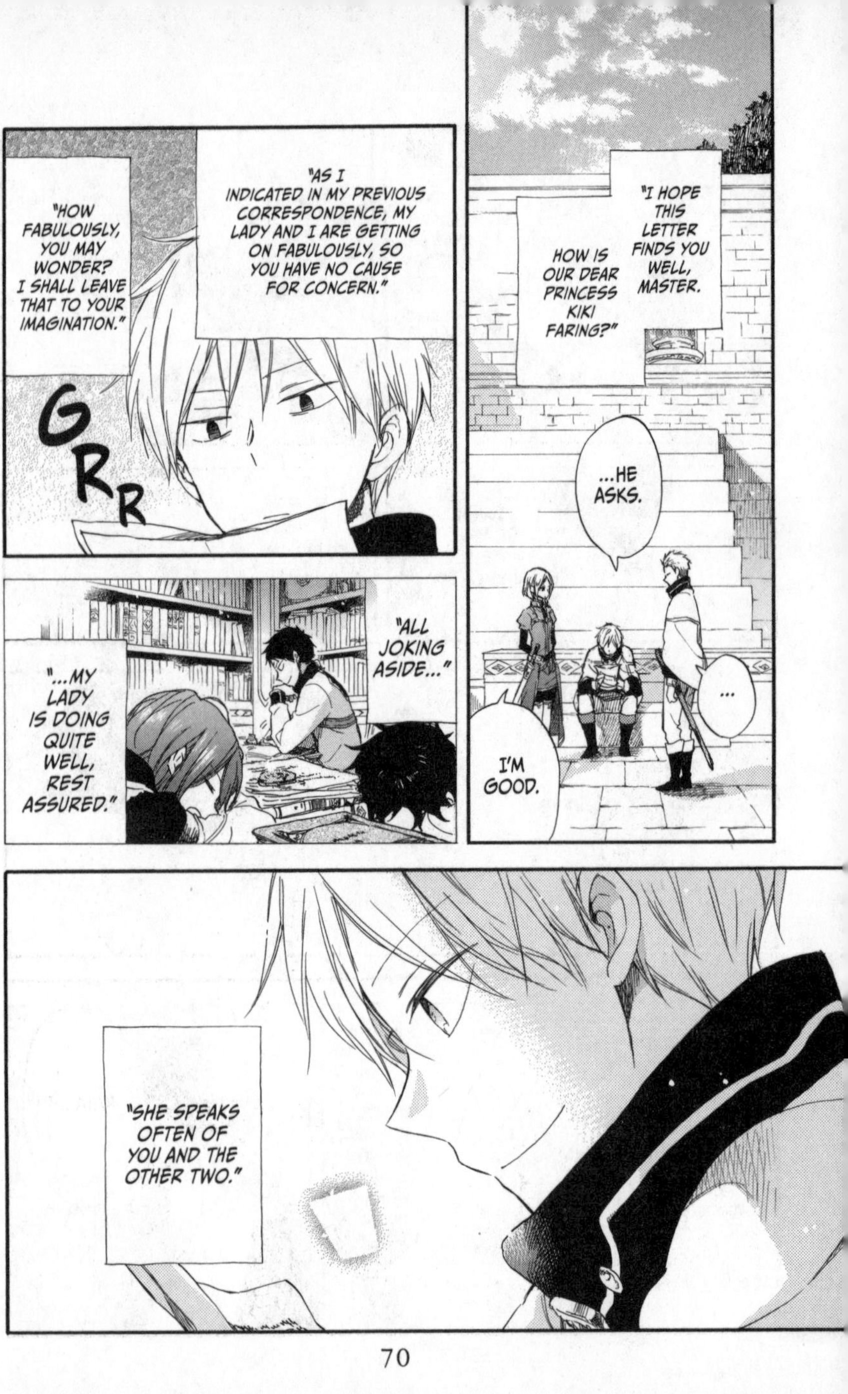
"I HOPE THIS LETTER FINDS YOU WELL, MASTER.
HOW IS OUR DEAR PRINCESS KIKI FARING?"
...HE ASKS.
...
I'M GOOD.
"AS I INDICATED IN MY PREVIOUS CORRESPONDENCE, MY LADY AND I ARE GETTING ON FABULOUSLY, SO YOU HAVE NO CAUSE FOR CONCERN."
"HOW FABULOUSLY, YOU MAY WONDER? I SHALL LEAVE THAT TO YOUR IMAGINATION."
GRR
"ALL JOKING ASIDE..."
"...MY LADY IS DOING QUITE WELL, REST ASSURED."
"SHE SPEAKS OFTEN OF YOU AND THE OTHER TWO."

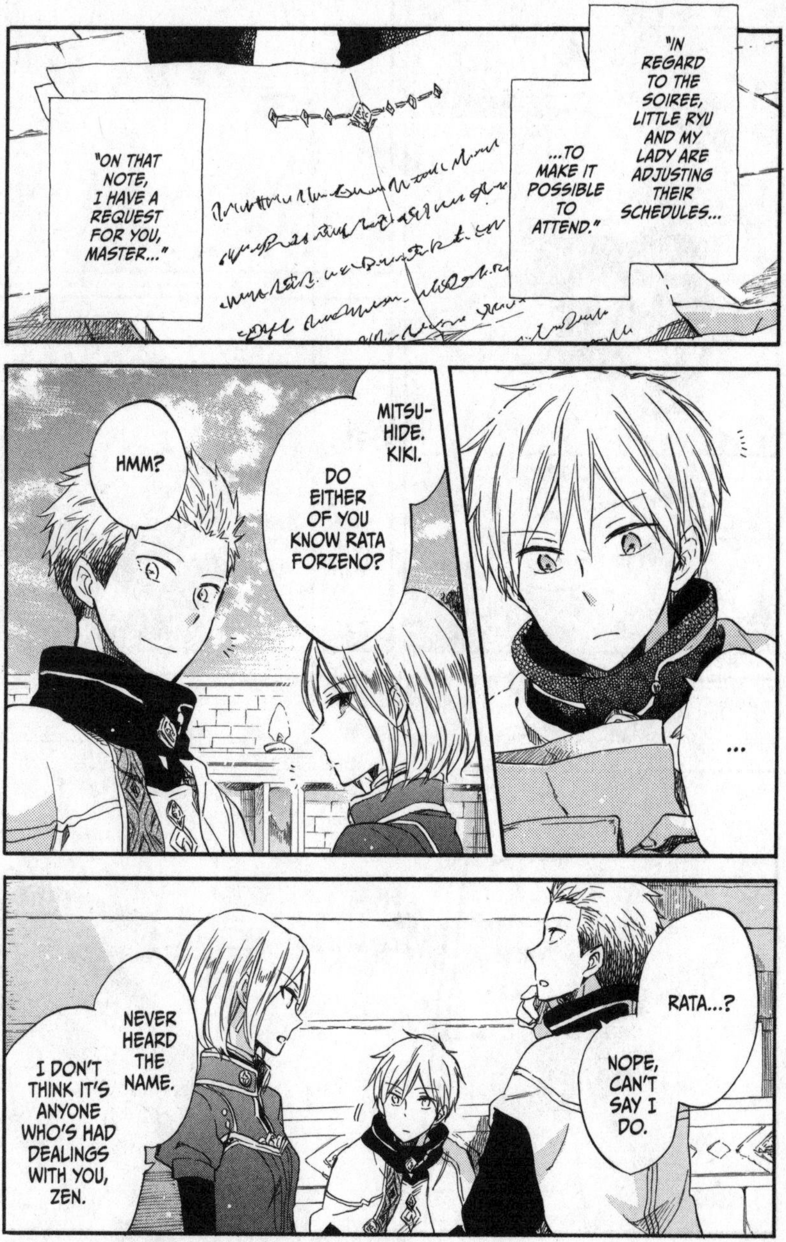
"IN REGARD TO THE SOIREE, LITTLE RYU AND MY LADY ARE ADJUSTING THEIR SCHEDULES...
...TO MAKE IT POSSIBLE TO ATTEND."
"ON THAT NOTE, I HAVE A REQUEST FOR YOU, MASTER..."
...
MITSU-HIDE. KIKI.
DO EITHER OF YOU KNOW RATA FORZENO?
HMM?
RATA...?
NOPE, CAN'T SAY I DO.
NEVER HEARD THE NAME.
I DON'T THINK IT'S ANYONE WHO'S HAD DEALINGS WITH YOU, ZEN.

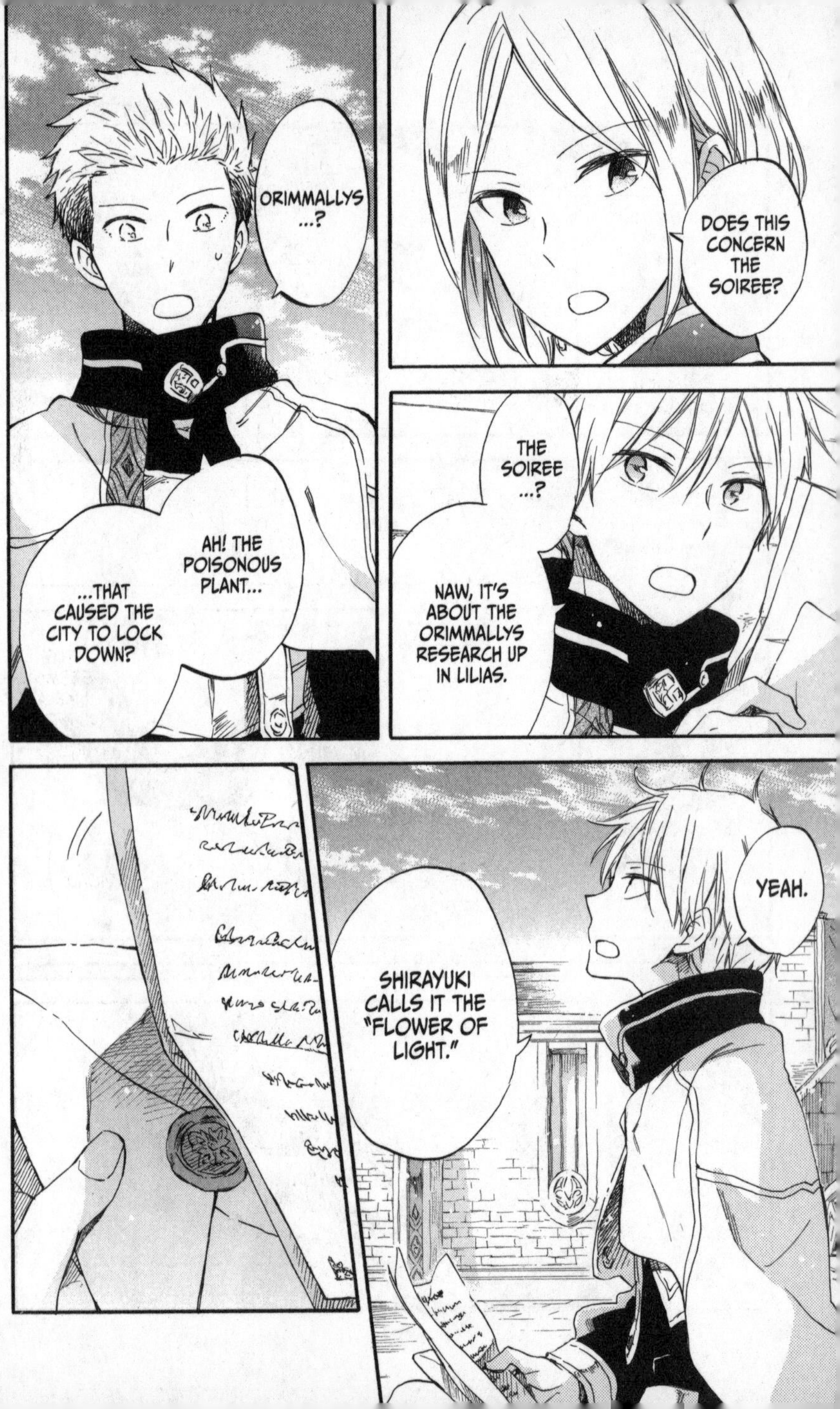
DOES THIS CONCERN THE SOIREE?
THE SOIREE ...?
NAW, IT'S ABOUT THE ORIMMALLYS RESEARCH UP IN LILIAS.
ORIMMALLYS ...?
AH! THE POISONOUS PLANT...
...THAT CAUSED THE CITY TO LOCK DOWN?
YEAH.
SHIRAYUKI CALLS IT THE "FLOWER OF LIGHT."

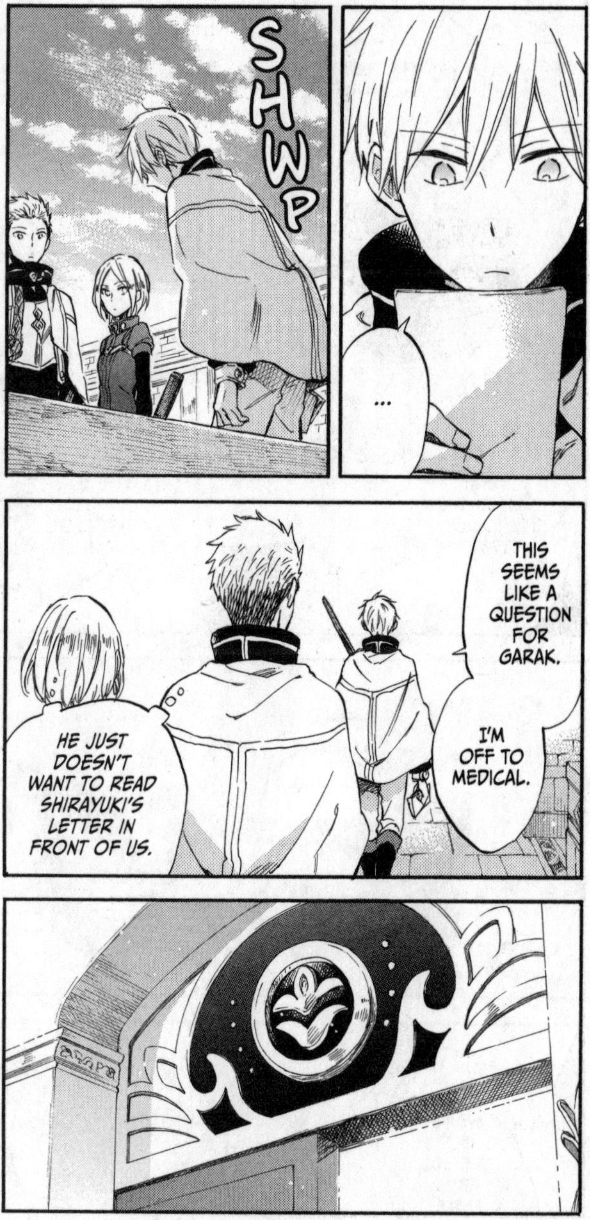
...
SHWP
THIS SEEMS LIKE A QUESTION FOR GARAK.
I'M OFF TO MEDICAL.
HE JUST DOESN'T WANT TO READ SHIRAYUKI'S LETTER IN FRONT OF US.

3

CHAPTER TALK

Spoilers Ahead

Chapter 61

Ryu is left speechless by Kirito's growth. He'll probably grow a lot more in the next two years, so as someone who's fond of itty-bitty scampering characters, I'm a little regretful? Reluctant? Never mind.

You grow up too, Ryu.

I think Kirito gets along better with Yuzuri than Suzu.

Where is Yuzuri anyhow?

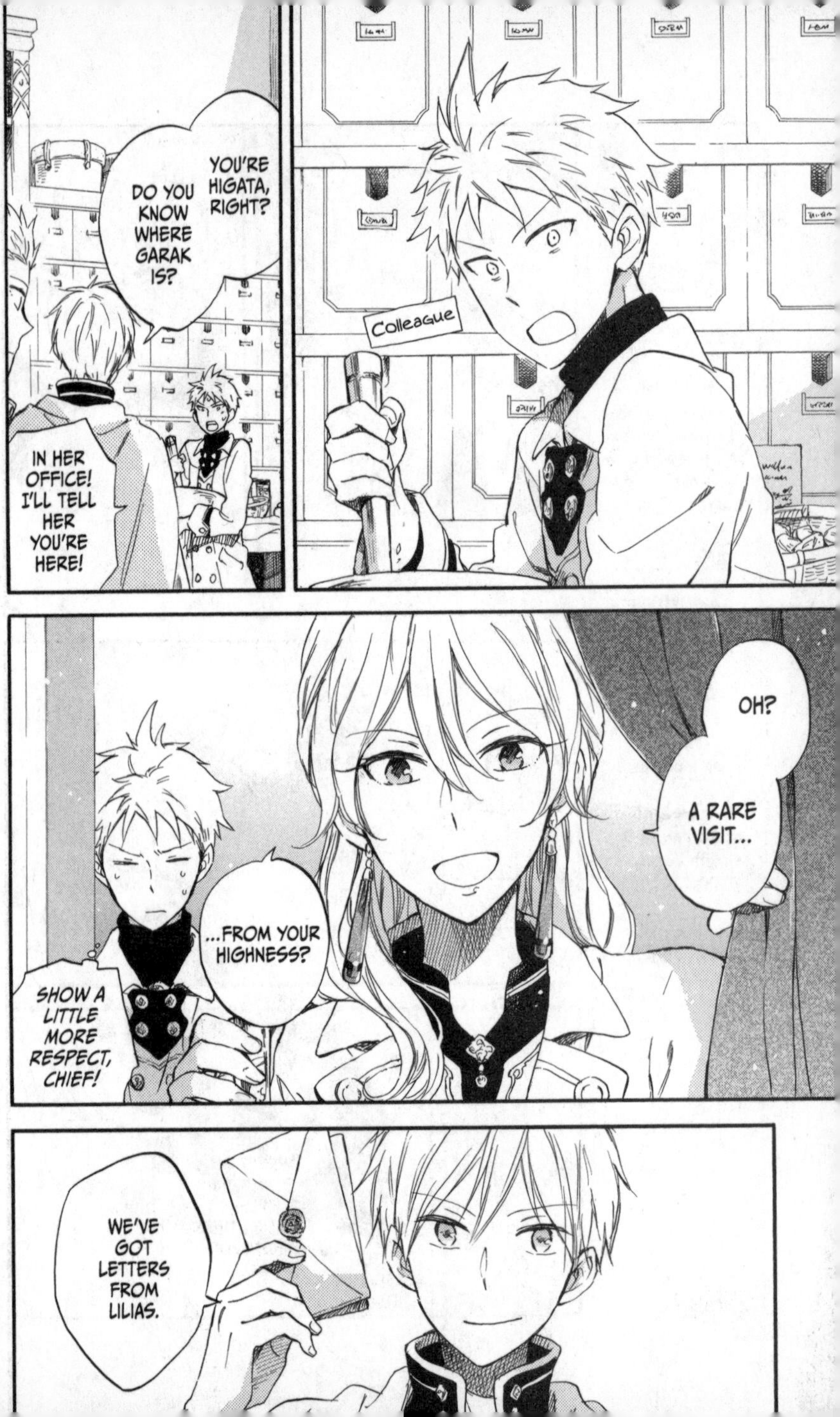
Colleague
YOU'RE HIGATA, RIGHT?
DO YOU KNOW WHERE GARAK IS?
IN HER OFFICE! I'LL TELL HER YOU'RE HERE!
OH?
A RARE VISIT...
...FROM YOUR HIGHNESS?
SHOW A LITTLE MORE RESPECT, CHIEF!
WE'VE GOT LETTERS FROM LILIAS.

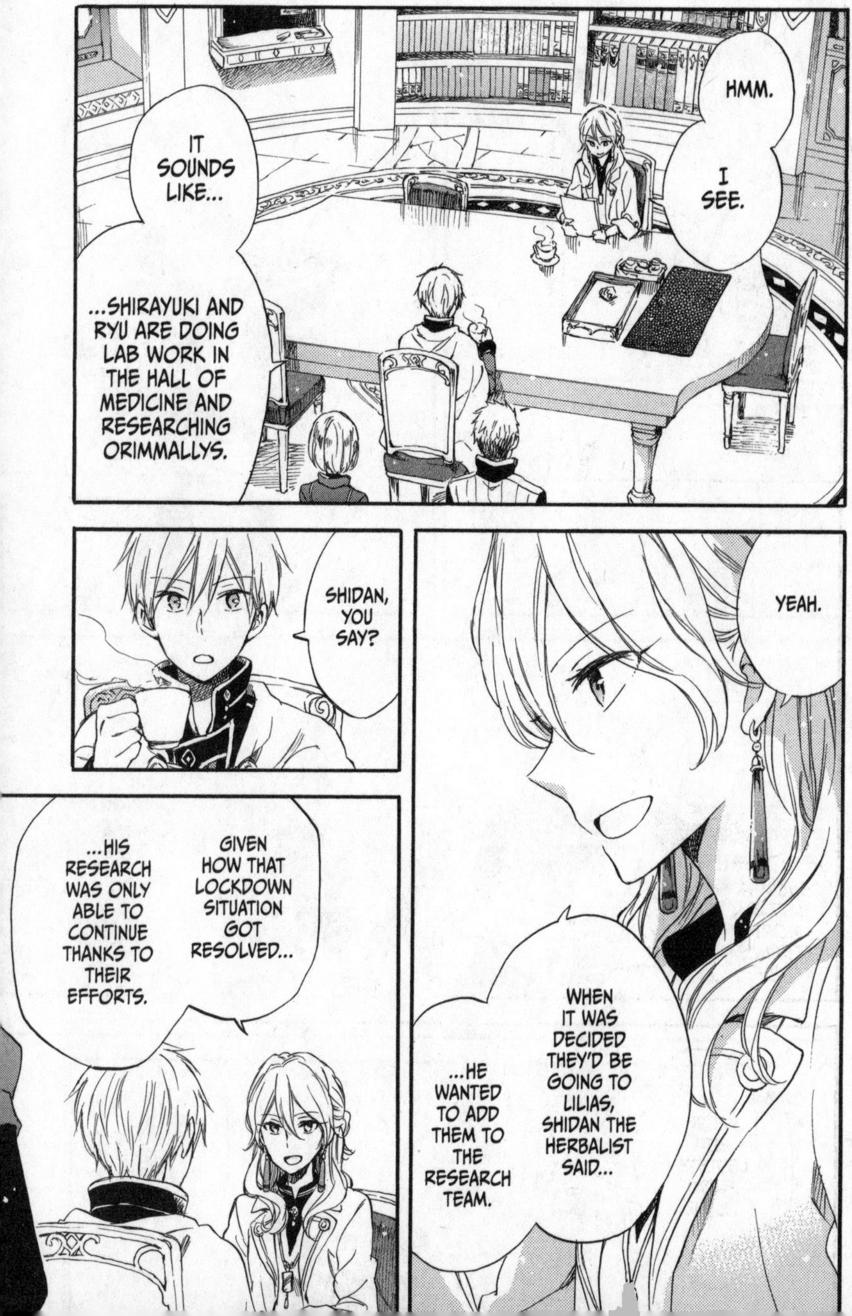
HMM.
I SEE.
IT SOUNDS LIKE...
...SHIRAYUKI AND RYU ARE DOING LAB WORK IN THE HALL OF MEDICINE AND RESEARCHING ORIMMALLYS.
YEAH.
WHEN IT WAS DECIDED THEY'D BE GOING TO LILIAS, SHIDAN THE HERBALIST SAID...
...HE WANTED TO ADD THEM TO THE RESEARCH TEAM.
SHIDAN, YOU SAY?
GIVEN HOW THAT LOCKDOWN SITUATION GOT RESOLVED...
...HIS RESEARCH WAS ONLY ABLE TO CONTINUE THANKS TO THEIR EFFORTS.

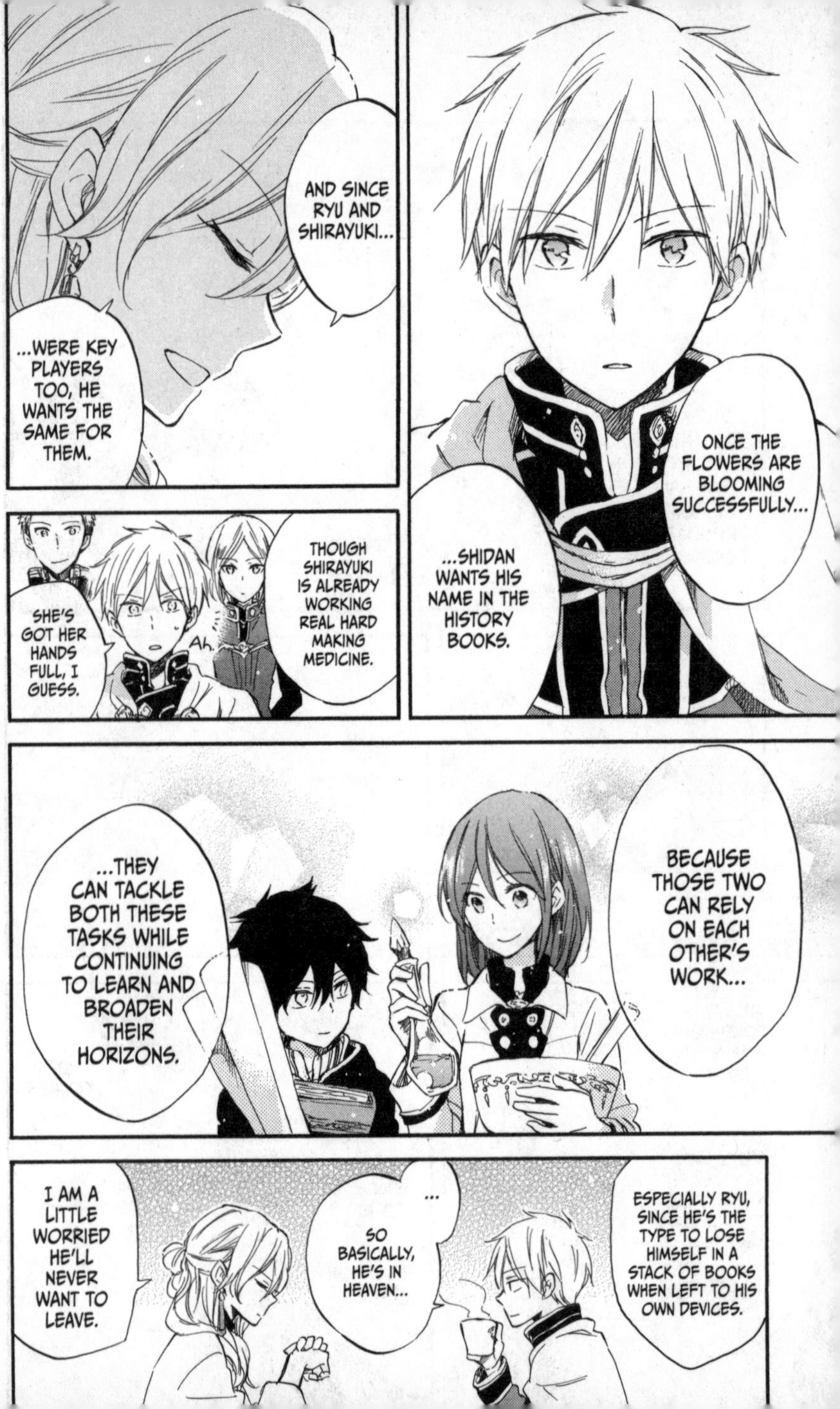
ONCE THE FLOWERS ARE BLOOMING SUCCESSFULLY...
...SHIDAN WANTS HIS NAME IN THE HISTORY BOOKS.
AND SINCE RYU AND SHIRAYUKI...
...WERE KEY PLAYERS TOO, HE WANTS THE SAME FOR THEM.
THOUGH SHIRAYUKI IS ALREADY WORKING REAL HARD MAKING MEDICINE.
Ah.
SHE'S GOT HER HANDS FULL, I GUESS.
BECAUSE THOSE TWO CAN RELY ON EACH OTHER'S WORK...
...THEY CAN TACKLE BOTH THESE TASKS WHILE CONTINUING TO LEARN AND BROADEN THEIR HORIZONS.
ESPECIALLY RYU, SINCE HE'S THE TYPE TO LOSE HIMSELF IN A STACK OF BOOKS WHEN LEFT TO HIS OWN DEVICES.
...
SO BASICALLY, HE'S IN HEAVEN...
I AM A LITTLE WORRIED HE'LL NEVER WANT TO LEAVE.

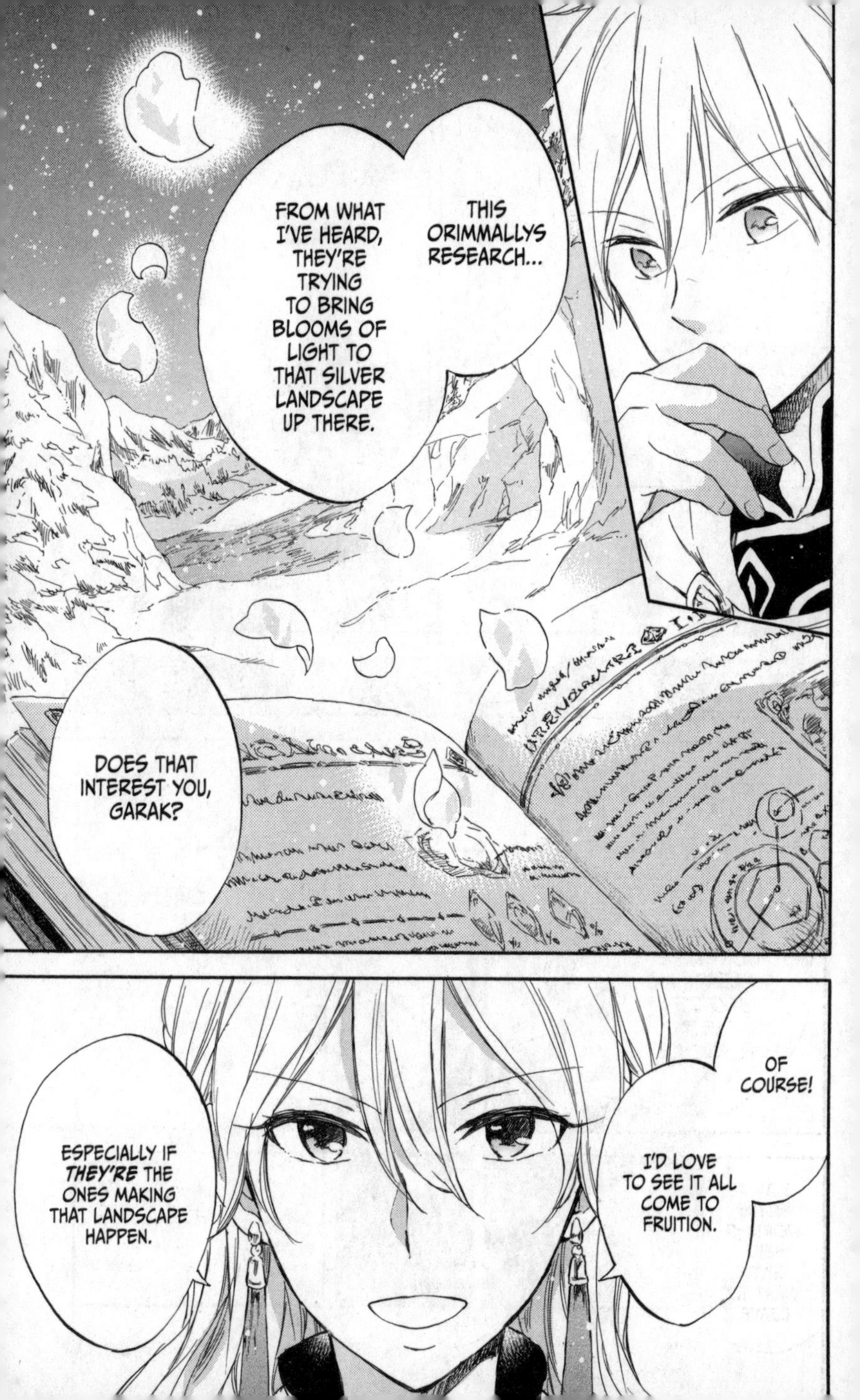
THIS ORIMMALLYS RESEARCH...
FROM WHAT I'VE HEARD, THEY'RE TRYING TO BRING BLOOMS OF LIGHT TO THAT SILVER LANDSCAPE UP THERE.
DOES THAT INTEREST YOU, GARAK?
OF COURSE!
I'D LOVE TO SEE IT ALL COME TO FRUITION.
ESPECIALLY IF *THEY'RE* THE ONES MAKING THAT LANDSCAPE HAPPEN.

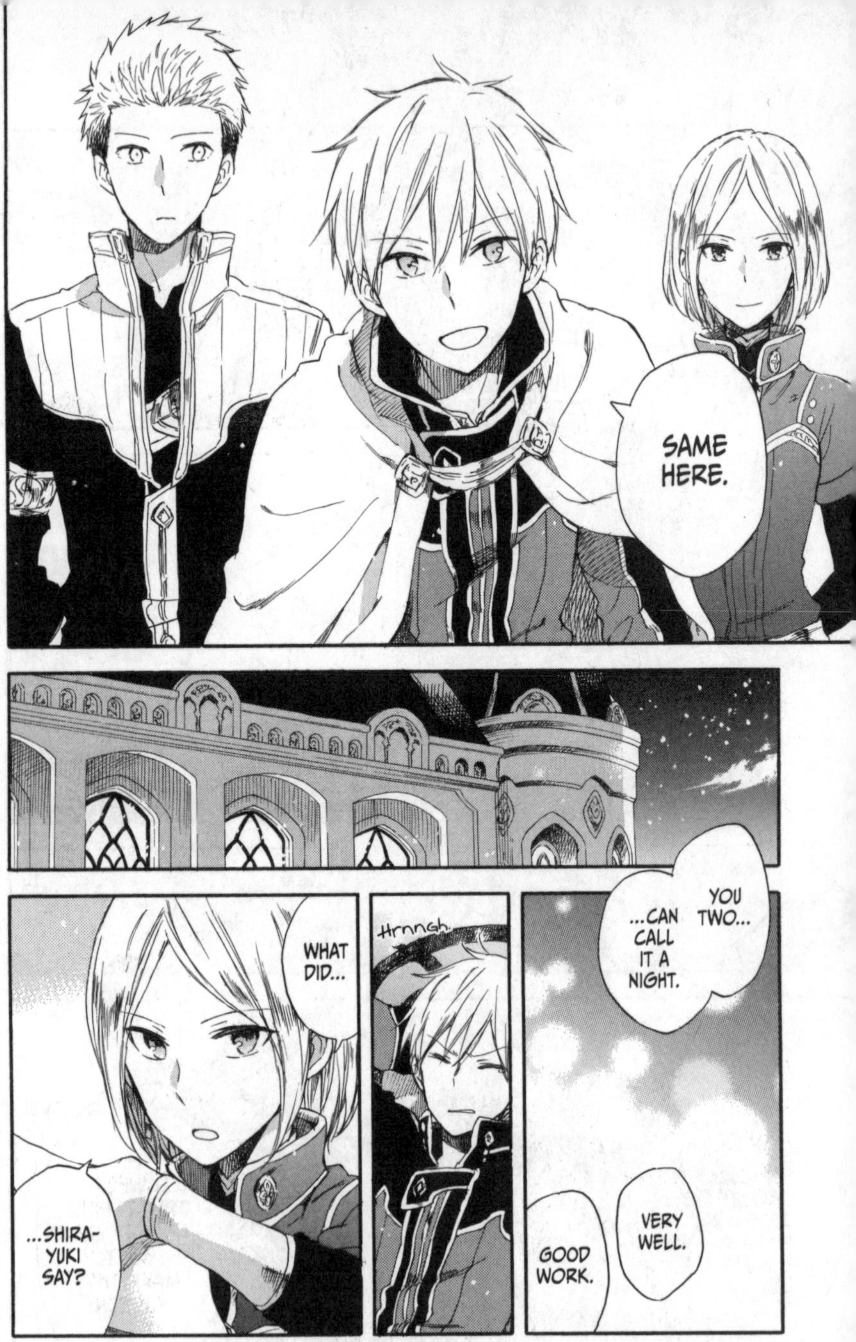
SAME HERE.
YOU TWO...
...CAN CALL IT A NIGHT.
VERY WELL.
GOOD WORK.
Hrnngh.
WHAT DID...
...SHIRA-YUKI SAY?

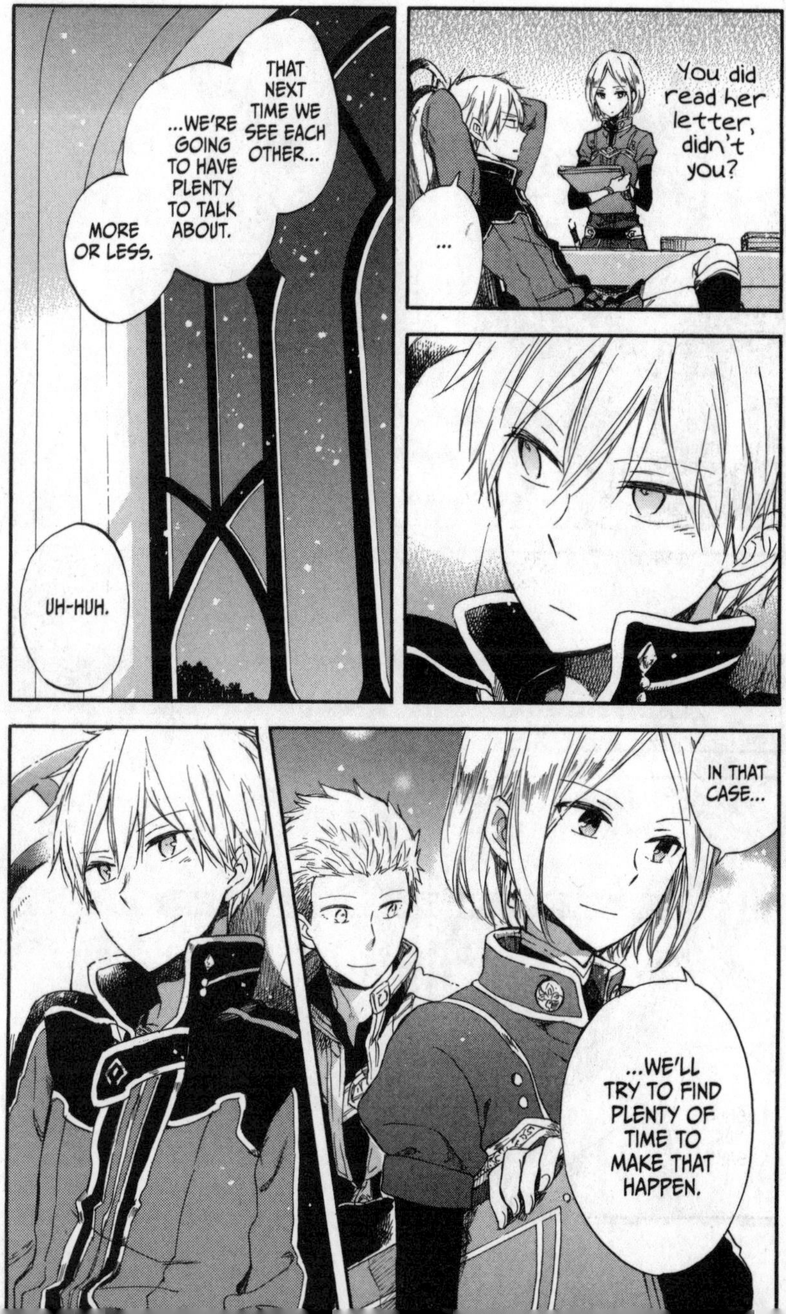
You did read her letter, didn't you?
...
THAT NEXT TIME WE SEE EACH OTHER...
...WE'RE GOING TO HAVE PLENTY TO TALK ABOUT.
MORE OR LESS.
UH-HUH.
IN THAT CASE...
...WE'LL TRY TO FIND PLENTY OF TIME TO MAKE THAT HAPPEN.

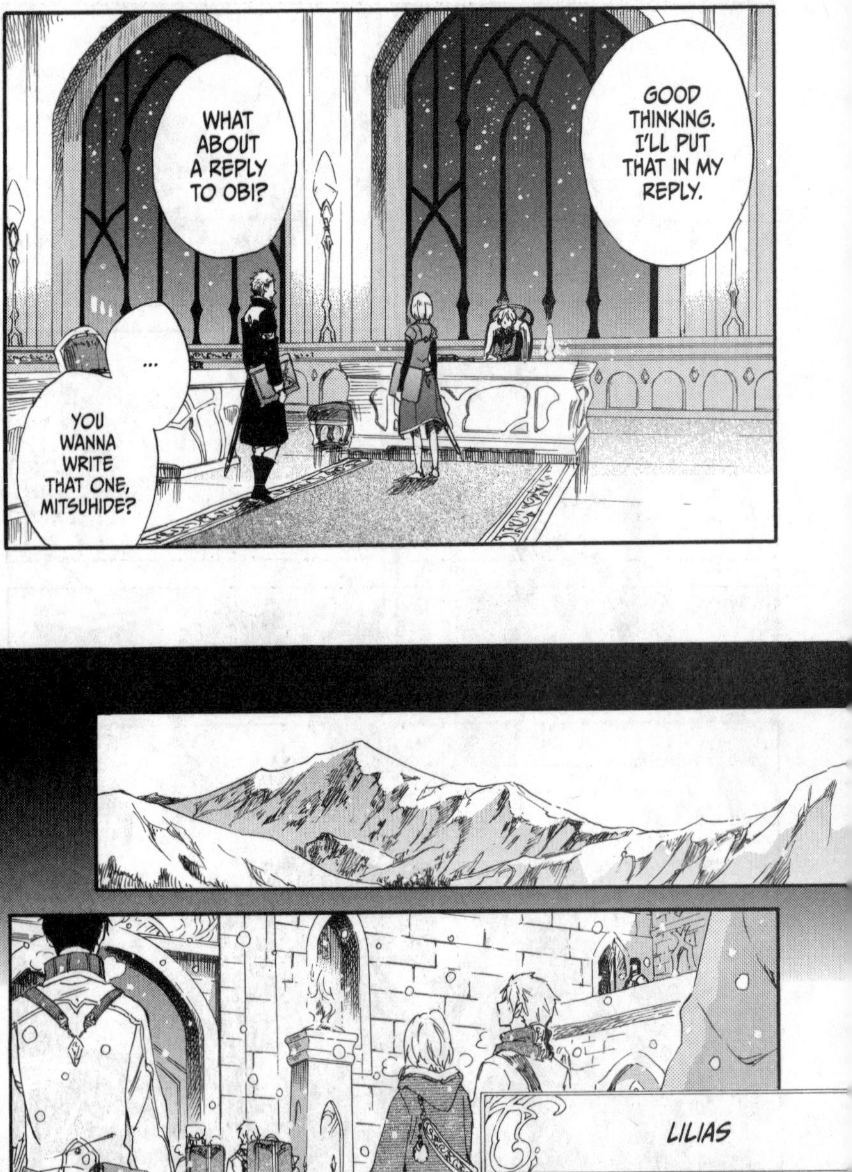
GOOD THINKING. I'LL PUT THAT IN MY REPLY.
WHAT ABOUT A REPLY TO OBI?
...
YOU WANNA WRITE THAT ONE, MITSUHIDE?
LILIAS

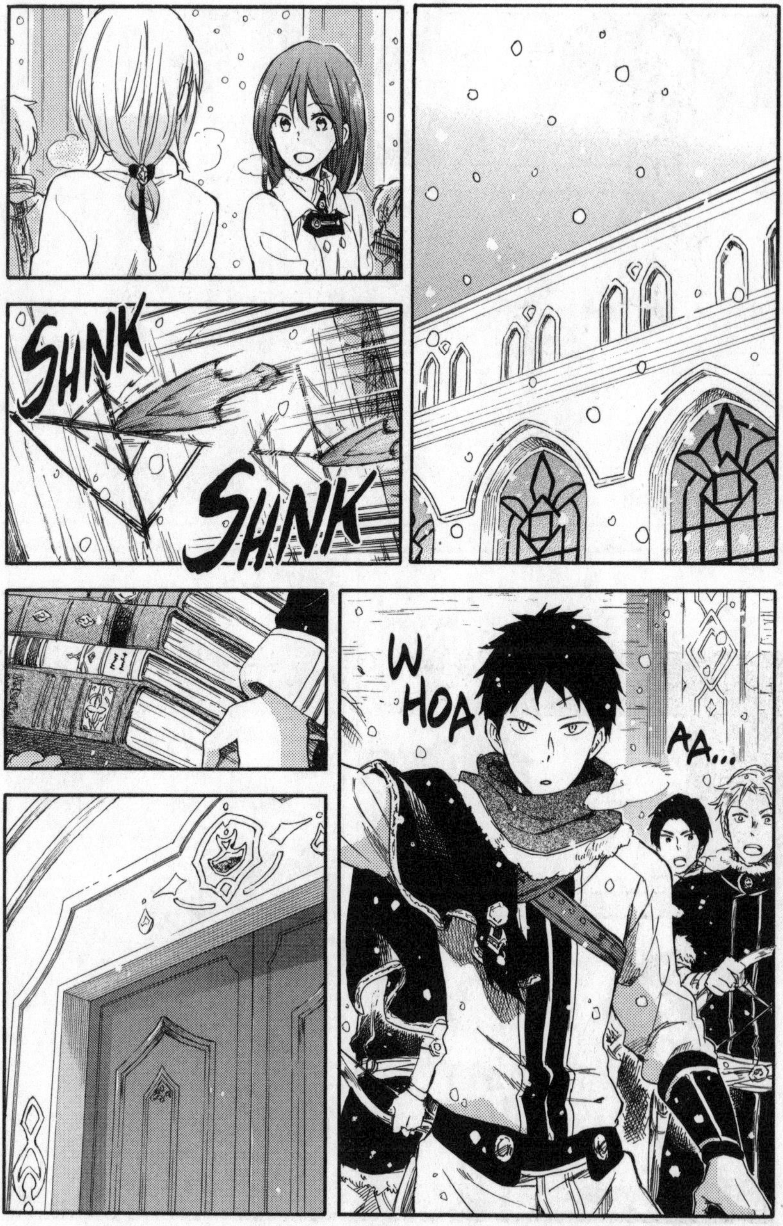
SHNK
SHNK
WHOA
AA...

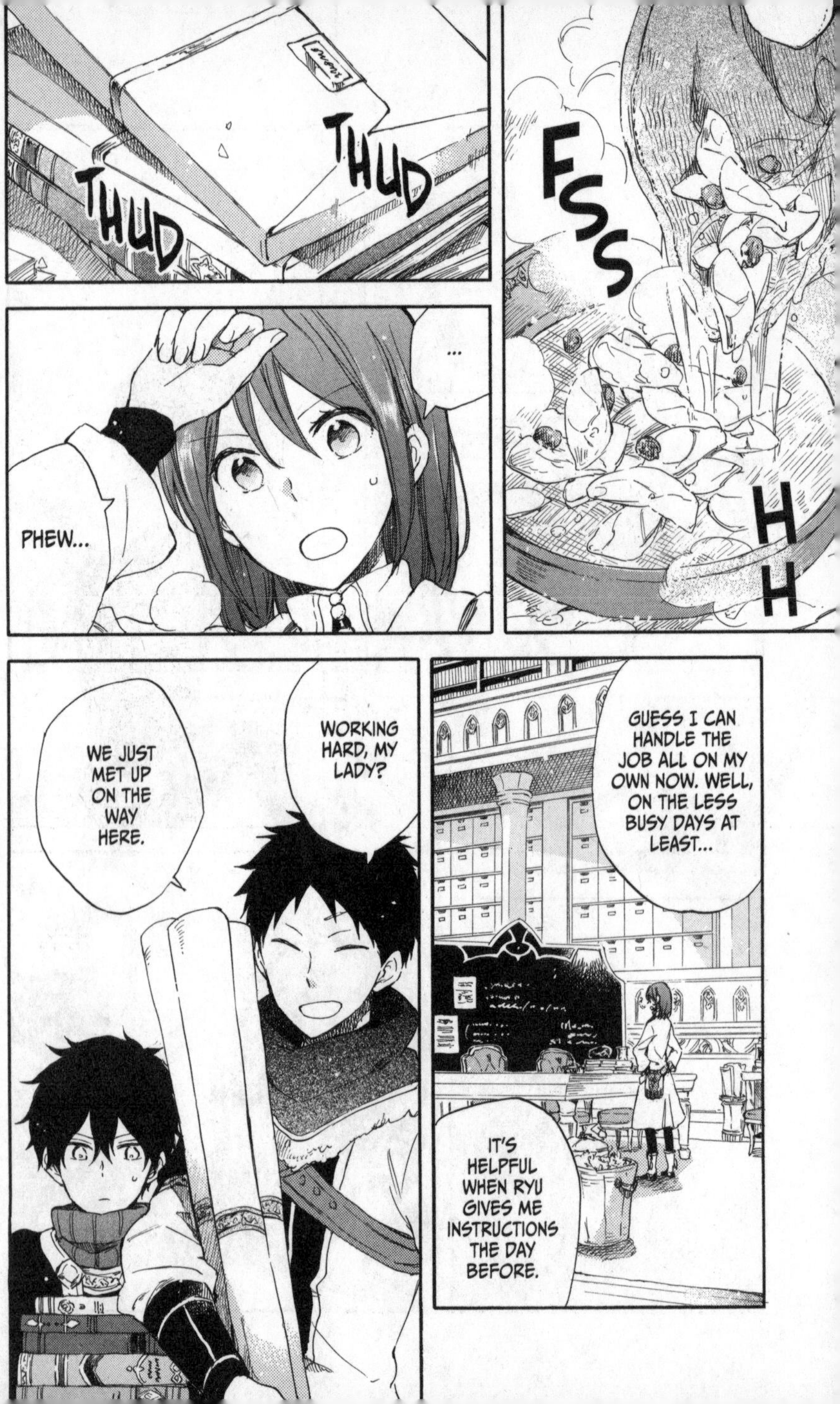
FSS
HH
THUD
THUD
...
PHEW...
GUESS I CAN HANDLE THE JOB ALL ON MY OWN NOW. WELL, ON THE LESS BUSY DAYS AT LEAST...
IT'S HELPFUL WHEN RYU GIVES ME INSTRUCTIONS THE DAY BEFORE.
WORKING HARD, MY LADY?
WE JUST MET UP ON THE WAY HERE.

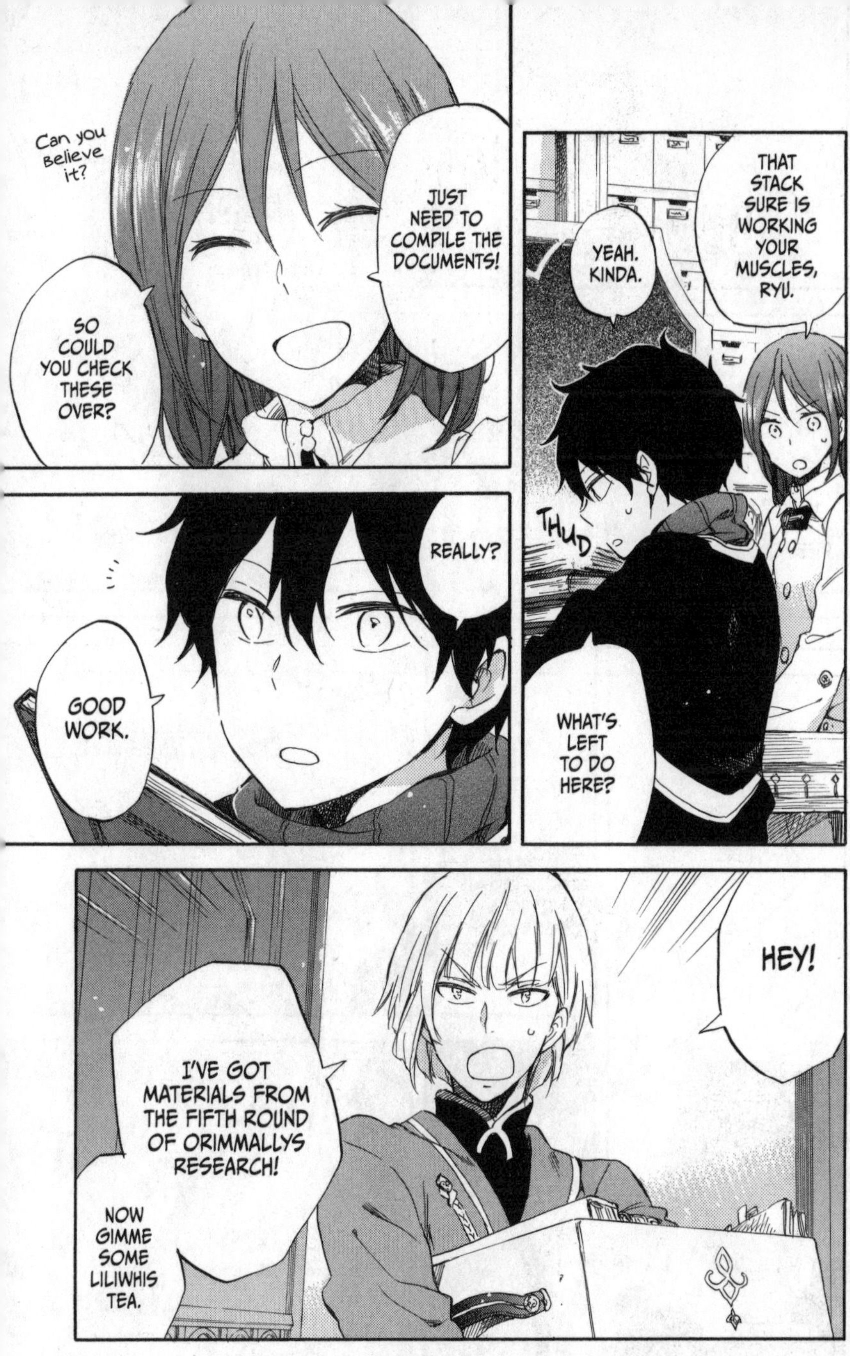
THAT STACK SURE IS WORKING YOUR MUSCLES, RYU.
YEAH. KINDA.
THUD
WHAT'S LEFT TO DO HERE?
JUST NEED TO COMPILE THE DOCUMENTS!
Can you believe it?
SO COULD YOU CHECK THESE OVER?
REALLY?
GOOD WORK.
HEY!
I'VE GOT MATERIALS FROM THE FIFTH ROUND OF ORIMMALLYS RESEARCH!
NOW GIMME SOME LILIWHIS TEA.

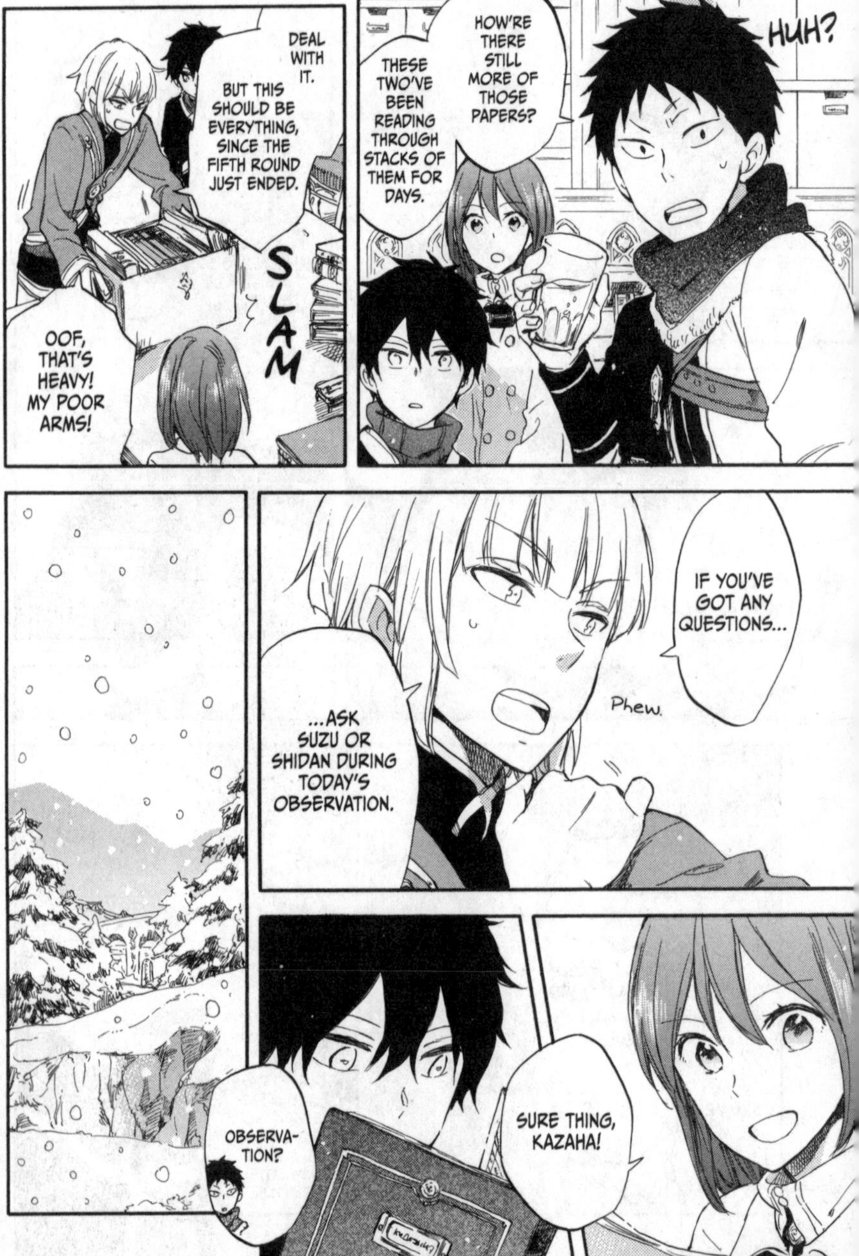
HUH?
HOW'RE THERE STILL MORE OF THOSE PAPERS?
THESE TWO'VE BEEN READING THROUGH STACKS OF THEM FOR DAYS.
DEAL WITH IT.
BUT THIS SHOULD BE EVERYTHING, SINCE THE FIFTH ROUND JUST ENDED.
SLAM
OOF, THAT'S HEAVY! MY POOR ARMS!
IF YOU'VE GOT ANY QUESTIONS...
Phew.
...ASK SUZU OR SHIDAN DURING TODAY'S OBSERVATION.
SURE THING, KAZAHA!
OBSERVA-TION?

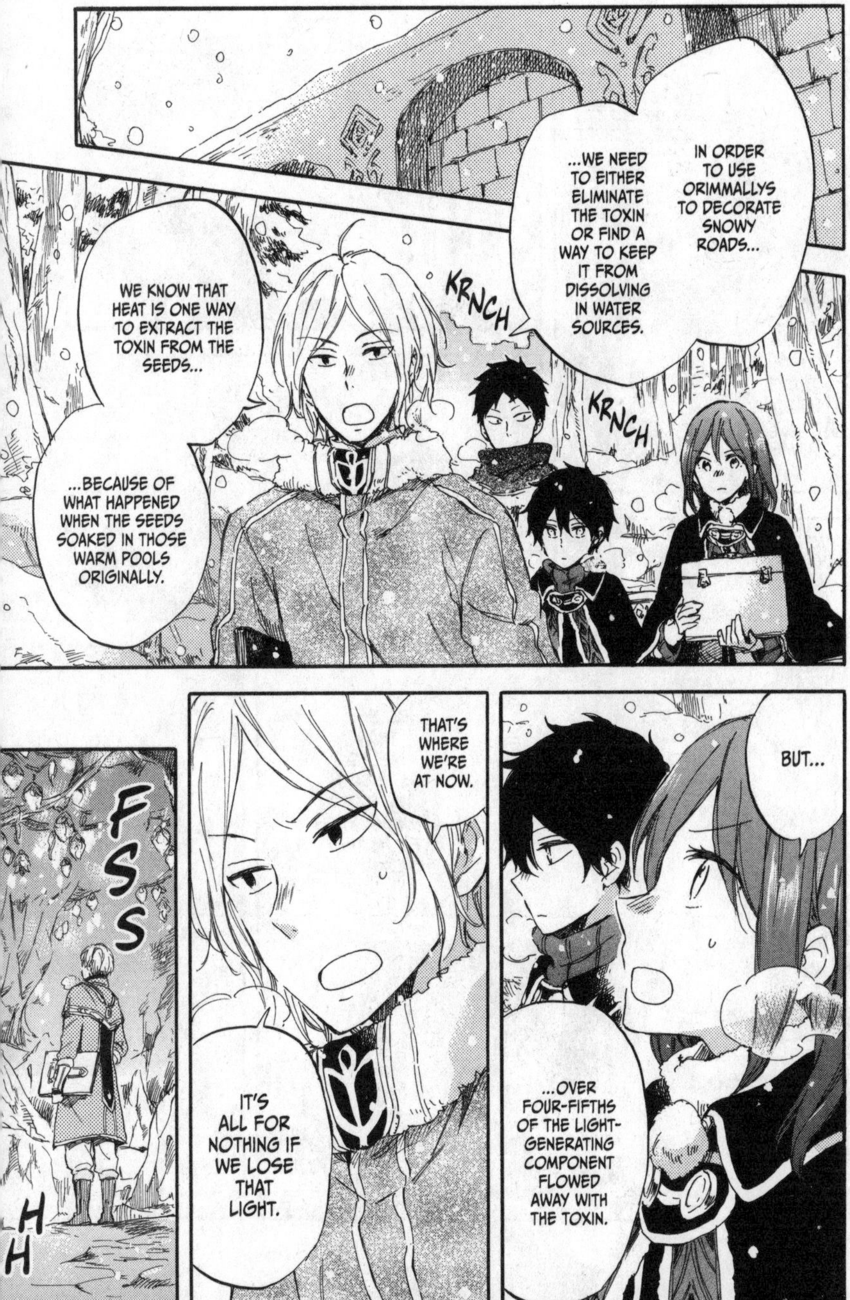
IN ORDER TO USE ORIMMALLYS TO DECORATE SNOWY ROADS...
...WE NEED TO EITHER ELIMINATE THE TOXIN OR FIND A WAY TO KEEP IT FROM DISSOLVING IN WATER SOURCES.
KRNCH
KRNCH
WE KNOW THAT HEAT IS ONE WAY TO EXTRACT THE TOXIN FROM THE SEEDS...
...BECAUSE OF WHAT HAPPENED WHEN THE SEEDS SOAKED IN THOSE WARM POOLS ORIGINALLY.
BUT...
...OVER FOUR-FIFTHS OF THE LIGHT-GENERATING COMPONENT FLOWED AWAY WITH THE TOXIN.
THAT'S WHERE WE'RE AT NOW.
IT'S ALL FOR NOTHING IF WE LOSE THAT LIGHT.
FSS
HH

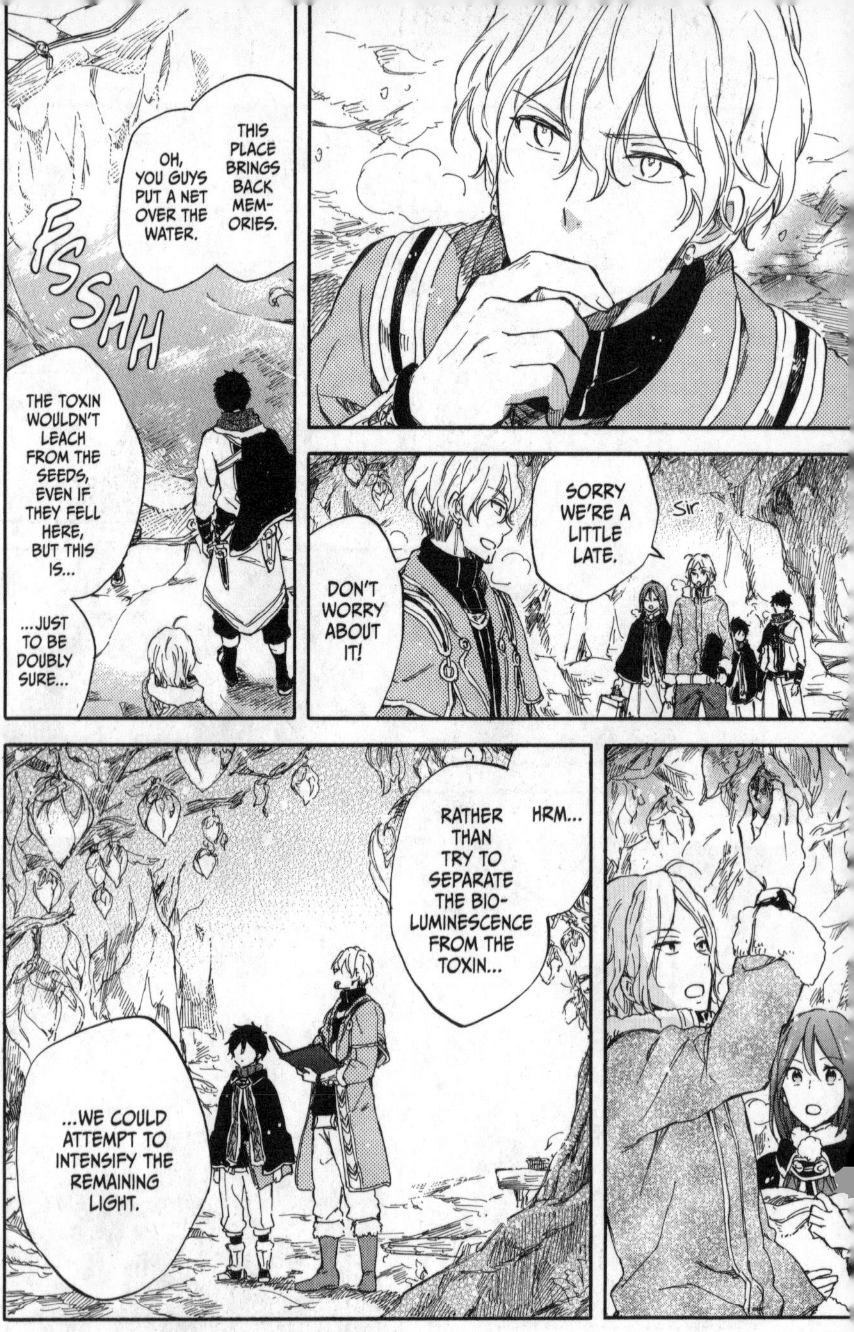
Sir.
SORRY WE'RE A LITTLE LATE.
DON'T WORRY ABOUT IT!
THIS PLACE BRINGS BACK MEM-ORIES.
OH, YOU GUYS PUT A NET OVER THE WATER.
FSSHH
THE TOXIN WOULDN'T LEACH FROM THE SEEDS, EVEN IF THEY FELL HERE, BUT THIS IS...
...JUST TO BE DOUBLY SURE...
HRM...
RATHER THAN TRY TO SEPARATE THE BIO-LUMINESCENCE FROM THE TOXIN...
...WE COULD ATTEMPT TO INTENSIFY THE REMAINING LIGHT.

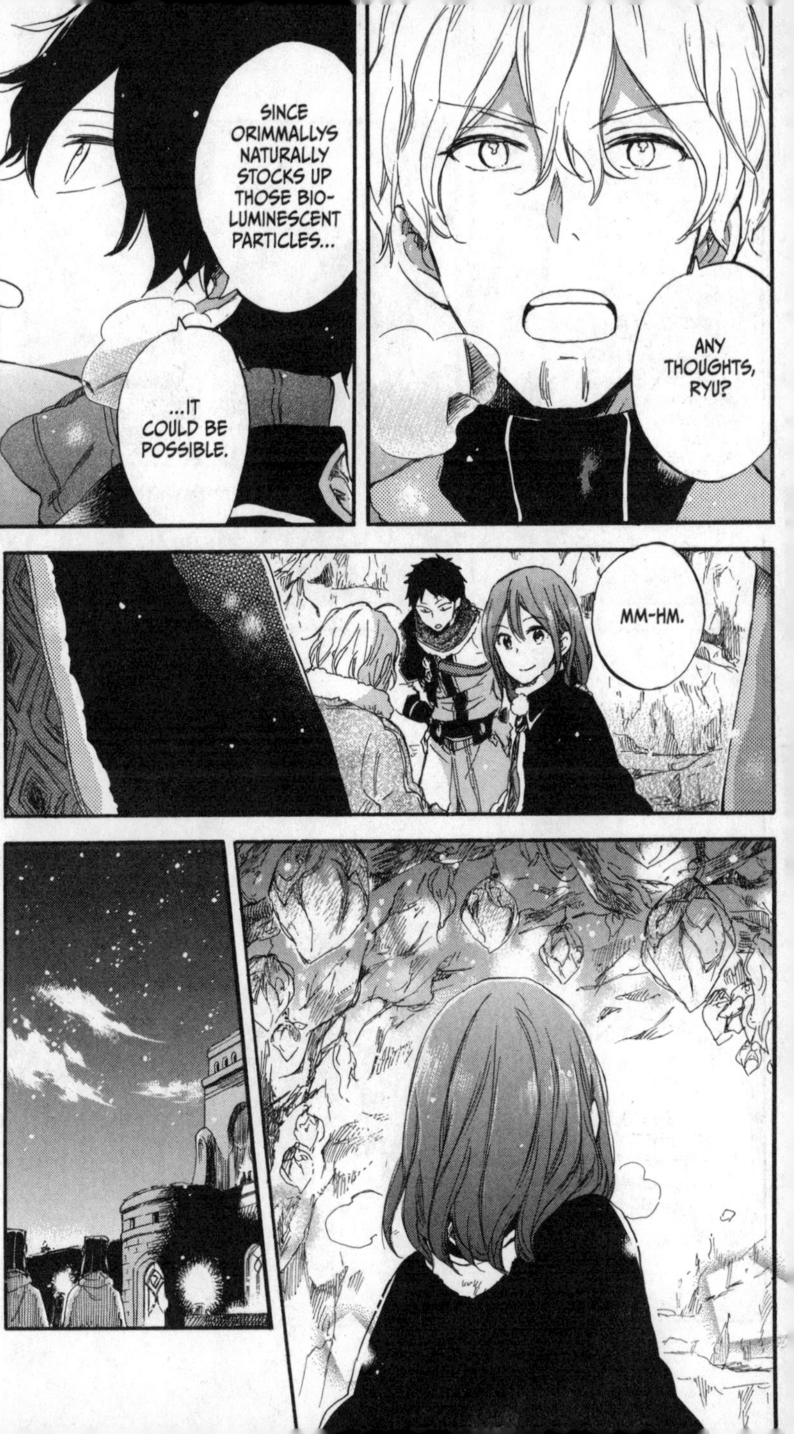
ANY THOUGHTS, RYU?
SINCE ORIMMALLYS NATURALLY STOCKS UP THOSE BIO-LUMINESCENT PARTICLES...
...IT COULD BE POSSIBLE.
MM-HM.

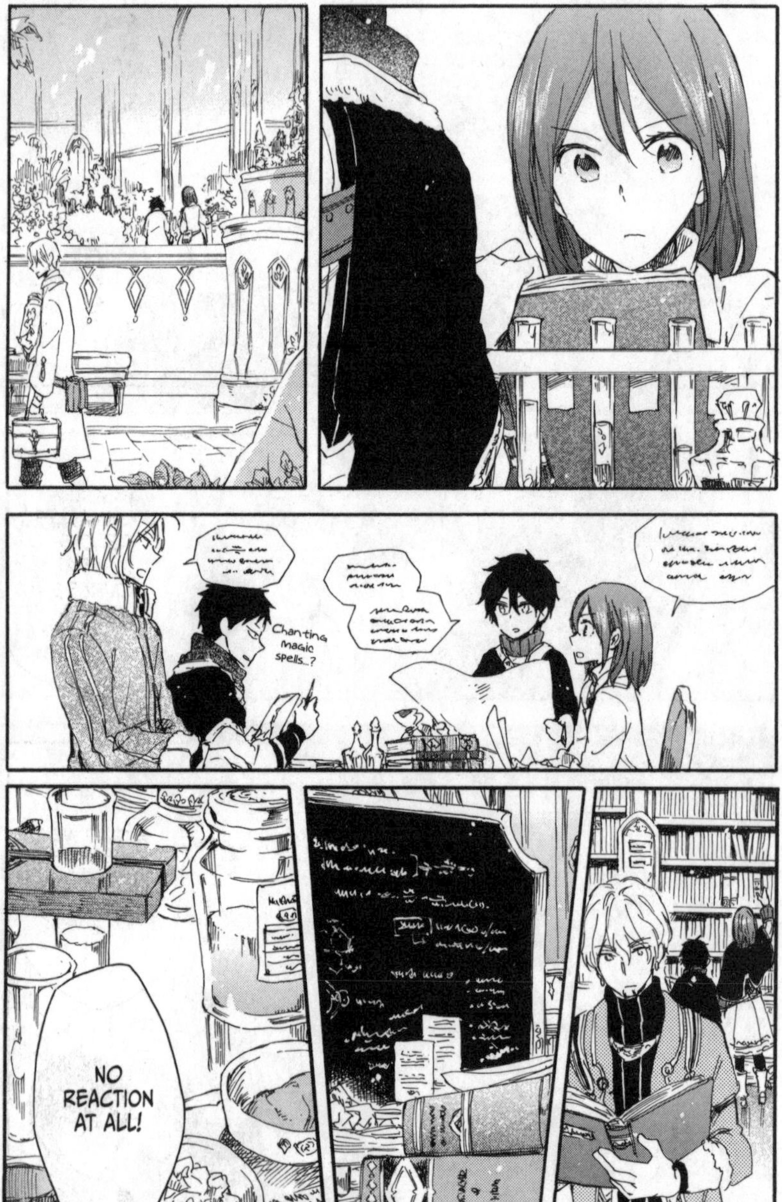
Chanting magic spells...?
NO REACTION AT ALL!

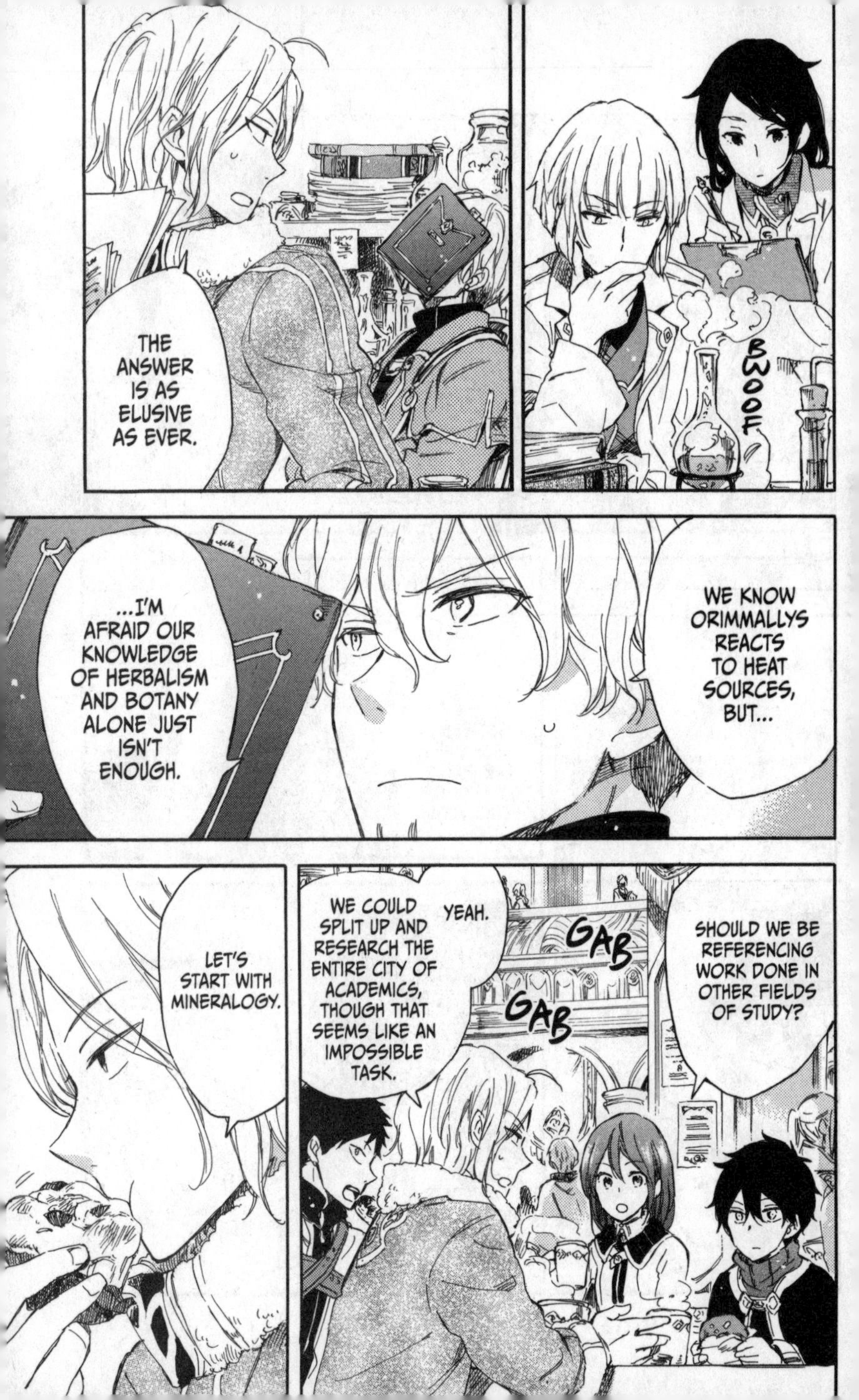
BWOOF
THE ANSWER IS AS ELUSIVE AS EVER.
WE KNOW ORIMMALLYS REACTS TO HEAT SOURCES, BUT...
...I'M AFRAID OUR KNOWLEDGE OF HERBALISM AND BOTANY ALONE JUST ISN'T ENOUGH.
SHOULD WE BE REFERENCING WORK DONE IN OTHER FIELDS OF STUDY?
GAB
GAB
YEAH.
WE COULD SPLIT UP AND RESEARCH THE ENTIRE CITY OF ACADEMICS, THOUGH THAT SEEMS LIKE AN IMPOSSIBLE TASK.
LET'S START WITH MINERALOGY.

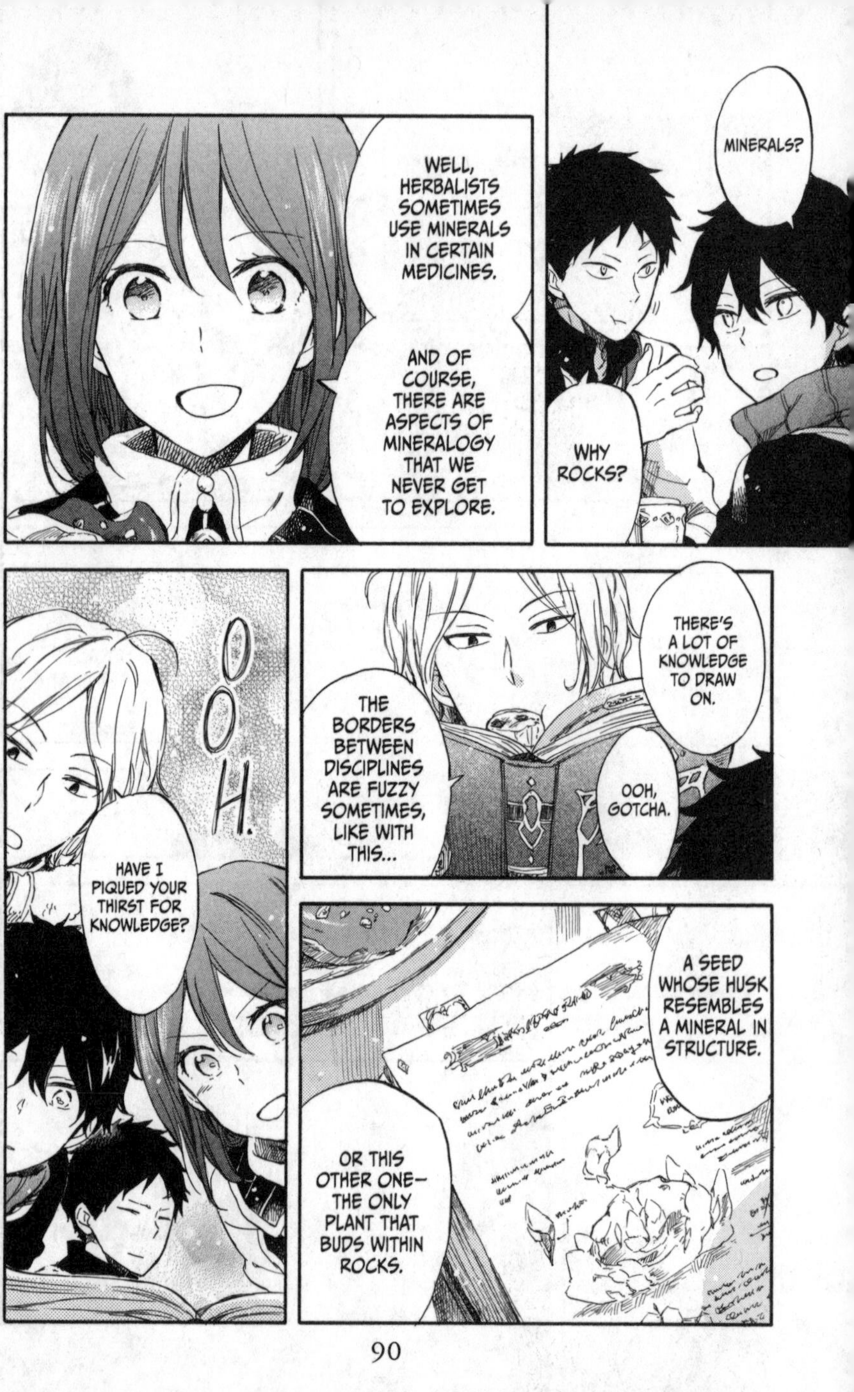
MINERALS?
WHY ROCKS?
WELL, HERBALISTS SOMETIMES USE MINERALS IN CERTAIN MEDICINES.
AND OF COURSE, THERE ARE ASPECTS OF MINERALOGY THAT WE NEVER GET TO EXPLORE.
THERE'S A LOT OF KNOWLEDGE TO DRAW ON.
THE BORDERS BETWEEN DISCIPLINES ARE FUZZY SOMETIMES, LIKE WITH THIS...
OOH, GOTCHA.
A SEED WHOSE HUSK RESEMBLES A MINERAL IN STRUCTURE.
OR THIS OTHER ONE— THE ONLY PLANT THAT BUDS WITHIN ROCKS.
OOOH.
HAVE I PIQUED YOUR THIRST FOR KNOWLEDGE?

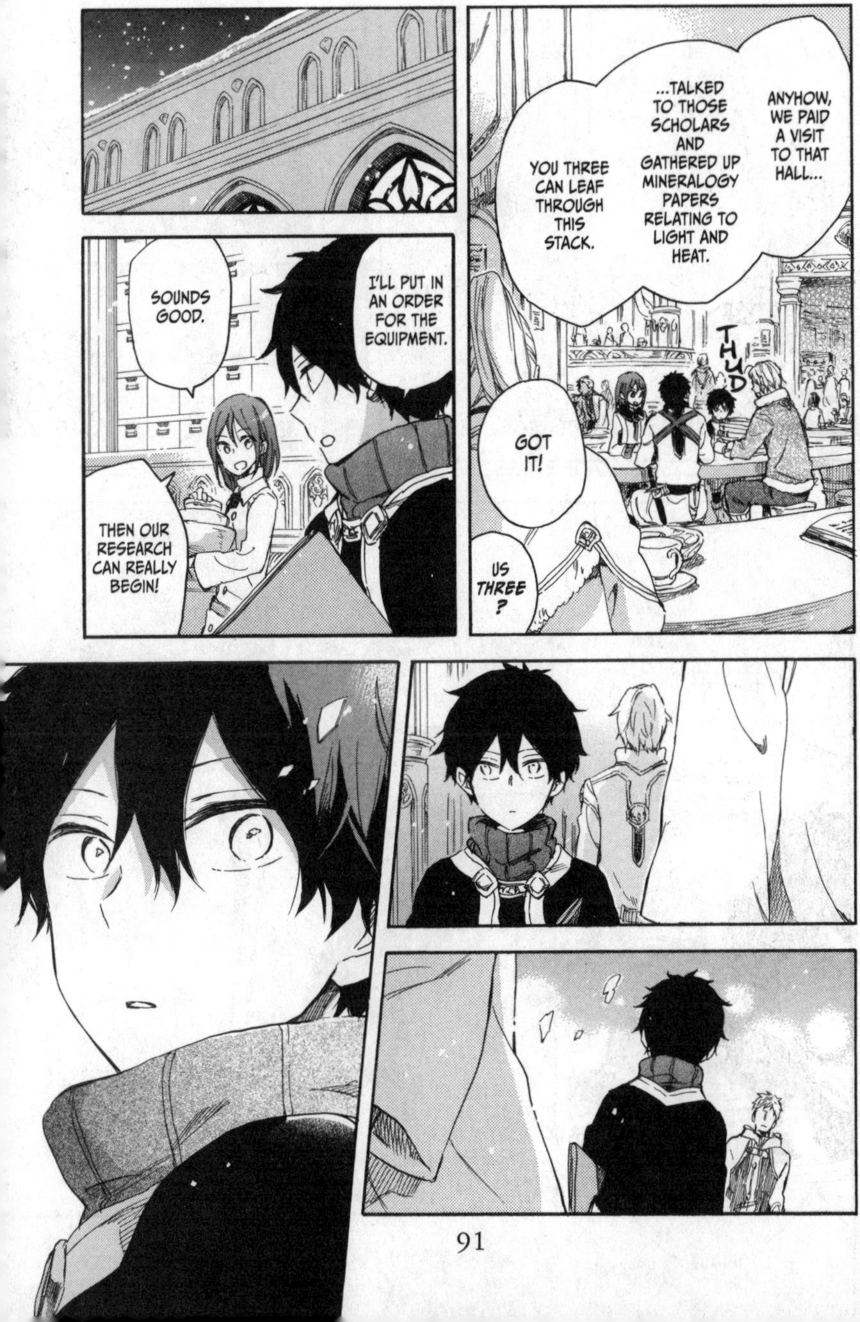
ANYHOW, WE PAID A VISIT TO THAT HALL...
...TALKED TO THOSE SCHOLARS AND GATHERED UP MINERALOGY PAPERS RELATING TO LIGHT AND HEAT.
YOU THREE CAN LEAF THROUGH THIS STACK.
THUD
GOT IT!
US THREE?
I'LL PUT IN AN ORDER FOR THE EQUIPMENT.
SOUNDS GOOD.
THEN OUR RESEARCH CAN REALLY BEGIN!

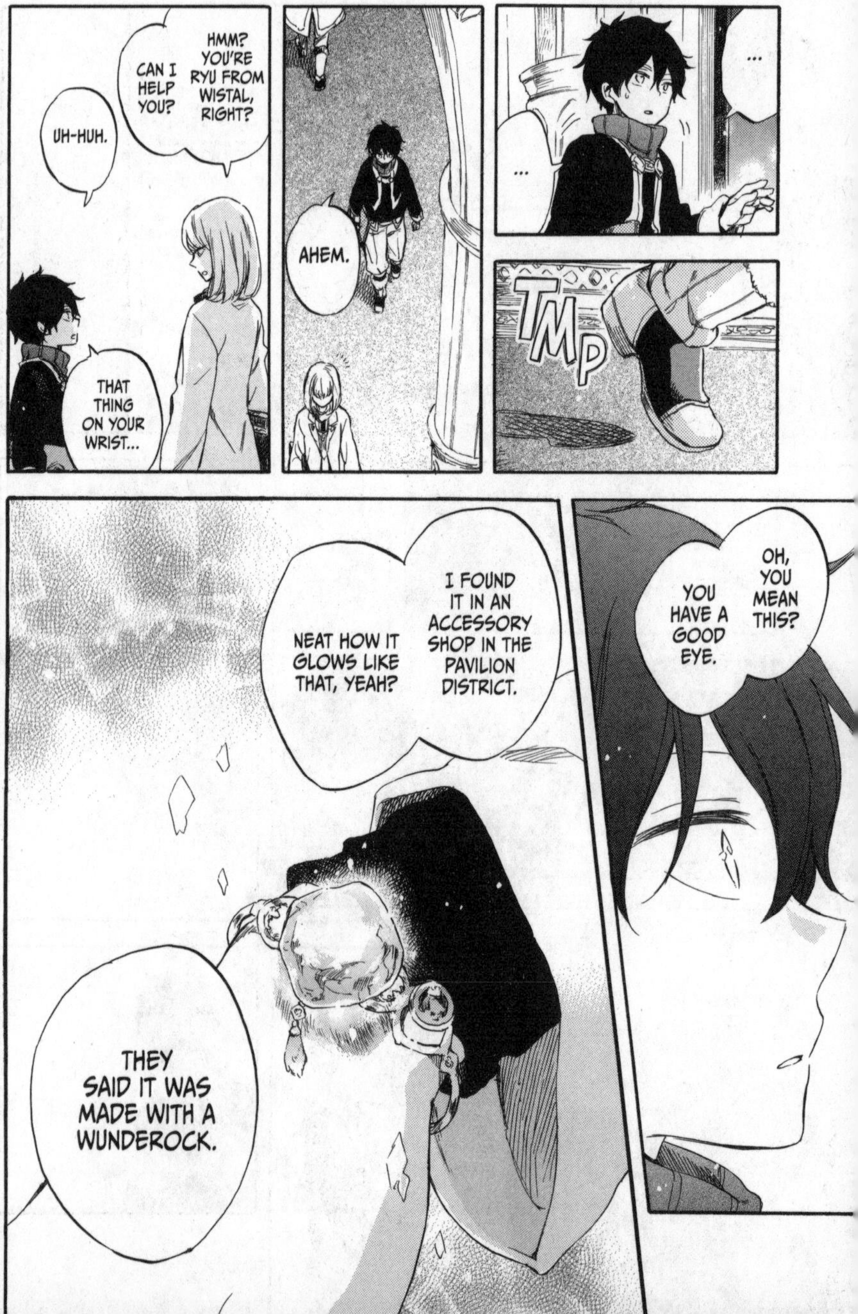
...
...
TMP
AHEM.
HMM? YOU'RE RYU FROM WISTAL, RIGHT?
CAN I HELP YOU?
UH-HUH.
THAT THING ON YOUR WRIST...
OH, YOU MEAN THIS?
YOU HAVE A GOOD EYE.
I FOUND IT IN AN ACCESSORY SHOP IN THE PAVILION DISTRICT.
NEAT HOW IT GLOWS LIKE THAT, YEAH?
THEY SAID IT WAS MADE WITH A WUNDEROCK.

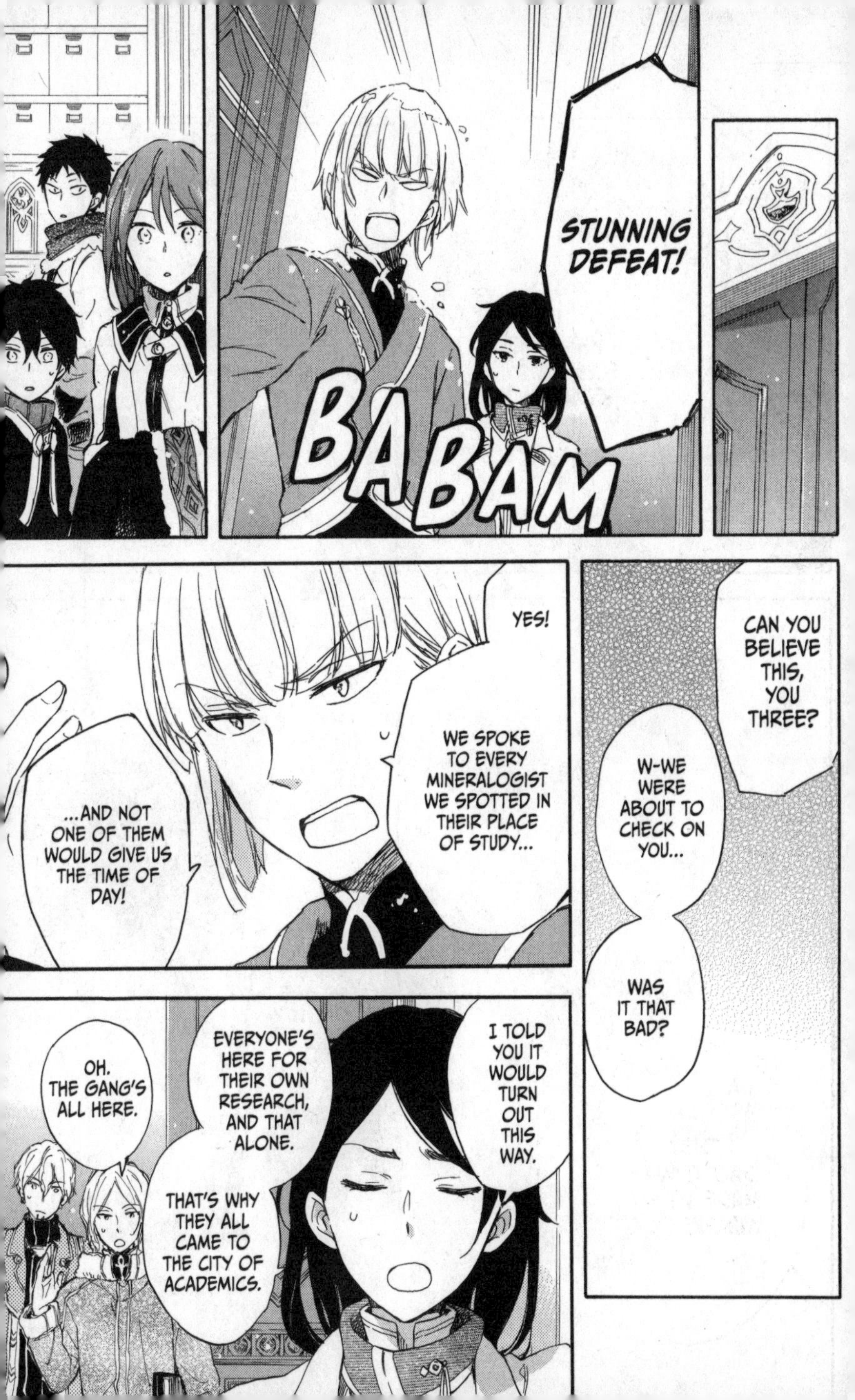
STUNNING DEFEAT!
BABAM
CAN YOU BELIEVE THIS, YOU THREE?
W-WE WERE ABOUT TO CHECK ON YOU...
WAS IT THAT BAD?
YES!
WE SPOKE TO EVERY MINERALOGIST WE SPOTTED IN THEIR PLACE OF STUDY...
...AND NOT ONE OF THEM WOULD GIVE US THE TIME OF DAY!
I TOLD YOU IT WOULD TURN OUT THIS WAY.
EVERYONE'S HERE FOR THEIR OWN RESEARCH, AND THAT ALONE.
THAT'S WHY THEY ALL CAME TO THE CITY OF ACADEMICS.
OH. THE GANG'S ALL HERE.

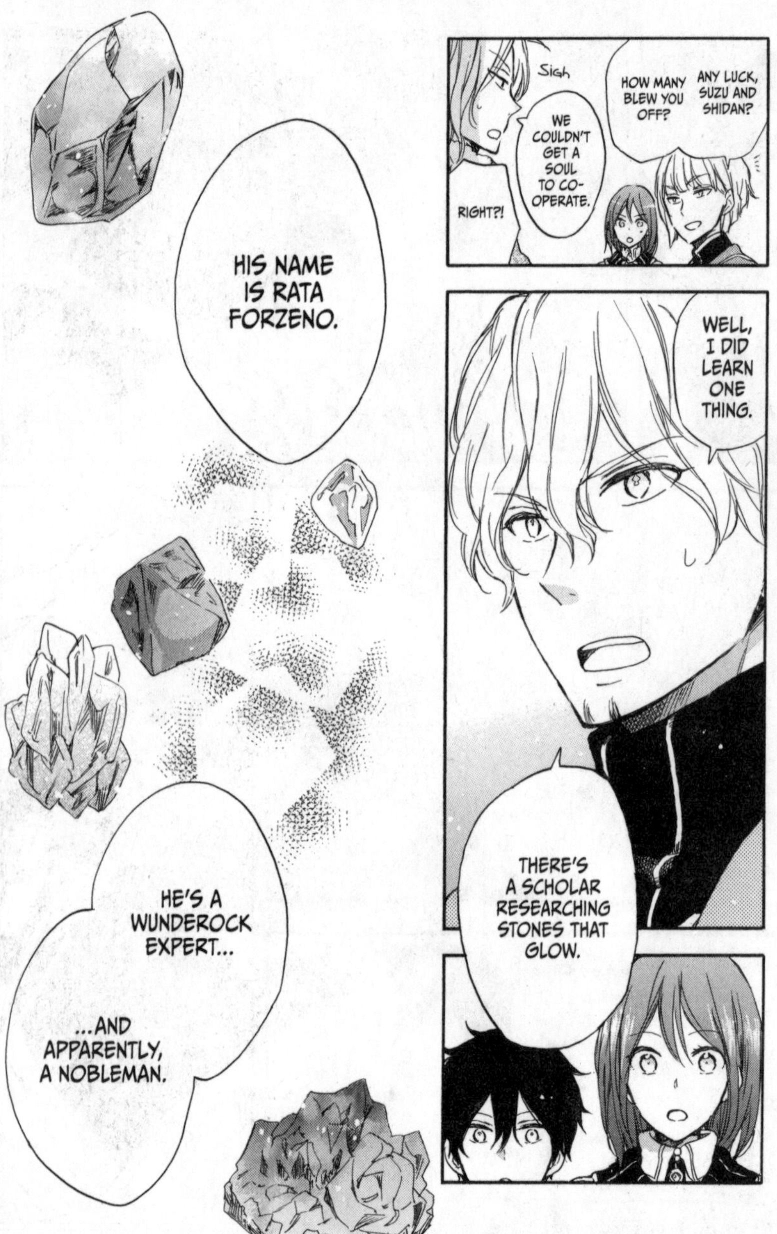
ANY LUCK, SUZU AND SHIDAN?
HOW MANY BLEW YOU OFF?
Sigh
WE COULDN'T GET A SOUL TO CO-OPERATE.
RIGHT?!
WELL, I DID LEARN ONE THING.
THERE'S A SCHOLAR RESEARCHING STONES THAT GLOW.
HIS NAME IS RATA FORZENO.
HE'S A WUNDEROCK EXPERT...
...AND APPARENTLY, A NOBLEMAN.

# Chapter 64

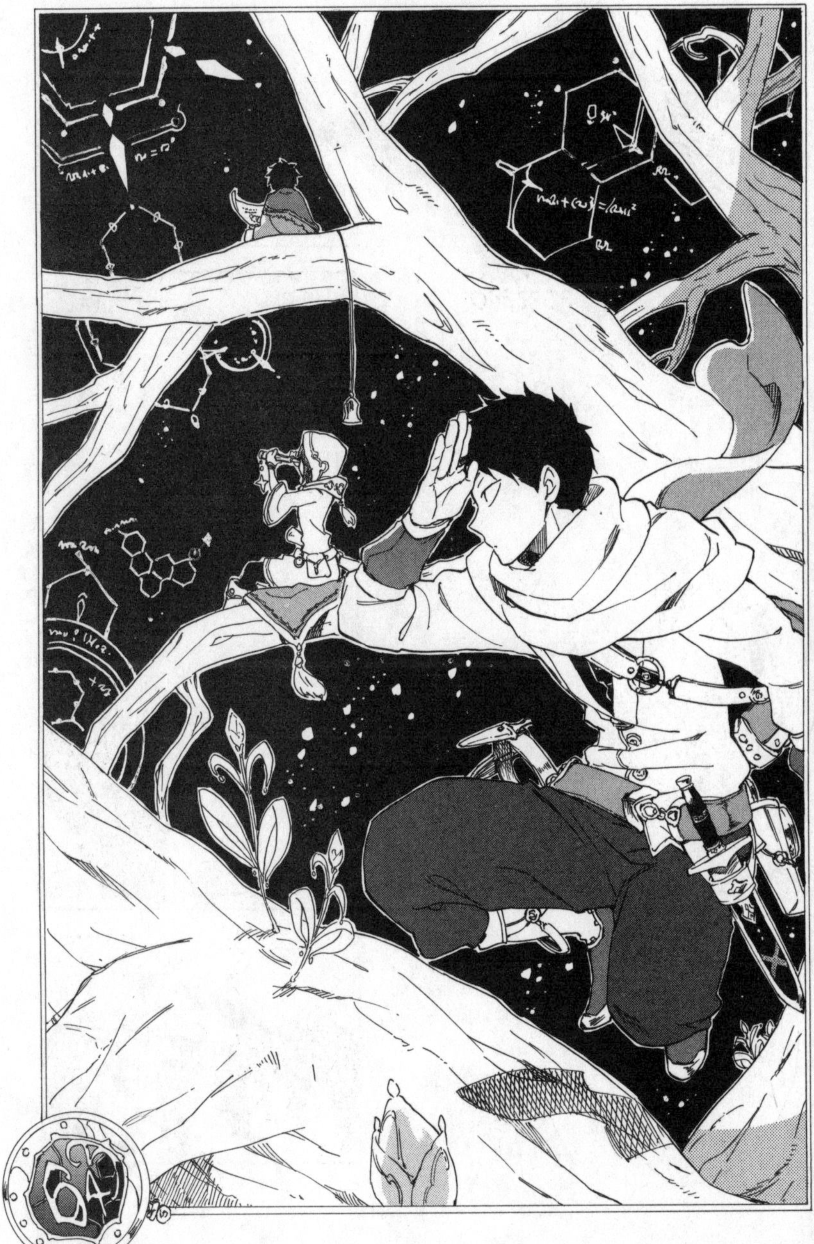
64

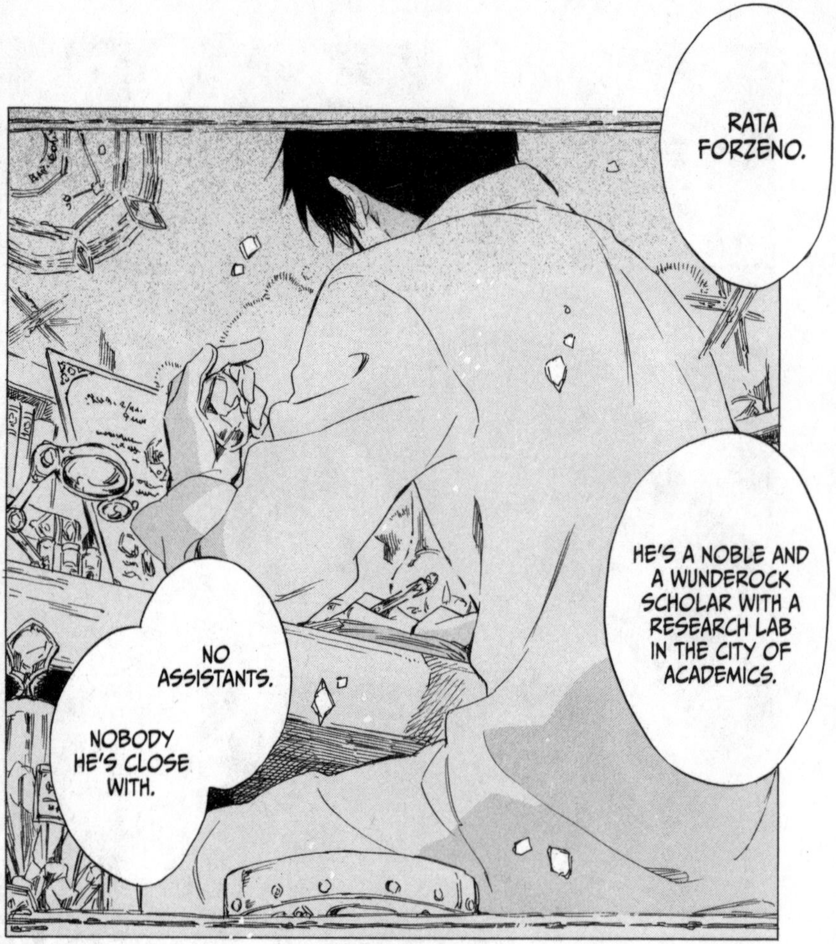
RATA FORZENO.
HE'S A NOBLE AND A WUNDEROCK SCHOLAR WITH A RESEARCH LAB IN THE CITY OF ACADEMICS.
NO ASSISTANTS.
NOBODY HE'S CLOSE WITH.

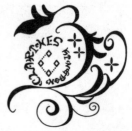

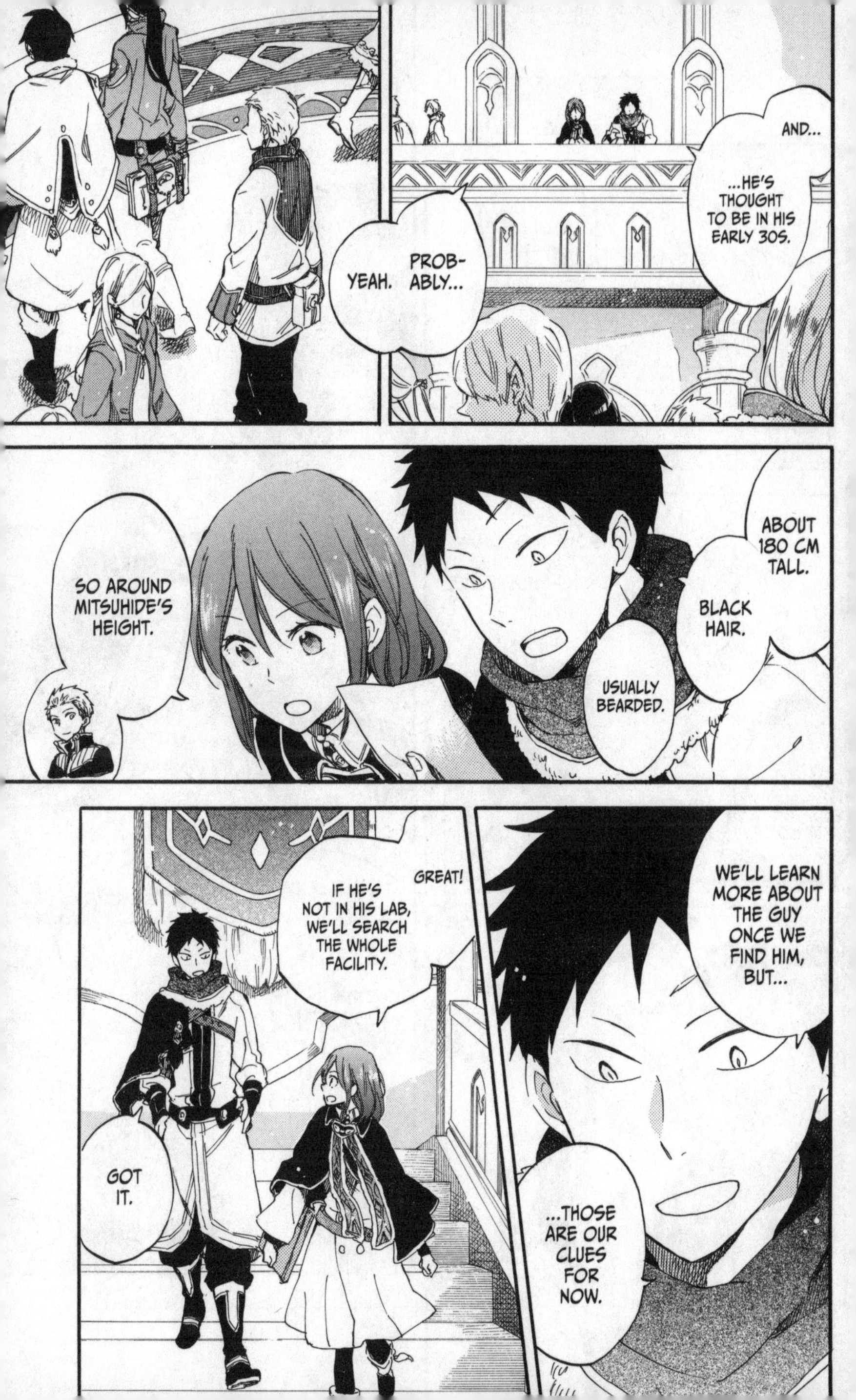
AND...
...HE'S THOUGHT TO BE IN HIS EARLY 30S.
PROB-ABLY... YEAH.
ABOUT 180 CM TALL.
BLACK HAIR.
USUALLY BEARDED.
SO AROUND MITSUHIDE'S HEIGHT.
WE'LL LEARN MORE ABOUT THE GUY ONCE WE FIND HIM, BUT...
...THOSE ARE OUR CLUES FOR NOW.
GREAT!
IF HE'S NOT IN HIS LAB, WE'LL SEARCH THE WHOLE FACILITY.
GOT IT.

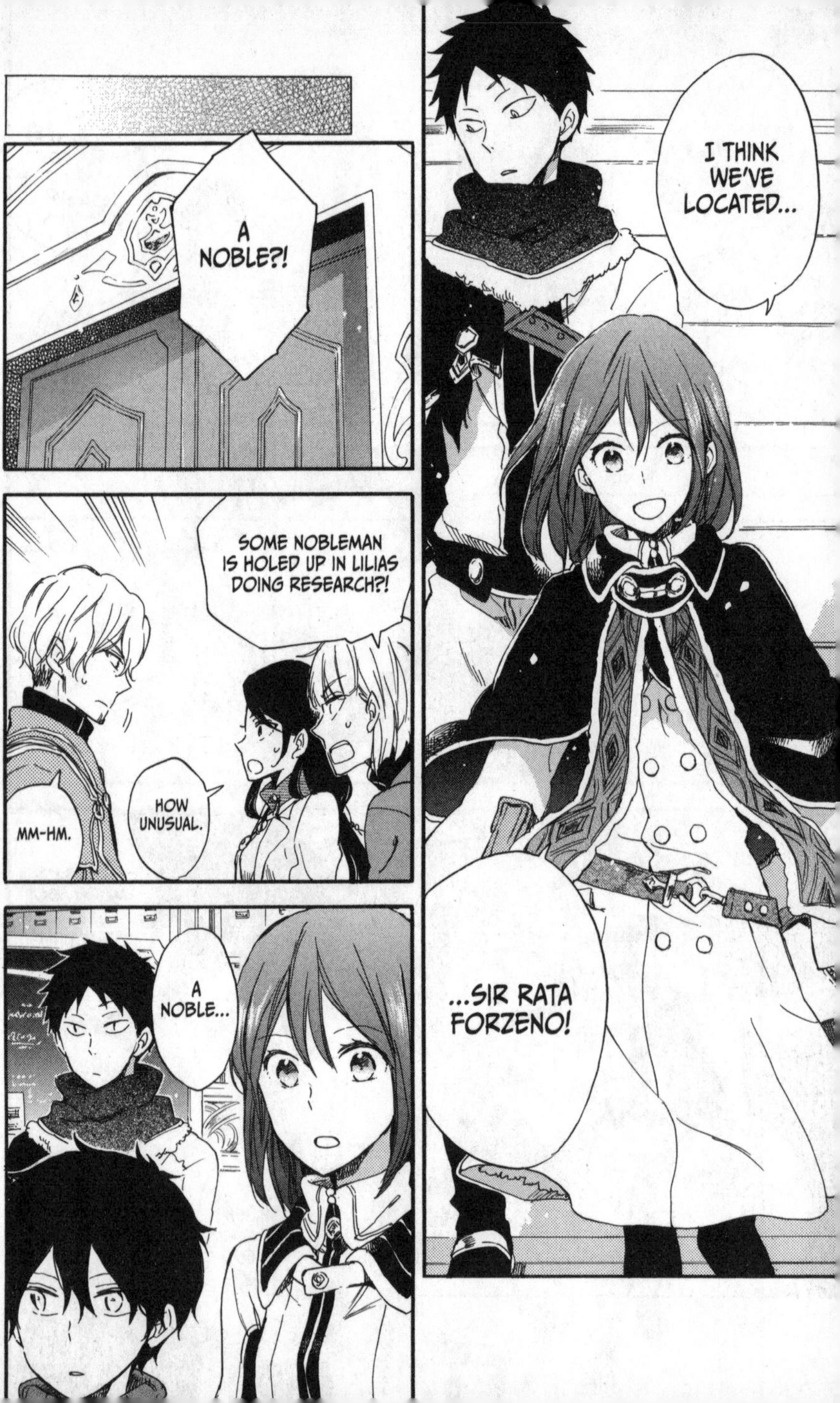
I THINK WE'VE LOCATED...
...SIR RATA FORZENO!
A NOBLE?!
SOME NOBLEMAN IS HOLED UP IN LILIAS DOING RESEARCH?!
HOW UNUSUAL.
MM-HM.
A NOBLE...

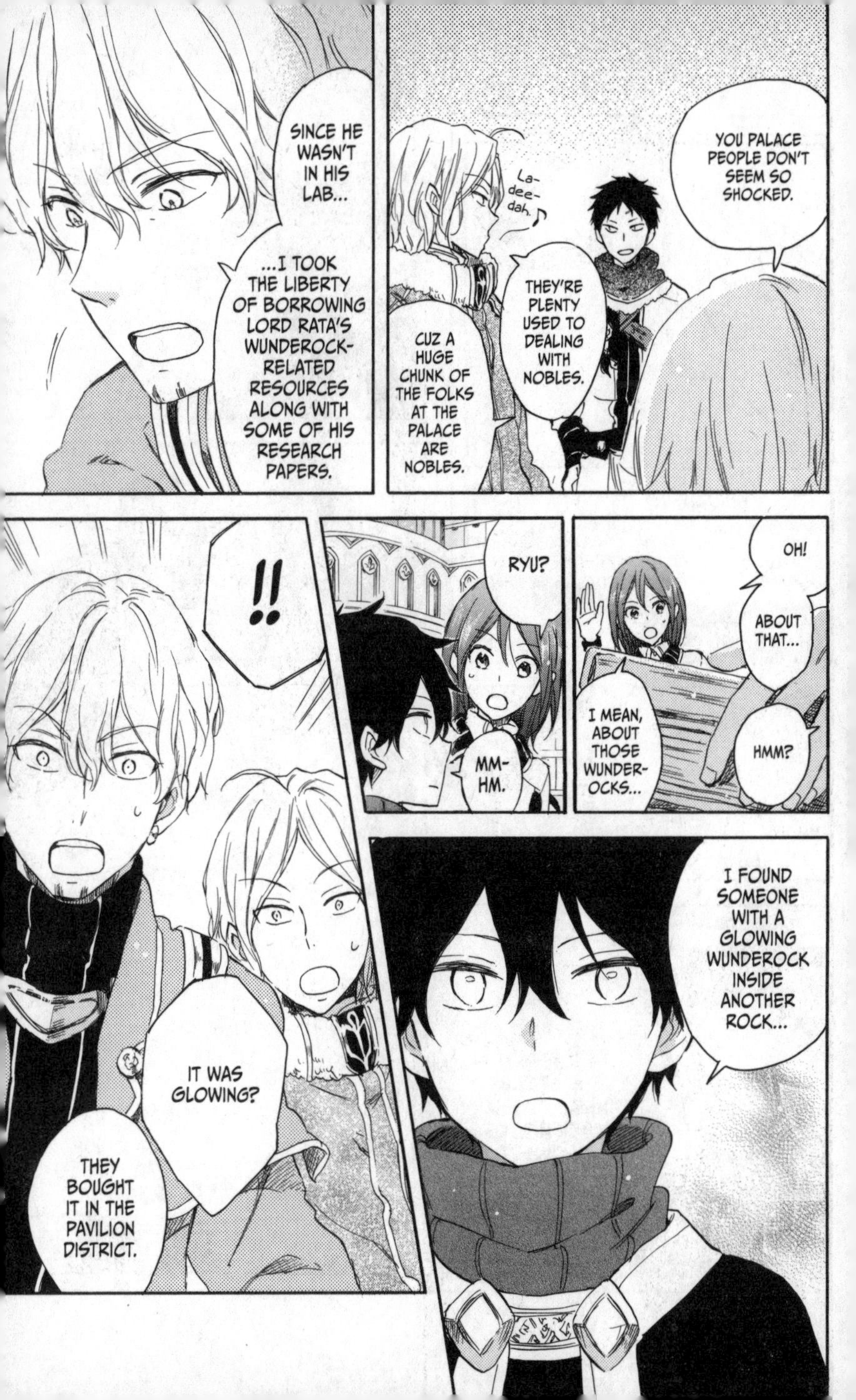
YOU PALACE PEOPLE DON'T SEEM SO SHOCKED.
La-dee-dah.♪
THEY'RE PLENTY USED TO DEALING WITH NOBLES.
CUZ A HUGE CHUNK OF THE FOLKS AT THE PALACE ARE NOBLES.
SINCE HE WASN'T IN HIS LAB...
...I TOOK THE LIBERTY OF BORROWING LORD RATA'S WUNDEROCK-RELATED RESOURCES ALONG WITH SOME OF HIS RESEARCH PAPERS.
OH!
ABOUT THAT...
HMM?
I MEAN, ABOUT THOSE WUNDER-OCKS...
RYU?
MM-HM.
I FOUND SOMEONE WITH A GLOWING WUNDEROCK INSIDE ANOTHER ROCK...
!!
IT WAS GLOWING?
THEY BOUGHT IT IN THE PAVILION DISTRICT.

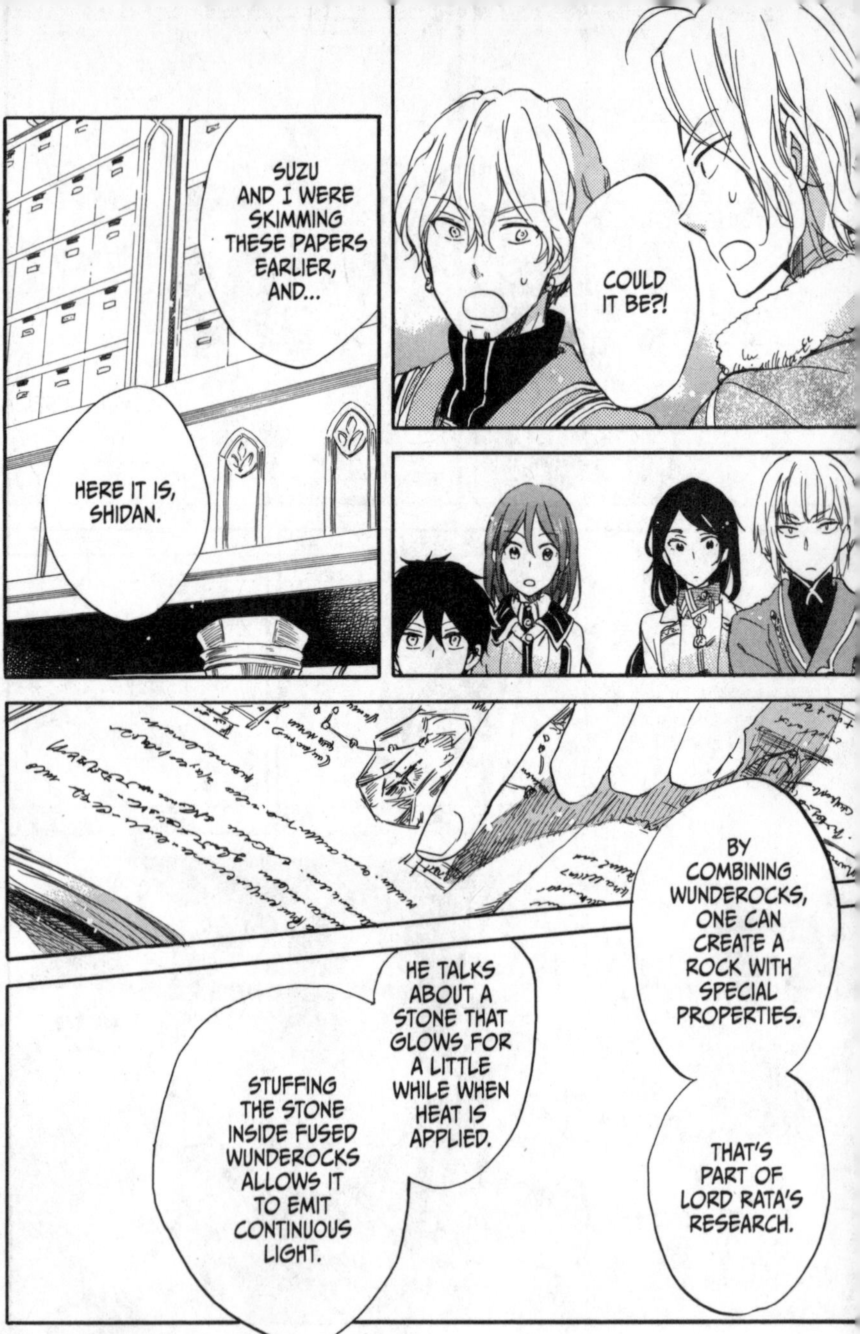
COULD IT BE?!
SUZU AND I WERE SKIMMING THESE PAPERS EARLIER, AND...
HERE IT IS, SHIDAN.
BY COMBINING WUNDEROCKS, ONE CAN CREATE A ROCK WITH SPECIAL PROPERTIES.
THAT'S PART OF LORD RATA'S RESEARCH.
HE TALKS ABOUT A STONE THAT GLOWS FOR A LITTLE WHILE WHEN HEAT IS APPLIED.
STUFFING THE STONE INSIDE FUSED WUNDEROCKS ALLOWS IT TO EMIT CONTINUOUS LIGHT.

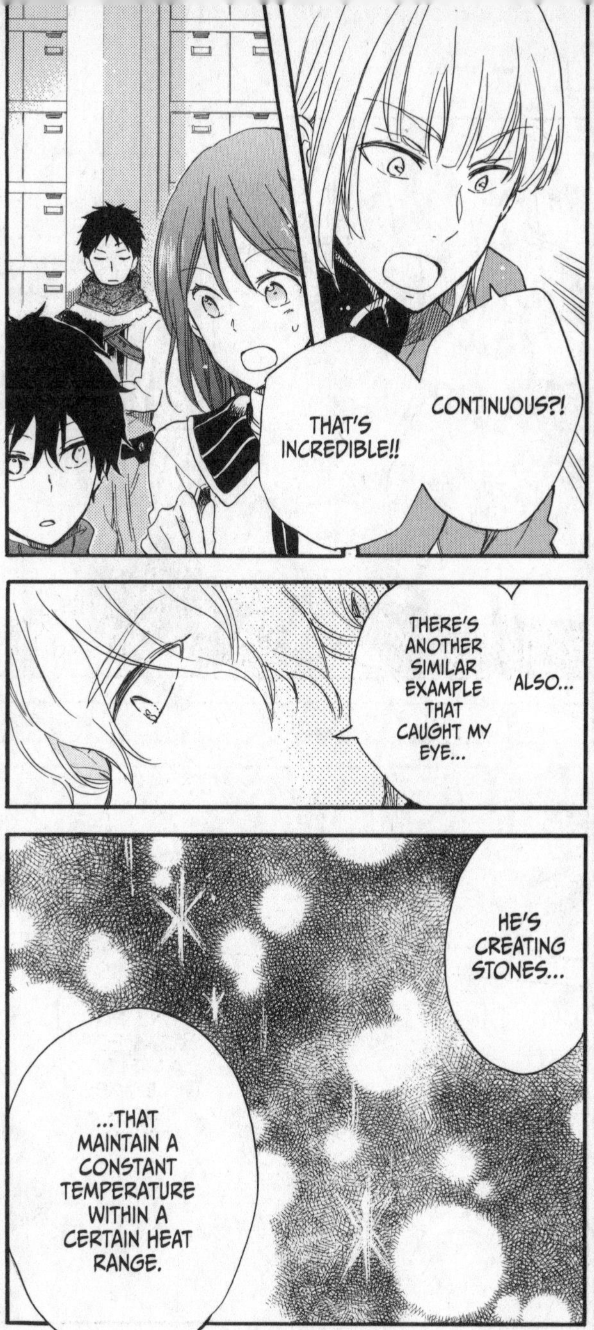
CONTINUOUS?!
THAT'S INCREDIBLE!!
ALSO...
THERE'S ANOTHER SIMILAR EXAMPLE THAT CAUGHT MY EYE...
HE'S CREATING STONES...
...THAT MAINTAIN A CONSTANT TEMPERATURE WITHIN A CERTAIN HEAT RANGE.

4

CHAPTER TALK

Chapter 62

Shirayuki and Obi's conversation.

With Obi by her side, it feels like Shirayuki will be doing a lot of running in all sorts of places.

Even adding Zen to the mix won't stop the running. I think that's just the kind of guy Obi is.

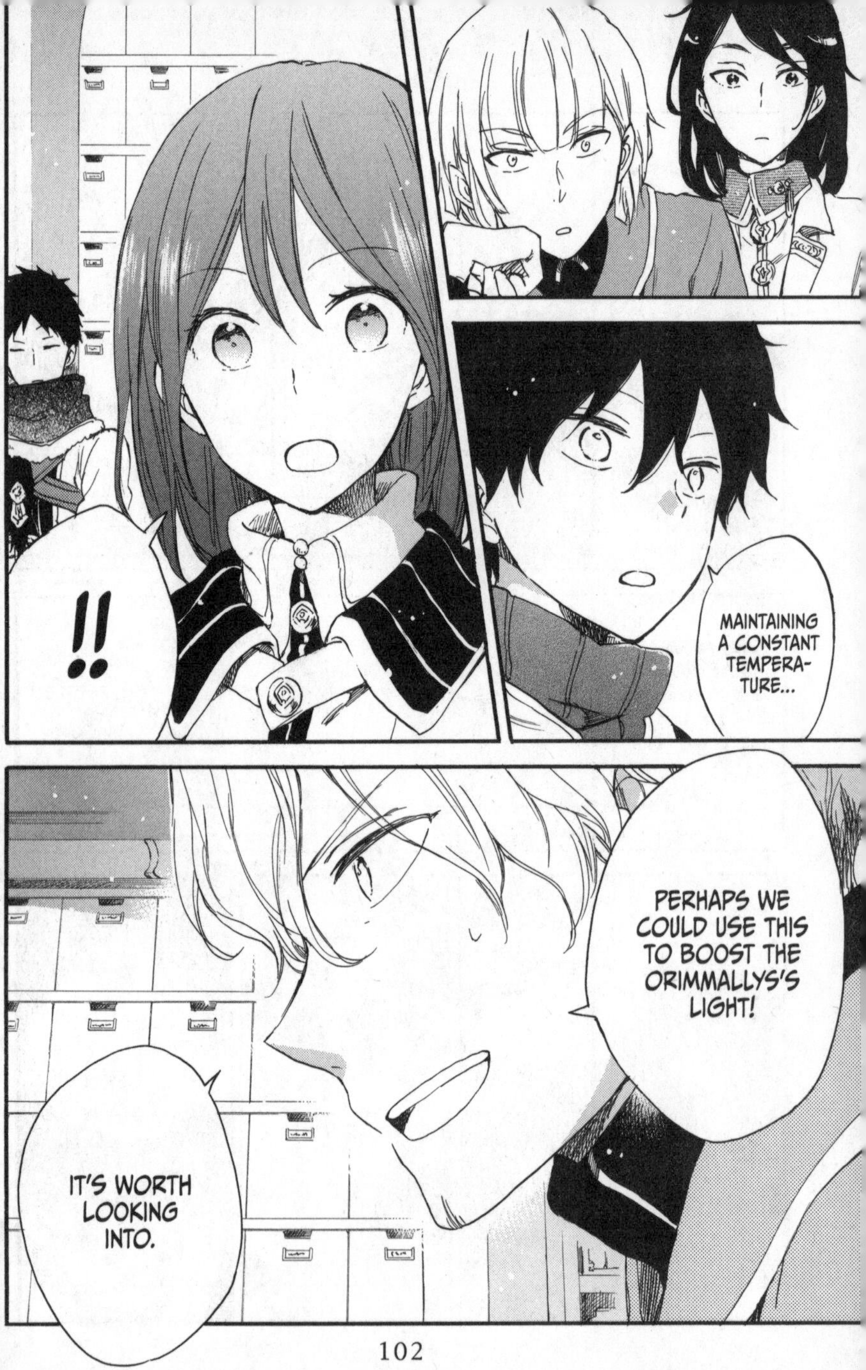
MAINTAINING A CONSTANT TEMPERA-TURE...
!!
PERHAPS WE COULD USE THIS TO BOOST THE ORIMMALLYS'S LIGHT!
IT'S WORTH LOOKING INTO.

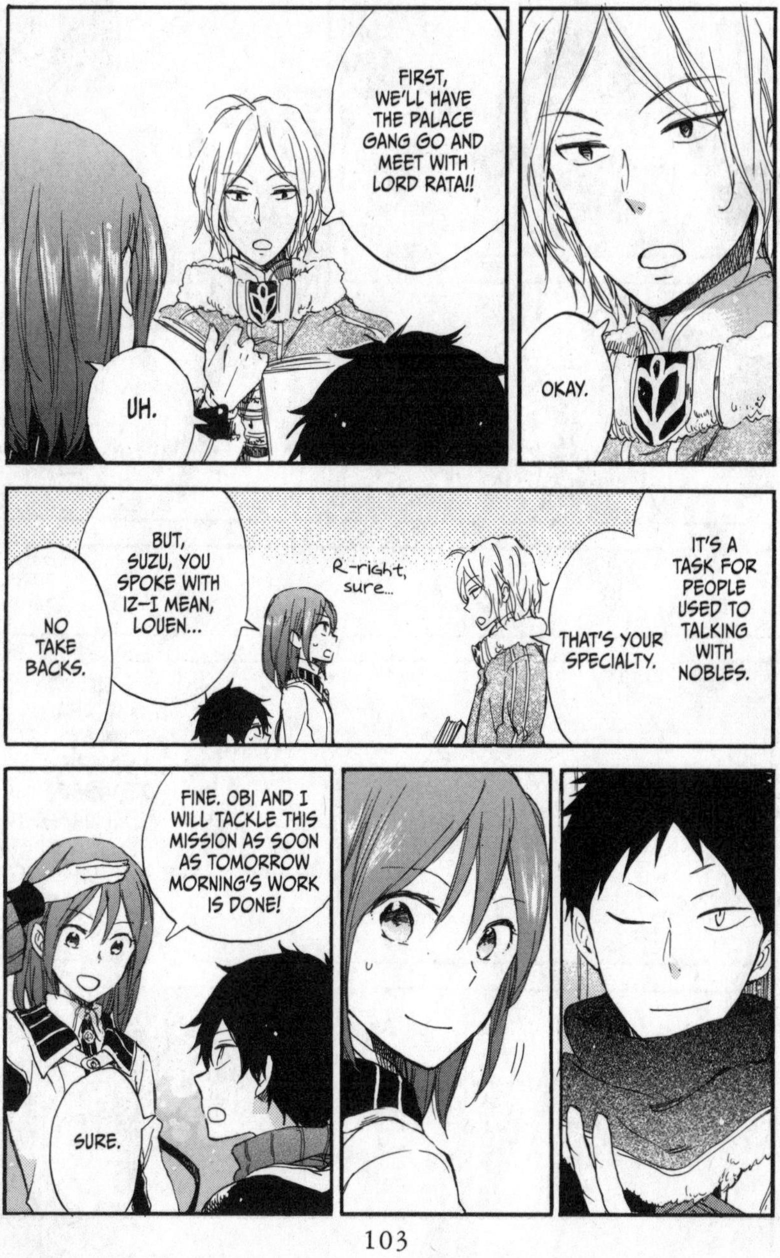
OKAY.
FIRST, WE'LL HAVE THE PALACE GANG GO AND MEET WITH LORD RATA!!
UH.
IT'S A TASK FOR PEOPLE USED TO TALKING WITH NOBLES.
THAT'S YOUR SPECIALTY.
R-right, sure...
BUT, SUZU, YOU SPOKE WITH IZ—I MEAN, LOUEN...
NO TAKE BACKS.
FINE. OBI AND I WILL TACKLE THIS MISSION AS SOON AS TOMORROW MORNING'S WORK IS DONE!
SURE.

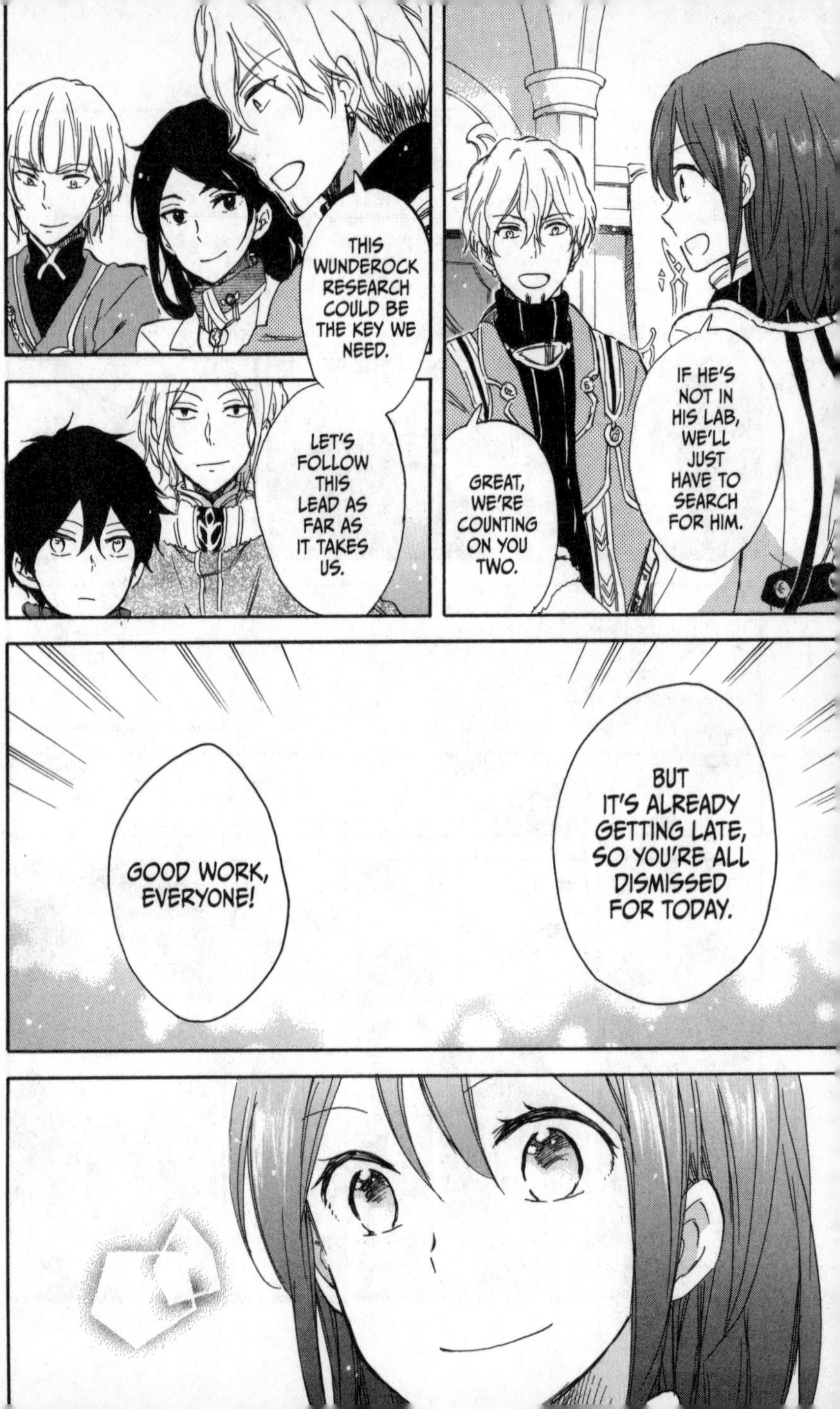
IF HE'S NOT IN HIS LAB, WE'LL JUST HAVE TO SEARCH FOR HIM.
GREAT, WE'RE COUNTING ON YOU TWO.
THIS WUNDEROCK RESEARCH COULD BE THE KEY WE NEED.
LET'S FOLLOW THIS LEAD AS FAR AS IT TAKES US.
BUT IT'S ALREADY GETTING LATE, SO YOU'RE ALL DISMISSED FOR TODAY.
GOOD WORK, EVERYONE!

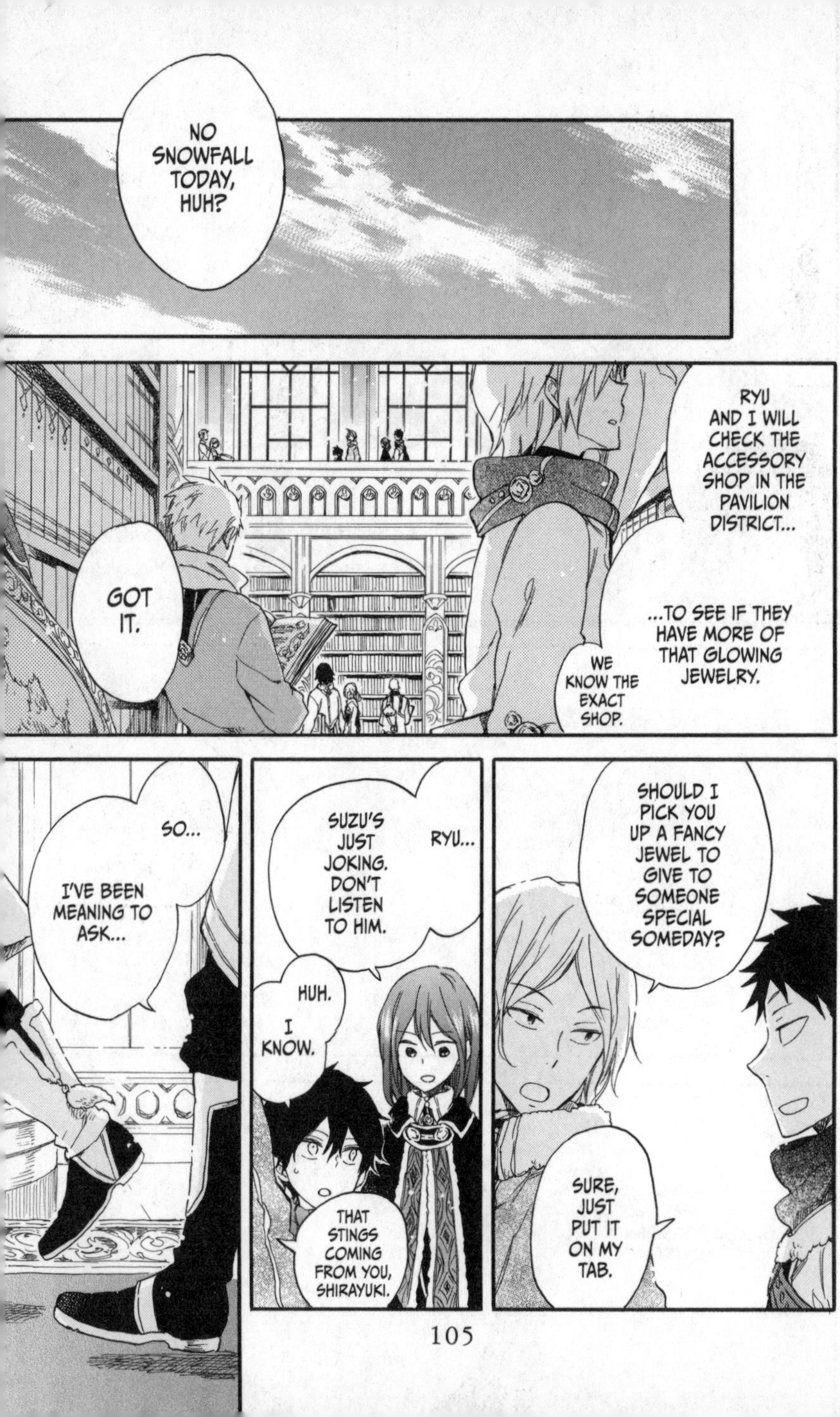
NO SNOWFALL TODAY, HUH?
RYU AND I WILL CHECK THE ACCESSORY SHOP IN THE PAVILION DISTRICT...
...TO SEE IF THEY HAVE MORE OF THAT GLOWING JEWELRY.
WE KNOW THE EXACT SHOP.
GOT IT.
SHOULD I PICK YOU UP A FANCY JEWEL TO GIVE TO SOMEONE SPECIAL SOMEDAY?
SURE, JUST PUT IT ON MY TAB.
RYU...
SUZU'S JUST JOKING. DON'T LISTEN TO HIM.
HUH.
I KNOW.
THAT STINGS COMING FROM YOU, SHIRAYUKI.
SO...
I'VE BEEN MEANING TO ASK...

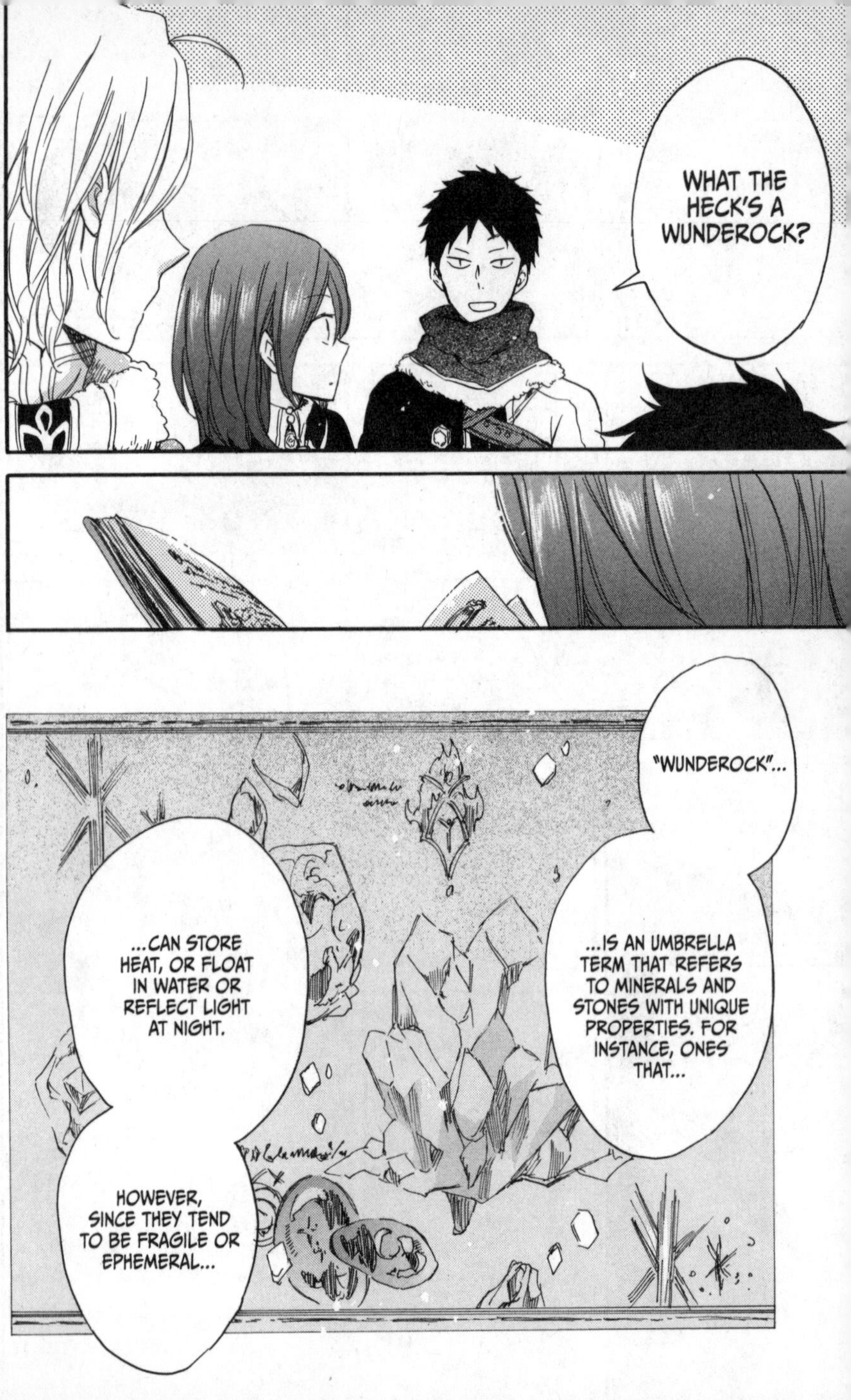
WHAT THE HECK'S A WUNDEROCK?
"WUNDEROCK"...
...IS AN UMBRELLA TERM THAT REFERS TO MINERALS AND STONES WITH UNIQUE PROPERTIES. FOR INSTANCE, ONES THAT...
...CAN STORE HEAT, OR FLOAT IN WATER OR REFLECT LIGHT AT NIGHT.
HOWEVER, SINCE THEY TEND TO BE FRAGILE OR EPHEMERAL...

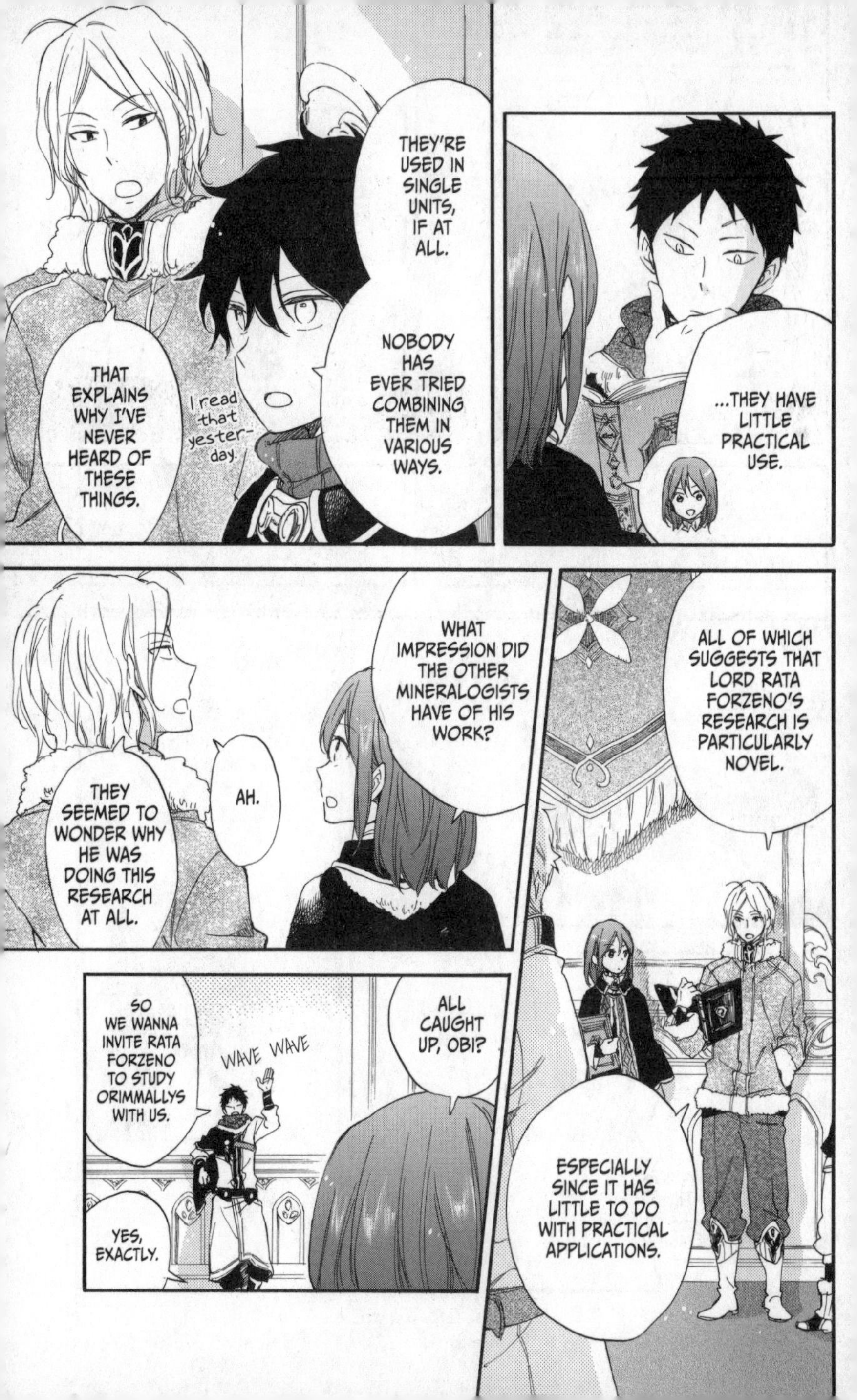
...THEY HAVE LITTLE PRACTICAL USE.
THEY'RE USED IN SINGLE UNITS, IF AT ALL.
NOBODY HAS EVER TRIED COMBINING THEM IN VARIOUS WAYS.
I read that yester-day.
THAT EXPLAINS WHY I'VE NEVER HEARD OF THESE THINGS.
ALL OF WHICH SUGGESTS THAT LORD RATA FORZENO'S RESEARCH IS PARTICULARLY NOVEL.
ESPECIALLY SINCE IT HAS LITTLE TO DO WITH PRACTICAL APPLICATIONS.
WHAT IMPRESSION DID THE OTHER MINERALOGISTS HAVE OF HIS WORK?
AH.
THEY SEEMED TO WONDER WHY HE WAS DOING THIS RESEARCH AT ALL.
ALL CAUGHT UP, OBI?
SO WE WANNA INVITE RATA FORZENO TO STUDY ORIMMALLYS WITH US.
WAVE WAVE
YES, EXACTLY.

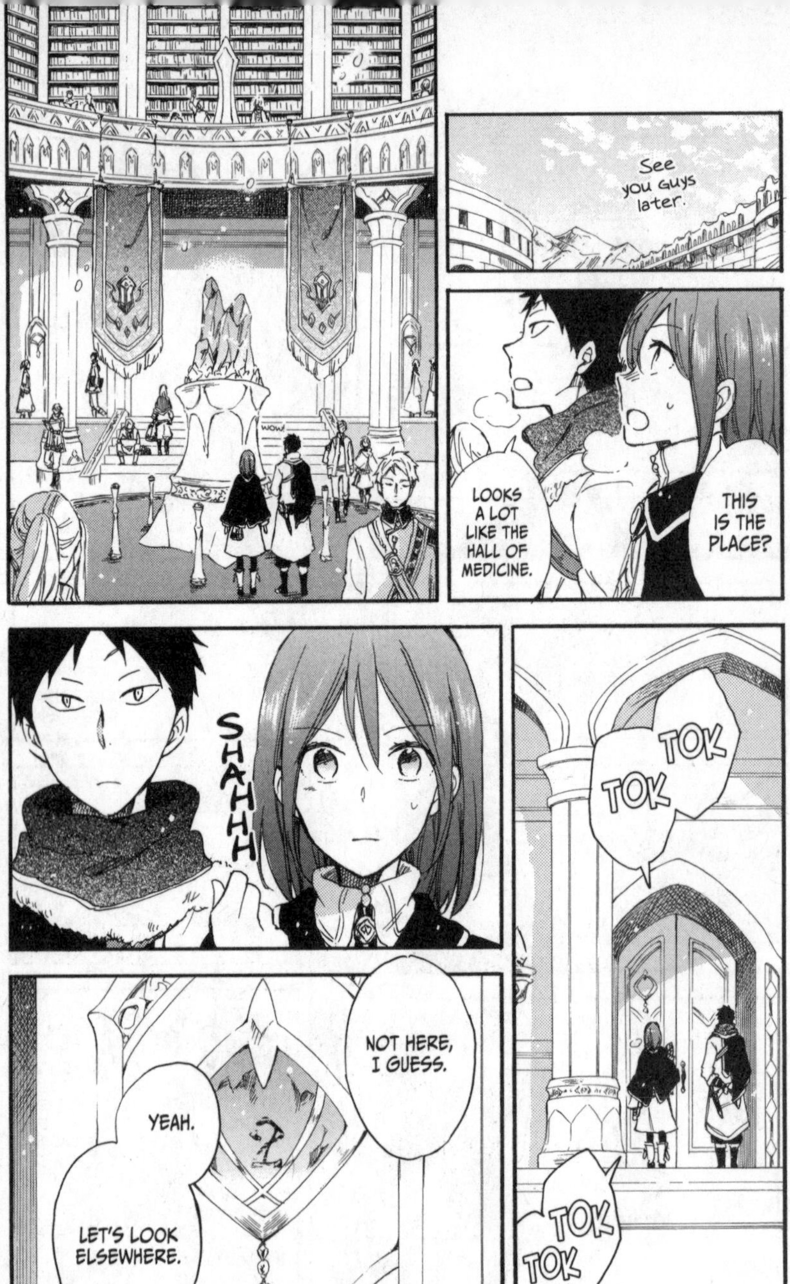

See you guys later.
THIS IS THE PLACE?
LOOKS A LOT LIKE THE HALL OF MEDICINE.
WOW!
TOK TOK
TOK TOK
SHAHHH
NOT HERE, I GUESS.
YEAH.
LET'S LOOK ELSEWHERE.

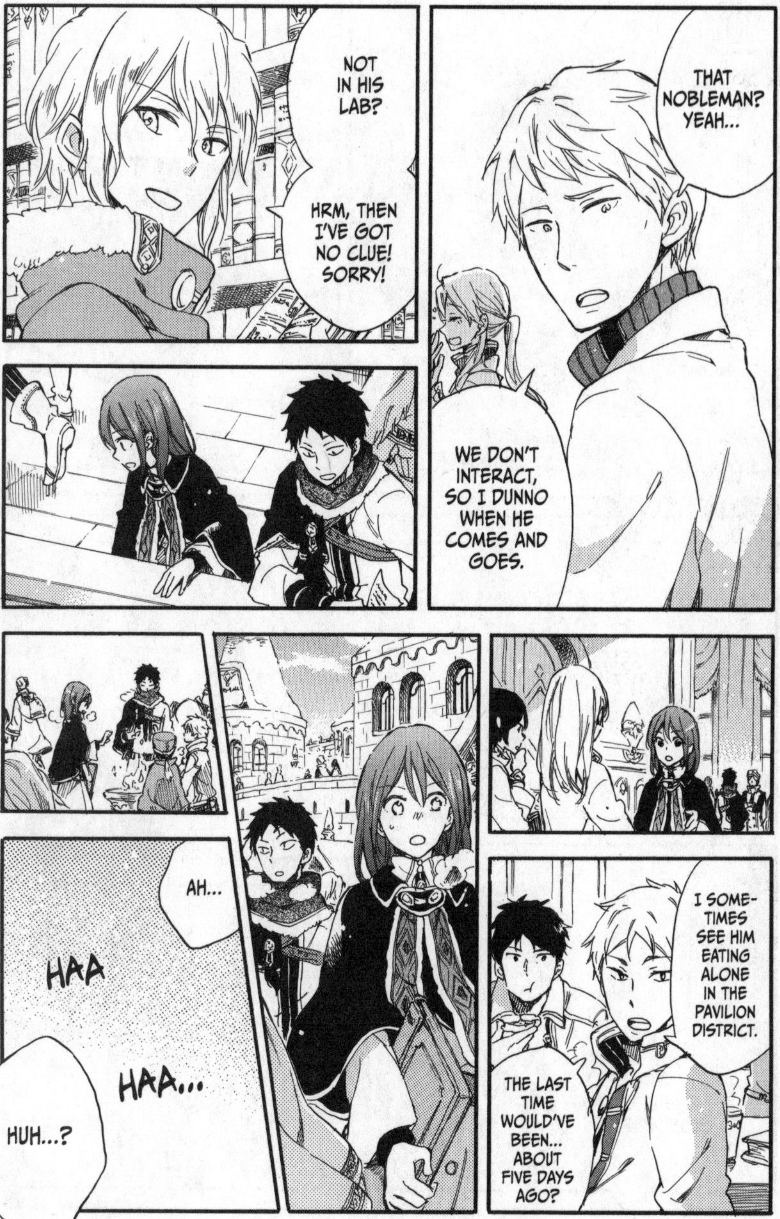
THAT NOBLEMAN? YEAH...
WE DON'T INTERACT, SO I DUNNO WHEN HE COMES AND GOES.
NOT IN HIS LAB?
HRM, THEN I'VE GOT NO CLUE! SORRY!
I SOMETIMES SEE HIM EATING ALONE IN THE PAVILION DISTRICT.
THE LAST TIME WOULD'VE BEEN... ABOUT FIVE DAYS AGO?
AH...
HAA
HAA...
HUH...?

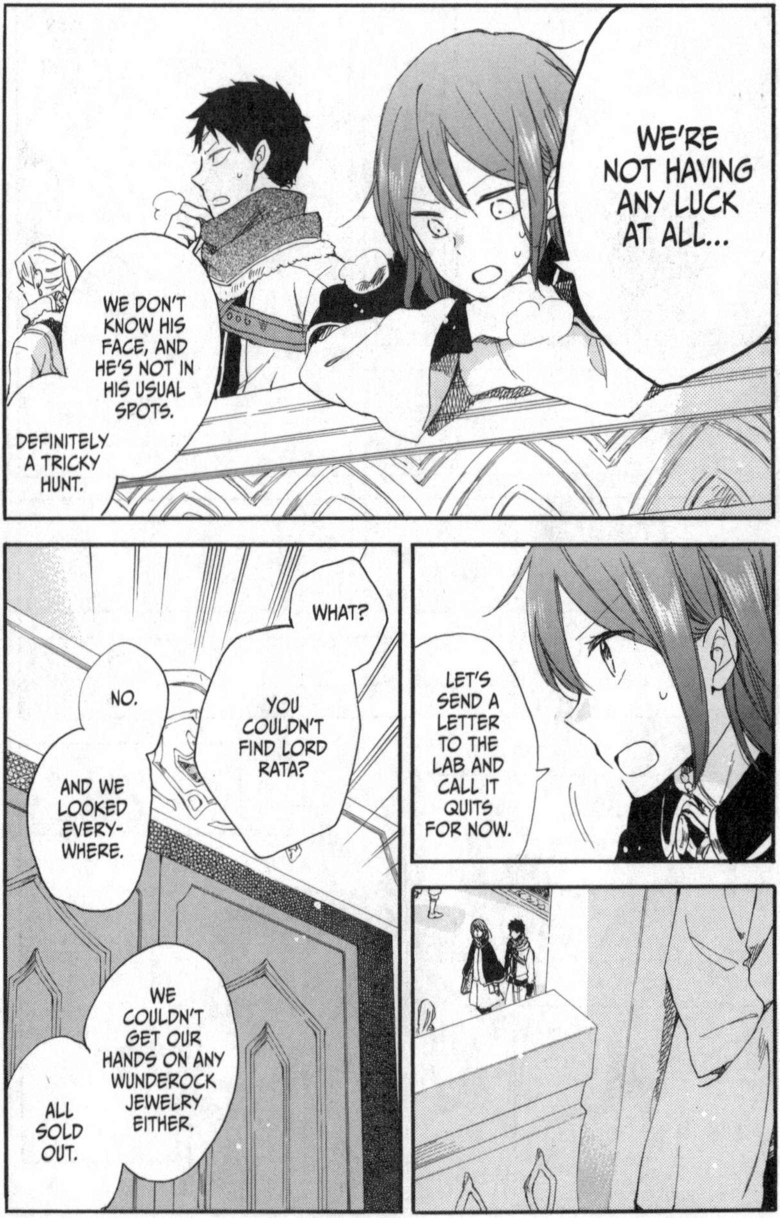
WE'RE NOT HAVING ANY LUCK AT ALL...
WE DON'T KNOW HIS FACE, AND HE'S NOT IN HIS USUAL SPOTS.
DEFINITELY A TRICKY HUNT.
LET'S SEND A LETTER TO THE LAB AND CALL IT QUITS FOR NOW.
WHAT?
YOU COULDN'T FIND LORD RATA?
NO.
AND WE LOOKED EVERY-WHERE.
WE COULDN'T GET OUR HANDS ON ANY WUNDEROCK JEWELRY EITHER.
ALL SOLD OUT.

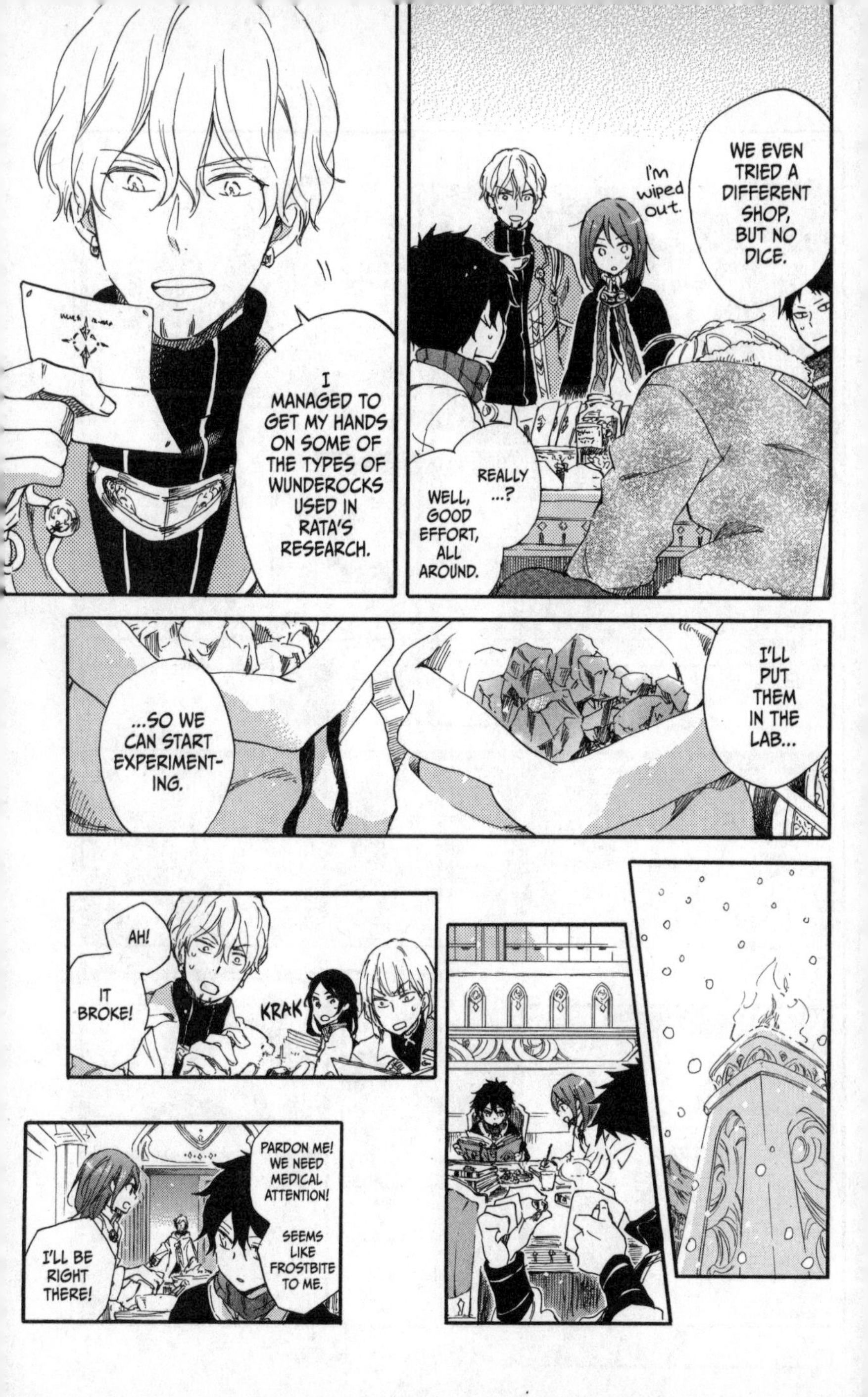
WE EVEN TRIED A DIFFERENT SHOP, BUT NO DICE.
I'm wiped out.
REALLY ...?
WELL, GOOD EFFORT, ALL AROUND.
I MANAGED TO GET MY HANDS ON SOME OF THE TYPES OF WUNDEROCKS USED IN RATA'S RESEARCH.
I'LL PUT THEM IN THE LAB...
...SO WE CAN START EXPERIMENT-ING.
AH!
IT BROKE!
KRAK
PARDON ME! WE NEED MEDICAL ATTENTION!
SEEMS LIKE FROSTBITE TO ME.
I'LL BE RIGHT THERE!

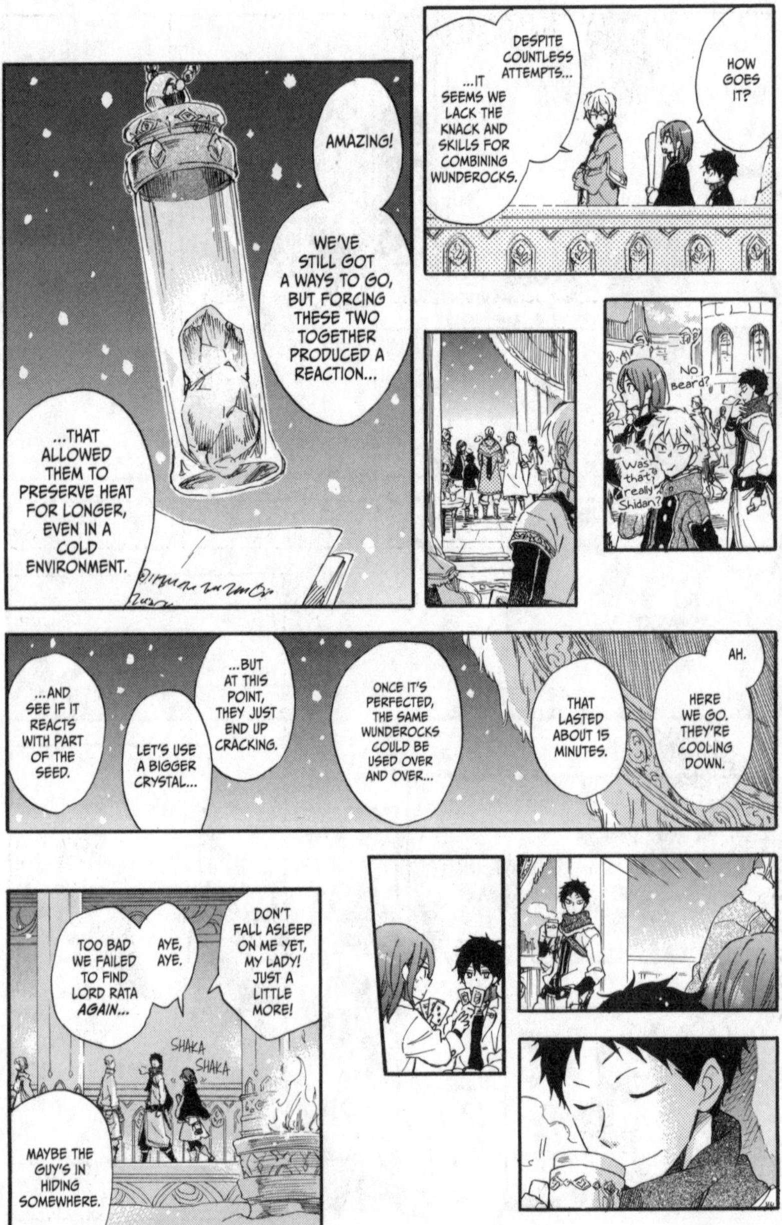
HOW GOES IT?
DESPITE COUNTLESS ATTEMPTS...
...IT SEEMS WE LACK THE KNACK AND SKILLS FOR COMBINING WUNDEROCKS.
No beard?
Was that really Shidan?
AMAZING!
WE'VE STILL GOT A WAYS TO GO, BUT FORCING THESE TWO TOGETHER PRODUCED A REACTION...
...THAT ALLOWED THEM TO PRESERVE HEAT FOR LONGER, EVEN IN A COLD ENVIRONMENT.
AH.
HERE WE GO. THEY'RE COOLING DOWN.
THAT LASTED ABOUT 15 MINUTES.
ONCE IT'S PERFECTED, THE SAME WUNDEROCKS COULD BE USED OVER AND OVER...
...BUT AT THIS POINT, THEY JUST END UP CRACKING.
LET'S USE A BIGGER CRYSTAL...
...AND SEE IF IT REACTS WITH PART OF THE SEED.
DON'T FALL ASLEEP ON ME YET, MY LADY! JUST A LITTLE MORE!
AYE, AYE.
TOO BAD WE FAILED TO FIND LORD RATA *AGAIN*...
SHAKA SHAKA
MAYBE THE GUY'S IN HIDING SOMEWHERE.

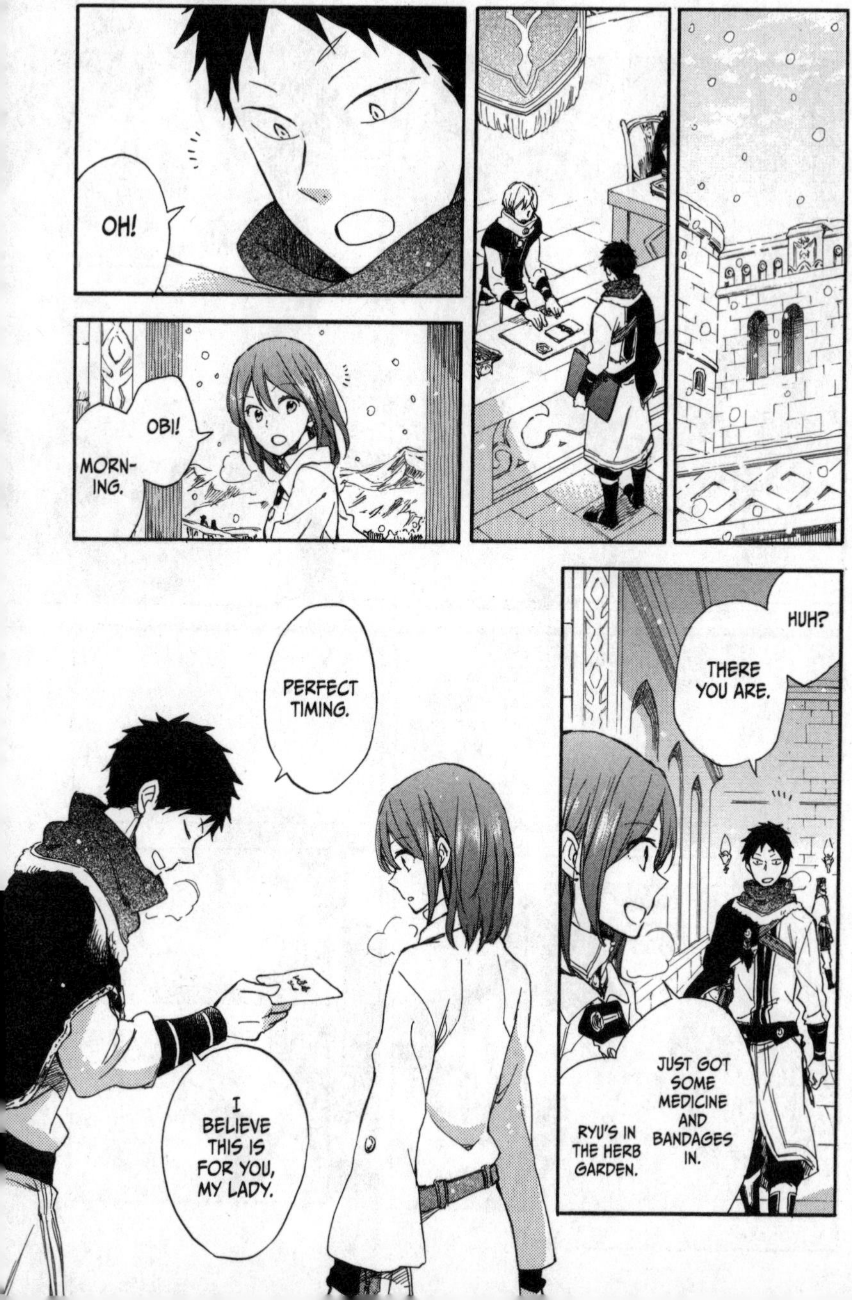
OH!
OBI!
MORNING.
HUH?
THERE YOU ARE.
JUST GOT SOME MEDICINE AND BANDAGES IN.
RYU'S IN THE HERB GARDEN.
PERFECT TIMING.
I BELIEVE THIS IS FOR YOU, MY LADY.

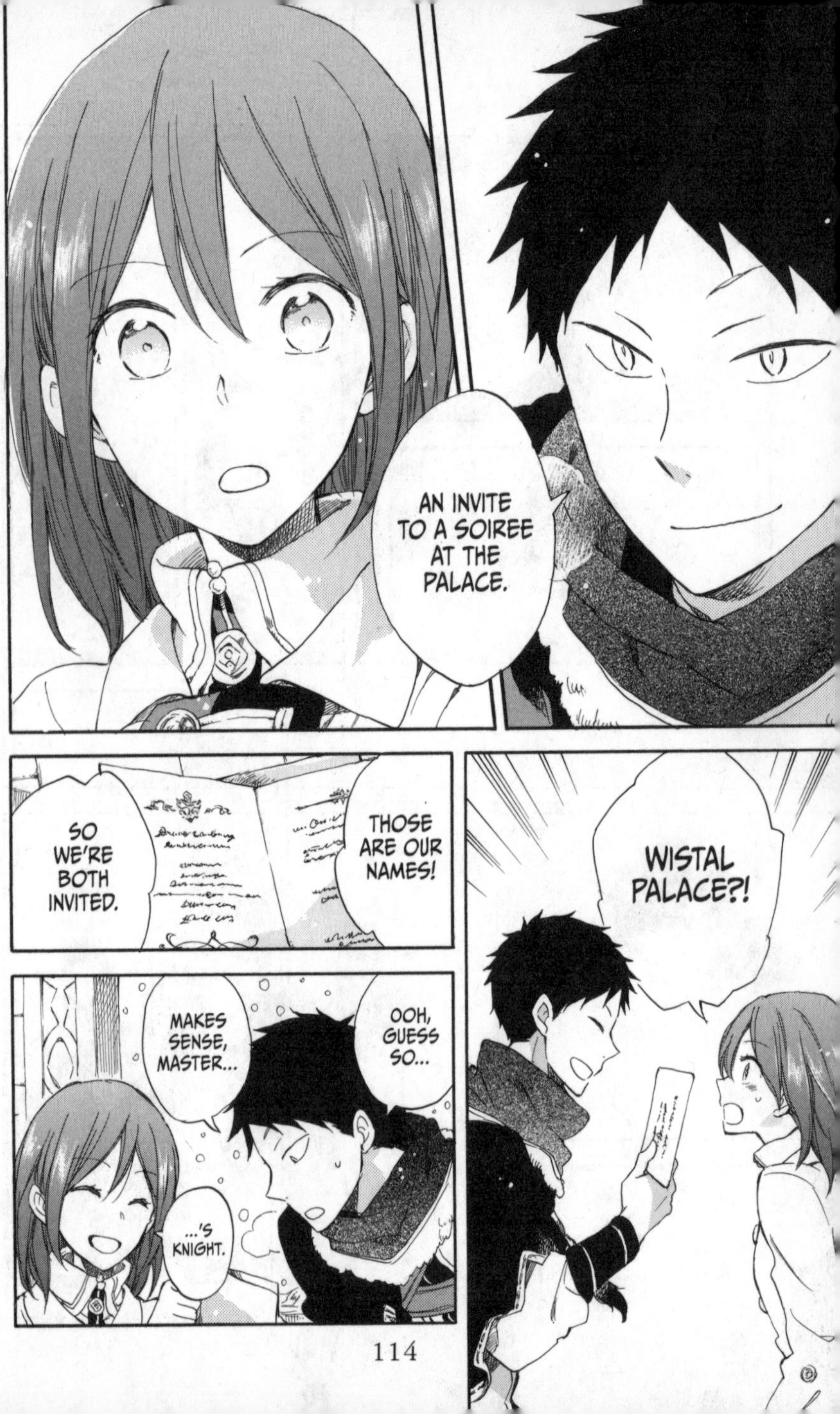
AN INVITE TO A SOIREE AT THE PALACE.
WISTAL PALACE?!
THOSE ARE OUR NAMES!
SO WE'RE BOTH INVITED.
OOH, GUESS SO...
MAKES SENSE, MASTER...
...'S KNIGHT.

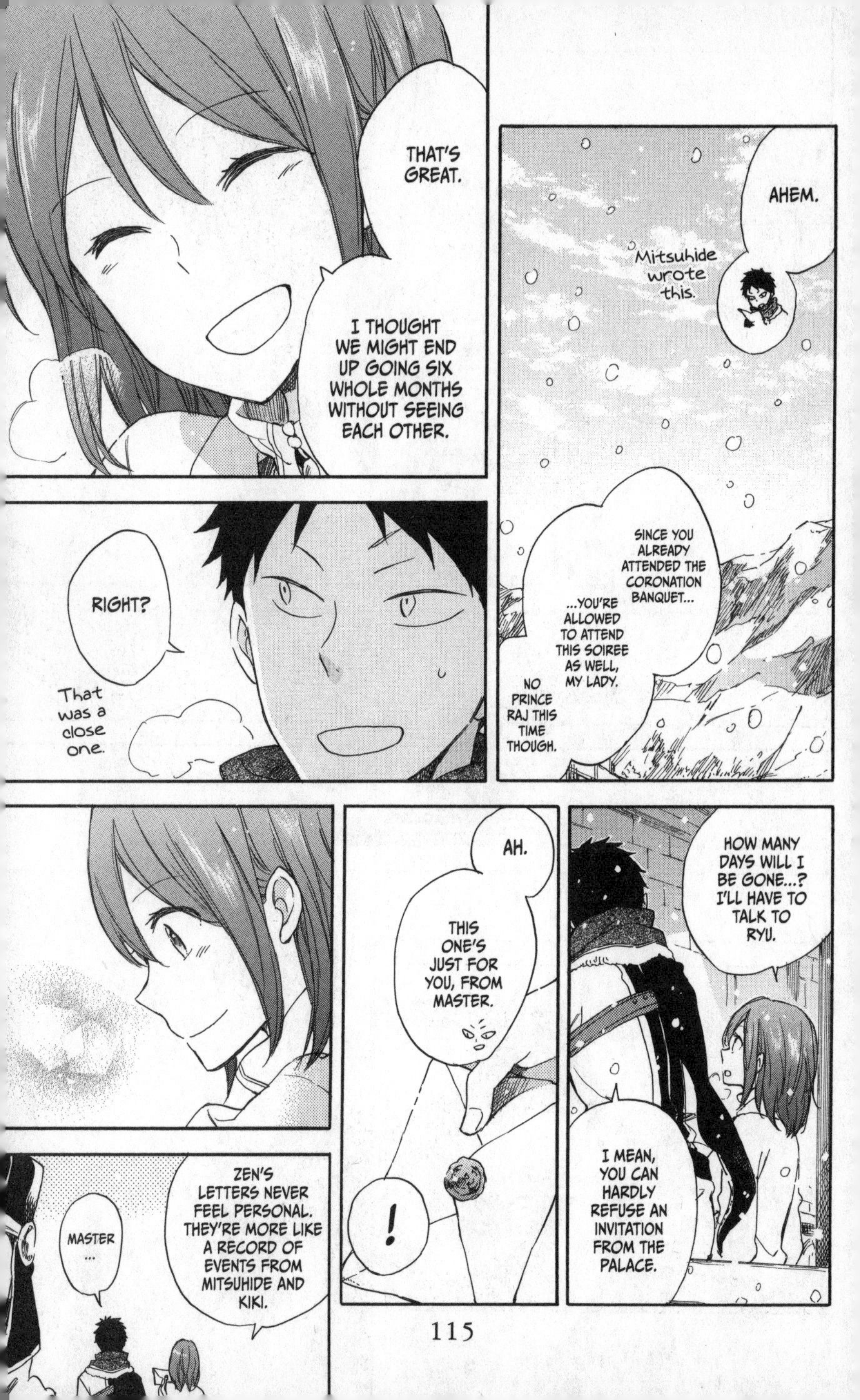
AHEM.
Mitsuhide wrote this.
SINCE YOU ALREADY ATTENDED THE CORONATION BANQUET...
...YOU'RE ALLOWED TO ATTEND THIS SOIREE AS WELL, MY LADY.
NO PRINCE RAJ THIS TIME THOUGH.
THAT'S GREAT.
I THOUGHT WE MIGHT END UP GOING SIX WHOLE MONTHS WITHOUT SEEING EACH OTHER.
RIGHT?
That was a close one.
HOW MANY DAYS WILL I BE GONE...? I'LL HAVE TO TALK TO RYU.
I MEAN, YOU CAN HARDLY REFUSE AN INVITATION FROM THE PALACE.
AH.
THIS ONE'S JUST FOR YOU, FROM MASTER.
!
ZEN'S LETTERS NEVER FEEL PERSONAL. THEY'RE MORE LIKE A RECORD OF EVENTS FROM MITSUHIDE AND KIKI.
MASTER ...

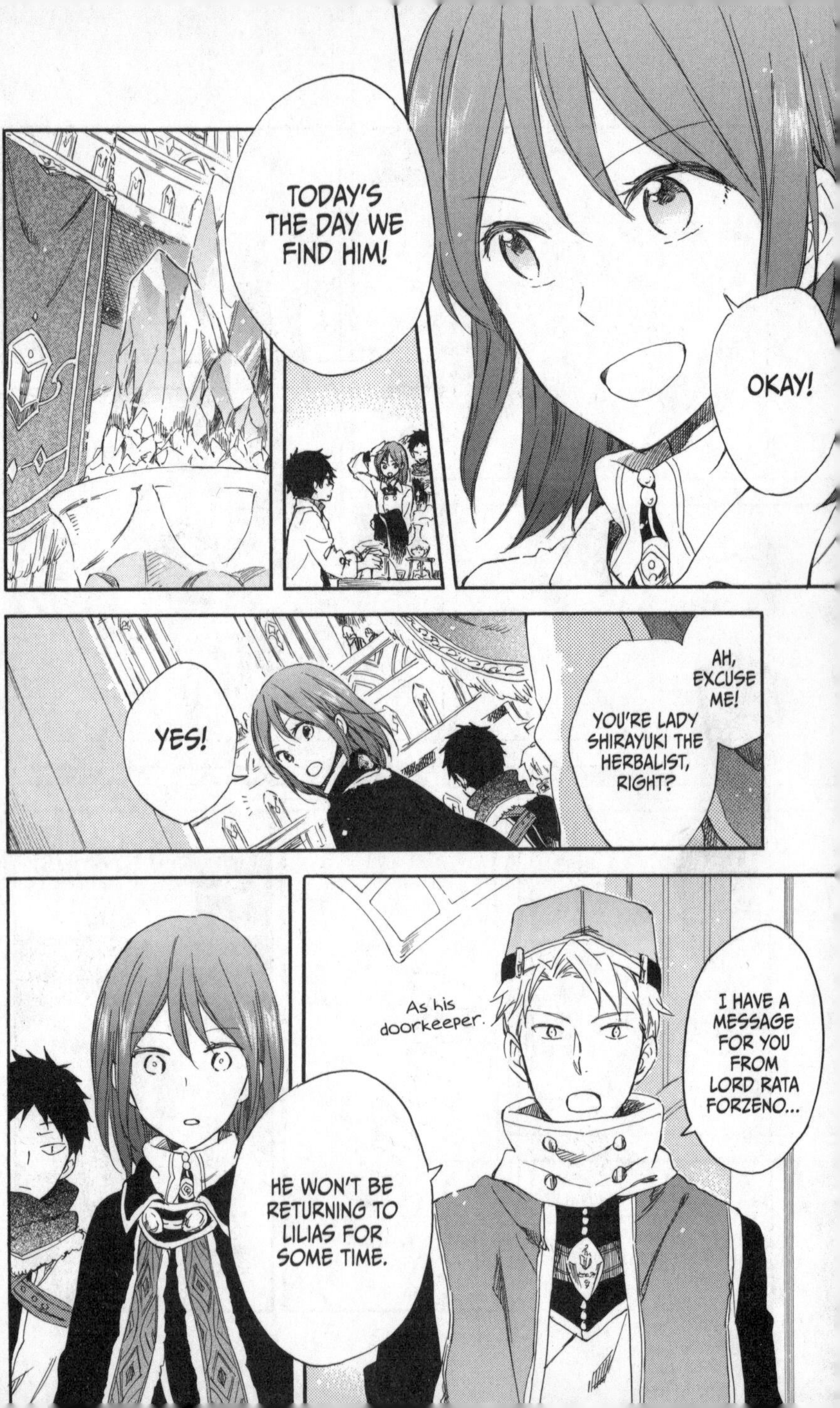
OKAY!
TODAY'S THE DAY WE FIND HIM!
AH, EXCUSE ME!
YOU'RE LADY SHIRAYUKI THE HERBALIST, RIGHT?
YES!
I HAVE A MESSAGE FOR YOU FROM LORD RATA FORZENO...
As his doorkeeper.
HE WON'T BE RETURNING TO LILIAS FOR SOME TIME.

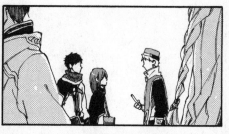

HUH?!
Y... YOU MEAN HE WENT SOME-WHERE?!
YES.
THOUGH I DON'T KNOW WHERE, PERSONALLY.
AND THIS...
...IS FOR YOU PEOPLE.
HE GAVE US THE SLIP?
Farewell.
CAN'T BE...
WE NEVER EVEN FOUND HIM OR SPOKE TO HIM.
Obnoxious.

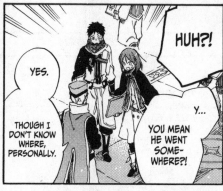

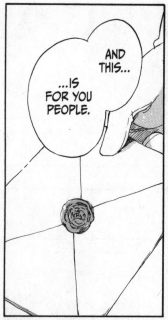

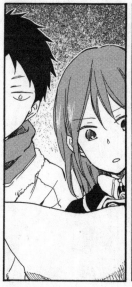

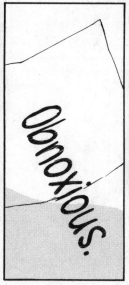

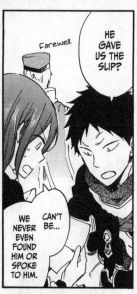

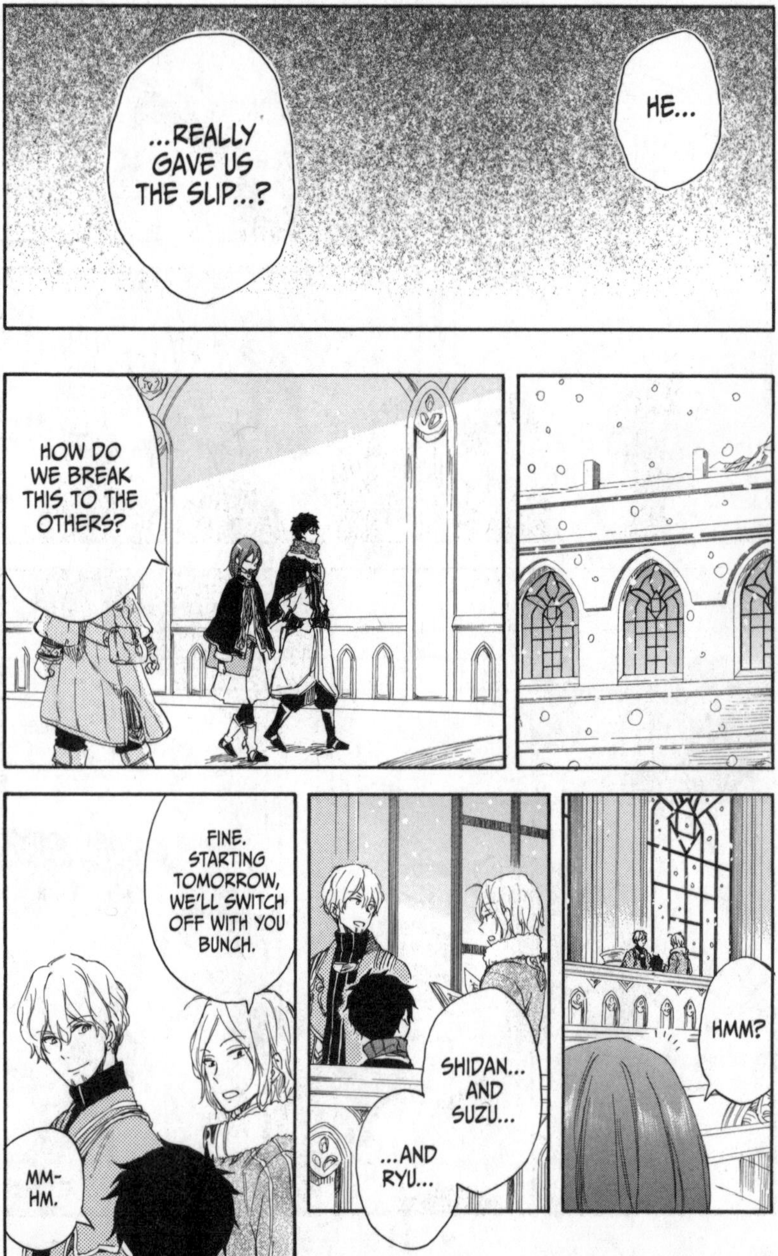
HE...
...REALLY GAVE US THE SLIP...?
HOW DO WE BREAK THIS TO THE OTHERS?
HMM?
SHIDAN... AND SUZU...
...AND RYU...
FINE. STARTING TOMORROW, WE'LL SWITCH OFF WITH YOU BUNCH.
MM-HM.

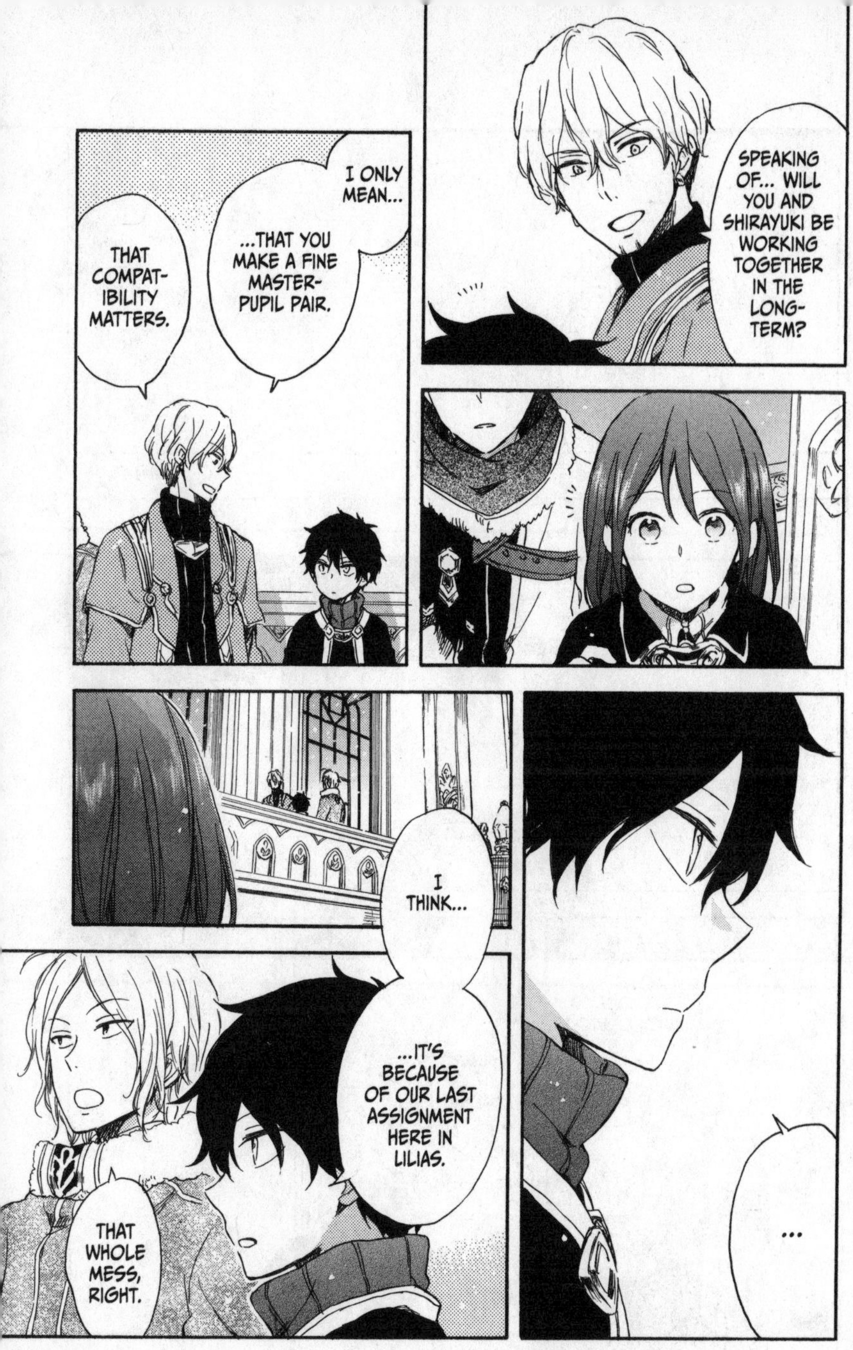
SPEAKING OF... WILL YOU AND SHIRAYUKI BE WORKING TOGETHER IN THE LONG-TERM?
I ONLY MEAN...
...THAT YOU MAKE A FINE MASTER-PUPIL PAIR.
THAT COMPAT-IBILITY MATTERS.
...
I THINK...
...IT'S BECAUSE OF OUR LAST ASSIGNMENT HERE IN LILIAS.
THAT WHOLE MESS, RIGHT.

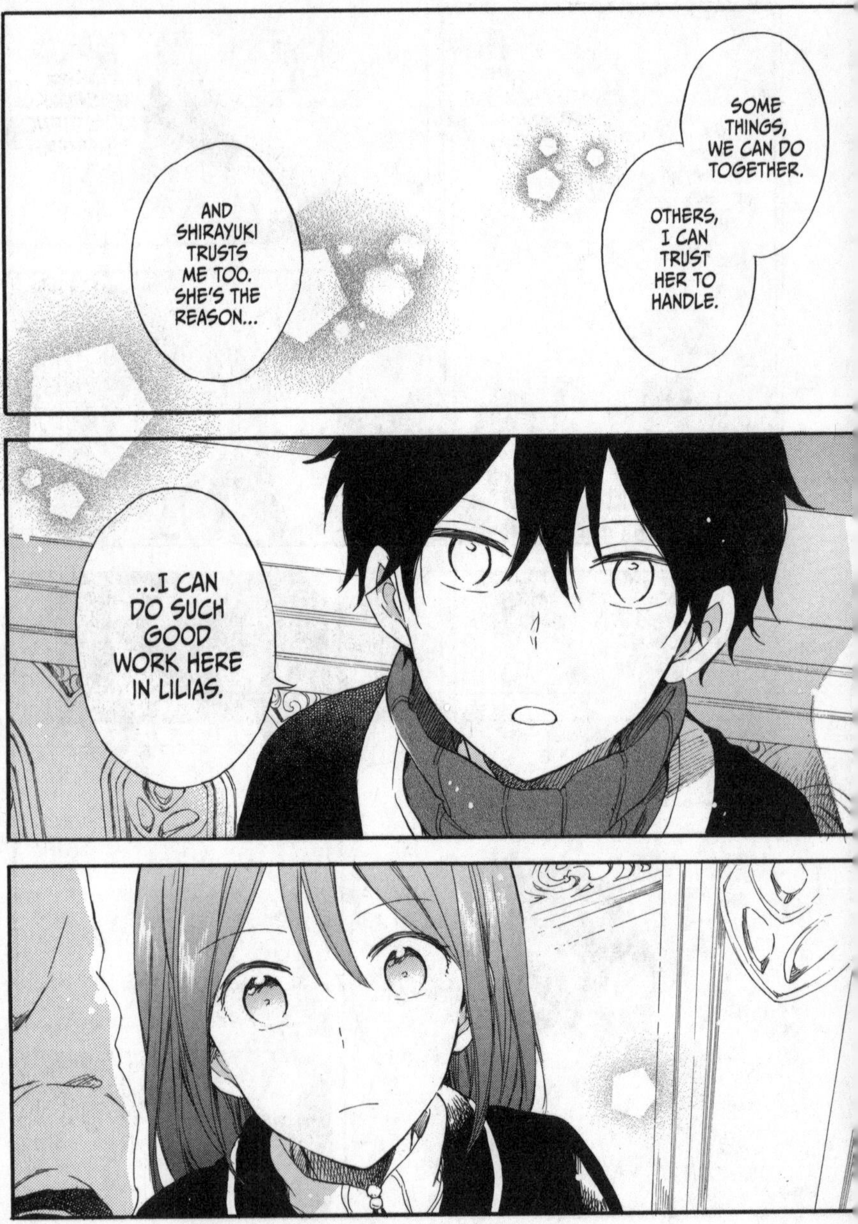
SOME THINGS, WE CAN DO TOGETHER.
OTHERS, I CAN TRUST HER TO HANDLE.
AND SHIRAYUKI TRUSTS ME TOO. SHE'S THE REASON...
...I CAN DO SUCH GOOD WORK HERE IN LILIAS.

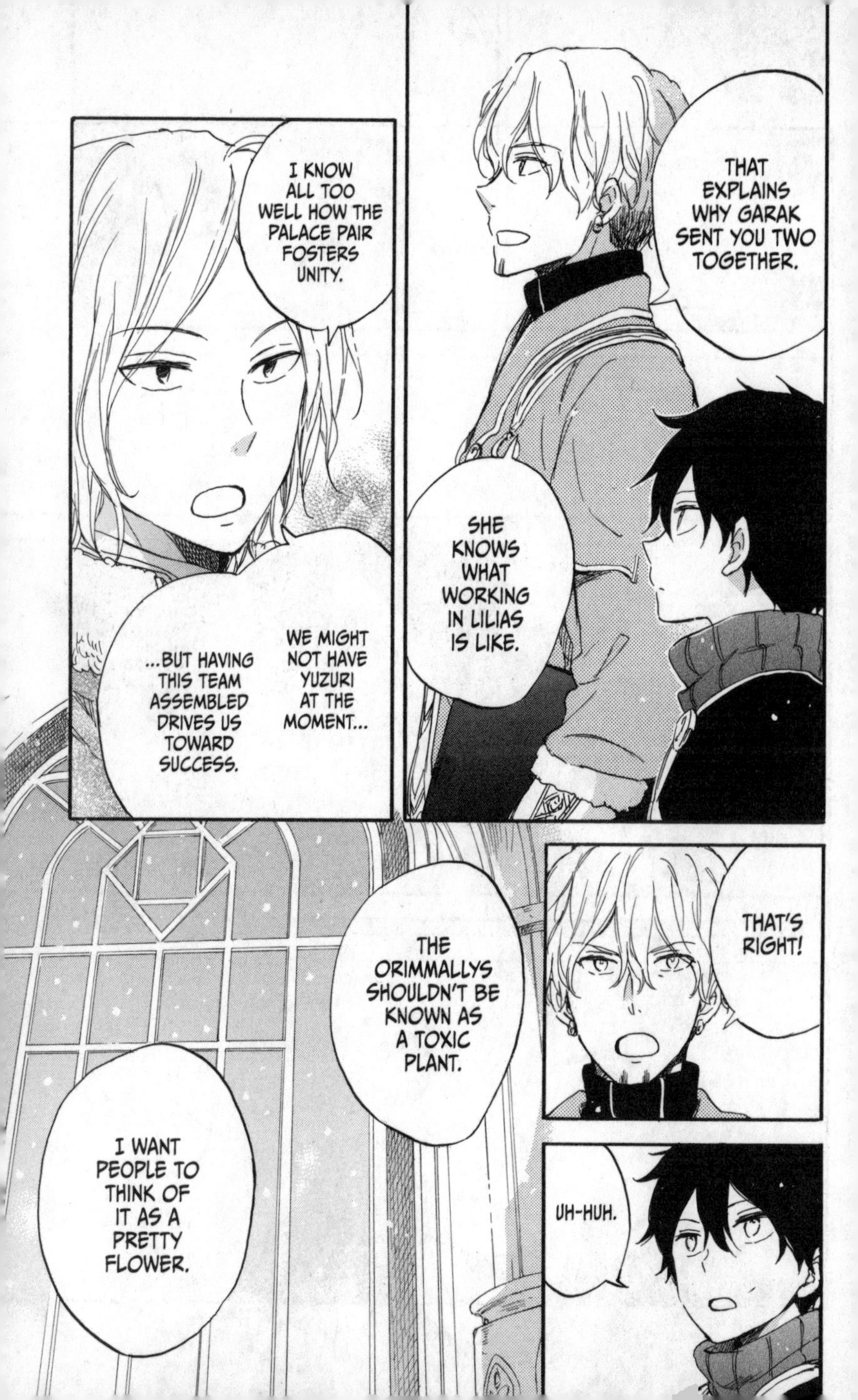
THAT EXPLAINS WHY GARAK SENT YOU TWO TOGETHER.
SHE KNOWS WHAT WORKING IN LILIAS IS LIKE.
I KNOW ALL TOO WELL HOW THE PALACE PAIR FOSTERS UNITY.
WE MIGHT NOT HAVE YUZURI AT THE MOMENT...
...BUT HAVING THIS TEAM ASSEMBLED DRIVES US TOWARD SUCCESS.
THAT'S RIGHT!
UH-HUH.
THE ORIMMALLYS SHOULDN'T BE KNOWN AS A TOXIC PLANT.
I WANT PEOPLE TO THINK OF IT AS A PRETTY FLOWER.

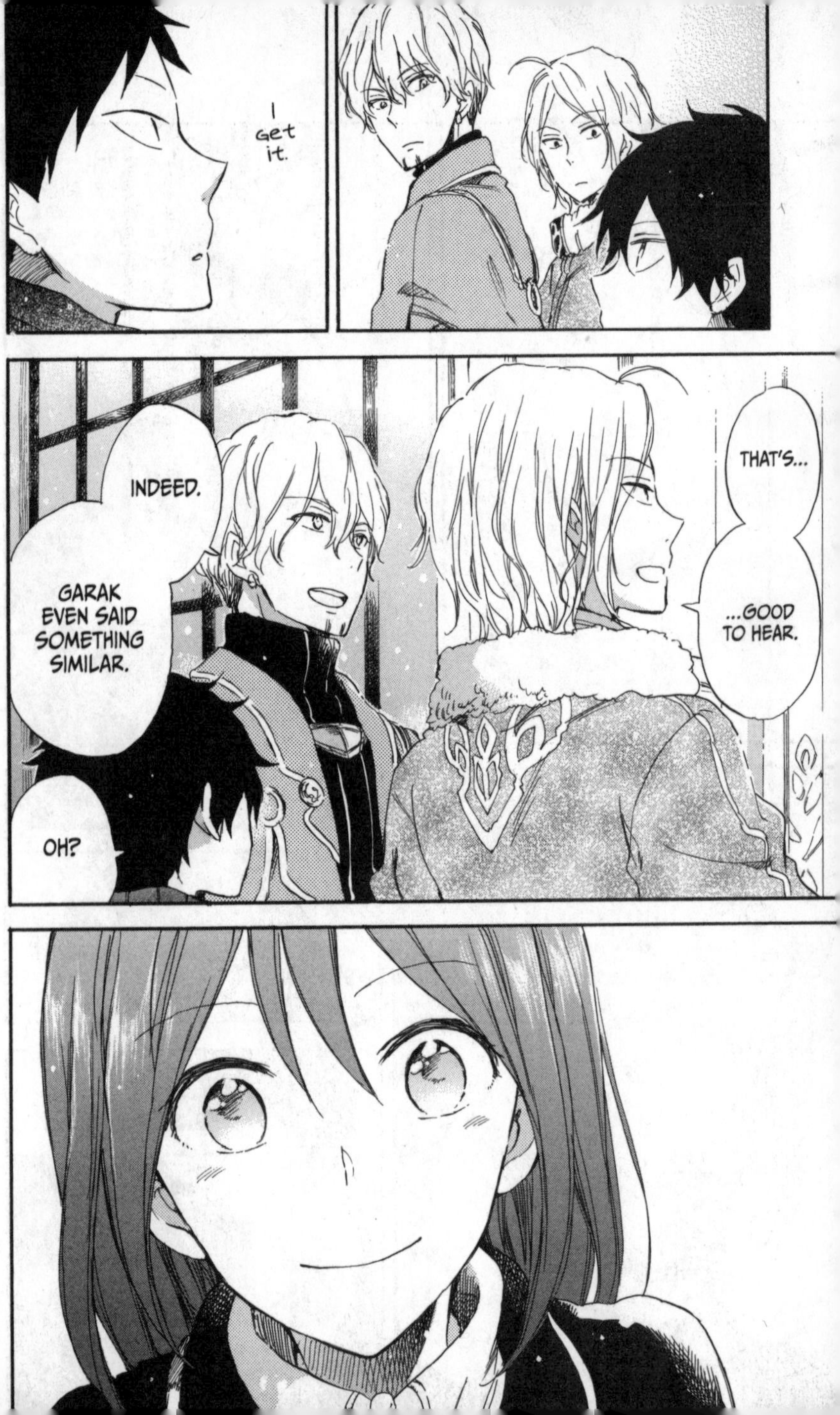
I get it.
THAT'S...
...GOOD TO HEAR.
INDEED.
GARAK EVEN SAID SOMETHING SIMILAR.
OH?

# Chapter 65

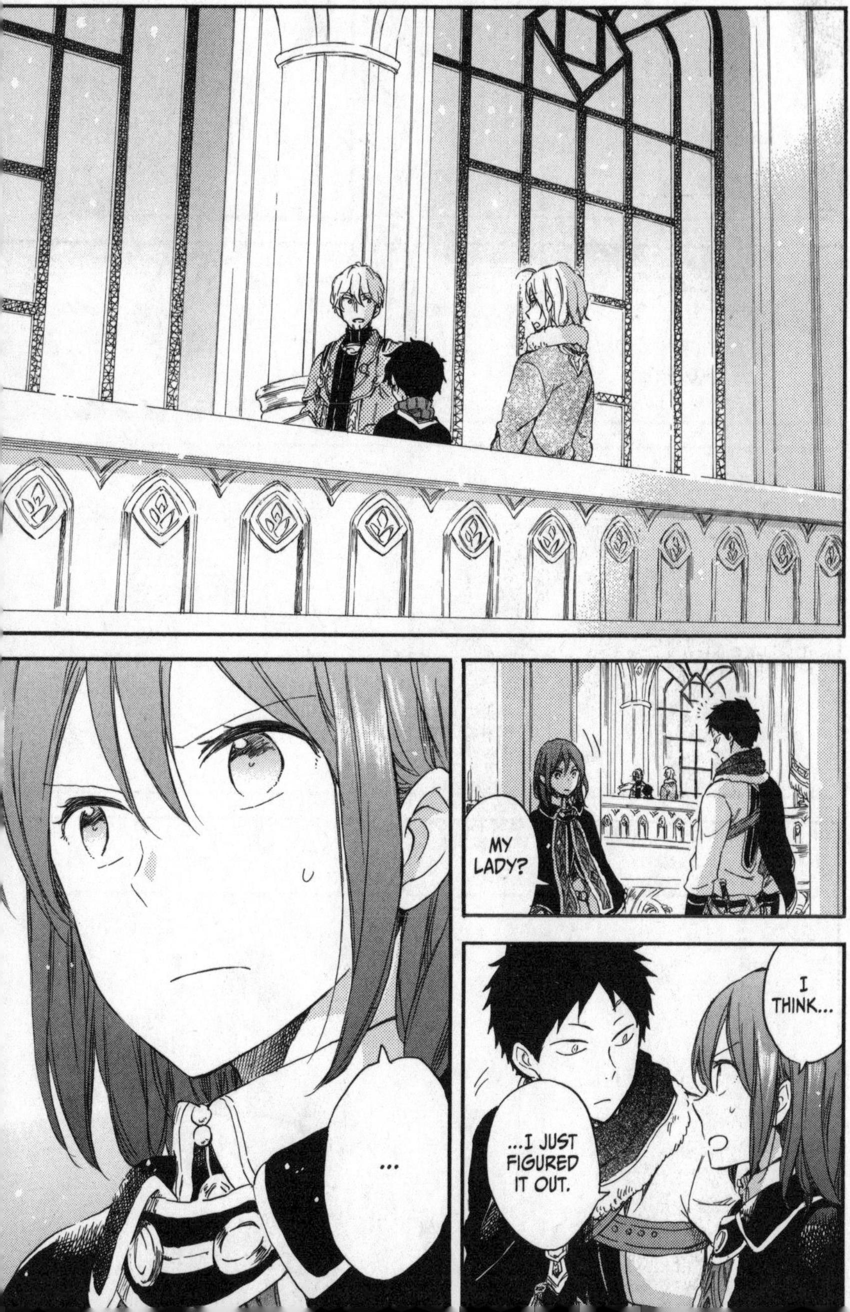

MY LADY?
I THINK...
...I JUST FIGURED IT OUT.
...

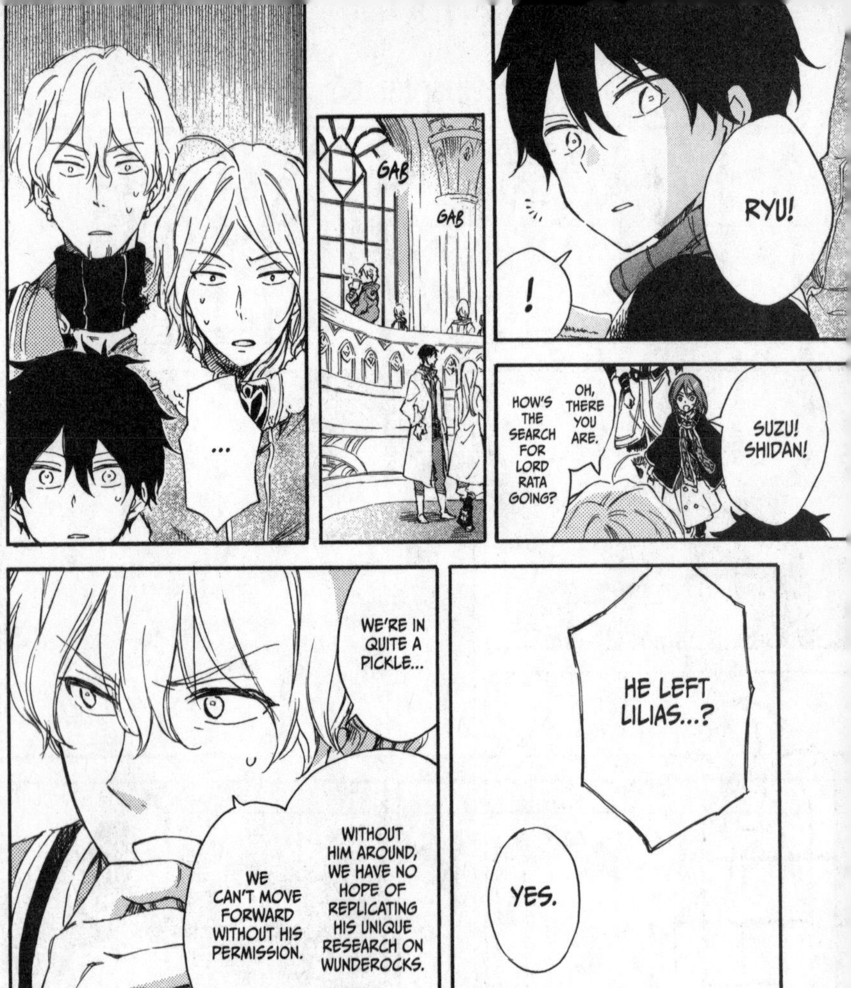
RYU!
!
SUZU! SHIDAN!
OH, THERE YOU ARE.
HOW'S THE SEARCH FOR LORD RATA GOING?
GAB
GAB
...
HE LEFT LILIAS...?
YES.
WE'RE IN QUITE A PICKLE...
WITHOUT HIM AROUND, WE HAVE NO HOPE OF REPLICATING HIS UNIQUE RESEARCH ON WUNDEROCKS.
WE CAN'T MOVE FORWARD WITHOUT HIS PERMISSION.

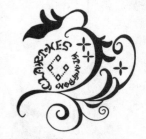

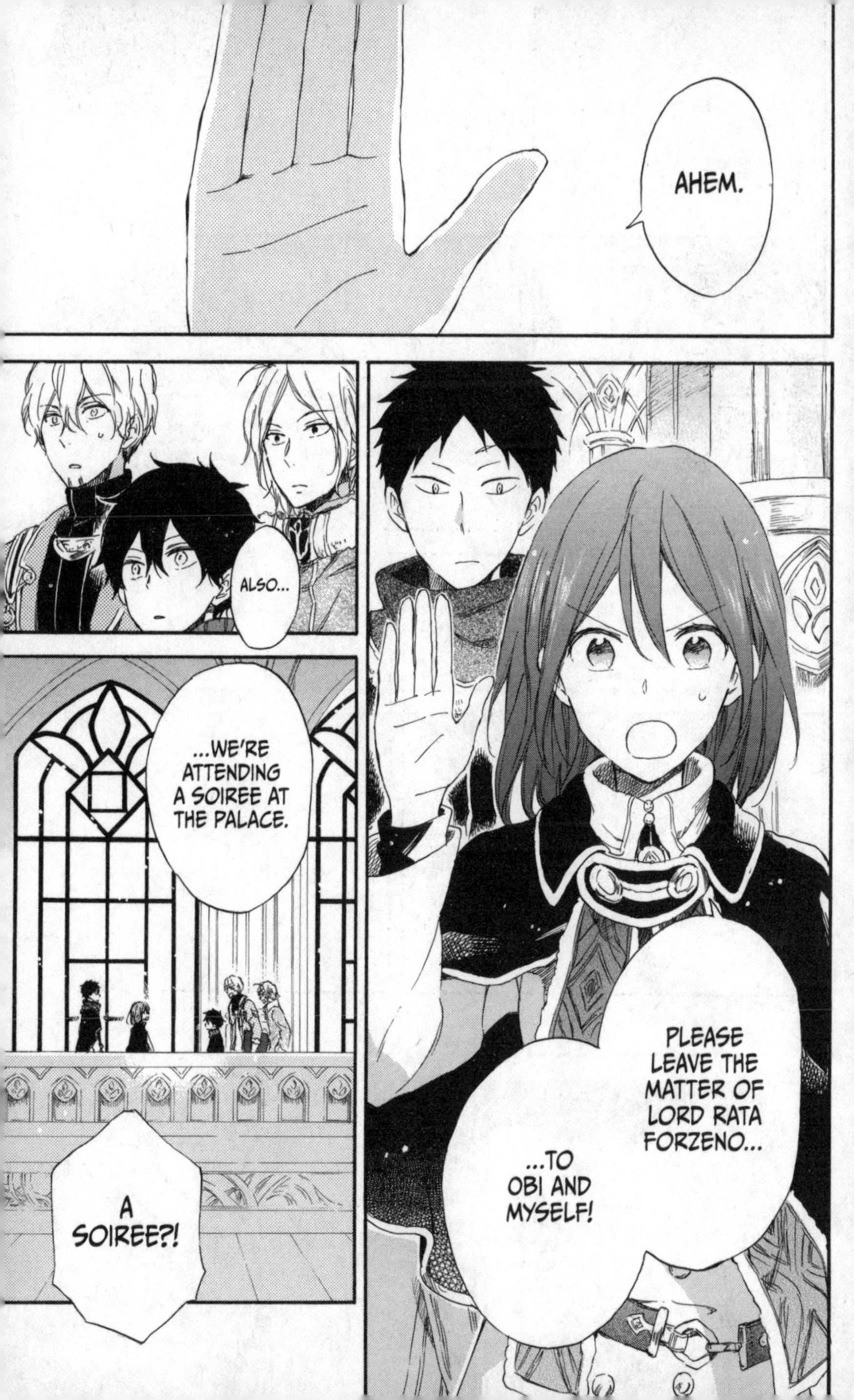
AHEM.
PLEASE LEAVE THE MATTER OF LORD RATA FORZENO...
...TO OBI AND MYSELF!
ALSO...
...WE'RE ATTENDING A SOIREE AT THE PALACE.
A SOIREE?!

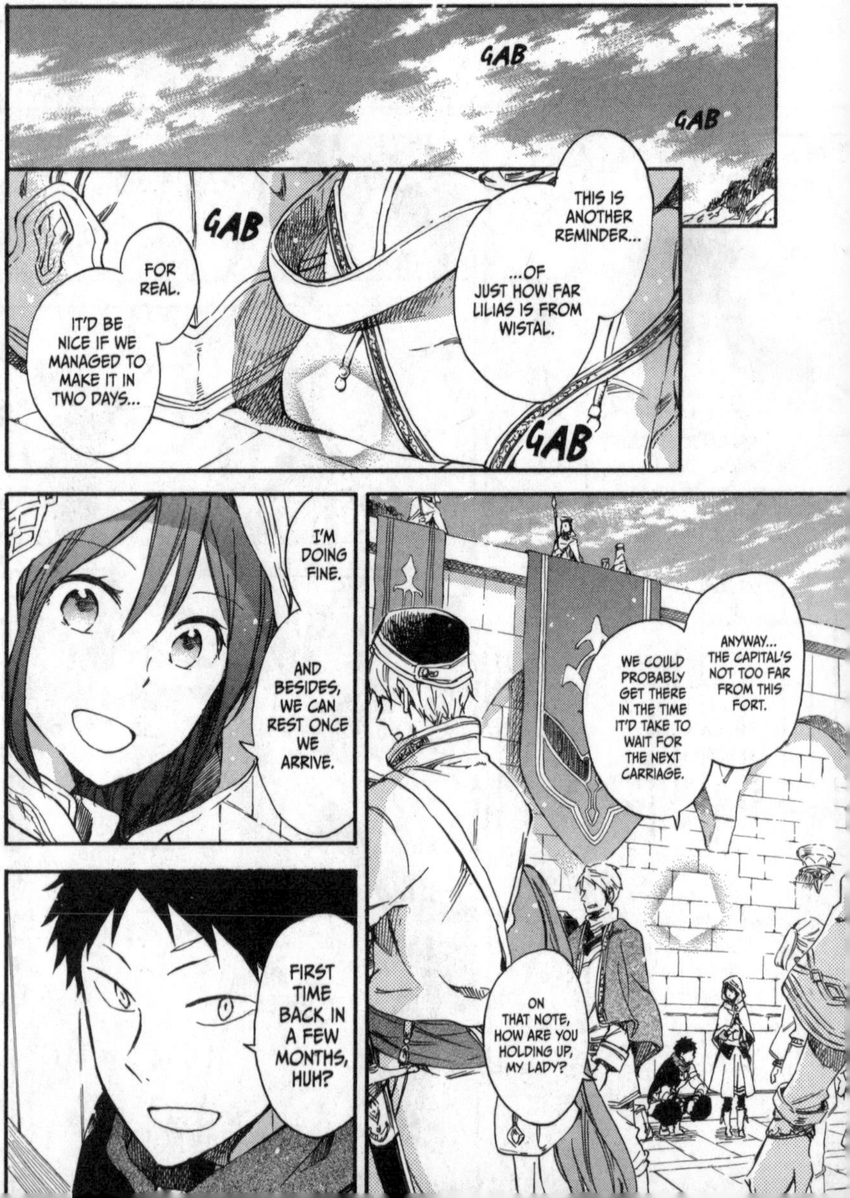
GAB
GAB
THIS IS ANOTHER REMINDER...
...OF JUST HOW FAR LILIAS IS FROM WISTAL.
GAB
FOR REAL.
IT'D BE NICE IF WE MANAGED TO MAKE IT IN TWO DAYS...
GAB
ANYWAY... THE CAPITAL'S NOT TOO FAR FROM THIS FORT.
WE COULD PROBABLY GET THERE IN THE TIME IT'D TAKE TO WAIT FOR THE NEXT CARRIAGE.
ON THAT NOTE, HOW ARE YOU HOLDING UP, MY LADY?
I'M DOING FINE.
AND BESIDES, WE CAN REST ONCE WE ARRIVE.
FIRST TIME BACK IN A FEW MONTHS, HUH?

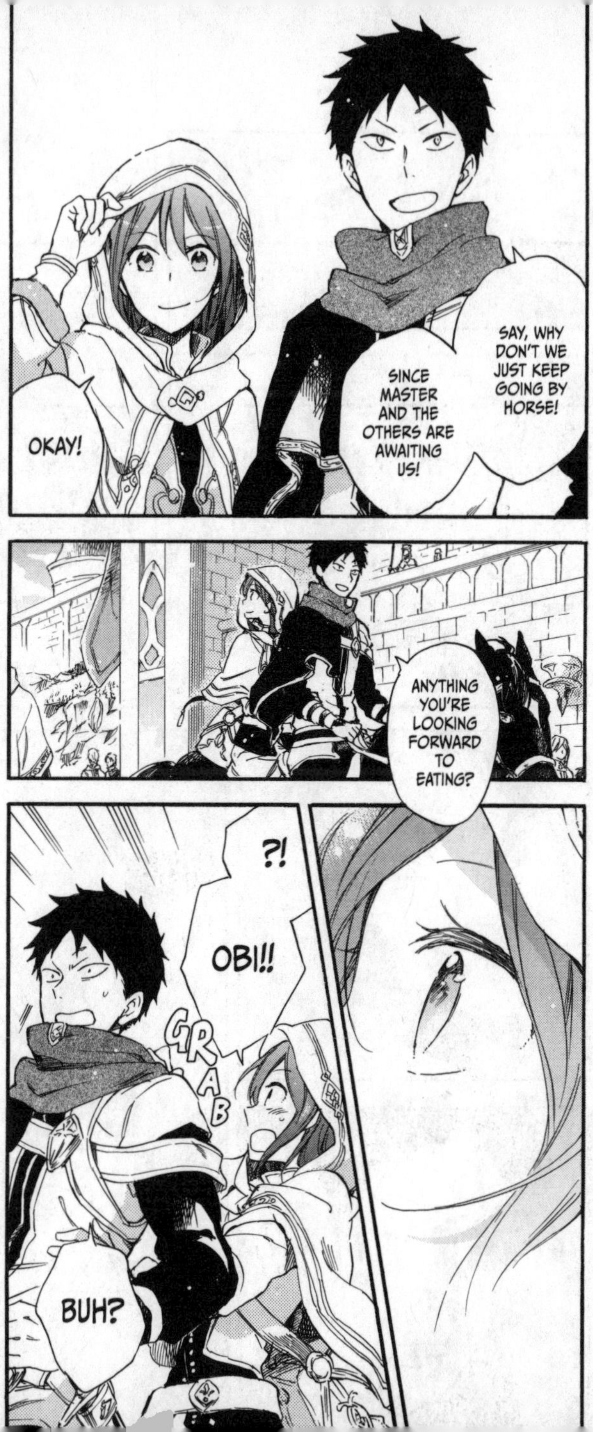
SAY, WHY DON'T WE JUST KEEP GOING BY HORSE!
SINCE MASTER AND THE OTHERS ARE AWAITING US!
OKAY!
ANYTHING YOU'RE LOOKING FORWARD TO EATING?
?!
OBI!!
GRAB
BUH?

5

CHAPTER TALK

Chapter 63

It's all orimmallys all the time in Lilias!

Meanwhile, back at the palace... When Izana took the throne, Zen moved his office and personal chamber (bedroom). And although I never showed it, you can assume that Izana changed rooms also. They're close to each other now, so there are more opportunities for them to chat!

Mitsuhide and Kiki are still in the east wing, but they come and go at wildly different times. They mostly see each other when they're attending to Zen.

Wait, what am I even talking about? This was supposed to be about chapter 63!

Chapter 63 was pure orimmallys!

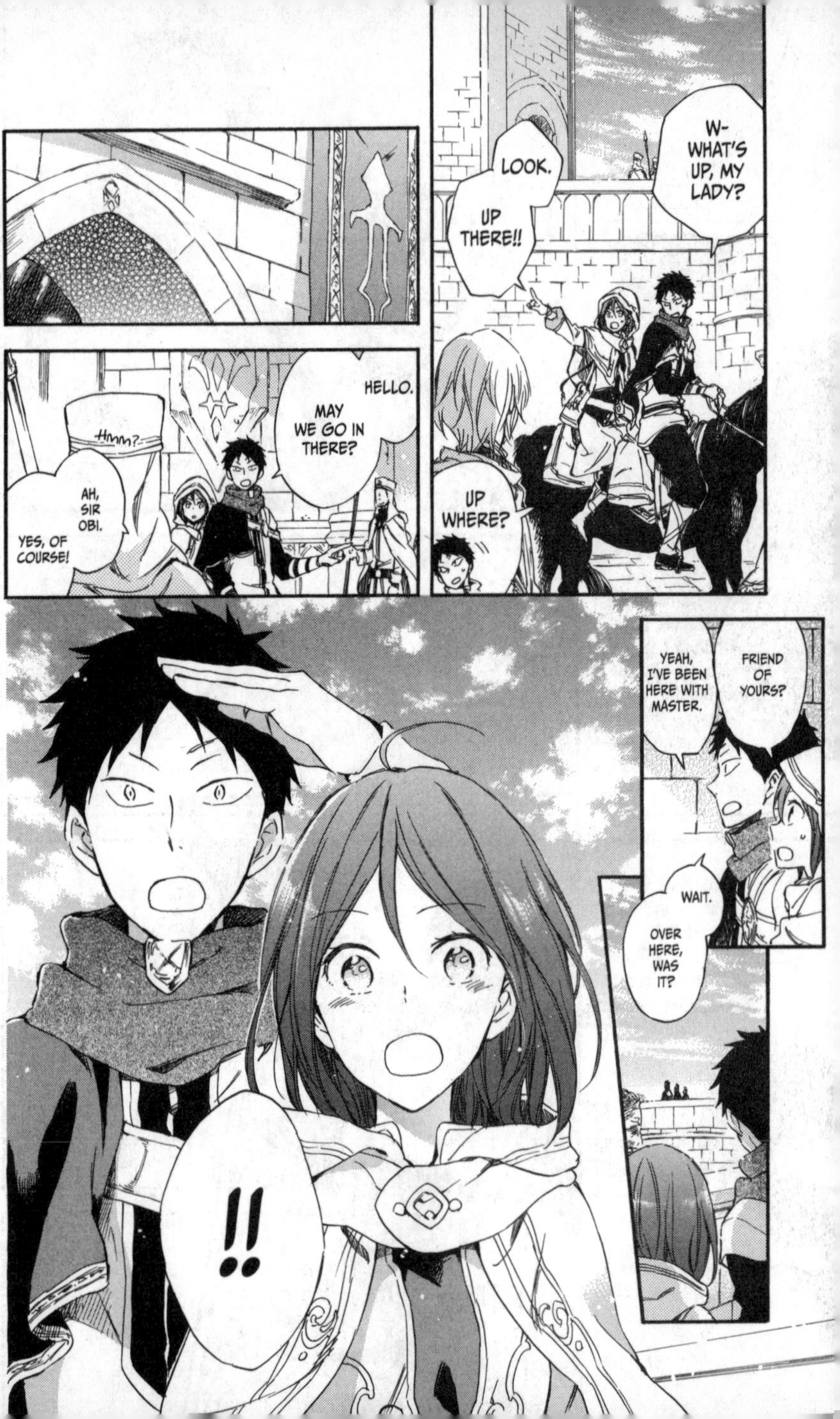
W- WHAT'S UP, MY LADY?
LOOK.
UP THERE!!
UP WHERE?
HELLO.
MAY WE GO IN THERE?
Hmm?
AH, SIR OBI.
YES, OF COURSE!
FRIEND OF YOURS?
YEAH, I'VE BEEN HERE WITH MASTER.
WAIT.
OVER HERE, WAS IT?
!!

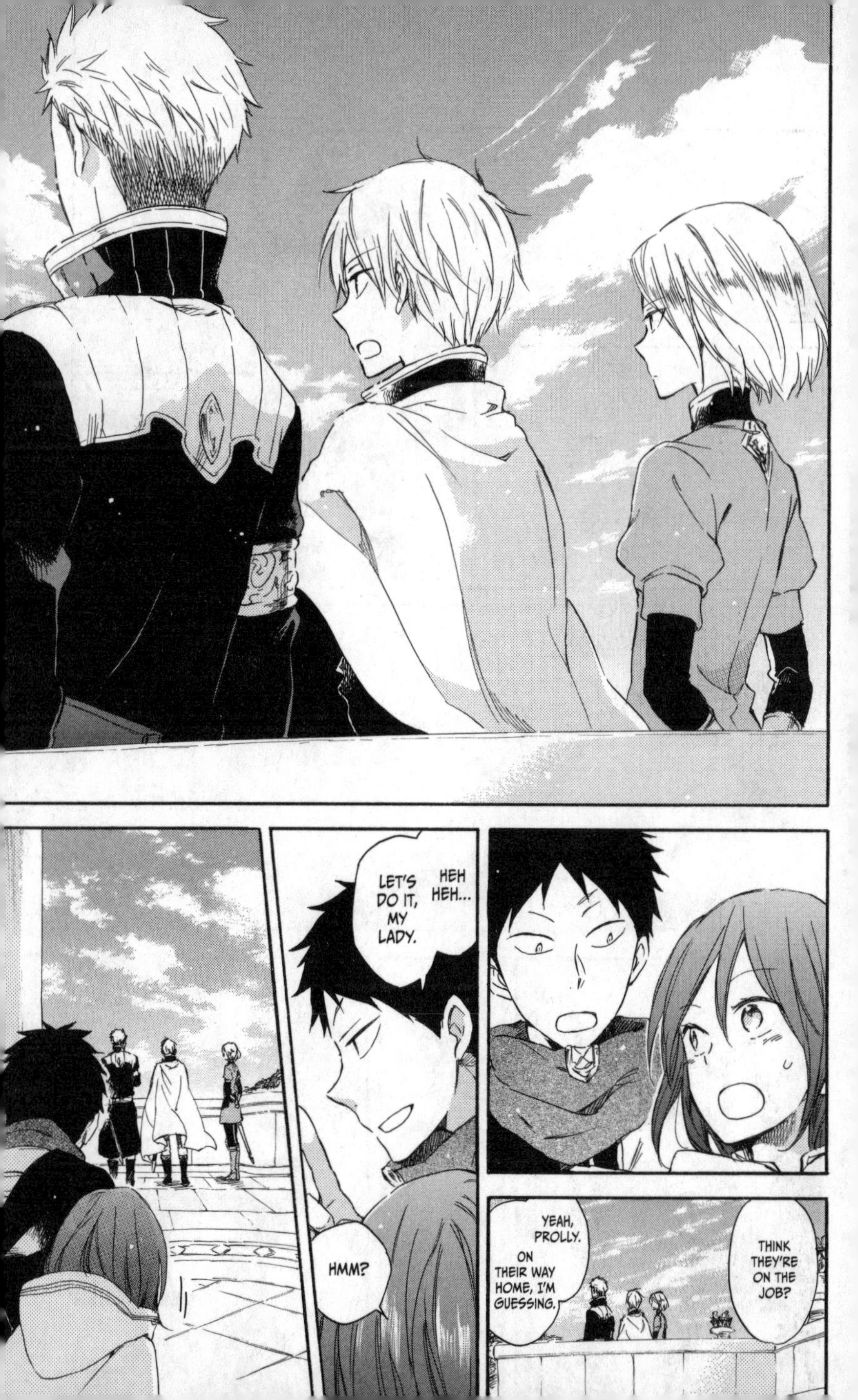
THINK THEY'RE ON THE JOB?
YEAH, PROLLY.
ON THEIR WAY HOME, I'M GUESSING.
HEH HEH...
LET'S DO IT, MY LADY.
HMM?

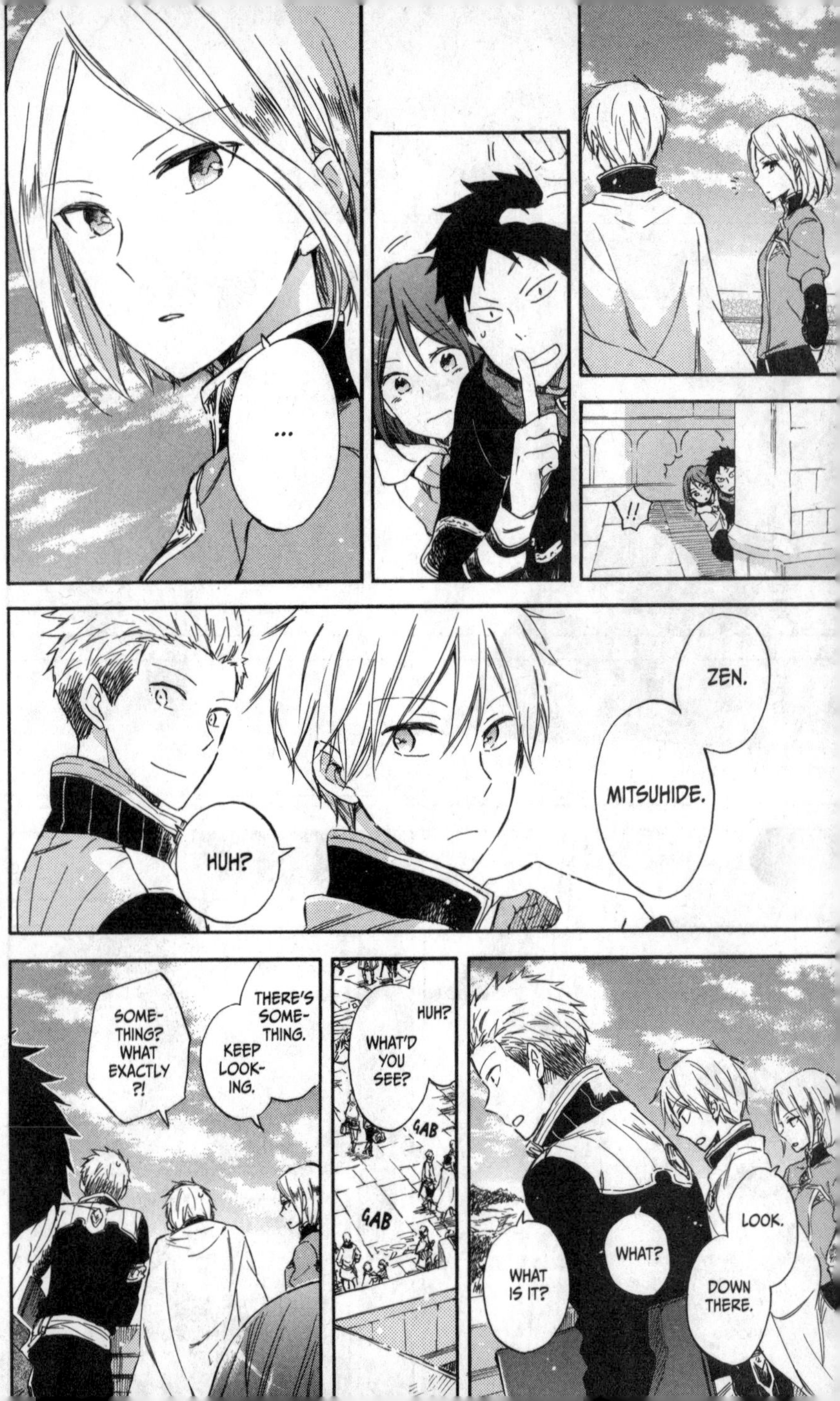
!!
...
ZEN.
MITSUHIDE.
HUH?
LOOK.
DOWN THERE.
WHAT?
WHAT IS IT?
HUH?
WHAT'D YOU SEE?
GAB
GAB
THERE'S SOMETHING.
KEEP LOOKING.
SOMETHING? WHAT EXACTLY ?!

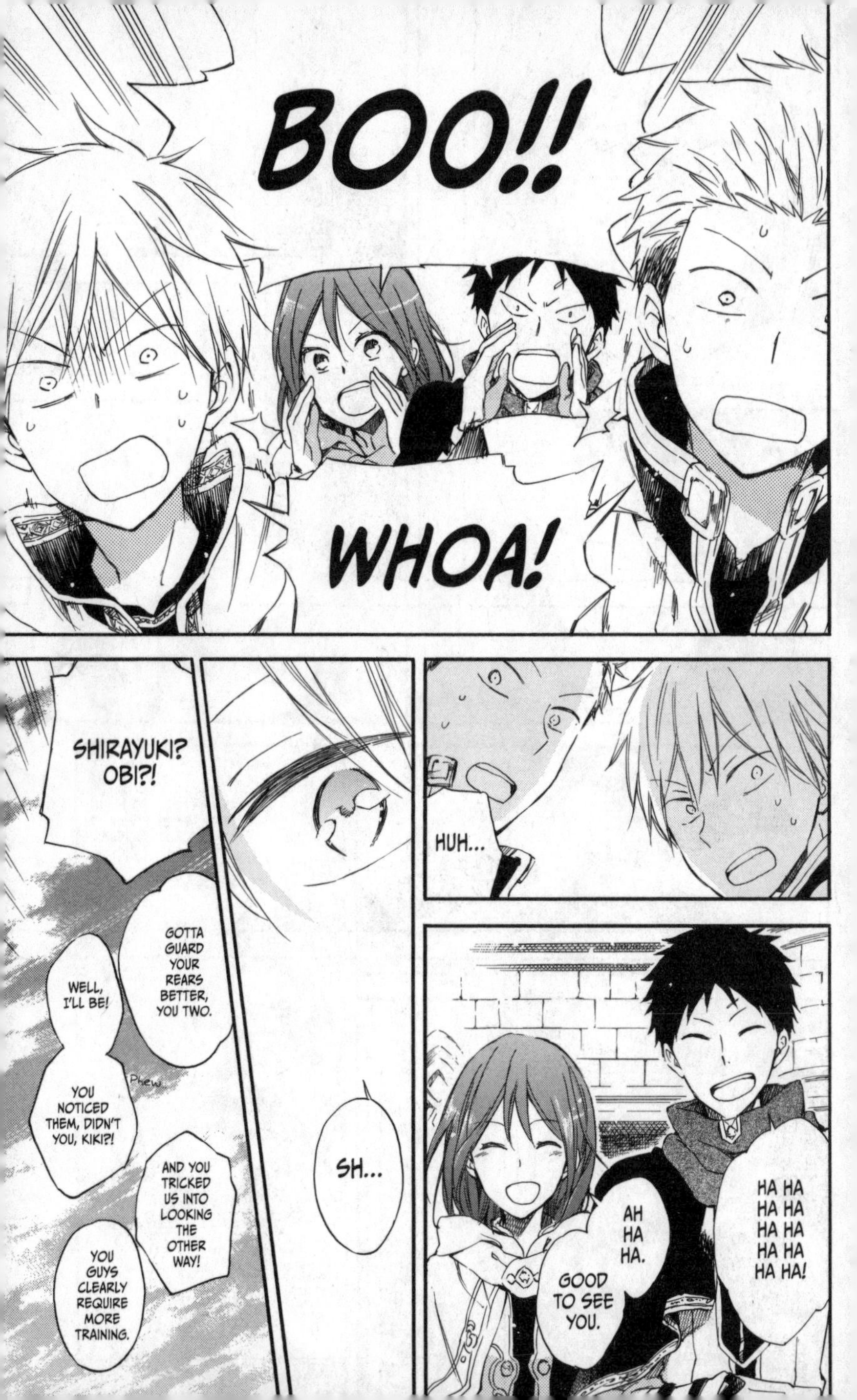
BOO!!
WHOA!
HUH...
HA HA HA HA HA HA HA HA HA HA!
AH HA HA.
GOOD TO SEE YOU.
SH...
SHIRAYUKI? OBI?!
GOTTA GUARD YOUR REARS BETTER, YOU TWO.
WELL, I'LL BE!
Phew...
YOU NOTICED THEM, DIDN'T YOU, KIKI?!
AND YOU TRICKED US INTO LOOKING THE OTHER WAY!
YOU GUYS CLEARLY REQUIRE MORE TRAINING.

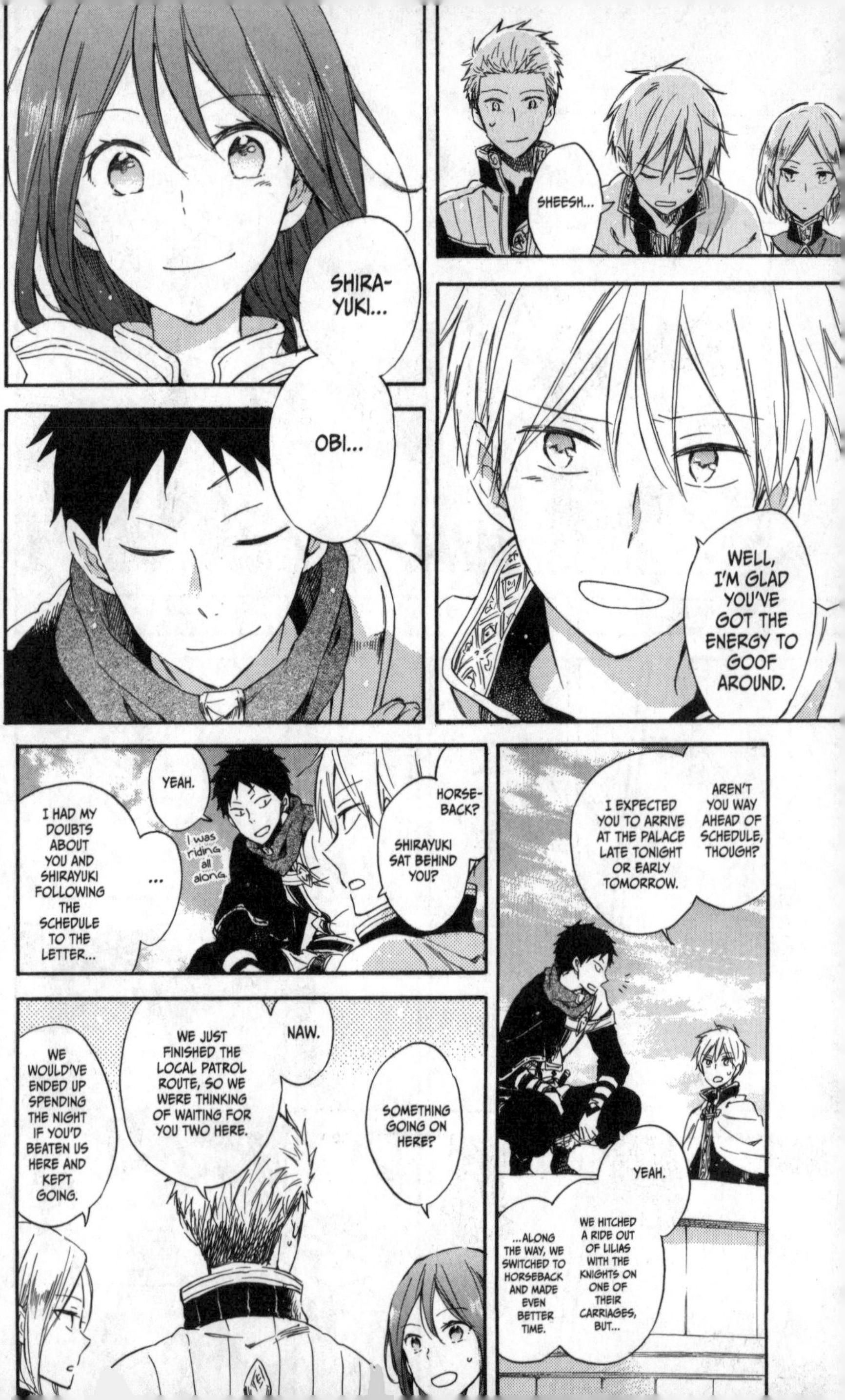
SHEESH...
SHIRA-YUKI...
OBI...
WELL, I'M GLAD YOU'VE GOT THE ENERGY TO GOOF AROUND.
AREN'T YOU WAY AHEAD OF SCHEDULE, THOUGH?
I EXPECTED YOU TO ARRIVE AT THE PALACE LATE TONIGHT OR EARLY TOMORROW.
YEAH.
WE HITCHED A RIDE OUT OF LILIAS WITH THE KNIGHTS ON ONE OF THEIR CARRIAGES, BUT...
...ALONG THE WAY, WE SWITCHED TO HORSEBACK AND MADE EVEN BETTER TIME.
HORSE-BACK?
SHIRAYUKI SAT BEHIND YOU?
YEAH.
I was riding all along
...
I HAD MY DOUBTS ABOUT YOU AND SHIRAYUKI FOLLOWING THE SCHEDULE TO THE LETTER...
SOMETHING GOING ON HERE?
NAW.
WE JUST FINISHED THE LOCAL PATROL ROUTE, SO WE WERE THINKING OF WAITING FOR YOU TWO HERE.
WE WOULD'VE ENDED UP SPENDING THE NIGHT IF YOU'D BEATEN US HERE AND KEPT GOING.

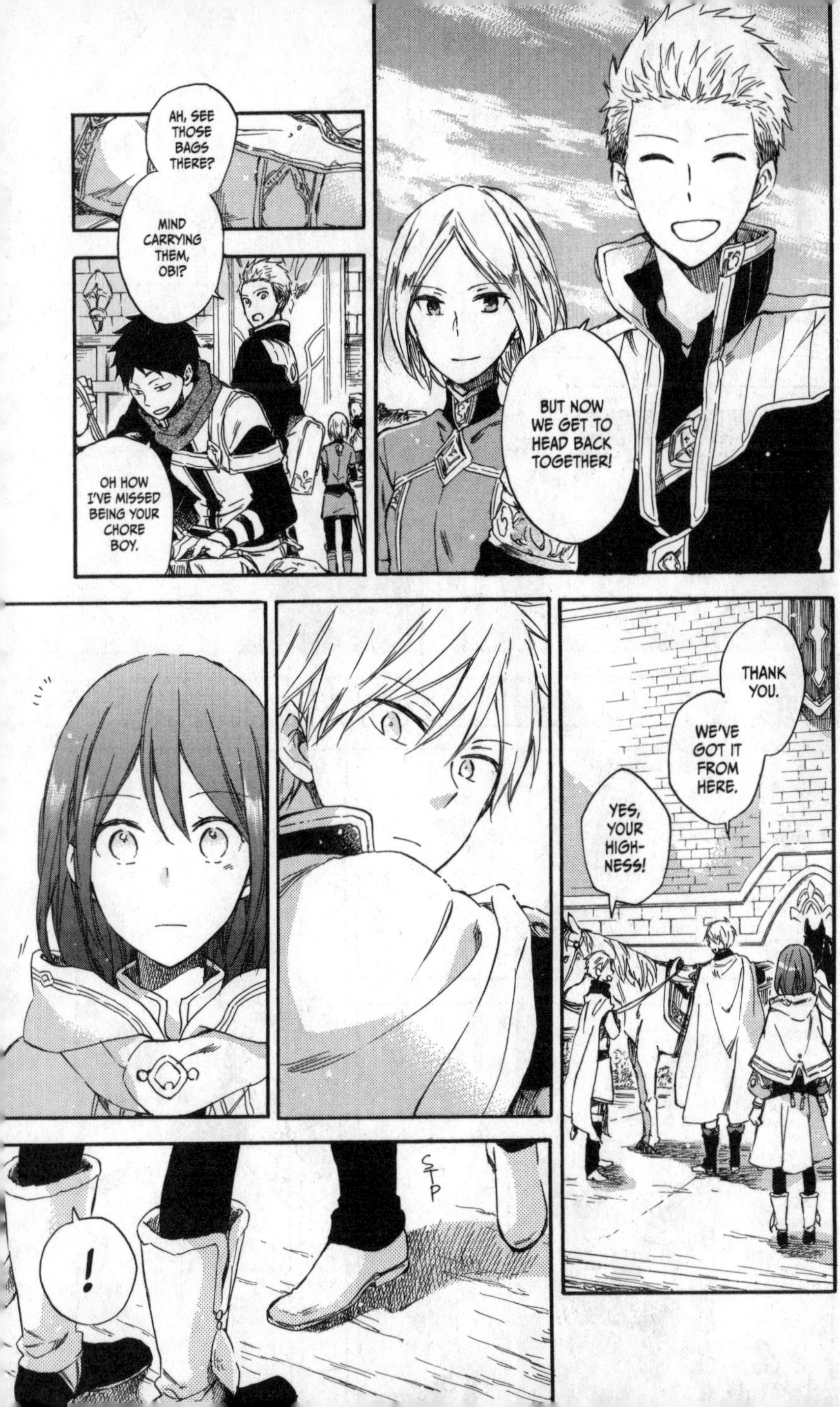
BUT NOW WE GET TO HEAD BACK TOGETHER!
AH, SEE THOSE BAGS THERE?
MIND CARRYING THEM, OBI?
OH HOW I'VE MISSED BEING YOUR CHORE BOY.
THANK YOU.
WE'VE GOT IT FROM HERE.
YES, YOUR HIGH-NESS!
STP
!

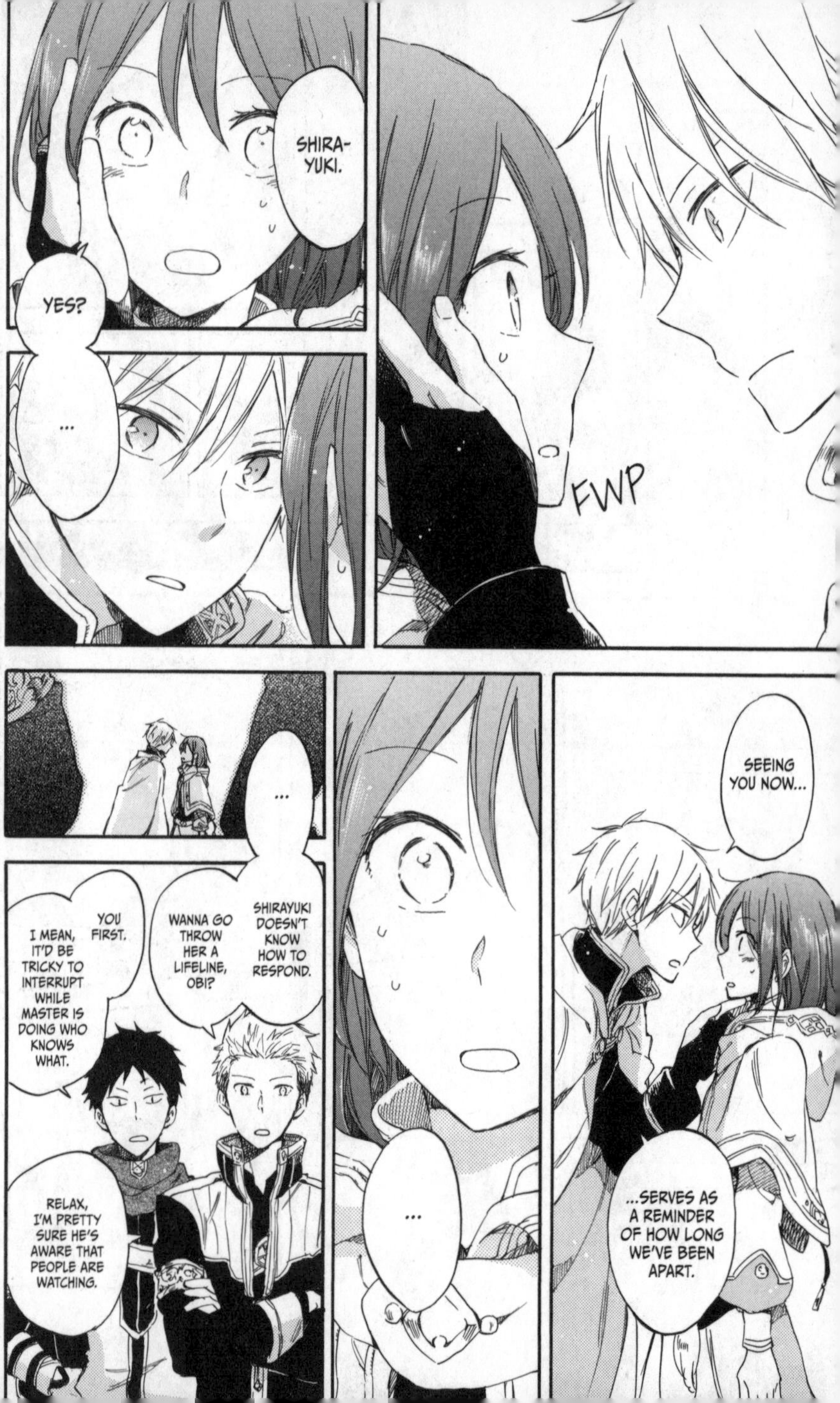
FWP
SHIRA-YUKI.
YES?
...
SEEING YOU NOW...
...SERVES AS A REMINDER OF HOW LONG WE'VE BEEN APART.
...
...
SHIRAYUKI DOESN'T KNOW HOW TO RESPOND.
WANNA GO THROW HER A LIFELINE, OBI?
YOU FIRST.
I MEAN, IT'D BE TRICKY TO INTERRUPT WHILE MASTER IS DOING WHO KNOWS WHAT.
RELAX, I'M PRETTY SURE HE'S AWARE THAT PEOPLE ARE WATCHING.

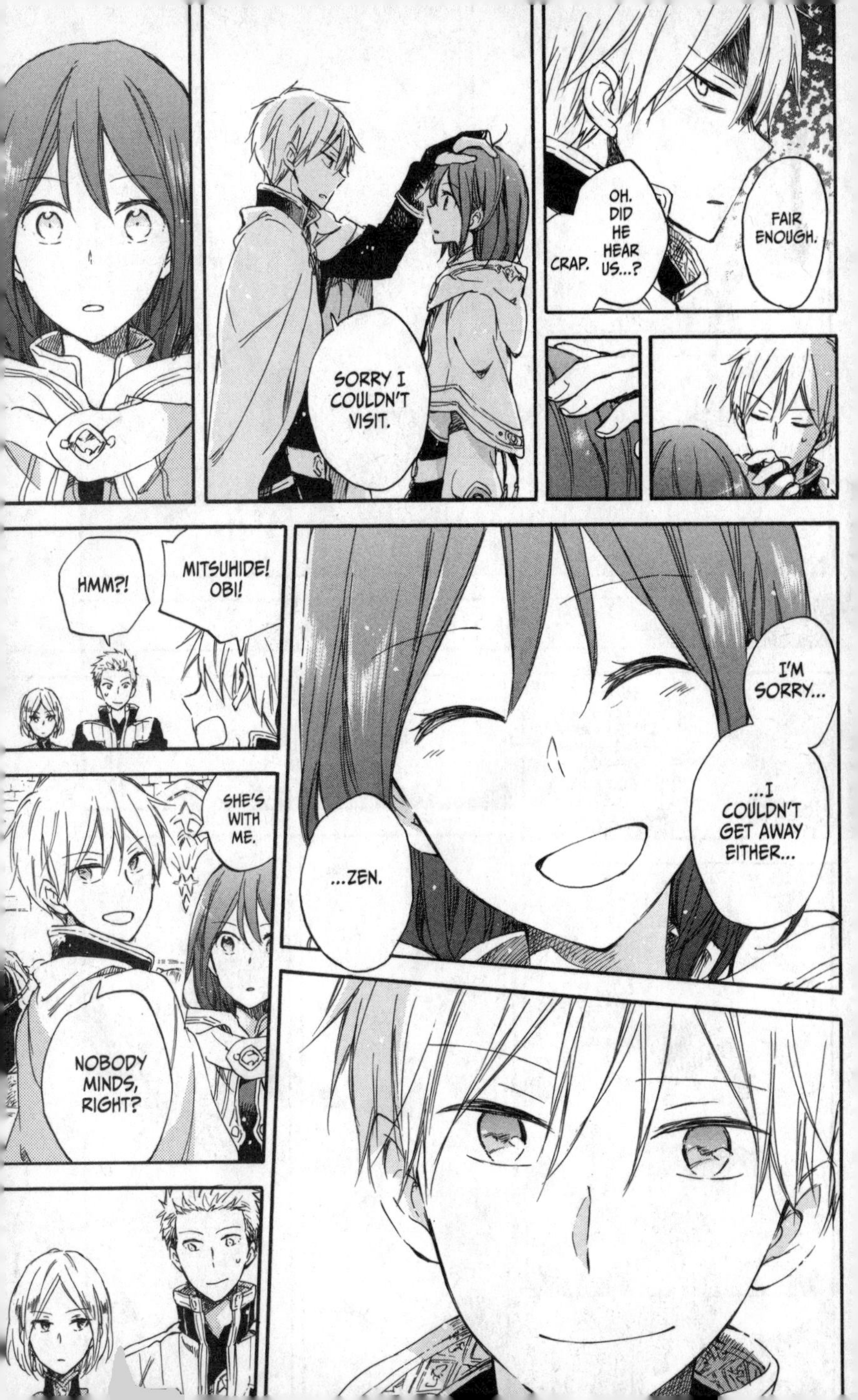
FAIR ENOUGH.
OH. DID HE HEAR US...?
CRAP.
SORRY I COULDN'T VISIT.
I'M SORRY...
...I COULDN'T GET AWAY EITHER...
...ZEN.
MITSUHIDE! OBI!
HMM?!
SHE'S WITH ME.
NOBODY MINDS, RIGHT?

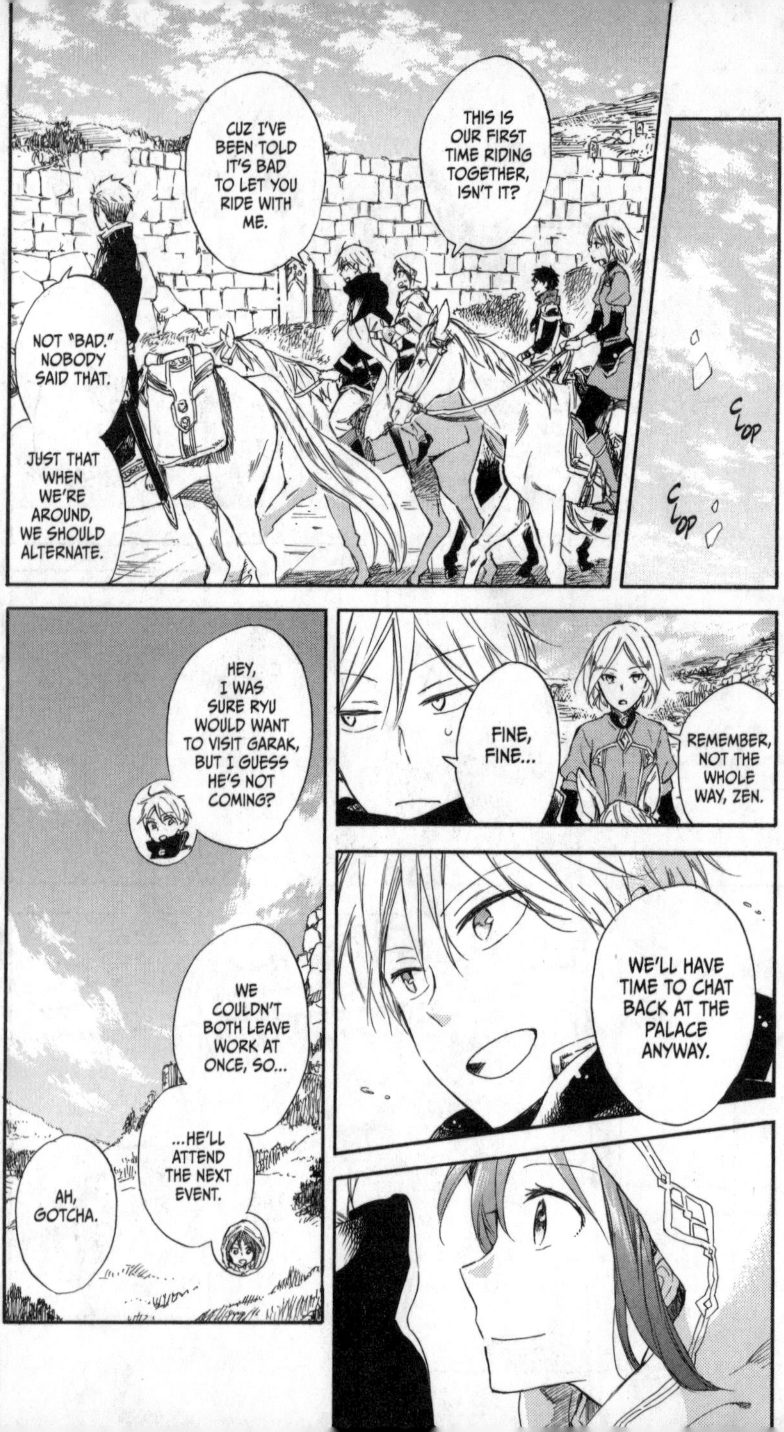
CLOP
CLOP
THIS IS OUR FIRST TIME RIDING TOGETHER, ISN'T IT?
CUZ I'VE BEEN TOLD IT'S BAD TO LET YOU RIDE WITH ME.
NOT "BAD." NOBODY SAID THAT.
JUST THAT WHEN WE'RE AROUND, WE SHOULD ALTERNATE.
REMEMBER, NOT THE WHOLE WAY, ZEN.
FINE, FINE...
WE'LL HAVE TIME TO CHAT BACK AT THE PALACE ANYWAY.
HEY, I WAS SURE RYU WOULD WANT TO VISIT GARAK, BUT I GUESS HE'S NOT COMING?
WE COULDN'T BOTH LEAVE WORK AT ONCE, SO...
...HE'LL ATTEND THE NEXT EVENT.
AH, GOTCHA.

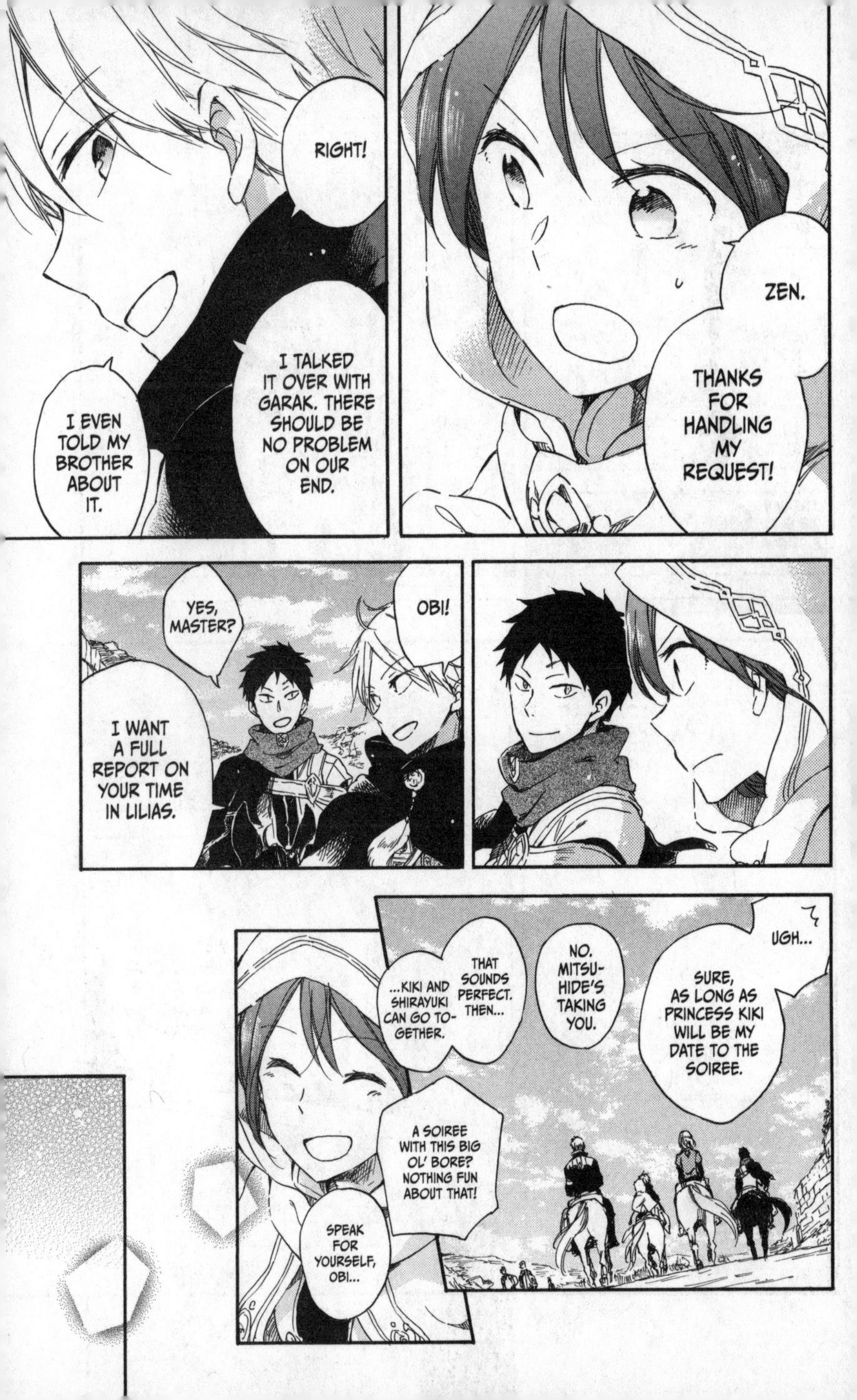
ZEN.
THANKS FOR HANDLING MY REQUEST!
RIGHT!
I TALKED IT OVER WITH GARAK. THERE SHOULD BE NO PROBLEM ON OUR END.
I EVEN TOLD MY BROTHER ABOUT IT.
OBI!
YES, MASTER?
I WANT A FULL REPORT ON YOUR TIME IN LILIAS.
UGH...
SURE, AS LONG AS PRINCESS KIKI WILL BE MY DATE TO THE SOIREE.
NO. MITSU-HIDE'S TAKING YOU.
THAT SOUNDS PERFECT. THEN...
...KIKI AND SHIRAYUKI CAN GO TO-GETHER.
A SOIREE WITH THIS BIG OL' BORE? NOTHING FUN ABOUT THAT!
SPEAK FOR YOURSELF, OBI...

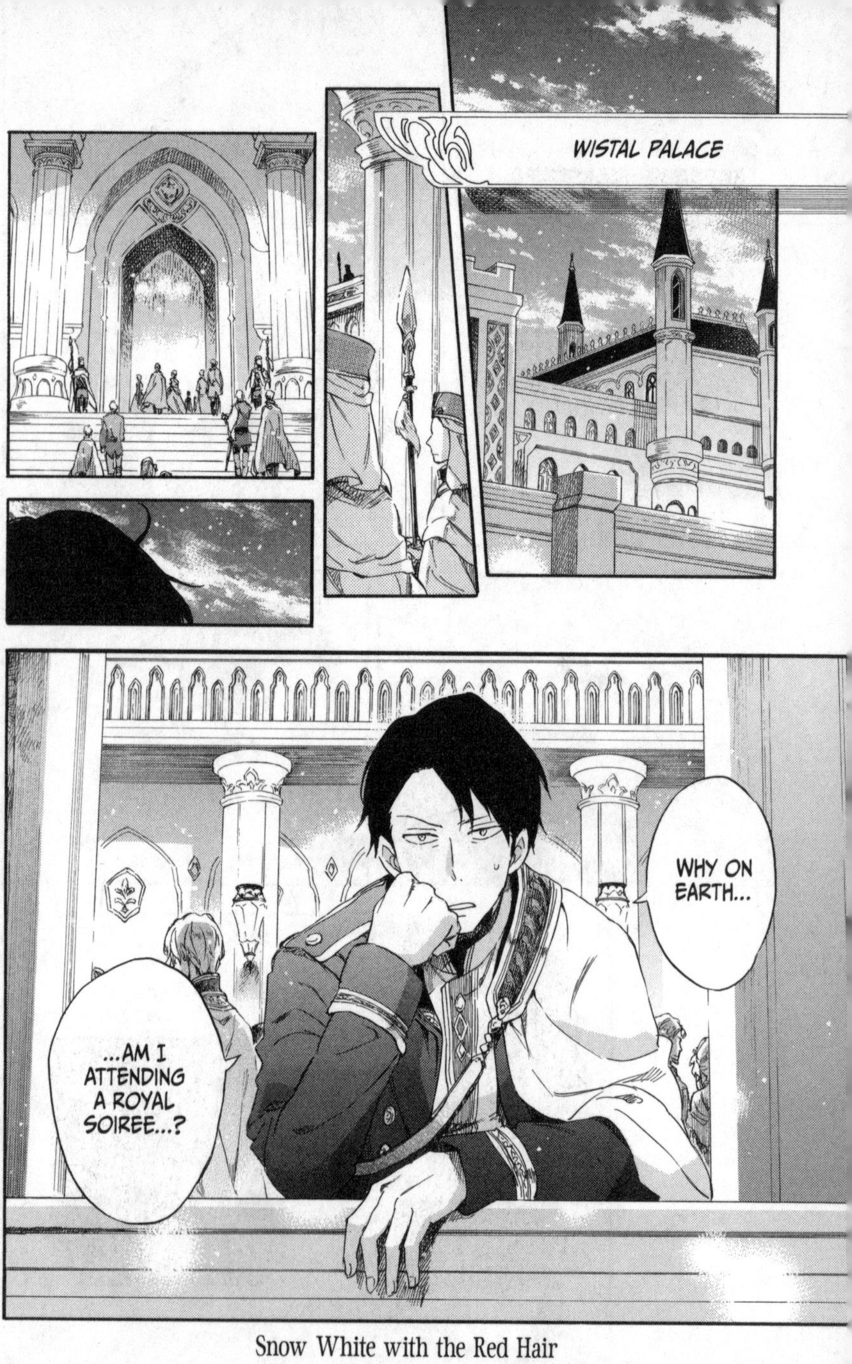
WISTAL PALACE
WHY ON EARTH...
...AM I ATTENDING A ROYAL SOIREE...?

Snow White with the Red Hair
Vol. 14: End

Snow White
with the Red Hair

Chapter 61
Preview Image

Snow White
with the Red Hair

Chapter 62
Preview Image

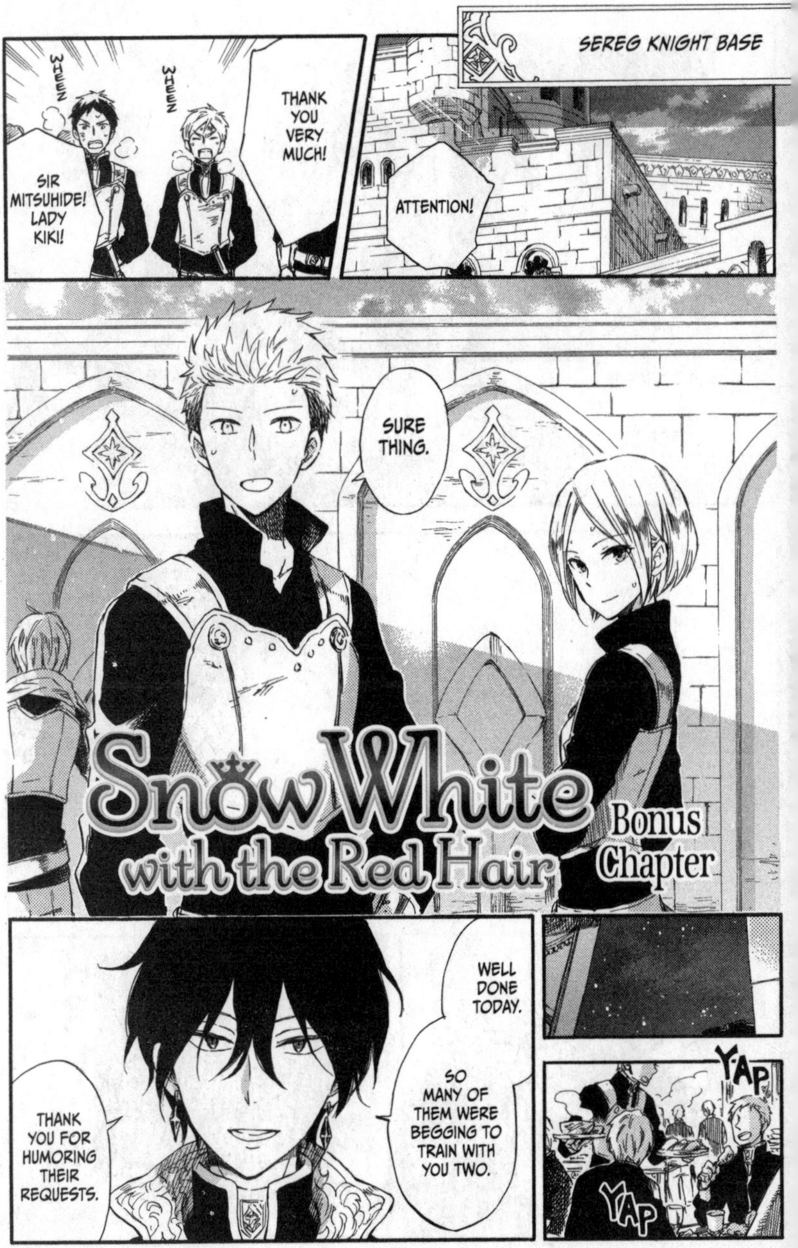
SEREG KNIGHT BASE
ATTENTION!
THANK YOU VERY MUCH!
WHEEZ
WHEEZ
SIR MITSUHIDE! LADY KIKI!
SURE THING.
Snow White with the Red Hair
Bonus Chapter
YAP
YAP
WELL DONE TODAY.
SO MANY OF THEM WERE BEGGING TO TRAIN WITH YOU TWO.
THANK YOU FOR HUMORING THEIR REQUESTS.

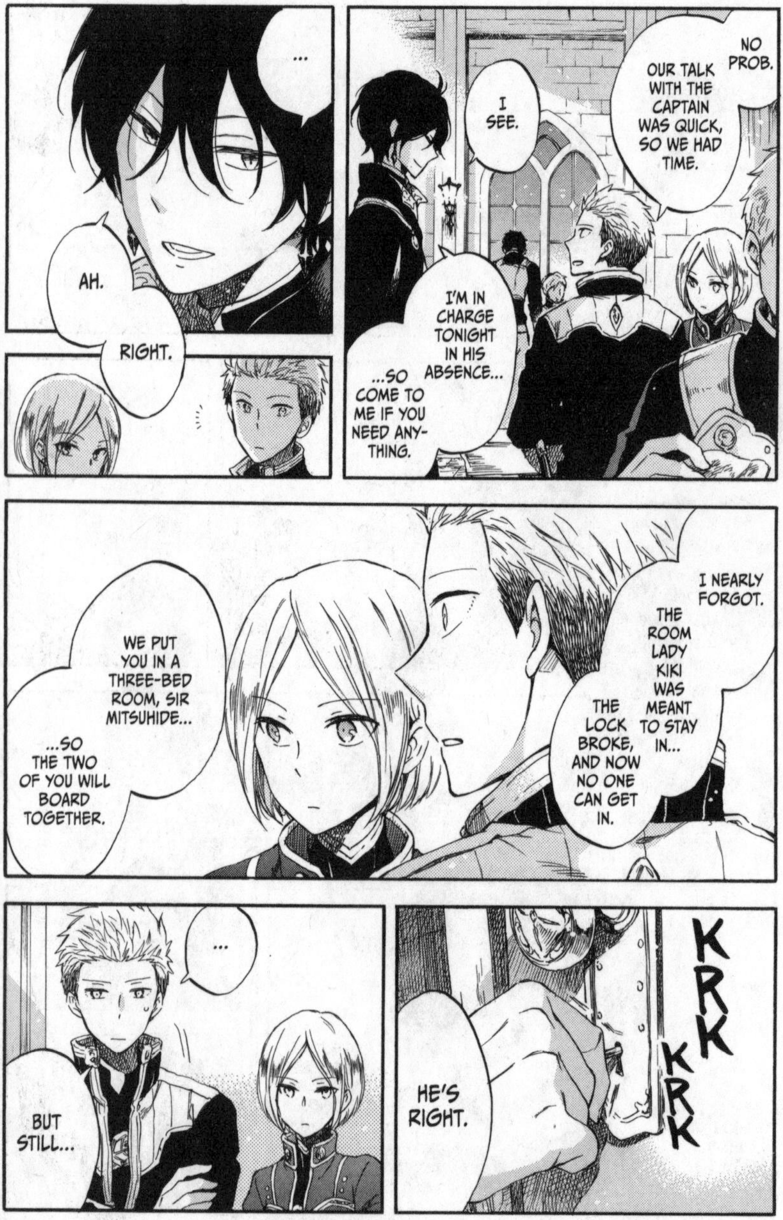
NO PROB.
OUR TALK WITH THE CAPTAIN WAS QUICK, SO WE HAD TIME.
I SEE.
I'M IN CHARGE TONIGHT IN HIS ABSENCE...
...SO COME TO ME IF YOU NEED ANY-THING.
...
AH.
RIGHT.
I NEARLY FORGOT.
THE ROOM LADY KIKI WAS MEANT TO STAY IN...
THE LOCK BROKE, AND NOW NO ONE CAN GET IN.
WE PUT YOU IN A THREE-BED ROOM, SIR MITSUHIDE...
...SO THE TWO OF YOU WILL BOARD TOGETHER.
KRK
KRK
KRK
HE'S RIGHT.
...
BUT STILL...

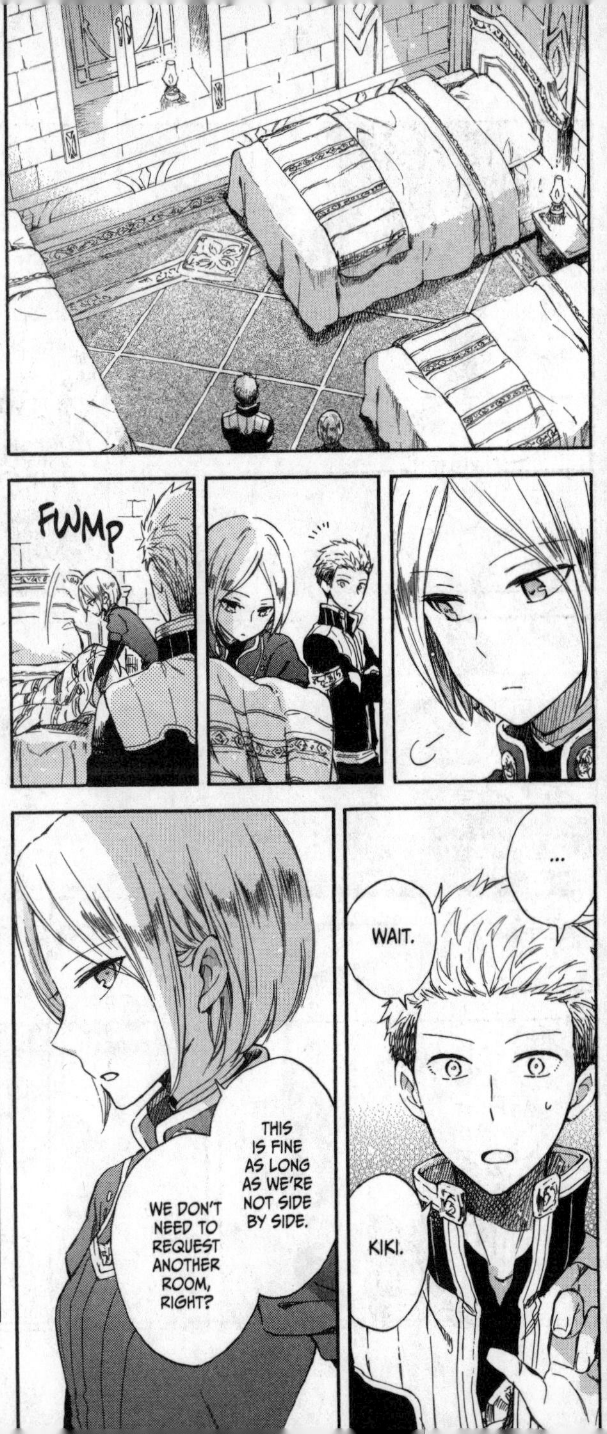
FWMP
...
WAIT.
KIKI.
THIS IS FINE AS LONG AS WE'RE NOT SIDE BY SIDE.
WE DON'T NEED TO REQUEST ANOTHER ROOM, RIGHT?

6

CHAPTER TALK

Spoilers!

Chapter 64

The search for Lord Rata!

Their brains were working in overdrive, which is why they were eating sweets. Donuts, donuts, donuts... Oh wait, that was chapter 63...

I drew Shirayuki and Ryu's bedroom for chapter 60, but it didn't show up in this volume at all.

Are they sleeping okay?

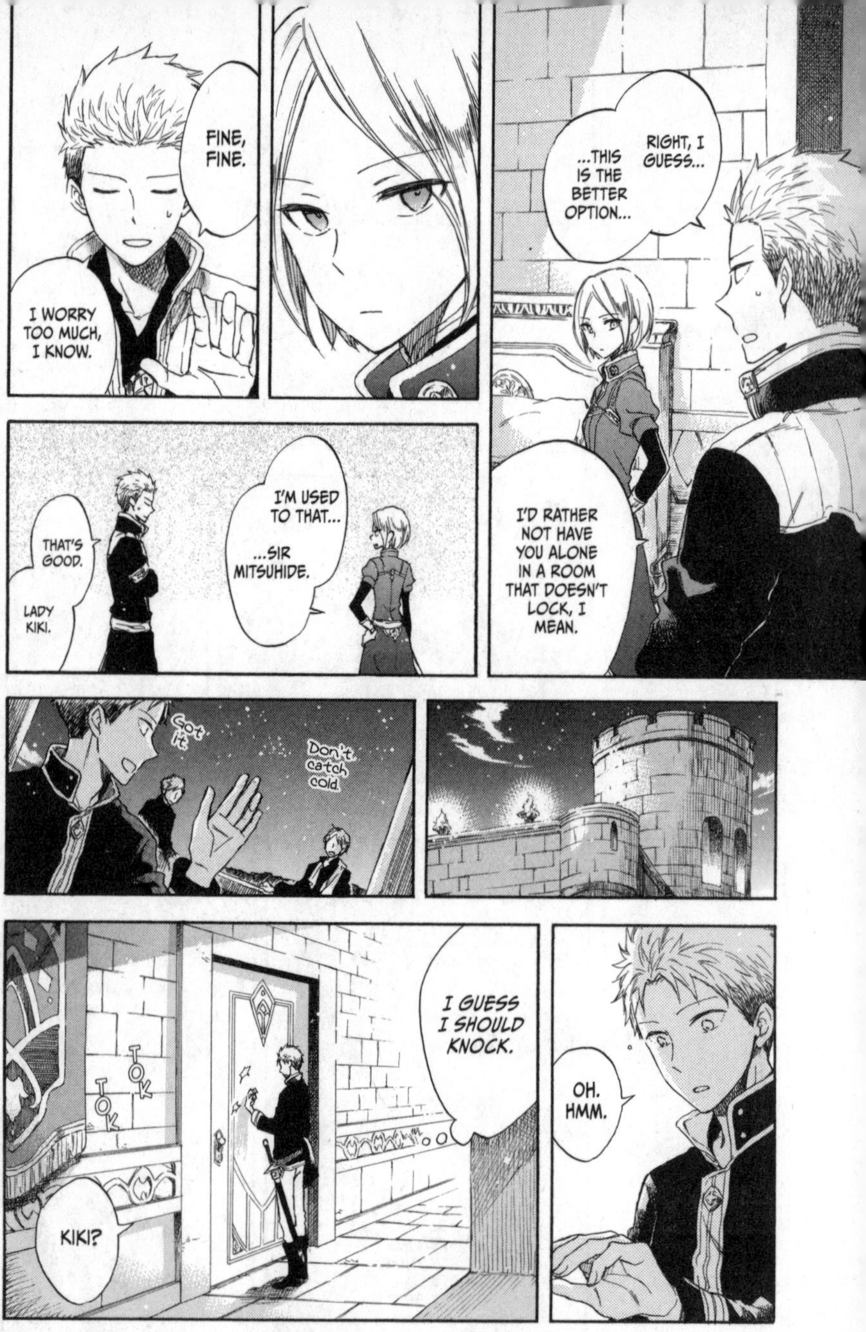
RIGHT, I GUESS... ...THIS IS THE BETTER OPTION...
I'D RATHER NOT HAVE YOU ALONE IN A ROOM THAT DOESN'T LOCK, I MEAN.
FINE, FINE.
I WORRY TOO MUCH, I KNOW.
I'M USED TO THAT...
...SIR MITSUHIDE.
THAT'S GOOD.
LADY KIKI.
Got it.
Don't catch cold.
OH. HMM.
I GUESS I SHOULD KNOCK.
TOK
TOK
KIKI?

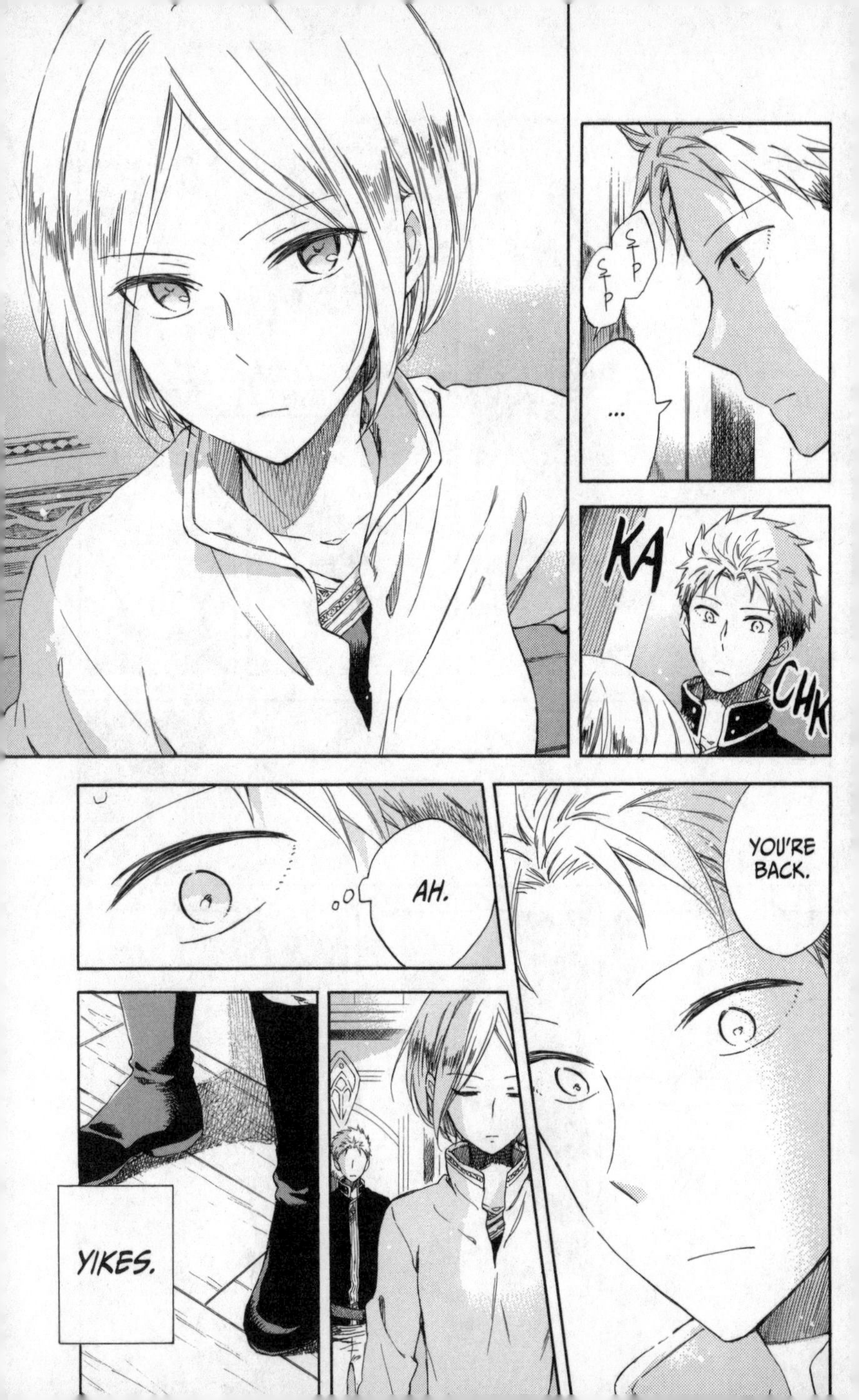
STP
STP
...
KA
CHK
YOU'RE BACK.
AH.
YIKES.

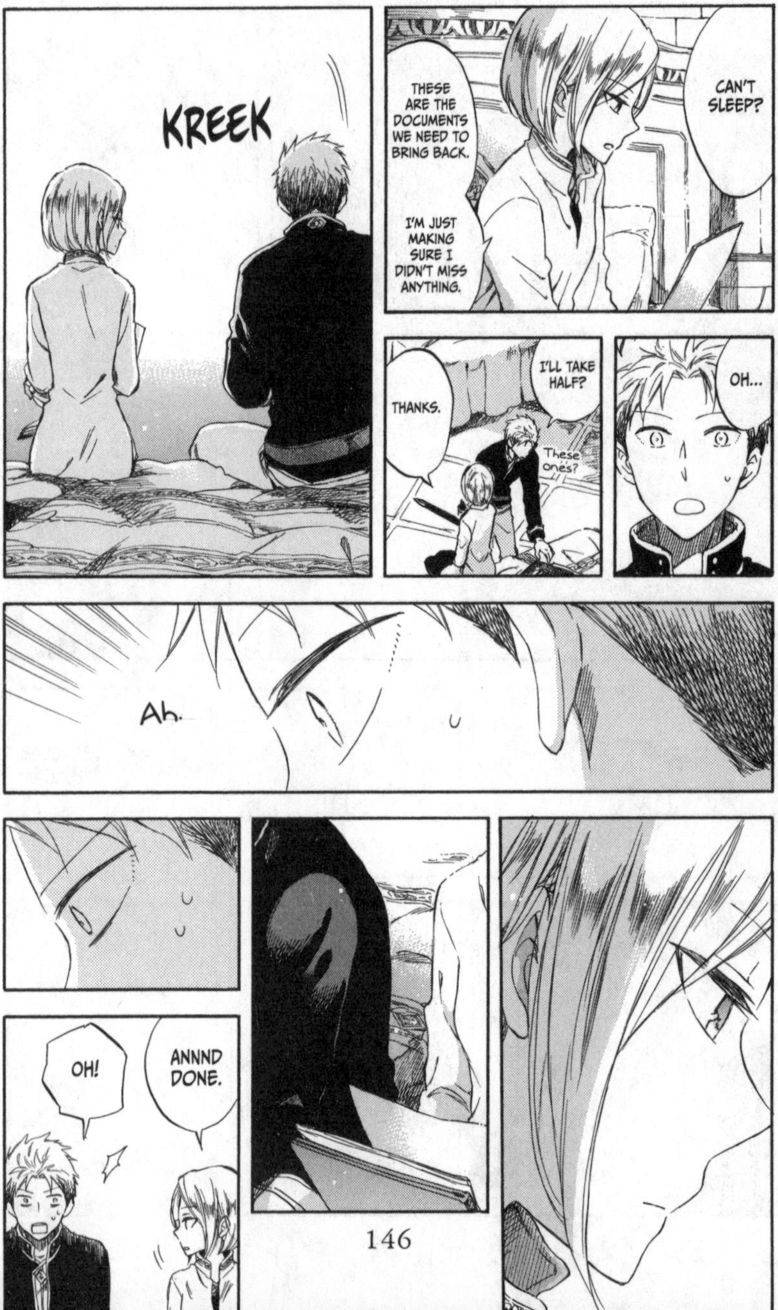
CAN'T SLEEP?
THESE ARE THE DOCUMENTS WE NEED TO BRING BACK.
I'M JUST MAKING SURE I DIDN'T MISS ANYTHING.
OH...
I'LL TAKE HALF?
These ones?
THANKS.
KREEK
Ah.
ANNND DONE.
OH!

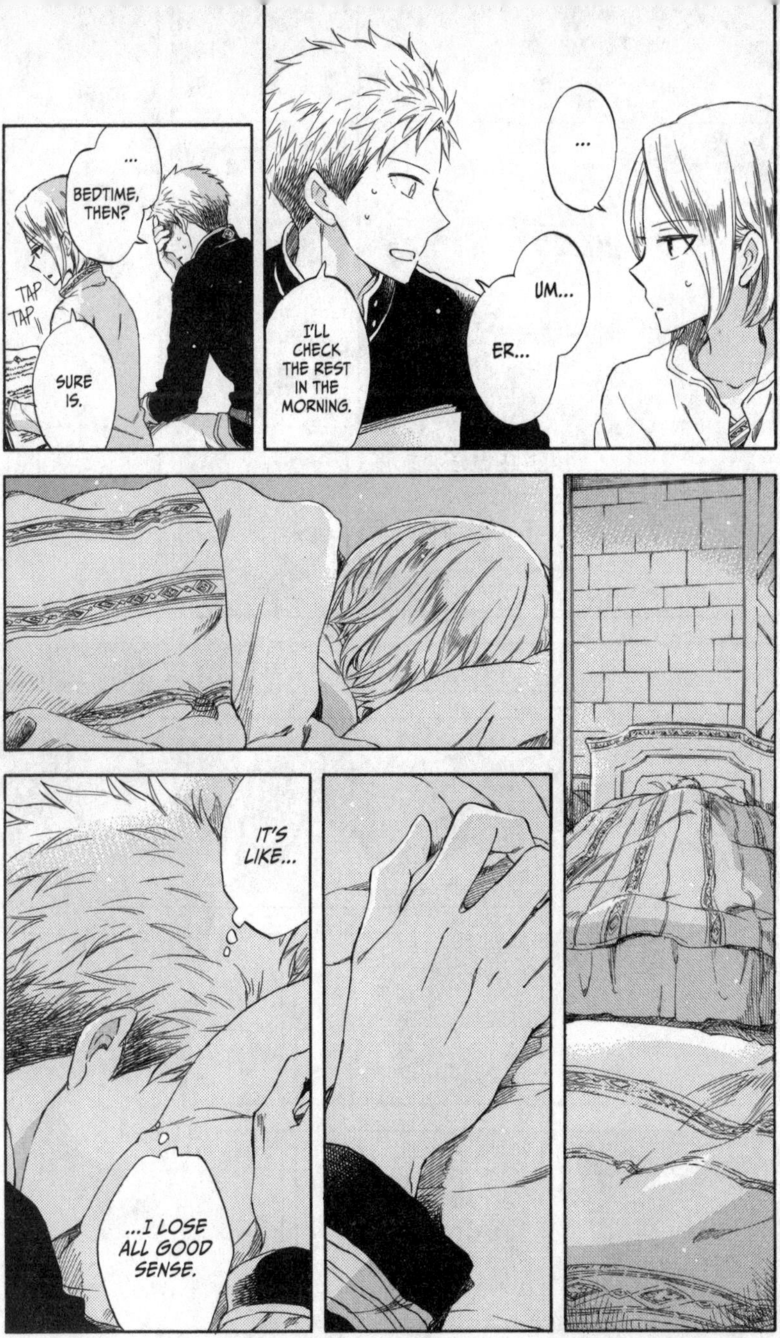
...
UM...
ER...
I'LL CHECK THE REST IN THE MORNING.
...
BEDTIME, THEN?
TAP TAP
SURE IS.
IT'S LIKE...
...I LOSE ALL GOOD SENSE.

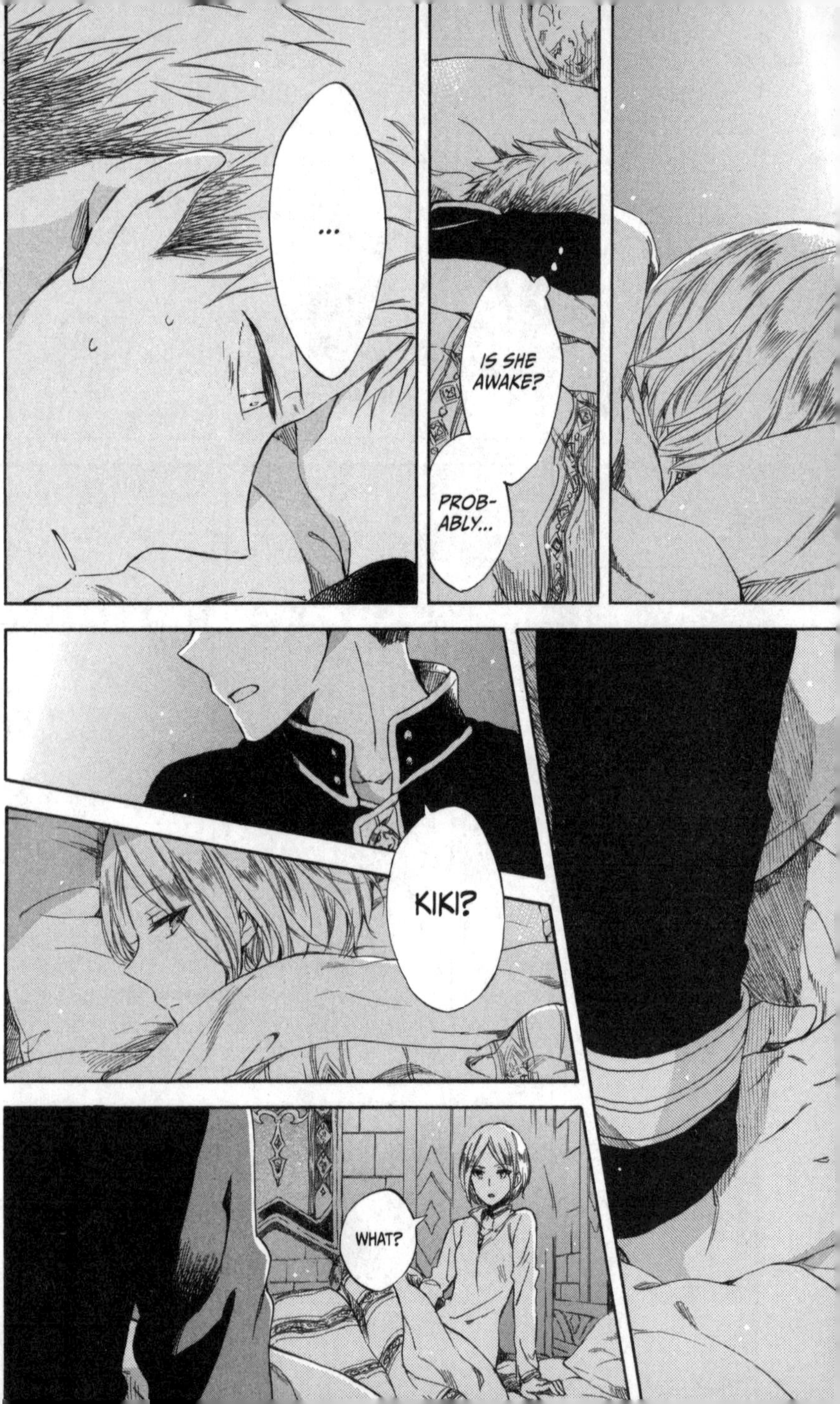
IS SHE AWAKE?
PROB-ABLY...
...
KIKI?
WHAT?

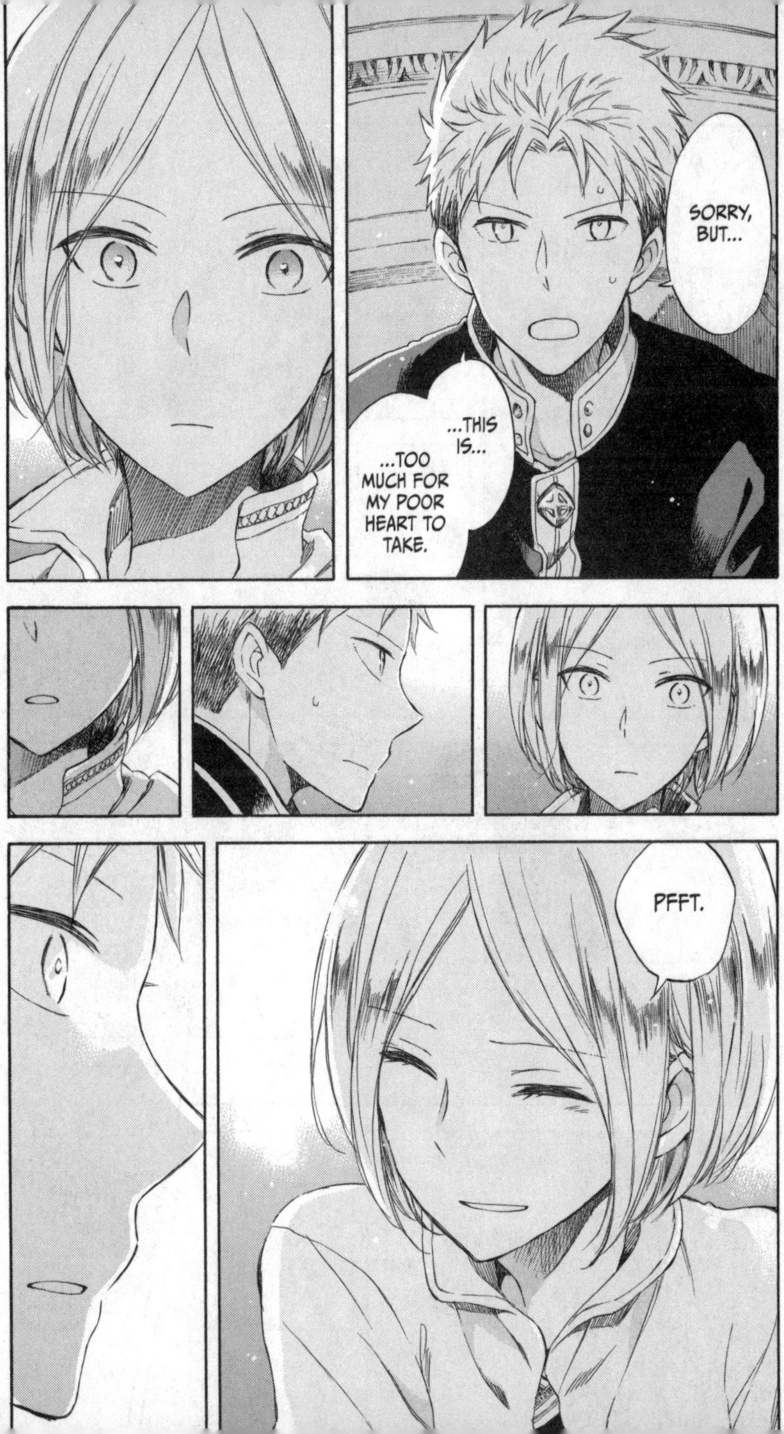
SORRY, BUT...
...THIS IS...
...TOO MUCH FOR MY POOR HEART TO TAKE.
PFFT.

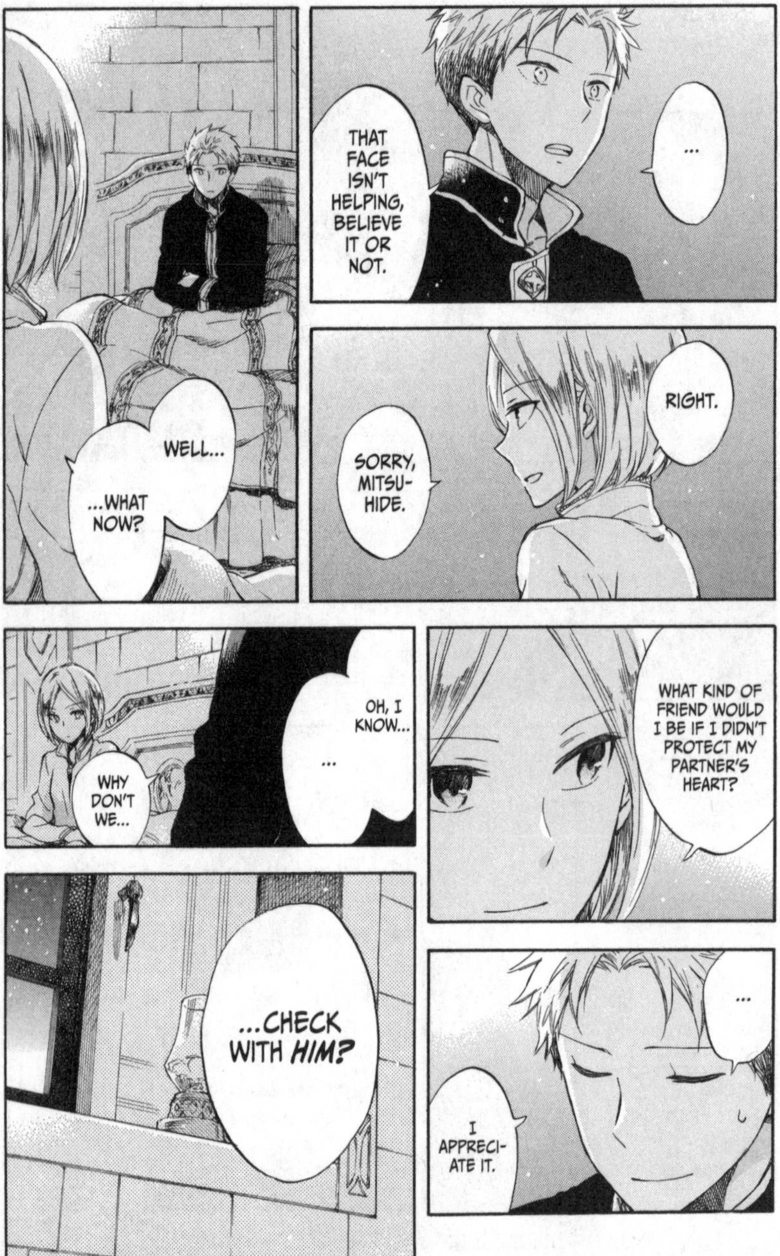
...
THAT FACE ISN'T HELPING, BELIEVE IT OR NOT.
RIGHT.
SORRY, MITSU-HIDE.
WELL...
...WHAT NOW?
WHAT KIND OF FRIEND WOULD I BE IF I DIDN'T PROTECT MY PARTNER'S HEART?
...
I APPRECI-ATE IT.
OH, I KNOW...
...
WHY DON'T WE...
...CHECK WITH *HIM?*

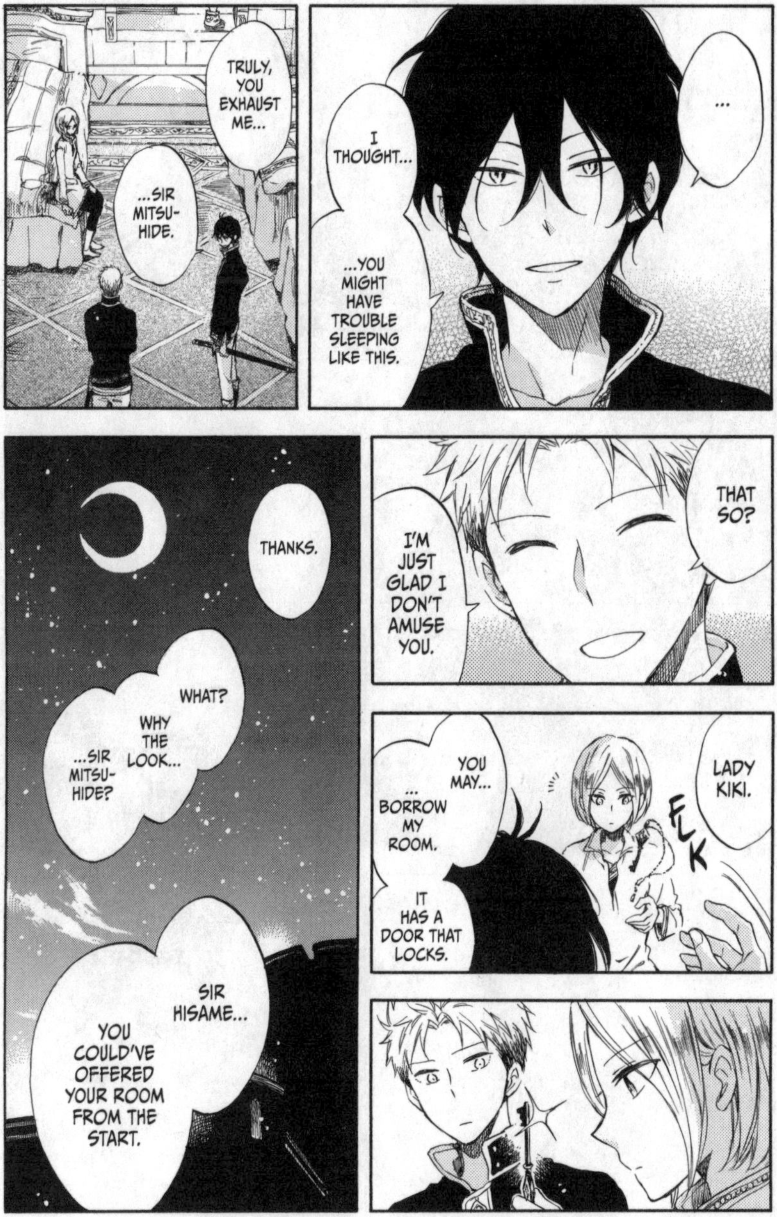
...
I THOUGHT...
...YOU MIGHT HAVE TROUBLE SLEEPING LIKE THIS.
TRULY, YOU EXHAUST ME...
...SIR MITSU-HIDE.
THAT SO?
I'M JUST GLAD I DON'T AMUSE YOU.
LADY KIKI.
FLK
YOU MAY...
... BORROW MY ROOM.
IT HAS A DOOR THAT LOCKS.
THANKS.
WHAT?
WHY THE LOOK...
...SIR MITSU-HIDE?
SIR HISAME...
YOU COULD'VE OFFERED YOUR ROOM FROM THE START.

Snow White with the Red Hair—Bonus Chapter/End

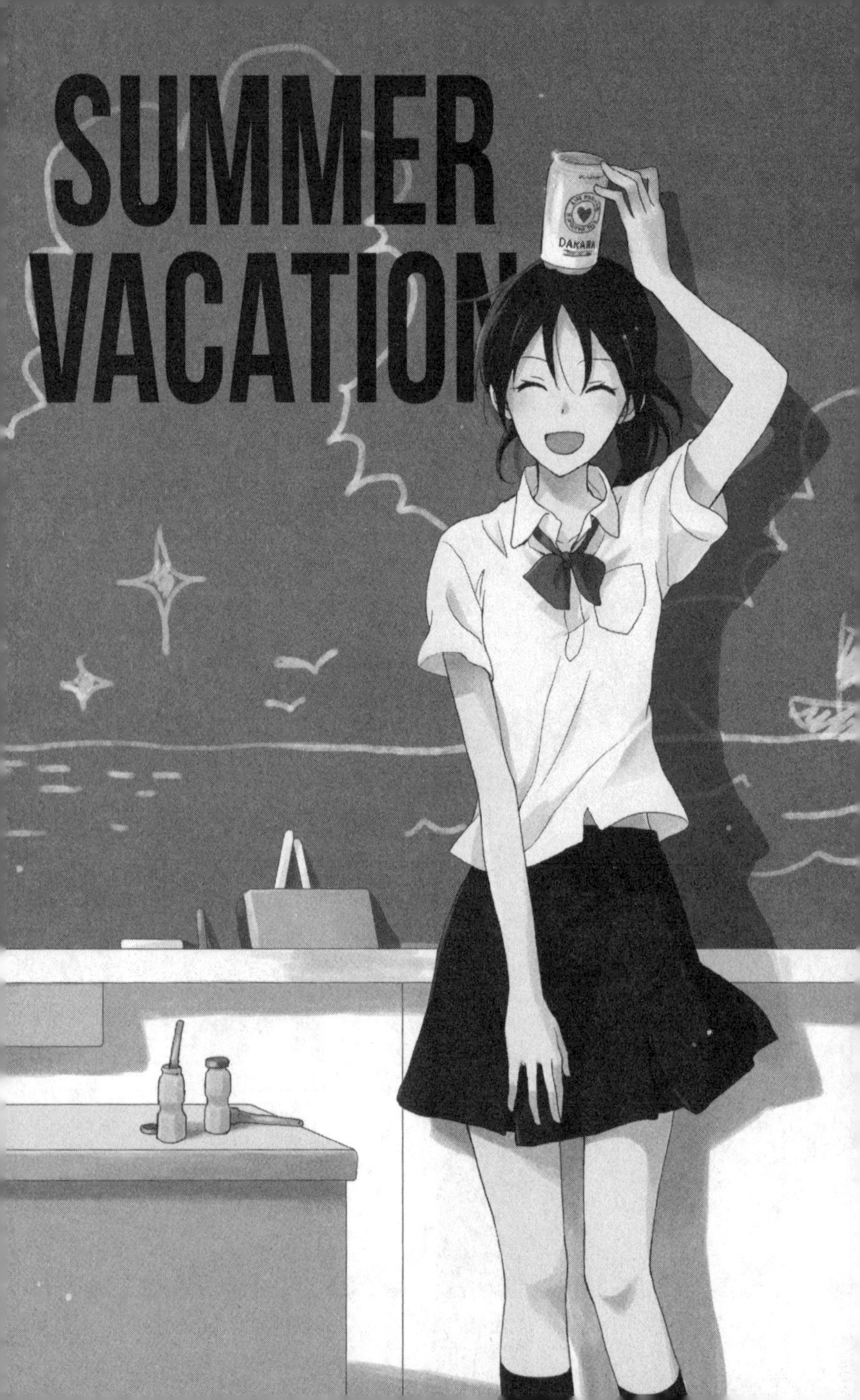
SUMMER
VACATION
DAKARA

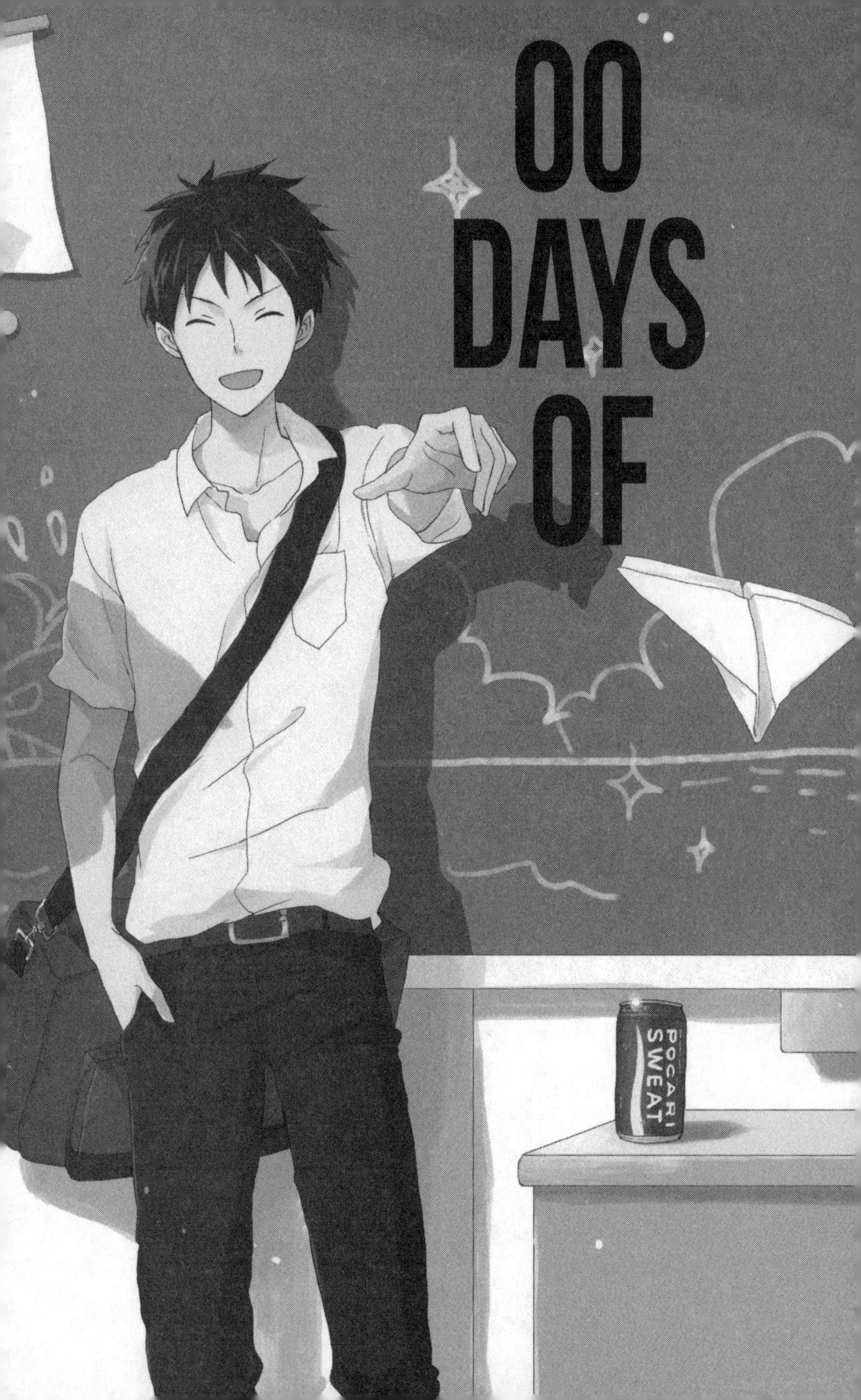
00
DAYS
OF
POCARI
SWEAT

00 DAYS OF SUMMER VACATION

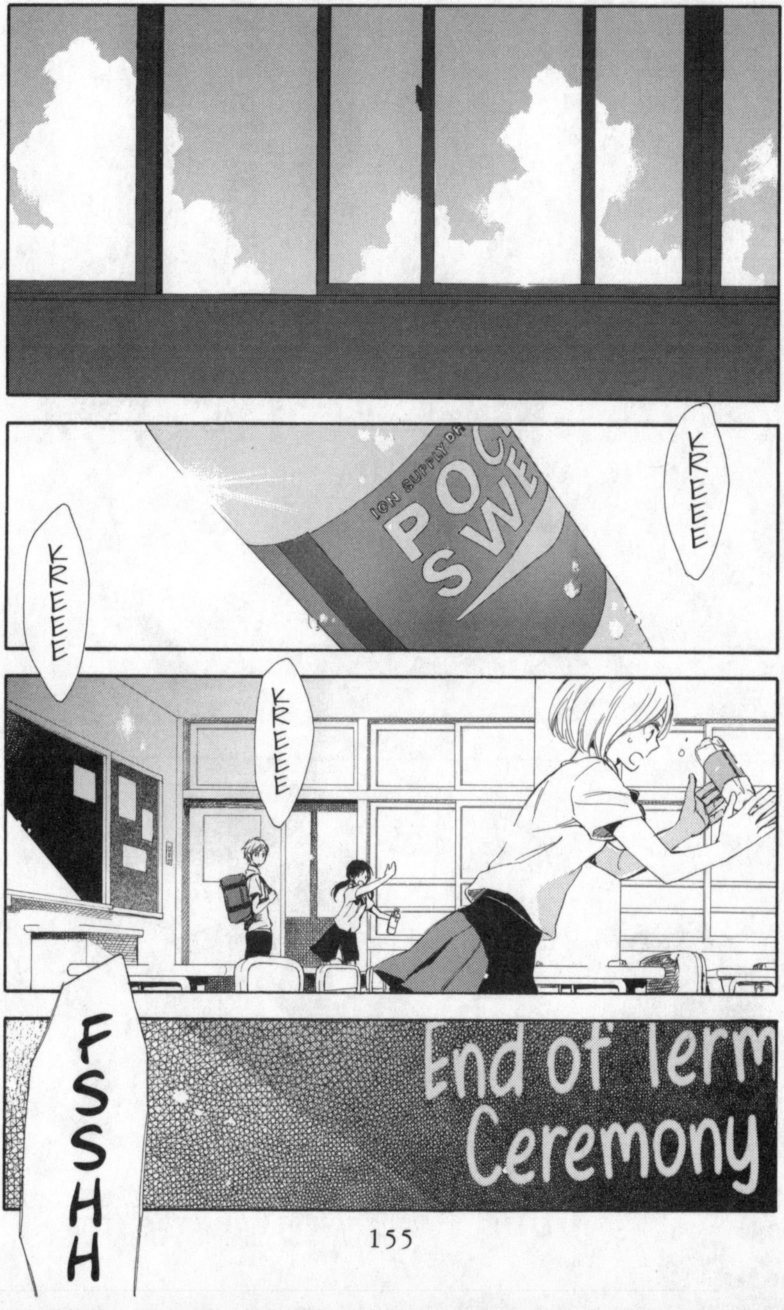
KREEE
KREEE
KREEE
End of Term Ceremony
FSSH

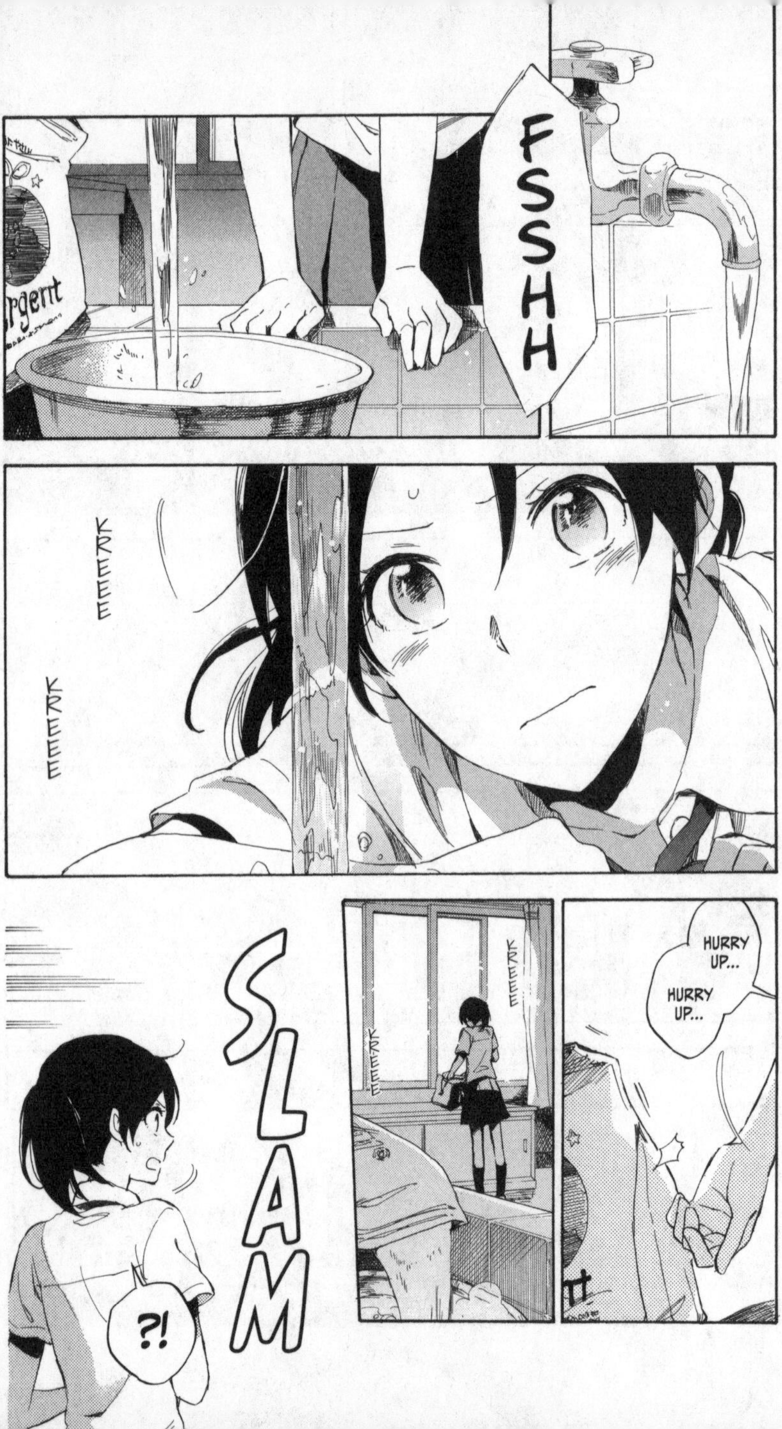
FSSH
KREEE
KREEE
HURRY UP...
HURRY UP...
KREEE
KREEE
SLAM
?!

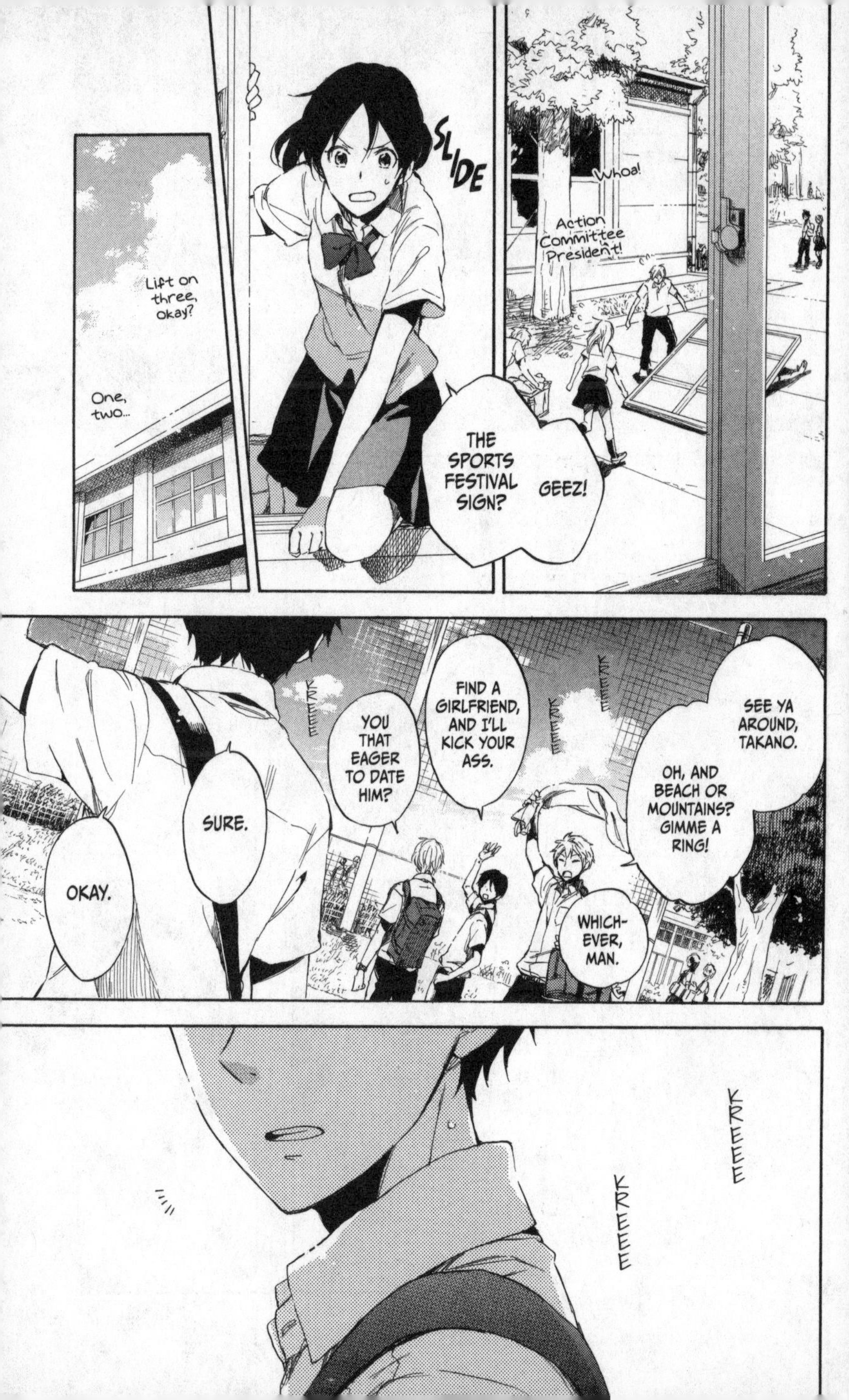
Whoa!
Action Committee President!
GEEZ!
THE SPORTS FESTIVAL SIGN?
SLIDE
Lift on three, okay?
One, two...
SEE YA AROUND, TAKANO.
OH, AND BEACH OR MOUNTAINS? GIMME A RING!
WHICH-EVER, MAN.
KREEE
KREEE
FIND A GIRLFRIEND, AND I'LL KICK YOUR ASS.
YOU THAT EAGER TO DATE HIM?
KREEE
SURE.
OKAY.
KREEE
KREEE

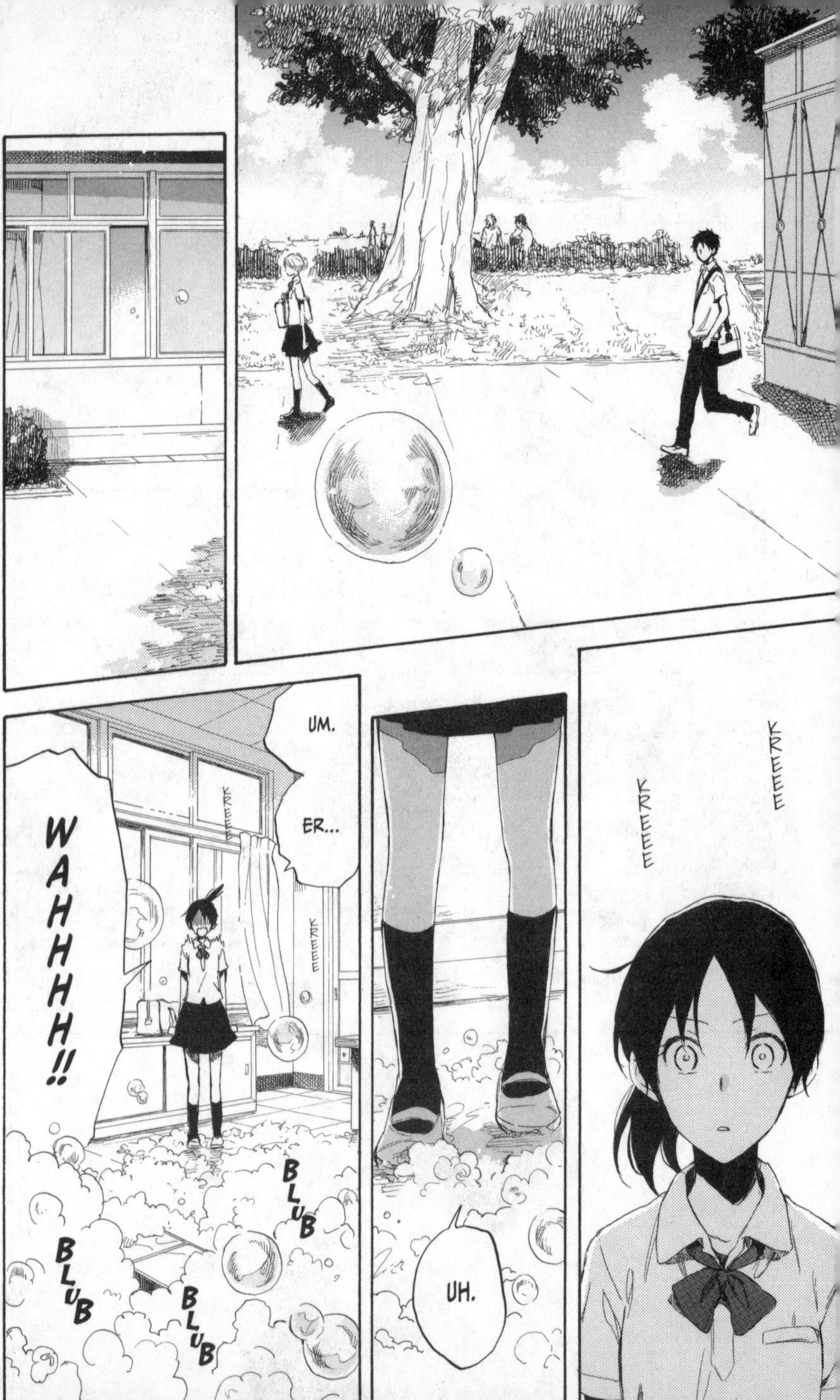
KREEE
KREEE
UH.
UM.
ER...
KREE
KREE
WAHHHH!!
BLUB
BLUB
BLUB

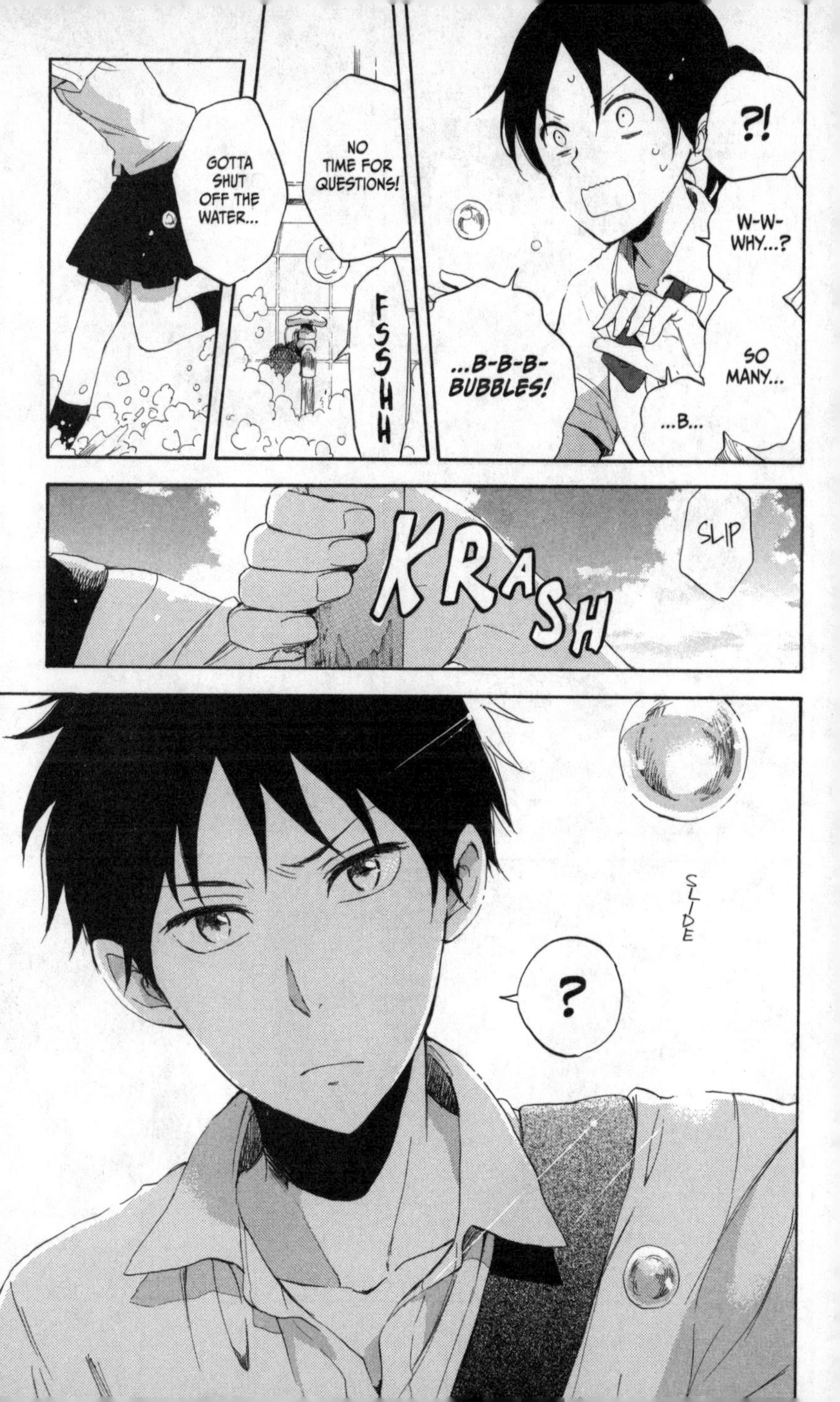
?!
W-W-WHY...?
SO MANY...
...B...
...B-B-B-BUBBLES!
NO TIME FOR QUESTIONS!
FSSHH
GOTTA SHUT OFF THE WATER...
SLIP
KRASH
SLIDE
?

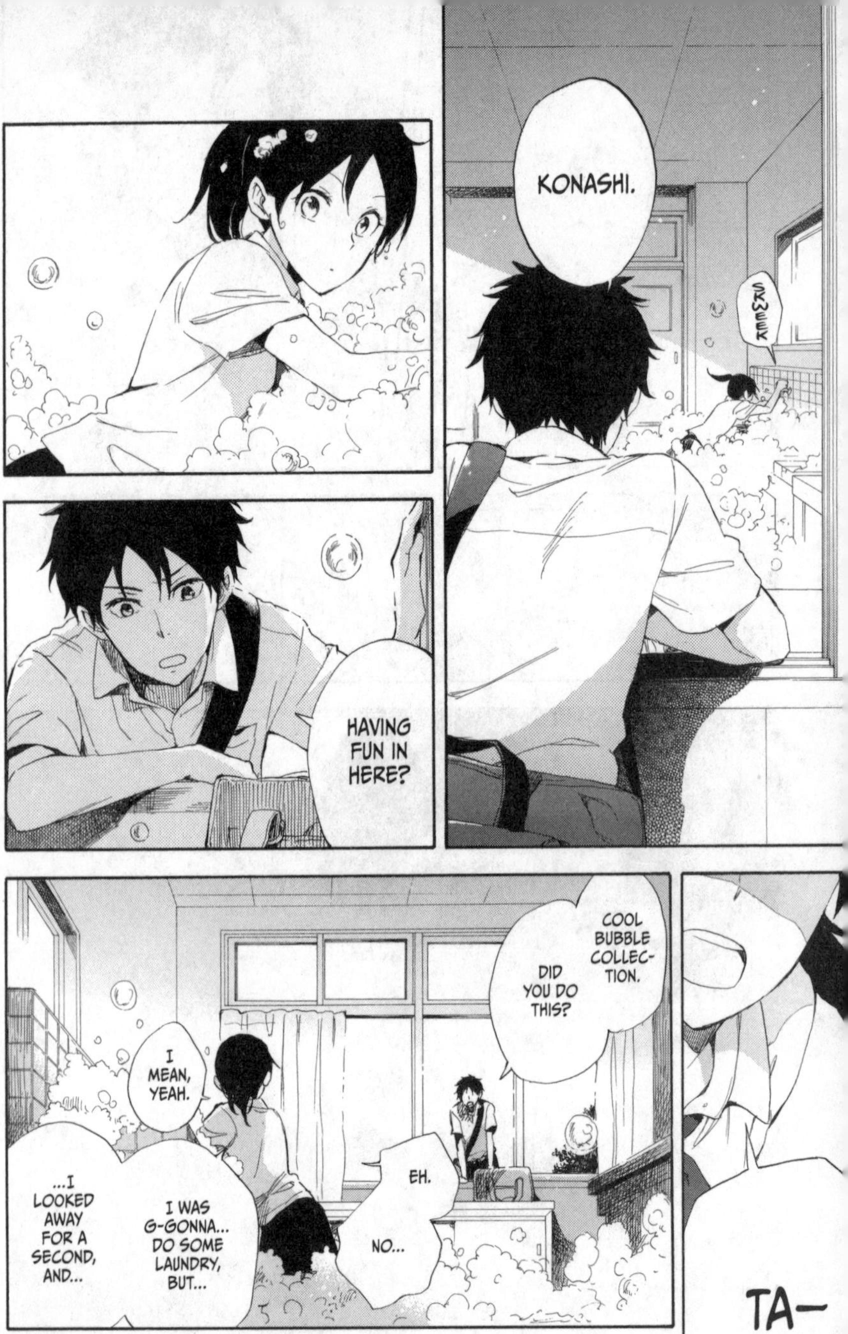
KONASHI.
SKWEEK
HAVING FUN IN HERE?
TA—
COOL BUBBLE COLLECTION.
DID YOU DO THIS?
EH.
NO...
I MEAN, YEAH.
I WAS G-GONNA... DO SOME LAUNDRY, BUT...
...I LOOKED AWAY FOR A SECOND, AND...

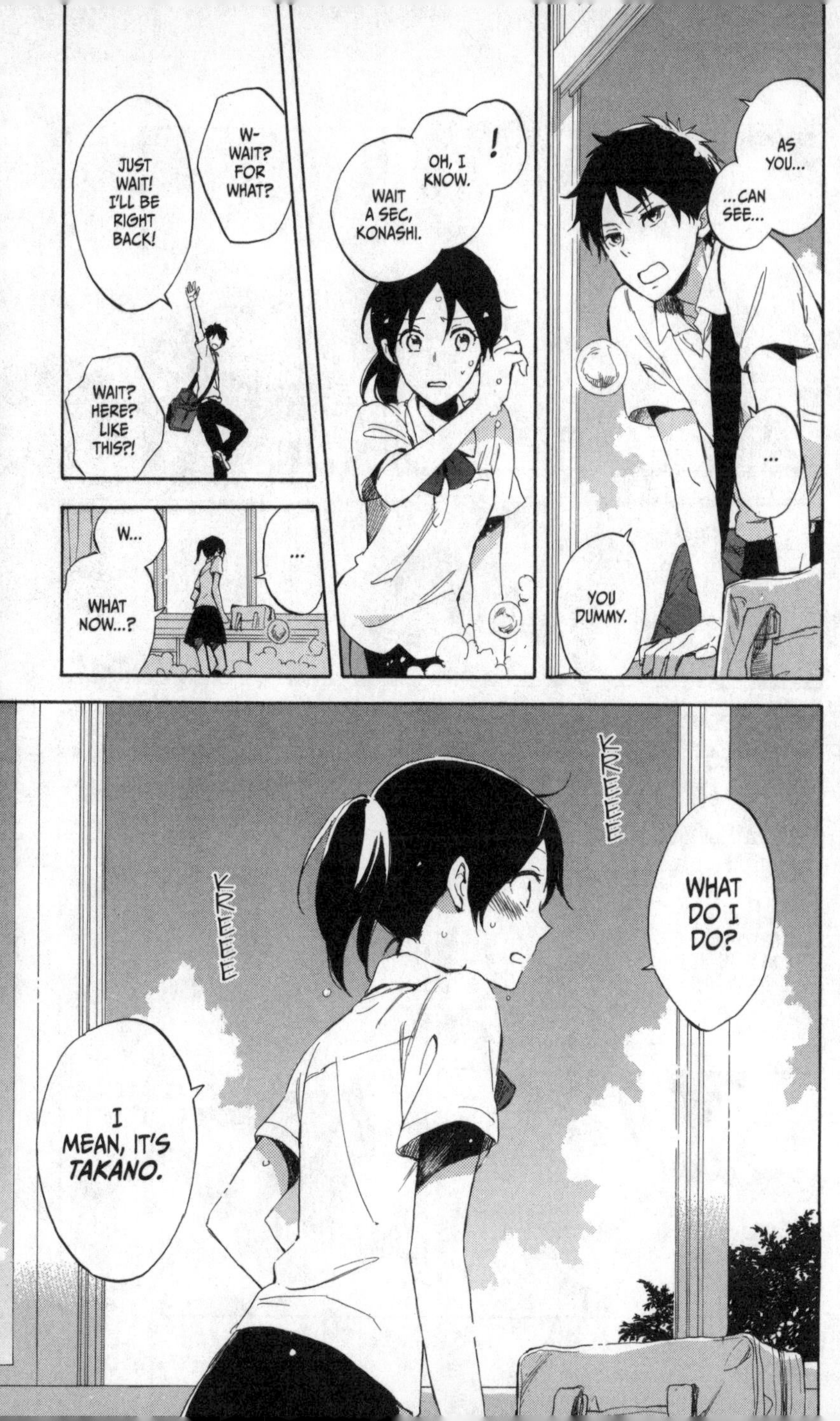
AS YOU...
...CAN SEE...
...
YOU DUMMY.
!
OH, I KNOW.
WAIT A SEC, KONASHI.
W-WAIT? FOR WHAT?
JUST WAIT! I'LL BE RIGHT BACK!
WAIT? HERE? LIKE THIS?!
...
W... WHAT NOW...?
KREEE
KREEE
WHAT DO I DO?
I MEAN, IT'S *TAKANO.*

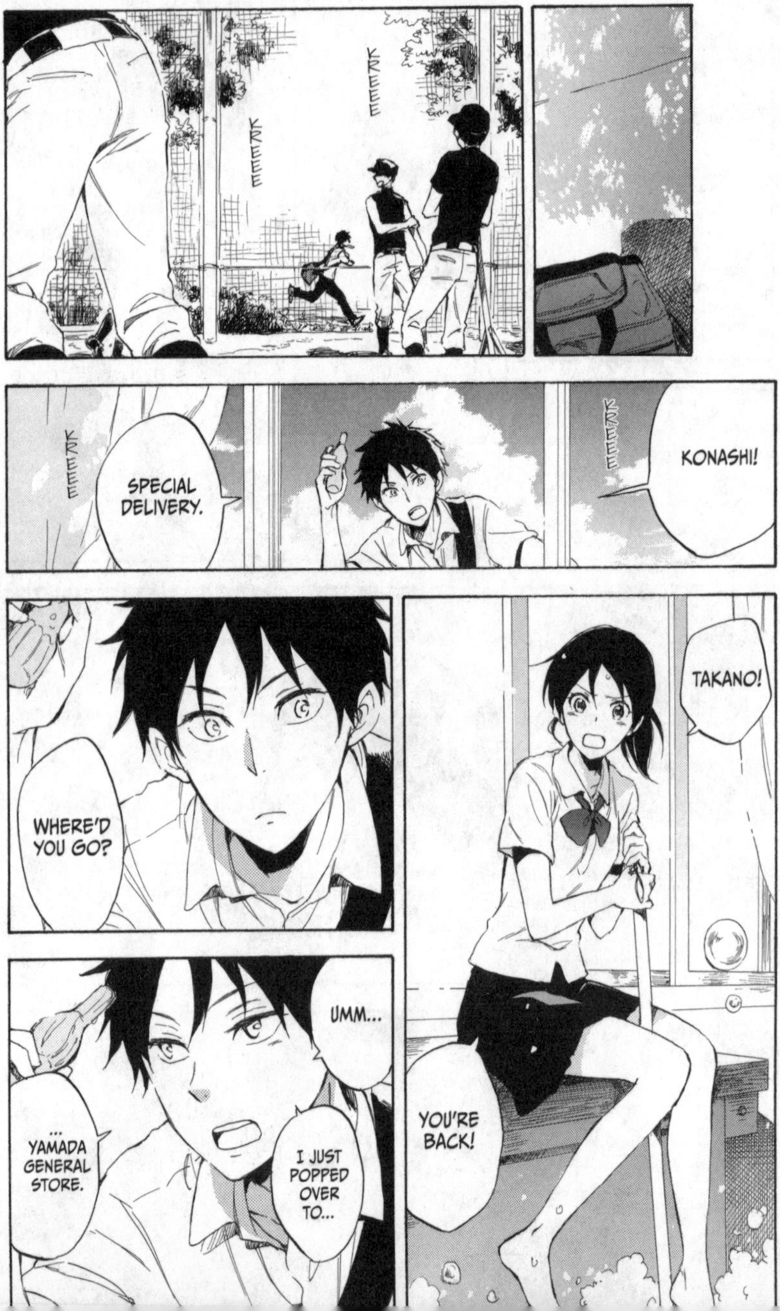
KREEE
KREEE
KONASHI!
KREEE
SPECIAL DELIVERY.
KREEE
TAKANO!
YOU'RE BACK!
WHERE'D YOU GO?
UMM...
I JUST POPPED OVER TO...
... YAMADA GENERAL STORE.

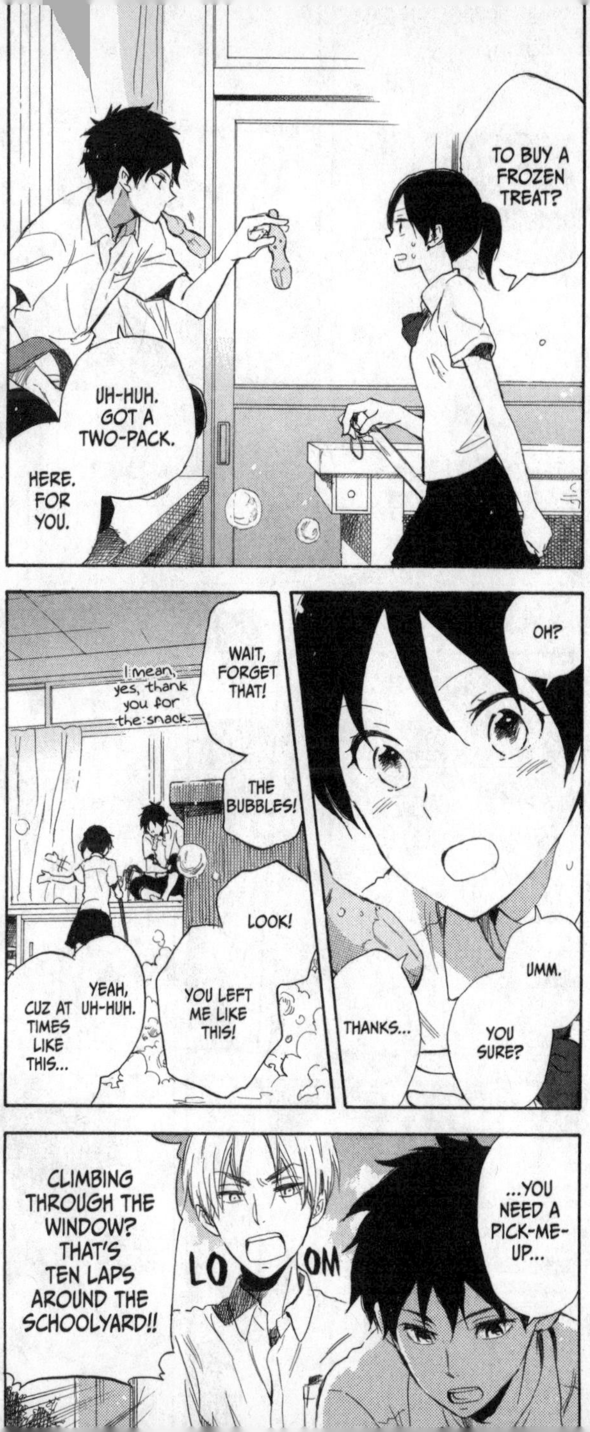
TO BUY A FROZEN TREAT?
UH-HUH. GOT A TWO-PACK.
HERE. FOR YOU.
OH?
UMM.
YOU SURE?
THANKS...
WAIT, FORGET THAT!
I mean, yes, thank you for the snack.
THE BUBBLES!
LOOK!
YOU LEFT ME LIKE THIS!
YEAH, UH-HUH.
CUZ AT TIMES LIKE THIS...
...YOU NEED A PICK-ME-UP...
CLIMBING THROUGH THE WINDOW? THAT'S TEN LAPS AROUND THE SCHOOLYARD!!
LO OM

7

CHAPTER TALK

Chapter 65

Short chapter, but they got their reunion.

Hooray!

There's something so heartwarming about having all five of them together. That's the vibe in chapter 65.

I think Kiki is prone to nonsense at times like that, and lo and behold...

Zen and Mitsuhide fell for it, hook, line and sinker!

And now, onward to the soiree in volume 15!

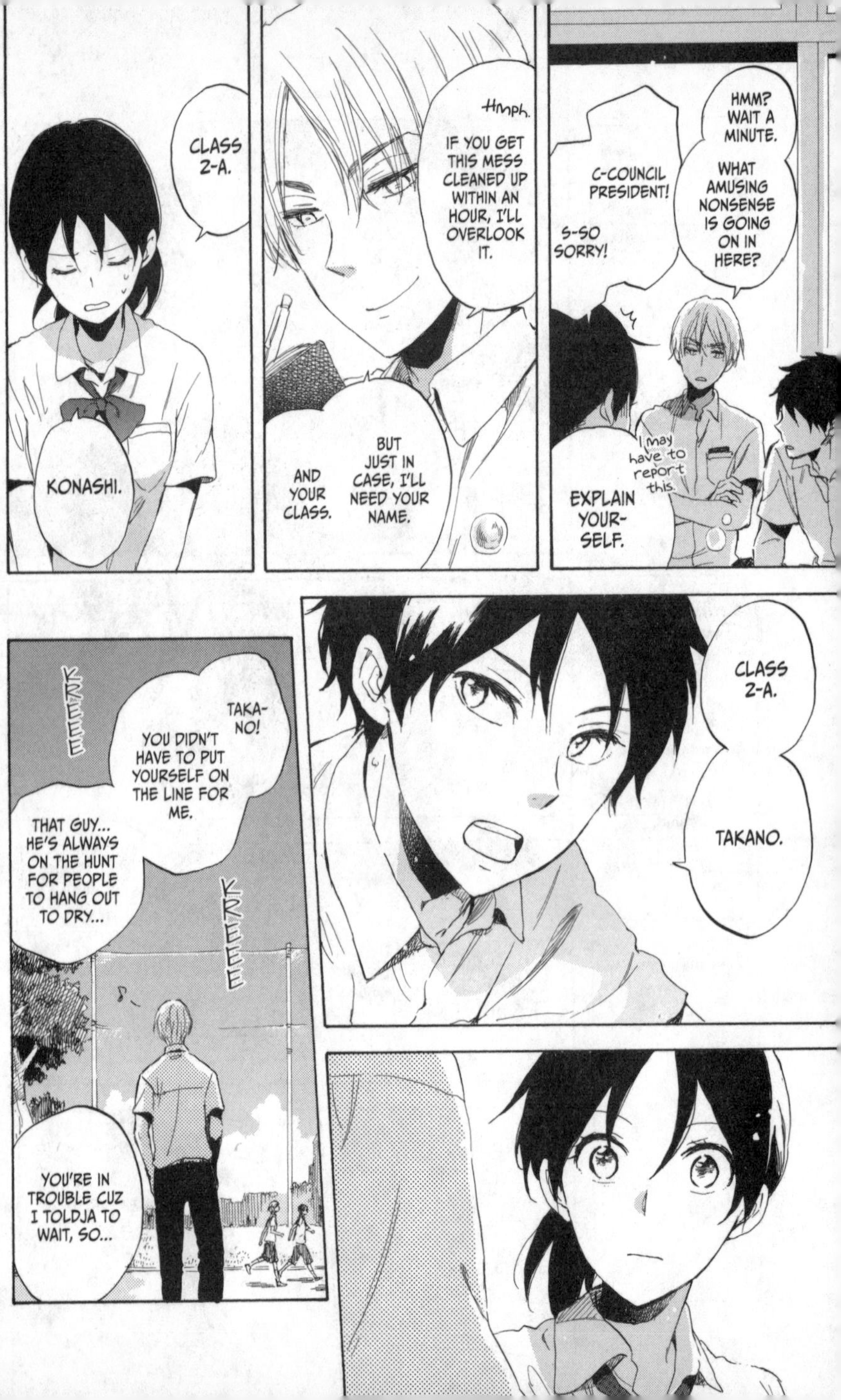
HMM? WAIT A MINUTE.
WHAT AMUSING NONSENSE IS GOING ON IN HERE?
C-COUNCIL PRESIDENT!
S-SO SORRY!
I may have to report this.
EXPLAIN YOURSELF.
Hmph.
IF YOU GET THIS MESS CLEANED UP WITHIN AN HOUR, I'LL OVERLOOK IT.
BUT JUST IN CASE, I'LL NEED YOUR NAME.
AND YOUR CLASS.
CLASS 2-A.
KONASHI.
CLASS 2-A.
TAKANO.
KREEE
TAKA-NO!
YOU DIDN'T HAVE TO PUT YOURSELF ON THE LINE FOR ME.
THAT GUY... HE'S ALWAYS ON THE HUNT FOR PEOPLE TO HANG OUT TO DRY...
KREEE
YOU'RE IN TROUBLE CUZ I TOLDJA TO WAIT, SO...

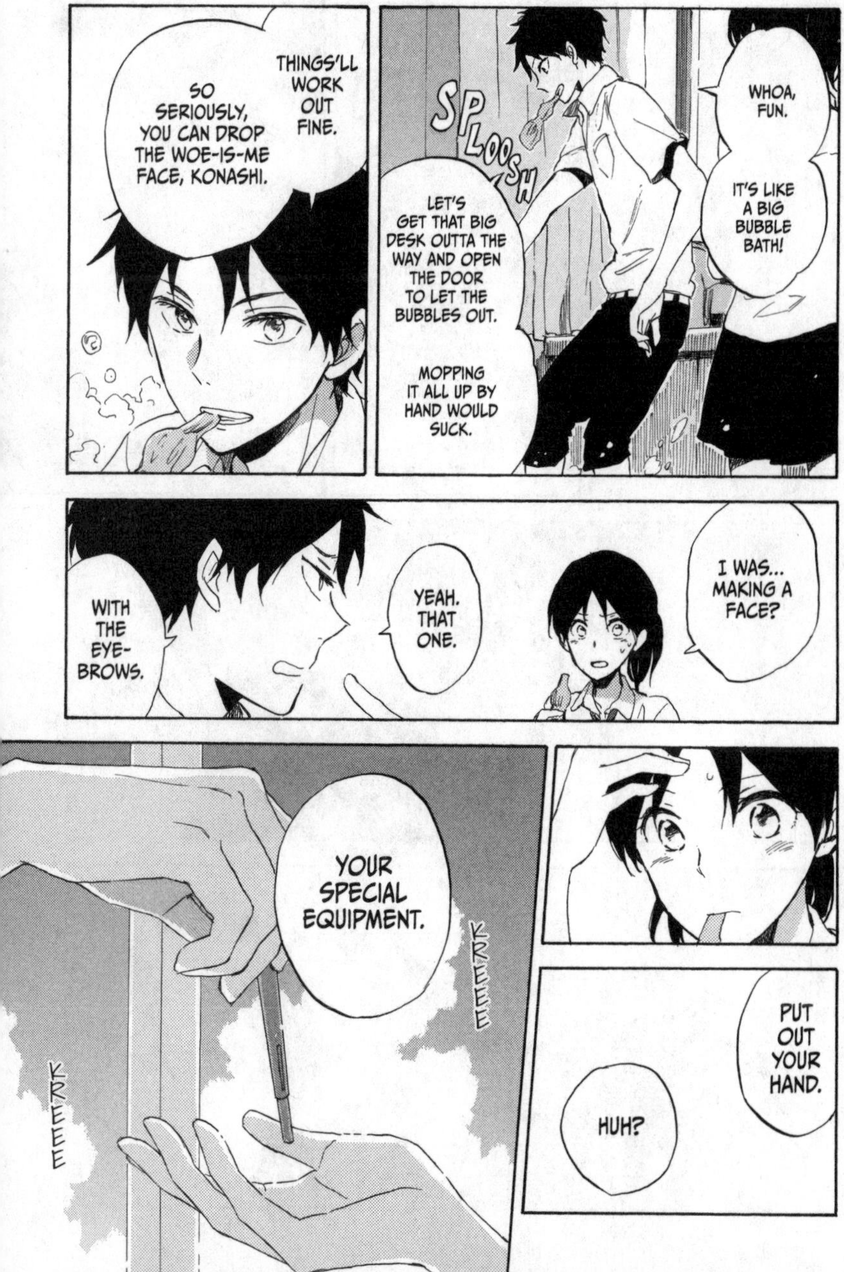
WHOA, FUN.
SPLOOSH
IT'S LIKE A BIG BUBBLE BATH!
LET'S GET THAT BIG DESK OUTTA THE WAY AND OPEN THE DOOR TO LET THE BUBBLES OUT.
MOPPING IT ALL UP BY HAND WOULD SUCK.
THINGS'LL WORK OUT FINE.
SO SERIOUSLY, YOU CAN DROP THE WOE-IS-ME FACE, KONASHI.
I WAS... MAKING A FACE?
YEAH. THAT ONE.
WITH THE EYE-BROWS.
PUT OUT YOUR HAND.
HUH?
KREEE
YOUR SPECIAL EQUIPMENT.
KREEE

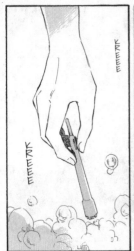

KREEE

KREEE

IS THIS FOR BLOWING BUBBLES?

I THOUGHT WE COULD USE 'EM, GIVEN ALL THE BUBBLES, Y'KNOW?

LIKE, AS WE CLEAN UP.

KREEE

KREEE

KREEE

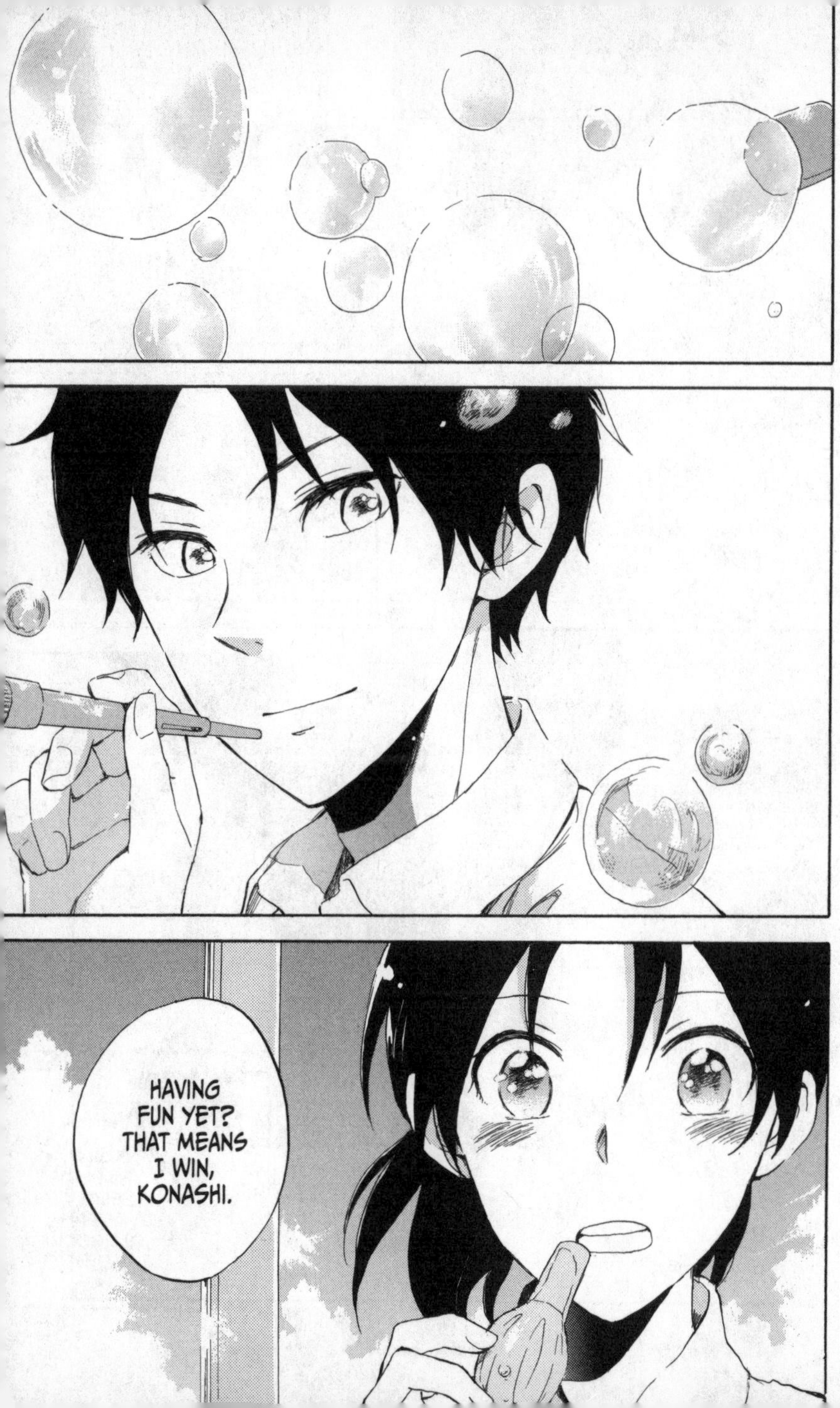
HAVING FUN YET? THAT MEANS I WIN, KONASHI.

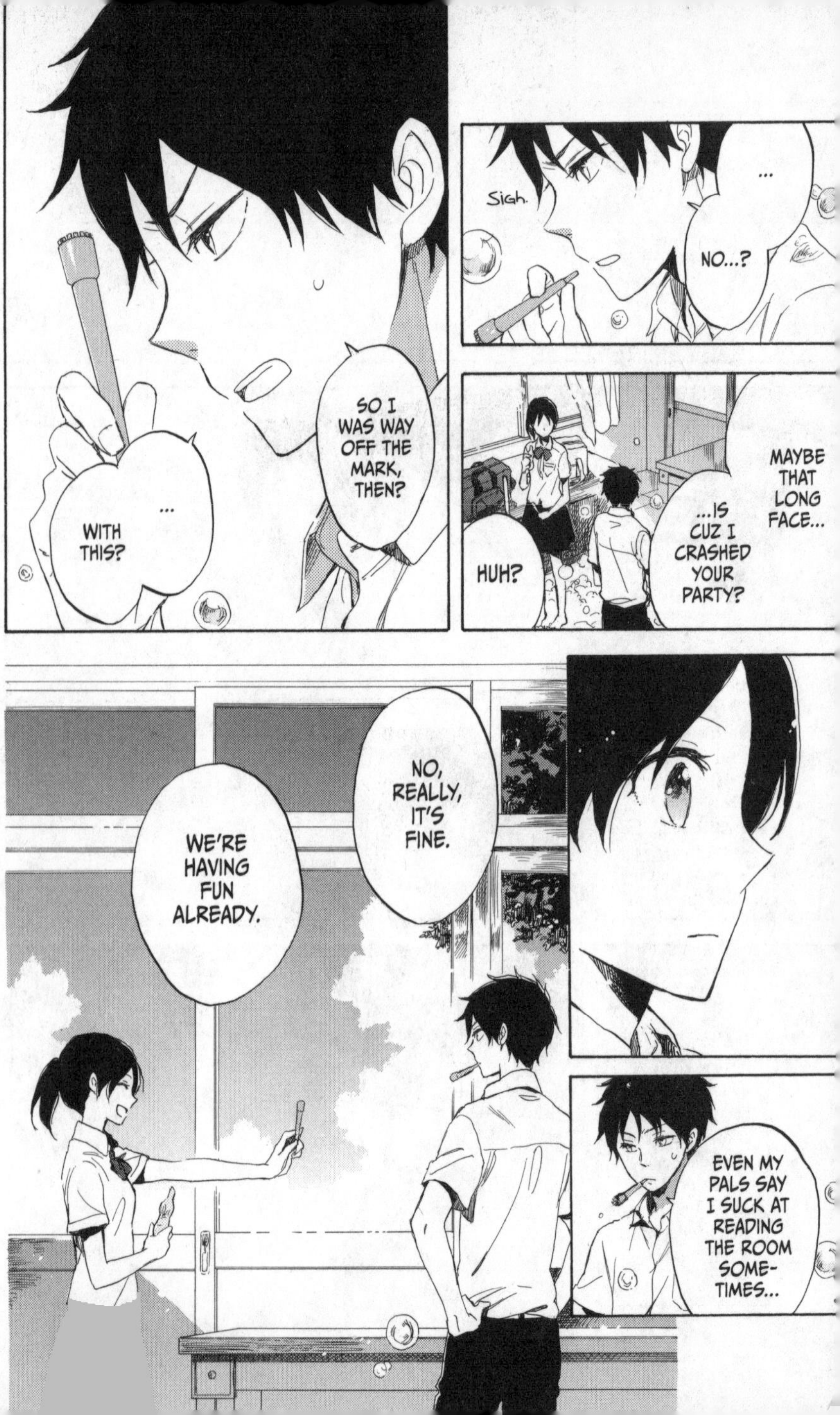
...
NO...?
Sigh.
MAYBE THAT LONG FACE...
...IS CUZ I CRASHED YOUR PARTY?
HUH?
SO I WAS WAY OFF THE MARK, THEN?
... WITH THIS?
EVEN MY PALS SAY I SUCK AT READING THE ROOM SOME-TIMES...
NO, REALLY, IT'S FINE.
WE'RE HAVING FUN ALREADY.

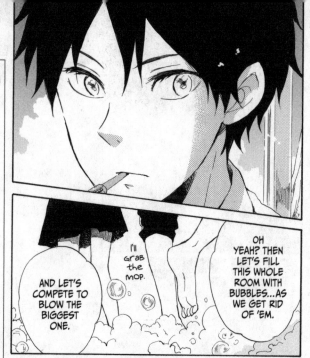

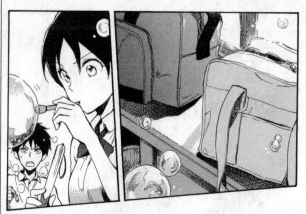

OH YEAH? THEN LET'S FILL THIS WHOLE ROOM WITH BUBBLES...AS WE GET RID OF 'EM.
I'll grab the mop.
AND LET'S COMPETE TO BLOW THE BIGGEST ONE.

8

MITSUHIDE'S TRICKY NIGHT

↑ Let's call that the subtitle.

I made Mitsuhide the star of this bonus chapter for a very specific reason (hint: the character popularity poll).

At first, the plot was just about Mitsuhide's relaxing day off, but should a bonus chapter really be that easygoing? I showed it to my sister, and she said, "Yikes! This is so boring!" So I started over from scratch, and this was the result.

I'm glad my current editor liked it!

Characters in *Snow White* are constantly cutting their hair or letting it grow, so maybe Mitsuhide should also grow his out...? Just hang in there for another two years.

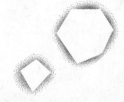

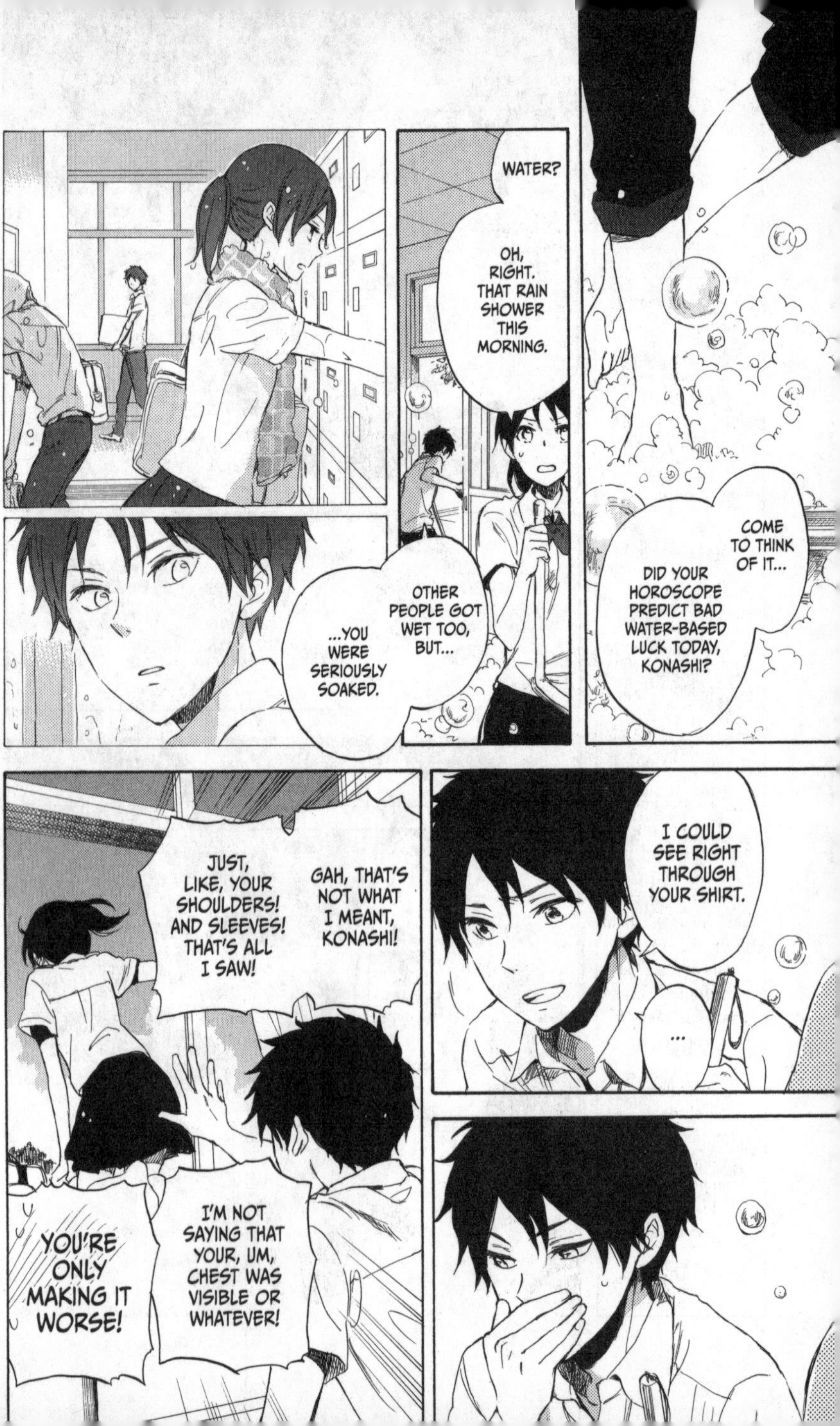
COME TO THINK OF IT...
DID YOUR HOROSCOPE PREDICT BAD WATER-BASED LUCK TODAY, KONASHI?
WATER?
OH, RIGHT. THAT RAIN SHOWER THIS MORNING.
OTHER PEOPLE GOT WET TOO, BUT...
...YOU WERE SERIOUSLY SOAKED.
I COULD SEE RIGHT THROUGH YOUR SHIRT.
...
GAH, THAT'S NOT WHAT I MEANT, KONASHI!
JUST, LIKE, YOUR SHOULDERS! AND SLEEVES! THAT'S ALL I SAW!
I'M NOT SAYING THAT YOUR, UM, CHEST WAS VISIBLE OR WHATEVER!
YOU'RE ONLY MAKING IT WORSE!

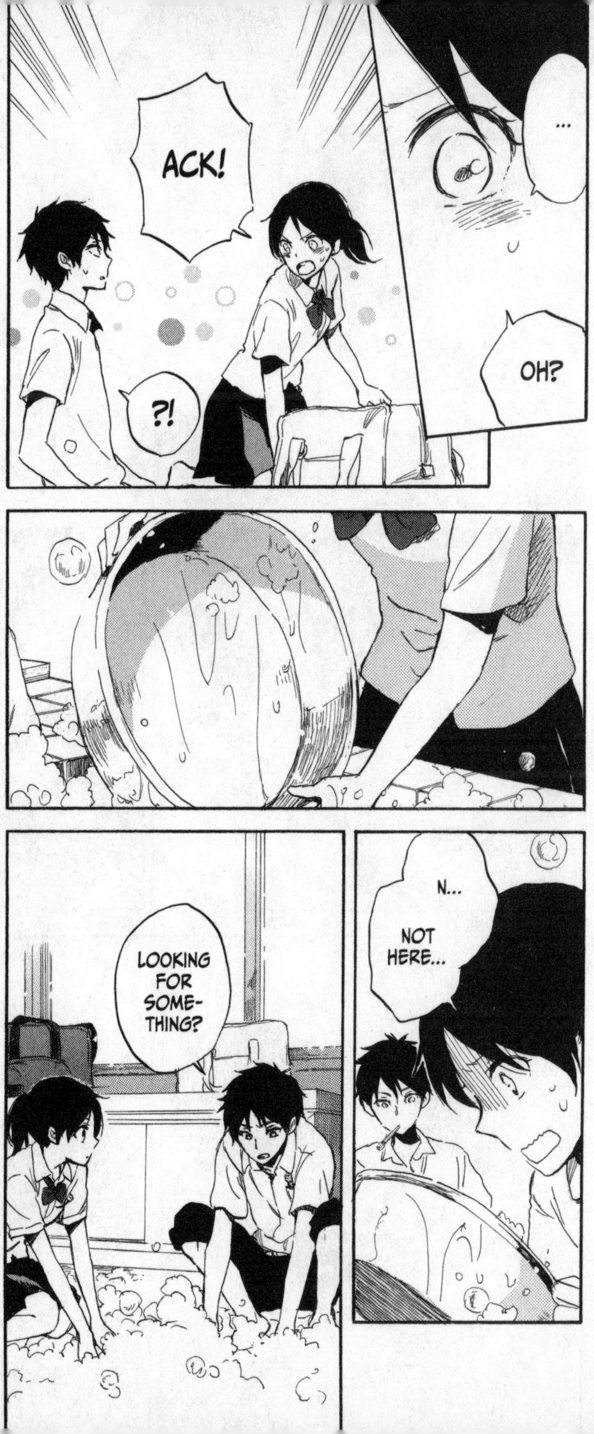
...
OH?
ACK!
?!
N...
NOT HERE...
LOOKING FOR SOME-THING?

9

*OO DAYS OF SUMMER VACATION*

This one-shot was for a special spring edition of *LaLa* featuring tales of blossoming youth. It had been a while since I had a story with a student protagonist, so this was a lot of fun.

Plus, it's summer! And the springtime of youth! And summer! Summer!

As I drew this one, I kept thinking about how great it is to look up at blue skies.

Pay attention to Takano's eyebrows. Do I like eyebrows, you might wonder? I usually don't focus on them much! But Takano's eyebrows are an exception. This was a fun story to work on.

Attention, all students. Your homework assignment for summer vacation is...to confess to your crush.

I like somen noodles.

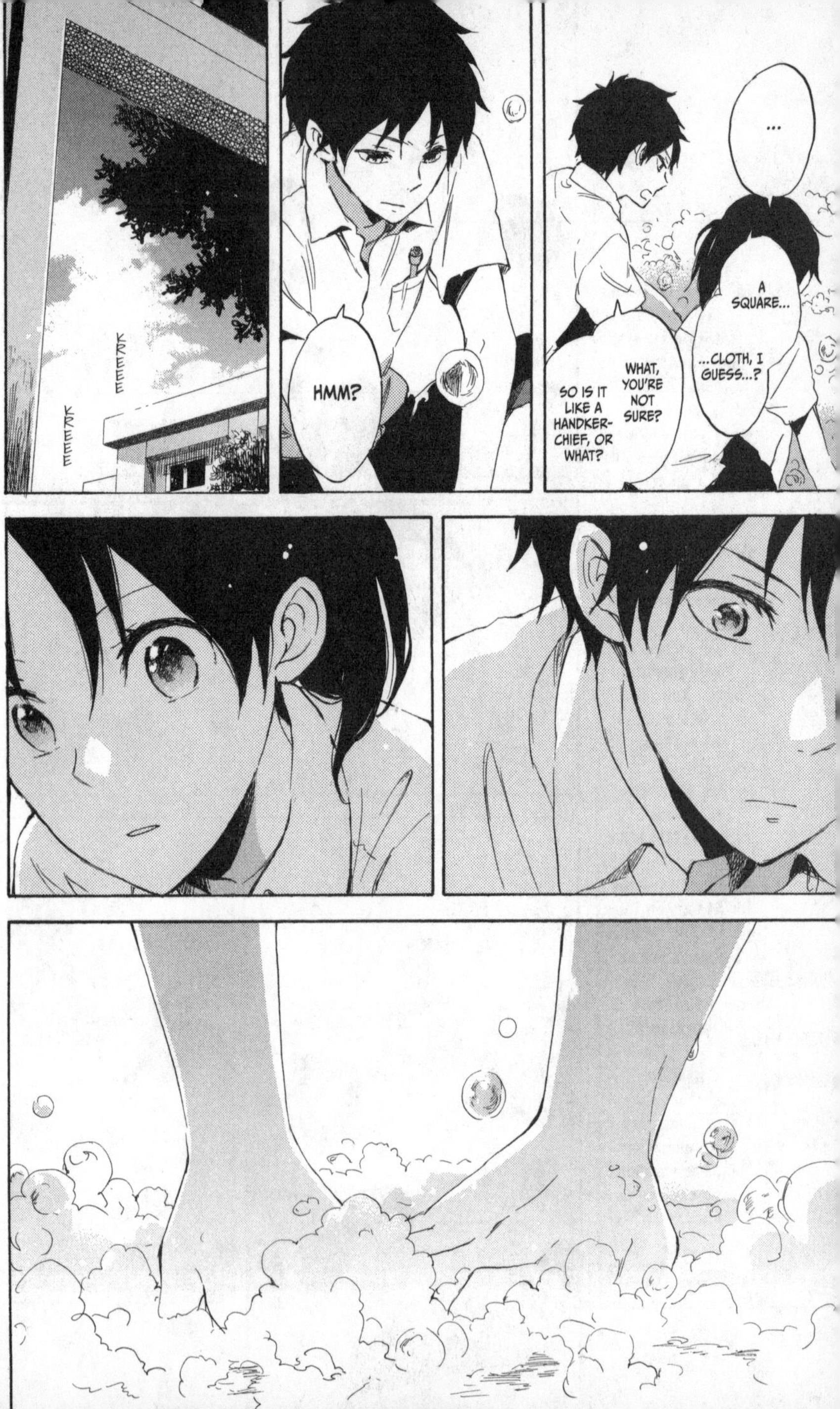
...
A SQUARE...
...CLOTH, I GUESS...?
WHAT, YOU'RE NOT SURE?
SO IS IT LIKE A HANDKERCHIEF, OR WHAT?
HMM?
KREEE
KREEE

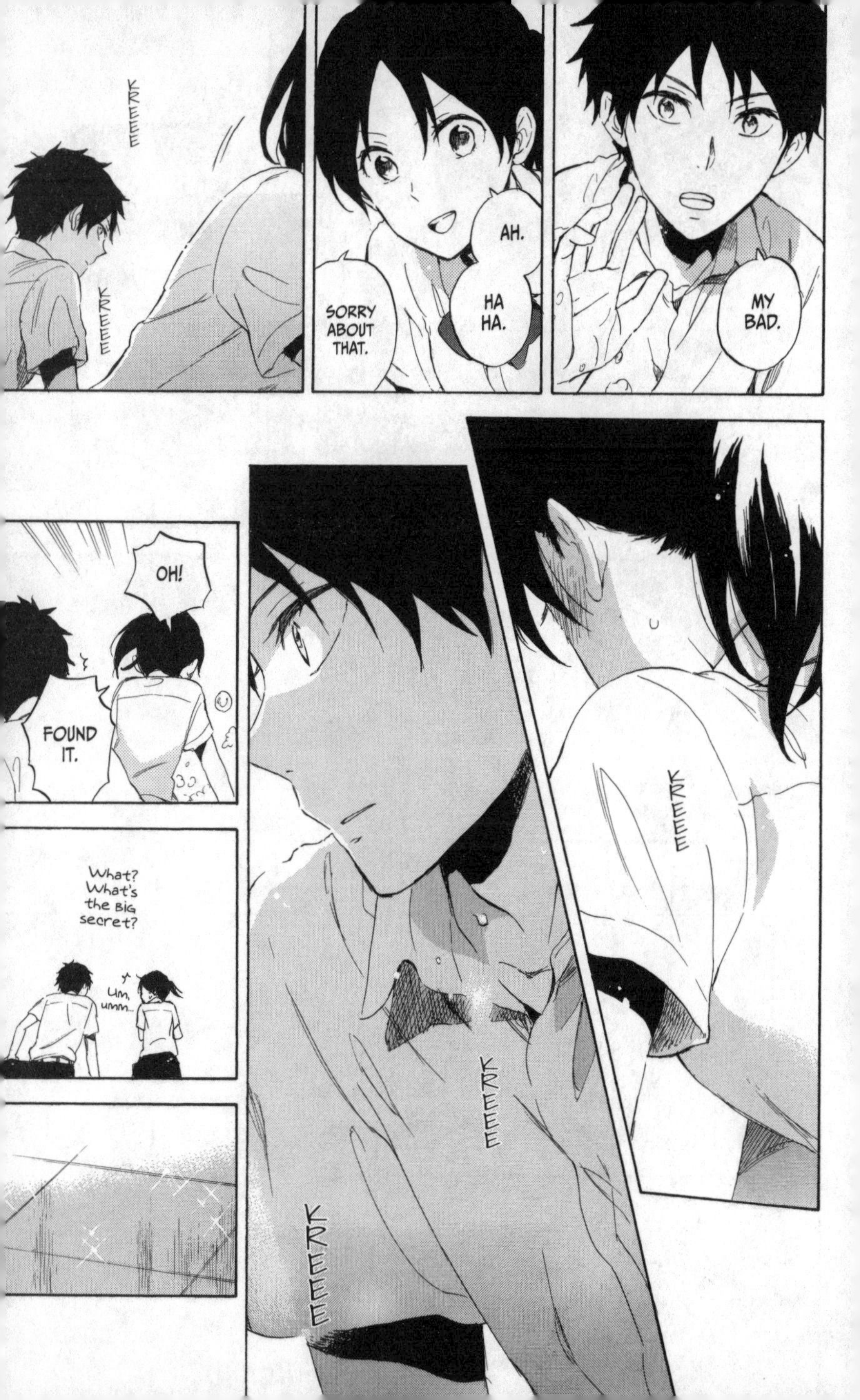
MY BAD.
AH.
HA HA.
SORRY ABOUT THAT.
KREEE
KREEE
KREEE
KREEE
KREEE
OH!
FOUND IT.
What? What's the big secret?
Um, umm...

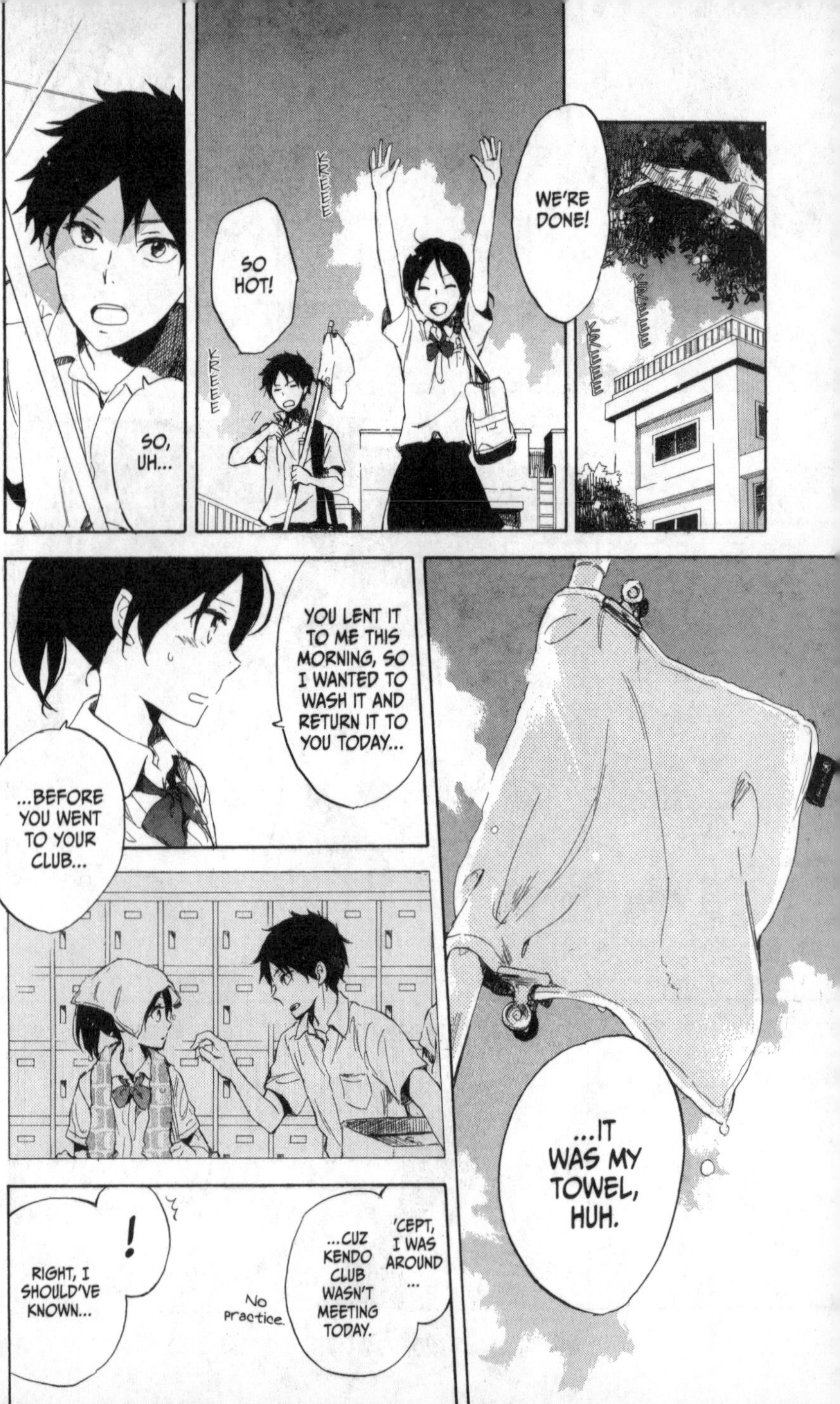
KREEE
KREEE
WE'RE DONE!
KREEE
SO HOT!
KREEE
SO, UH...
...IT WAS MY TOWEL, HUH.
YOU LENT IT TO ME THIS MORNING, SO I WANTED TO WASH IT AND RETURN IT TO YOU TODAY...
...BEFORE YOU WENT TO YOUR CLUB...
'CEPT, I WAS AROUND...
...CUZ KENDO CLUB WASN'T MEETING TODAY.
No practice.
!
RIGHT, I SHOULD'VE KNOWN...

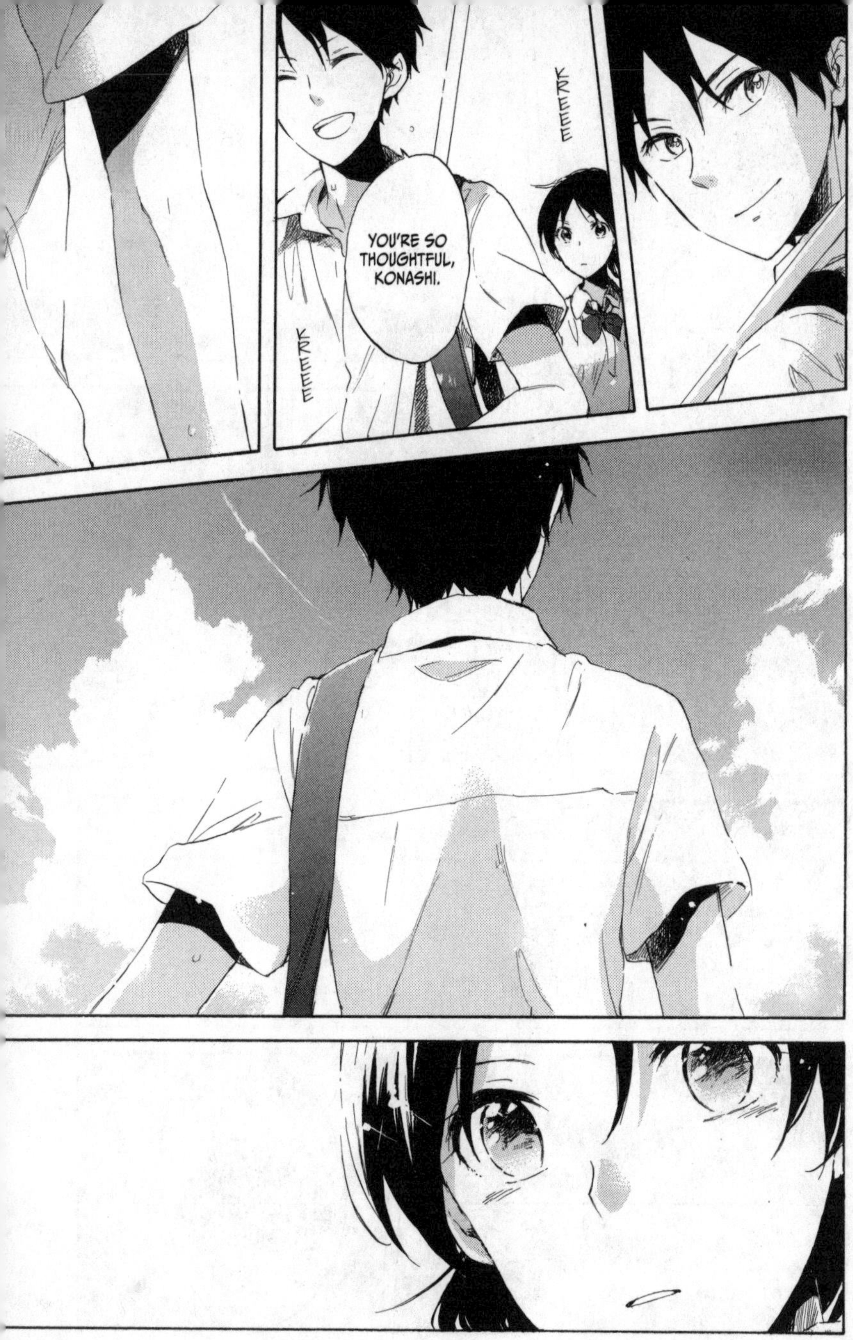
KREEE
YOU'RE SO THOUGHTFUL, KONASHI.
KREEE

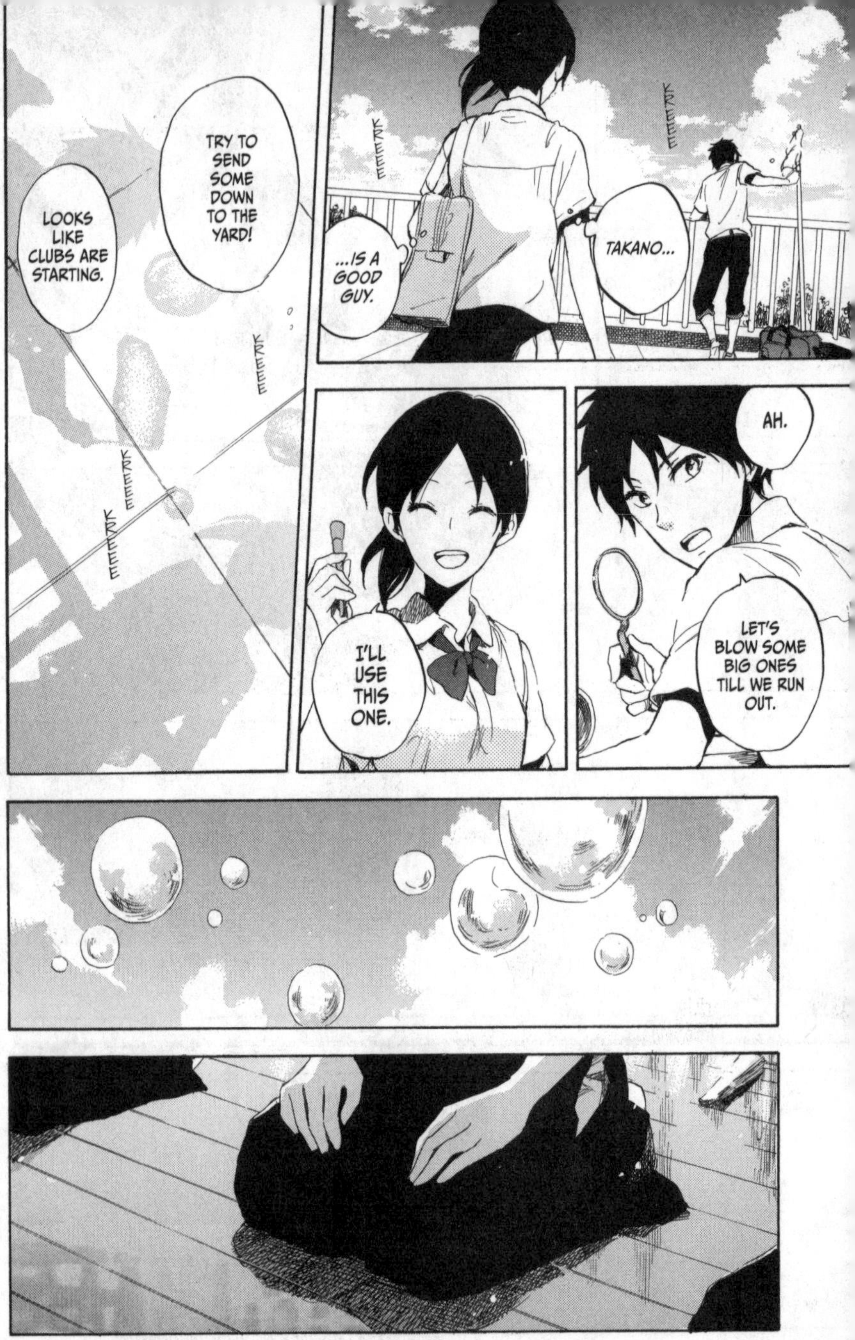
KREEE
KREEE
TAKANO...
...IS A GOOD GUY.
AH.
LET'S BLOW SOME BIG ONES TILL WE RUN OUT.
I'LL USE THIS ONE.
TRY TO SEND SOME DOWN TO THE YARD!
LOOKS LIKE CLUBS ARE STARTING.
KREEE
KREEE
KREEE

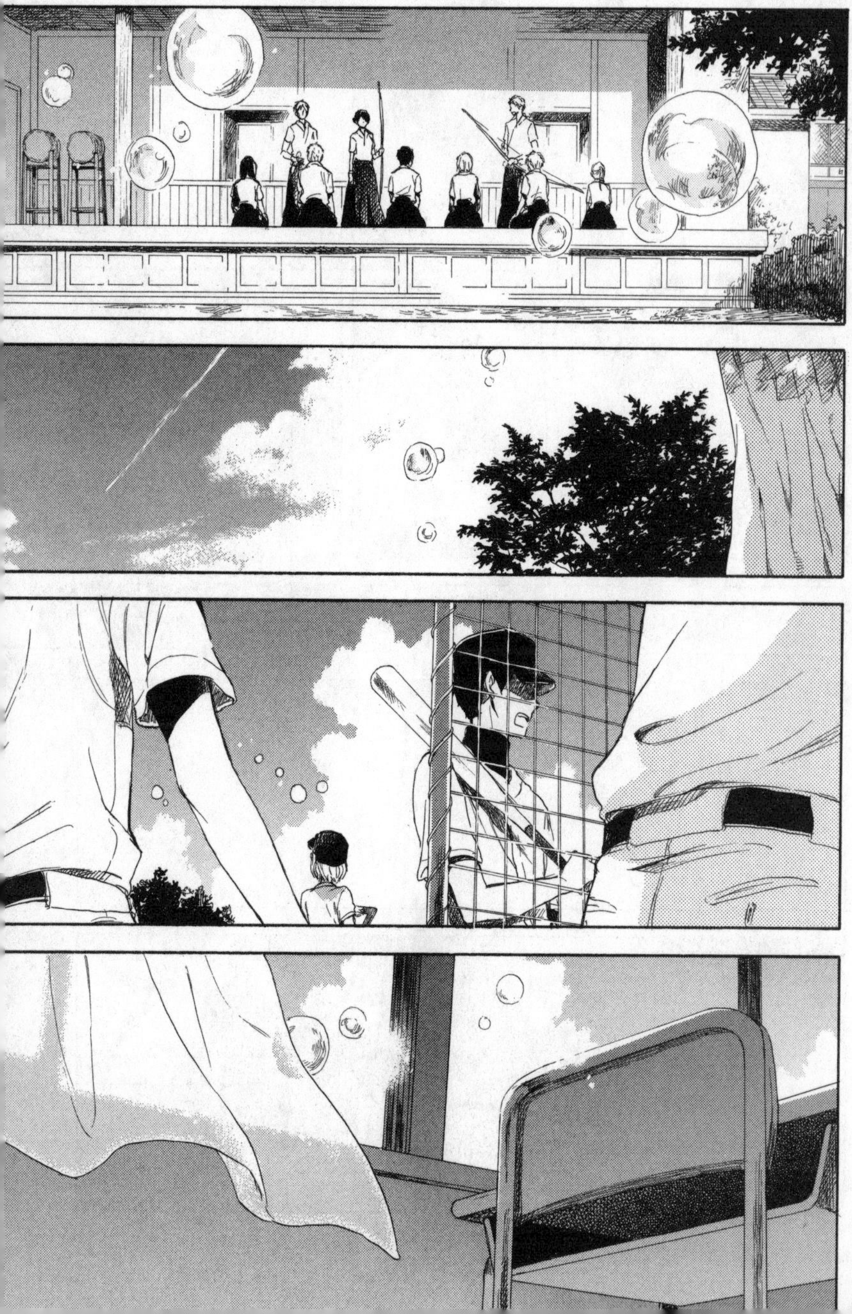

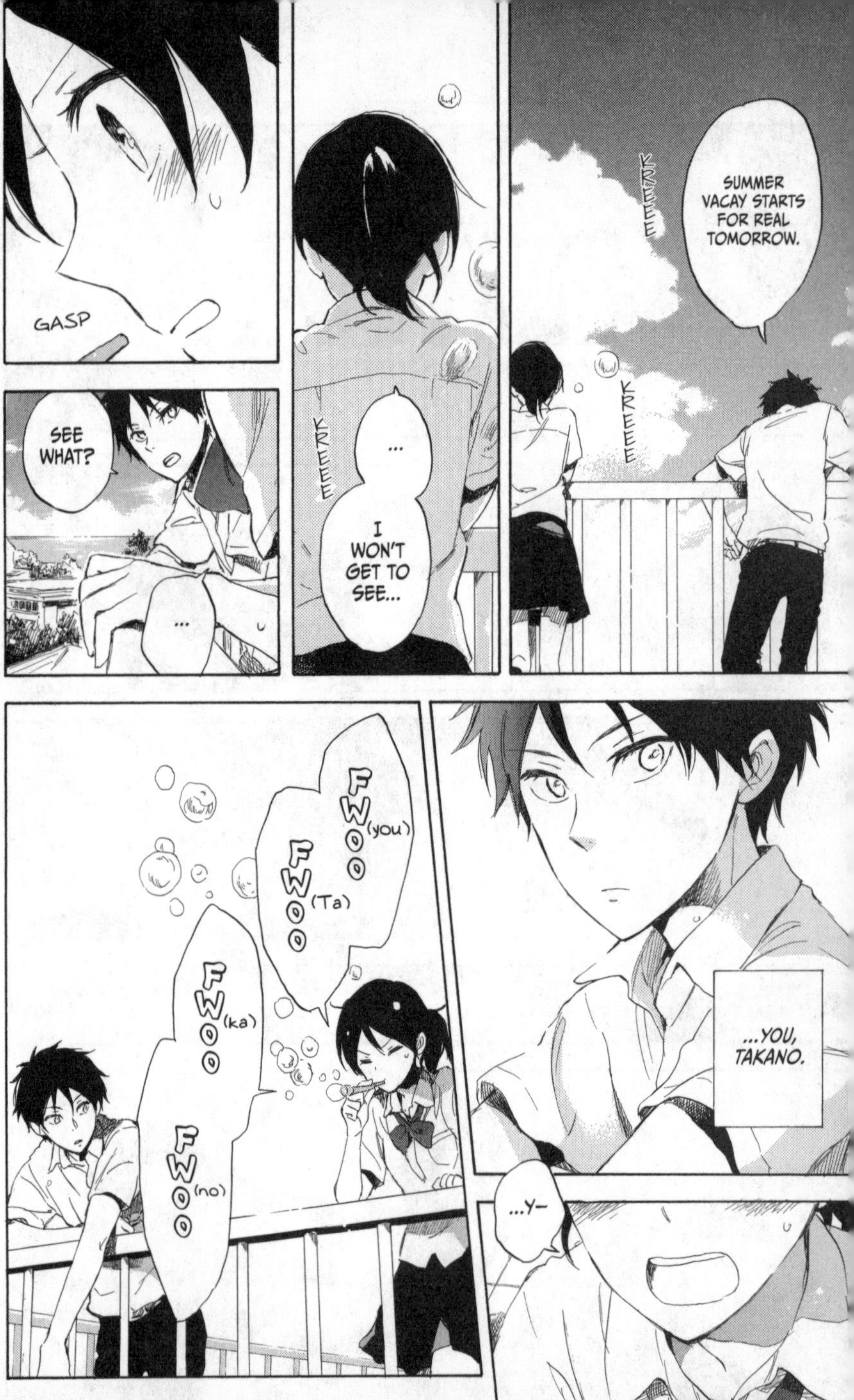
SUMMER VACAY STARTS FOR REAL TOMORROW.
KREEEE
KREEE
...
I WON'T GET TO SEE...
KREEE
GASP
SEE WHAT?
...
...YOU, TAKANO.
...Y–
FWOO (you)
FWOO (Ta)
FWOO (ka)
FWOO (no)

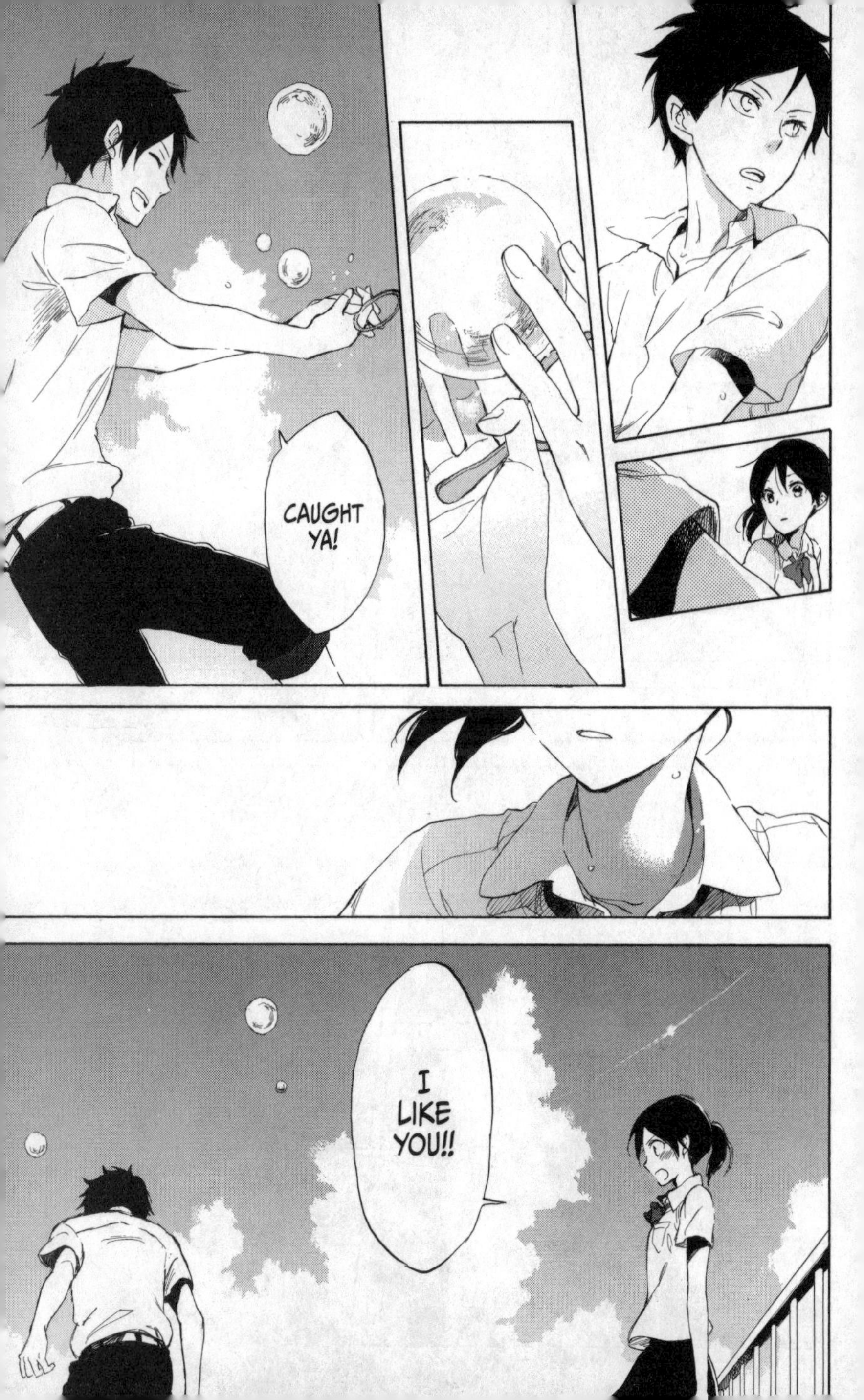
CAUGHT YA!
I LIKE YOU!!

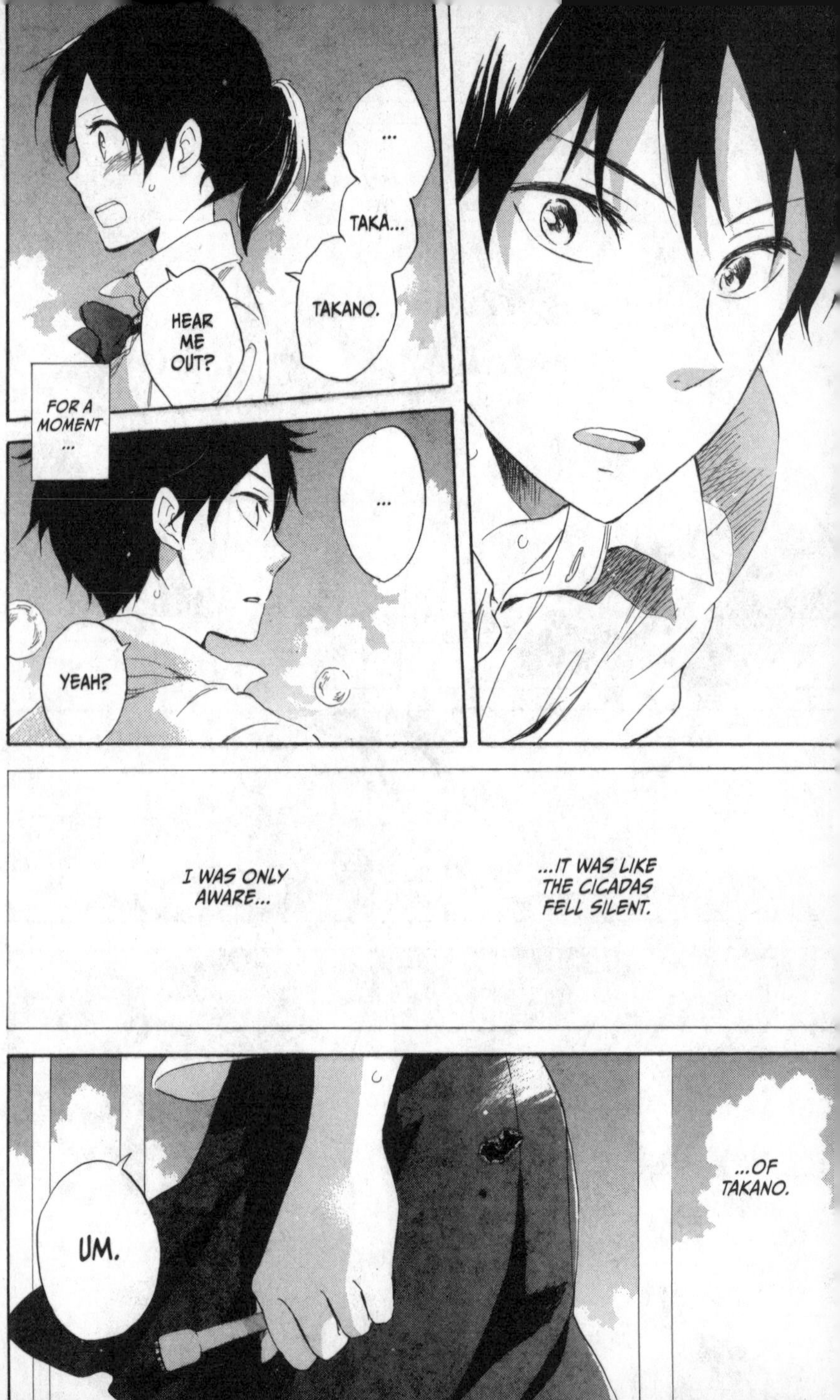
...
TAKA...
TAKANO.
HEAR ME OUT?
FOR A MOMENT ...
...
YEAH?
...IT WAS LIKE THE CICADAS FELL SILENT.
I WAS ONLY AWARE...
...OF TAKANO.
UM.

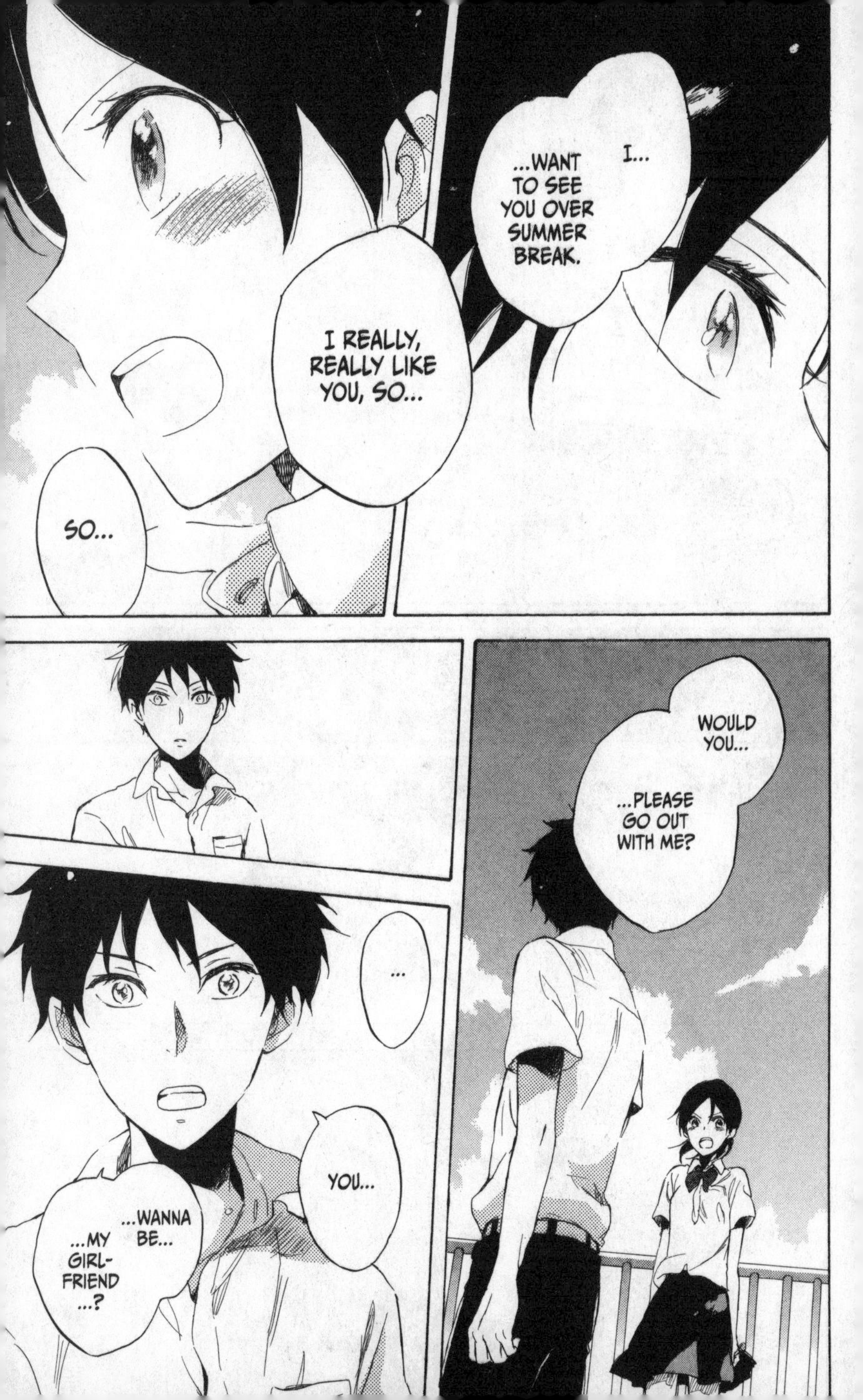
I...
...WANT TO SEE YOU OVER SUMMER BREAK.
I REALLY, REALLY LIKE YOU, SO...
SO...
WOULD YOU...
...PLEASE GO OUT WITH ME?
...
YOU...
...WANNA BE...
...MY GIRL-FRIEND ...?

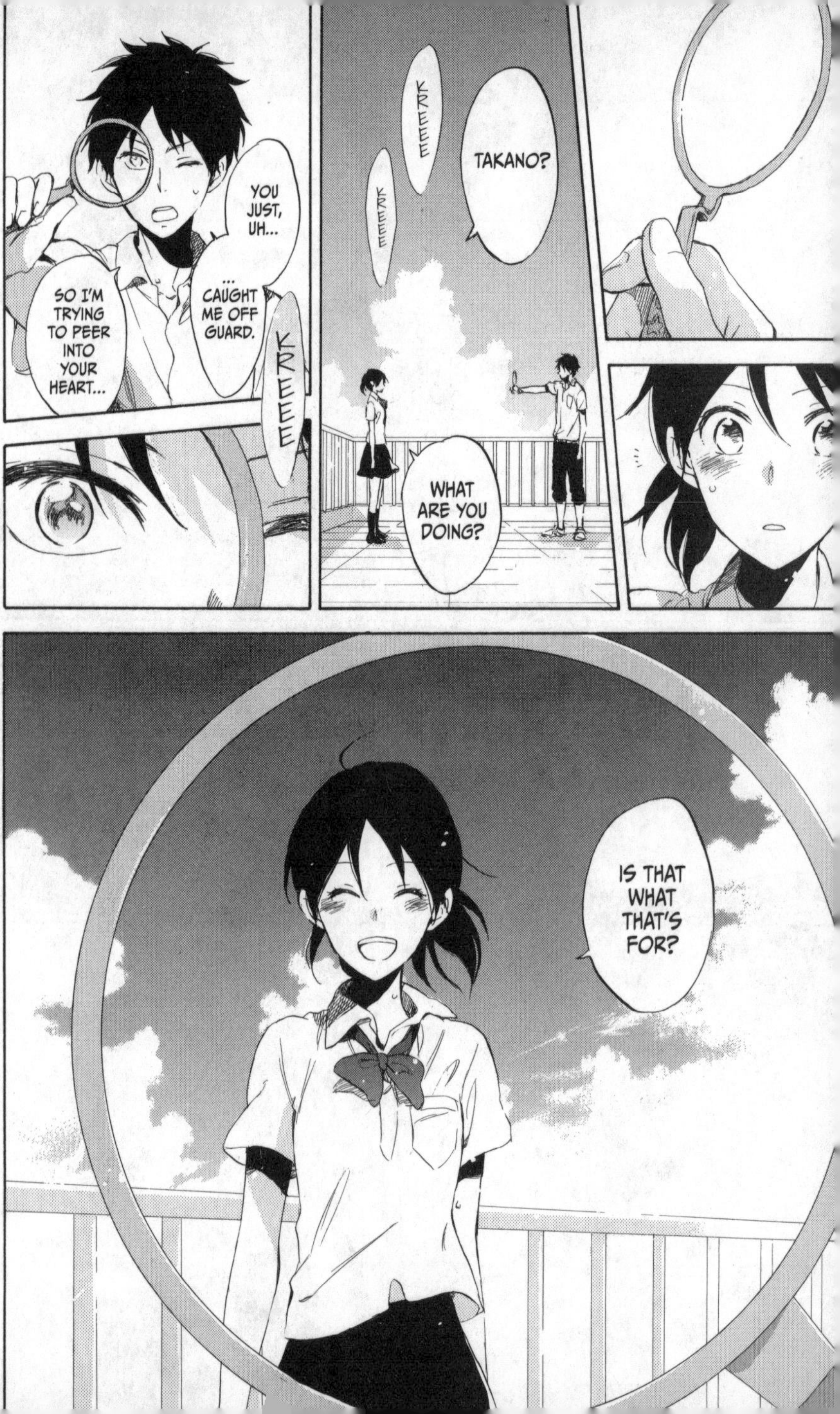
TAKANO?
KREEE
KREEE
WHAT ARE YOU DOING?
YOU JUST, UH...
...CAUGHT ME OFF GUARD.
SO I'M TRYING TO PEER INTO YOUR HEART...
KREEE
IS THAT WHAT THAT'S FOR?

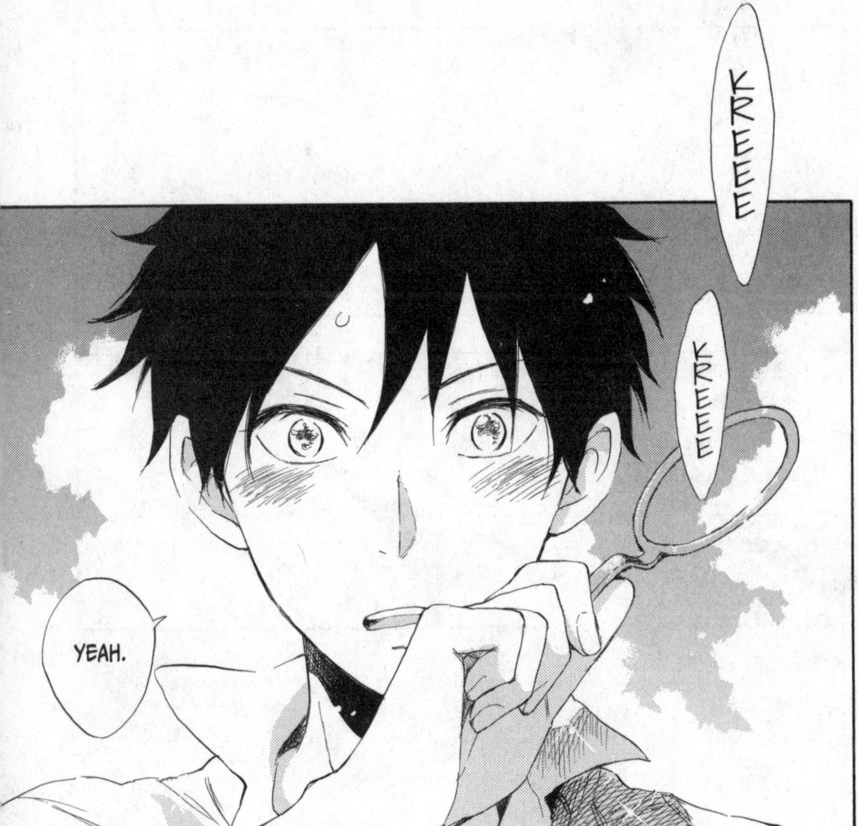
KREEE
KREEE
YEAH.

YOUTH IS SO HOT...

...IT BURNS.

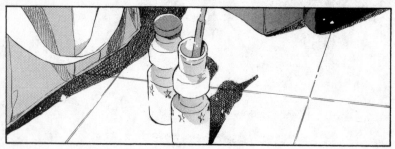

*SUMMER VACATION: DAY 0*

00 Days of Summer Vacation/End

# The Snow White with the Red Hair anime starts July 2015!

Animation Studio ✦ Bones

Director ✦ Masahiro Andou

Cast: Shirayuki ✦ Saori Hayami

Zen ✦ Ryota Osaka

Check out the official website!

http://clarines-kingdom.com

At long last!
Can't wait
to see it!!

 Big
Thanks To:

-Ide-sama, Iwakiri-sama

-The editorial staff at *LaLa*

-Everyone in Publishing/Sales

-Yamashita-sama

-Noro-sama

-All the anime staff

-My mother, father and sister

-All the readers out there!

Sorata Akiduki

**Sorata Akiduki** was born on March 21 and is an accomplished shojo manga author. She made her debut in January 2002 with a one-shot titled "Utopia." Her previous works include *Vahlia no Hanamuko* (Vahlia's Bridegroom), *Seishun Kouryakubon* (Youth Strategy Guide) and *Natsu Yasumi Zero Zero Nichime* (00 Days of Summer Vacation). *Snow White with the Red Hair* began serialization in August 2006 in *LaLa DX* in Japan and has since moved to *LaLa*.

# Snow White
## with the Red Hair

14

### SHOJO BEAT EDITION

STORY AND ART BY
**Sorata Akiduki**

TRANSLATION **Caleb Cook**
TOUCH-UP ART & LETTERING **Brandon Bovia**
DESIGN **Alice Lewis**
EDITOR **Karla Clark**

Akagami no Shirayukihime by Sorata Akiduki
© Sorata Akiduki 2015
All rights reserved.
First published in Japan in 2015 by HAKUSENSHA, Inc., Tokyo.
English language translation rights arranged with HAKUSENSHA, Inc., Tokyo.

The stories, characters and incidents mentioned
in this publication are entirely fictional.

Printed in Canada

Published by VIZ Media, LLC
P.O. Box 77010
San Francisco, CA 94107

10 9 8 7 6 5 4 3 2 1
First printing, July 2021

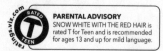

PARENTAL ADVISORY
SNOW WHITE WITH THE RED HAIR is
rated T for Teen and is recommended
for ages 13 and up for mild language.

viz.com          shojobeat.com

# Behind the Scenes!!

STORY AND ART BY **BISCO HATORI**

From the creator of Ouran High School Host Club

Ranmaru Kurisu comes from a family of hardy, rough-and-tumble fisherfolk and he sticks out at home like a delicate, artistic sore thumb. It's given him a raging inferiority complex and a permanently pessimistic outlook. Now that he's in college, he's hoping to find a sense of belonging. But after a whole life of being left out, does he even know how to fit in?!

# YOU'RE READING THE WRONG WAY!

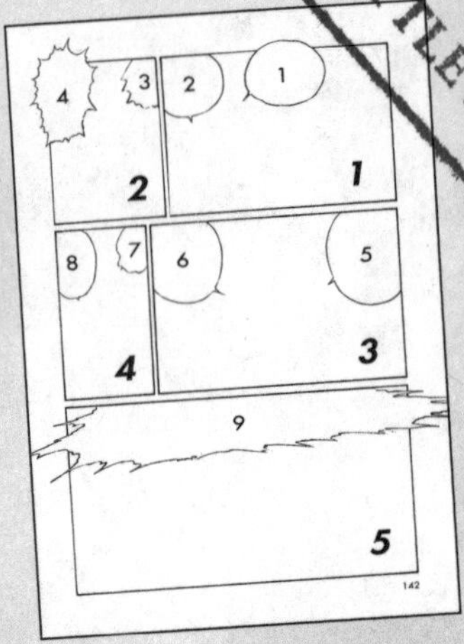
1
2
1
3
4
2
5
6
3
7
8
4
9
5
142

*Snow White with the Red Hair* reads from right to left, starting in the upper-right corner. Japanese is read from right to left, meaning that action, sound effects and word-balloon order are completely reversed from English order.



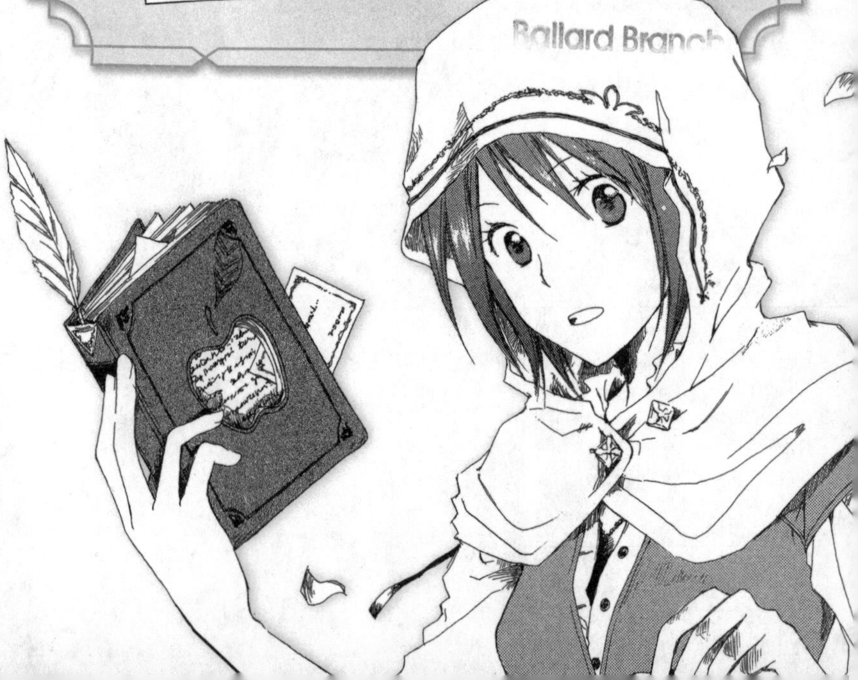